Insurance Operations

Insurance Operations

Edited by

Susan J. Kearney, CPCU, MBA, ARM, AU, AAI

2nd Edition • 3rd Printing

The Institutes
720 Providence Road, Suite 100
Malvern, Pennsylvania 19355-3433

2nd Edition • 3rd Printing • November 2016

Library of Congress Control Number: 2013950278

ISBN 978-0-89463-707-0

Foreword

The Institutes are the trusted leader in delivering proven knowledge solutions that drive powerful business results for the risk management and property-casualty insurance industry. For more than 100 years, The Institutes have been meeting the industry's changing professional development needs with customer-driven products and services.

In conjunction with industry experts and members of the academic community, our Knowledge Resources Department develops our course and program content, including Institutes study materials. Practical and technical knowledge gained from Institutes courses enhances qualifications, improves performance, and contributes to professional growth—all of which drive results.

The Institutes' proven knowledge helps individuals and organizations achieve powerful results with a variety of flexible, customer-focused options:

Recognized Credentials—The Institutes offer an unmatched range of widely recognized and industry-respected specialty credentials. The Institutes' Chartered Property Casualty Underwriter (CPCU®) professional designation is designed to provide a broad understanding of the property-casualty insurance industry. Depending on professional needs, CPCU students may select either a commercial insurance focus or a personal risk management and insurance focus and may choose from a variety of electives.

In addition, The Institutes offer certificate or designation programs in a variety of disciplines, including these:

- Claims
- Commercial underwriting
- Fidelity and surety bonding
- General insurance
- Insurance accounting and finance
- Insurance information technology
- Insurance production and agency management
- Insurance regulation and compliance
- Management
- Marine insurance
- Personal insurance
- Premium auditing
- Quality insurance services
- Reinsurance
- Risk management
- Surplus lines

Ethics—Ethical behavior is crucial to preserving not only the trust on which insurance transactions are based, but also the public's trust in our industry as a whole. All Institutes designations now have an ethics requirement, which is delivered online and free of charge. The ethics requirement content is designed specifically for insurance practitioners and uses insurance-based case studies to outline an ethical framework. More information is available in the Programs section of our website, TheInstitutes.org.

Flexible Online Learning—The Institutes have an unmatched variety of technical insurance content covering topics from accounting to underwriting, which we now deliver through hundreds of online courses. These cost-effective self-study courses are a convenient way to fill gaps in technical knowledge in a matter of hours without ever leaving the office.

Continuing Education—A majority of The Institutes' courses are filed for CE credit in most states. We also deliver quality, affordable, online CE courses quickly and conveniently through CEU. Visit CEU.com to learn more. CEU is powered by The Institutes.

College Credits—Most Institutes courses carry college credit recommendations from the American Council on Education. A variety of courses also qualify for credits toward certain associate, bachelor's, and master's degrees at several prestigious colleges and universities. More information is available in the Student Services section of our website, TheInstitutes.org.

Custom Applications—The Institutes collaborate with corporate customers to use our trusted course content and flexible delivery options in developing customized solutions that help them achieve their unique organizational goals.

Insightful Analysis—Our Insurance Research Council (IRC) division conducts public policy research on important contemporary issues in property-casualty insurance and risk management. Visit www.insurance-research.org to learn more or purchase its most recent studies.

The Institutes look forward to serving the risk management and property-casualty insurance industry for another 100 years. We welcome comments from our students and course leaders; your feedback helps us continue to improve the quality of our study materials.

Peter L. Miller, CPCU
President and CEO
The Institutes

Preface

Insurance Operations is the assigned textbook for CPCU 520, one of the four foundation courses in The Institutes' Chartered Property Casualty Underwriter (CPCU®) designation program.

The goal of CPCU 520 is to enable learners to improve their operational effectiveness by increasing their knowledge of how the various property-casualty insurance functions work together to create and deliver insurance products efficiently. The ten assignments in *Insurance Operations* support this goal.

Assignment 1 provides an overview of insurance operations, including classifications of insurers; insurers' major goals and the constraints on achieving those goals; and measurements used to evaluate insurers' success in meeting goals. Assignment 2 discusses insurance regulation and the regulatory activities that affect insurance operations.

Assignment 3 examines the characteristics of the competitive property-casualty insurance marketplace and the marketing and distribution systems and channels that insurers use. Assignment 4 provides an overview of the important role that the the underwriting function plays in an insurer's operations and the steps in the underwriting process.

Assignment 5 examines the risk control and premium audit functions and how they support insurance operations. Assignment 6 provides an overview of the important role that the claim function plays in an insurer's operations and the activities performed in the claim handling process.

Assignment 7 examines the two most prominent actuarial functions of insurers—ratemaking and estimation of loss reserves. Assignment 8 describes the principal functions of reinsurance, the various types of reinsurance, alternative methods to reinsurance, and the factors that should be considered in the design of reinsurance programs.

Assignment 9 examines the importance of aligning information technology strategy with the goals of the insurance organization. Assignment 10 broadens the functional view of insurance and examines the strategic management process insurers can use to establish goals and to determine strategies for creating a competitive advantage.

The Institutes are grateful to the following industry experts, whose thoughtful review of the content and suggestions for improving it contributed to making this content current, accurate, and relevant:

Edwin B. Barber, CPCU, ARe

Carolyn J. Bergh, FCAS, MAAA

Marsha A. Cohen, CPCU, ARe

Anne Crabbs, CPCU, CIC

Dennis Dunham, CPCU, FCAS, MAAA

Michael Goldman, CPCU, MBA, ERM

Lawrence P. Johnsen, Esq., CPCU, ARe

William Kelso, APA

Daniel P. Konzen, MBA, PhD (ABD)

Michelle L. Krajewski, CPCU, ARM-E

Gerald S. Kraut

David R. Lesieur, FCAS

Gregory J. Massey, CPCU, CIC, ARM, CRM, CLCS, PMP

Claire Mead, CPCU, MBA, CPIW, AIS, ACS, PCS

Gary E. Shook, FCAS, MAAA

Jeffrey Spangler, CPCU, CSP, REM

Lynn T. Splittstoesser, PhD, CPCU, CLU, ChFC, FLMI, AFSB

Donald S. Sutton, CPCU, APA, CIPA

Sean S. Sweeney, MBA, CPCU, RPLU, ARe

Paul Walther, CPCU, ARe

Matthew T. Wulf, Esq.

The Institutes remain equally thankful to the many insurance professionals who contributed to the development of earlier versions of this content. Although they are too numerous to name here, their valuable insights remain in the current content.

For more information about The Institutes' programs, please call our Customer Success Department at (800) 644-2101, email us at CustomerSuccess@TheInstitutes.org, or visit our website at TheInstitutes.org.

Contributors

Susan J. Kearney The Institutes acknowledge with deep appreciation the contributions made to the content of this text by the following persons:

Pamela J. Brooks, CPCU, MBA, AAM, AIM, AIS

Cheryl Ferguson, CPCU, EdD, AU, API, AAI, AIM

Doug Froggatt, CPCU, AINS

Lynn Knauf, CPCU, ARP

Eric C. Nordman, CPCU, CIE

Judith M. Vaughan, CPCU, AIC

Lawrence White, CPCU, ACAS, MAAA, ARM, AIAF, ARe

Contents

Overview of Insurance Operations

Educational Objectives

After learning the content of this assignment, you should be able to:

▷ Explain how insurers have organized to provide property-casualty insurance.

▷ Describe the major goals of an insurer.

▷ Describe the internal and external constraints that impede insurers from achieving their major goals.

▷ Describe the measurements used to evaluate how successful an insurer is at meeting its established goals.

▷ Describe the core and supporting functions performed by insurers.

Overview of Insurance Operations

CLASSIFICATIONS OF INSURERS

Insurance is a system under which participants (such as individuals, families, and businesses) make payments in exchange for the commitment to reimburse for specific types of losses under certain circumstances. Insurers, which are organizations within the financial services industry, may be classified in various manners.

The insurance organization or the entity that facilitates the pooling of funds and the payment of benefits is called an insurer. Participants in this mechanism, called insureds, benefit through reimbursement of covered losses that occur, reduction of uncertainty, additional services provided by the insurer to reduce the frequency or severity of losses, and financial protection against legal liability for damages to others. Additionally, insureds can benefit from the potential availability of credit from lenders, which may help enable them to purchase property. Because the risk of loss to property is transferred to the insurer, lenders are willing to loan money to insureds with greater confidence that the loan will be repaid.

The principal function of every insurer is the same: the acceptance of risks that others transfer to it through the insurance mechanism. This task is divided into core operations consisting of underwriting, claims, and marketing, which, in turn, are supported by several other functions. These operations are described in other sections.

Property-casualty insurers can be classified in these four ways:

- Legal form of ownership
- Place of incorporation
- Licensing status
- Insurance distribution systems and channels

The exhibit shows the general classifications of insurers. An insurer might be further classified by what types of insurance it writes or its specialty. See the exhibit "Classifications of Insurers."

Legal Form of Ownership

The first classification of insurers is by legal form of ownership. The two major types of insurers in this classification are proprietary and cooperative insurers.

Classifications of Insurers

Classification	Type	
Legal Form of Ownership	Proprietary	Stock Insurers
		Lloyd's of London and American Lloyds
		Insurance Exchanges
	Cooperative	Mutual Insurers
		Reciprocal Insurance Exchanges
		Fraternal Organizations
		Other Cooperatives
		Captive Insurers
		Risk Retention Groups
		Purchasing Groups
	Other	Pools
		Government Insurers
Place of Incorporation	Domestic	
	Foreign	
	Alien	
Licensing Status	Admitted	
	Nonadmitted	
Insurance Distribution Systems and Channels	Independent Agency and Brokerage Marketing System	
	Direct Writer Marketing System	
	Exclusive Agency Marketing System	

[DA06276]

Proprietary Insurers

Proprietary insurers include stock insurers, Lloyd's of London and American Lloyds, and insurance exchanges.

Stock insurers are the most prevalent type of proprietary insurer in the United States. These insurers are owned by their stockholders. By purchasing stock in a for-profit insurer, stockholders supply the capital needed to form the insurer or the additional capital the insurer needs to expand its operations. Stockholders expect to receive a return on their investment in the form of stock dividends, increased stock value, or both.

Stockholders have the right to elect the board of directors, which has the authority to control the insurer's activities. The board of directors creates and

Proprietary insurer

Insurer formed for the purpose of earning a profit for its owners.

oversees corporate goals and objectives and appoints a chief executive officer (CEO) to carry out the insurer's operations and implement the programs necessary to operate the company.

Among the proprietary types of insurance ownership is a unique type known as Lloyds. Two types of Lloyds associations exist: Lloyd's of London and American Lloyds.

Lloyd's of London (Lloyd's) is technically not an insurer. However, it does provide the physical and procedural facilities for its members to write insurance. It is a marketplace, similar to a stock exchange. The members are investors who hope to earn a profit from the insurance operations.

In the past, all of the insurance written at Lloyd's was written by or on behalf of individual members, and the insurance each member wrote was backed by his or her personal fortune. Individual members were not liable for the obligations assumed by any other member. Today, a declining proportion of Lloyd's accounts are still underwritten and secured by individuals. A larger portion of Lloyd's members today are corporations, and the liability of each of these members is limited to the amount that the member agrees to write. Lloyd's provides coverage for many unusual or difficult loss exposures and underwrites much of the global marine and aviation insurance.

American Lloyds associations are smaller than Lloyd's of London, and most are domiciled in Texas because of the favorable regulatory climate. Most of these associations were formed or have been acquired by insurers. Like most investors of Lloyd's of London today, members (called underwriters) of American Lloyds are not liable beyond their investment in the association.

An insurance exchange is a proprietary insurer similar to Lloyd's because it acts as an insurance marketplace. Exchange members underwrite any insurance or reinsurance purchased on the exchange. Members can be individuals, partnerships, or corporations, and they have limited liability. Members belong to syndicates and delegate day-to-day operations to the syndicate manager.

For example, INEX (formerly the Illinois Insurance Exchange) was formed in 1979. This exchange serves as an excess and surplus lines market, writing various types of insurance. Member syndicates operate as separate businesses that focus on a particular group of loss exposures.

Cooperative Insurers

Cooperative insurers are the second type of insurer in the legal form of ownership classification. This type of insurer is owned by its policyholders and is usually formed to provide insurance protection to its policyholders at minimum cost. This classification includes mutual insurers, reciprocal insurance exchanges, fraternal organizations, and other cooperatives.

Mutual insurers constitute the largest number of cooperative insurers and provide low-cost insurance to their policyholders, who are the owners of the

Mutual insurer

An insurer that is owned by its policyholders and formed as a corporation for the purpose of providing insurance to them.

insurer. Because a traditional mutual insurer issues no common stock, it has no stockholders. Its policyholders have voting rights similar to those of a stock company's stockholders, and, like stockholders, they elect the insurer's board of directors that appoints officers to manage the company. Some profit is retained to increase surplus, and excess profit is usually returned to policyholders as dividends. Mutual insurers include some large national insurers and many regional insurers.

Although initially formed to provide insurance for their owners, who otherwise could not obtain insurance, mutual insurers today generally seek to earn profits in their ongoing operations, just as stock companies do. A mutual insurer's retained profits ensure the future financial health of the organization.

Reciprocal insurance exchange (interinsurance exchange)

An insurer owned by its policyholders, formed as an unincorporated association for the purpose of providing insurance coverage to its members (called subscribers), and managed by an attorney-in-fact. Members agree to mutually insure each other, and they share profits and losses in the same proportion as the amount of insurance purchased from the exchange by that member.

A **reciprocal insurance exchange**, also simply called a reciprocal, consists of a series of private contracts in which subscribers, or members of the group, agree to insure each other. The term "reciprocal" comes from the reciprocity of responsibility of all subscribers to each other. Each member of the reciprocal is both an insured and an insurer. Because the subscribers are not experts in running an insurance operation, they contract with an individual or organization to operate the reciprocal. This manager is called an attorney-in-fact. The subscribers empower the attorney-in-fact to handle all the duties necessary to manage the reciprocal. An insurer may be formed as a reciprocal to receive favorable tax treatment.

Fraternal organizations resemble mutual companies, but they combine a lodge or social function with their insurance function. They write primarily life and health insurance.

Cooperative insurers include captive insurers, risk retention groups, and purchasing groups.

When a business organization or a group of affiliated organizations forms a subsidiary company to provide all or part of its insurance, the subsidiary is known as a captive insurer, or captive. This arrangement is sometimes referred to as "formalized self-insurance." For example, a large retail chain may decide it can insure itself at a more reasonable cost by using a captive rather than an unaffiliated insurer. The captive may also be formed to cover losses that other insurers will not cover at any price.

Captive insurers can take several forms, and their ultimate purpose is to fund the losses of their owners. Some states have enacted legislation to facilitate the formation and operation of captive insurers within their jurisdictions, while others do not permit the formation of captives.

Legislation has also allowed risk retention groups and purchasing groups to form. These cooperatives can be stock companies, mutuals, or reciprocal exchanges. They are usually organized so that a limited group or type of insured is eligible to purchase insurance from them. These types of insurers are becoming more significant in the evolving insurance marketplace.

Other Insurers

Other insurers are the third type of insurer in the legal form of ownership classification. Insurers that fall into this classification include pools and government insurers.

A pool consists of several insurers, not otherwise related, that join together to insure loss exposures that individual insurers are unwilling to insure. These loss exposures present the potential for losses that either occur too frequently or are too severe (catastrophic) for individual insurers to accept the risk. A major airplane crash is an example of such a catastrophic loss that might be insured under a pool arrangement.

Another catastrophic loss exposure that insurers may be unwilling to insure individually is a large nuclear power plant, for which losses could amount to billions of dollars for property and liability damage. Because no single insurer was willing to assume such tremendous liability, nuclear energy pools were formed. These pools allow many member insurers to spread any losses among members. Additionally, the pools buy reinsurance from nonmembers to increase their capacity.

Pools can be formed either voluntarily or to meet statutory requirements. They operate either as a syndicate or through reinsurance. A syndicate pool issues a joint (or syndicate) policy to the insured, listing all pool members and specifying the part of the insurance for which each member is responsible. Under such policies, the insured has a contractual relationship with each pool member and can sue any or all of them directly if a disagreement arises.

Under a reinsurance pool, one member of the pool issues the policy to the insured, and the other pool members reinsure an agreed proportion of the policy's insured loss exposures. The insured has a contractual relationship only with the member that issued the policy. The policyholder has no legal rights against the other members of the pool and might not even know that they exist.

Many pools are required by law. Virtually all states require some kind of pooling arrangement to provide auto liability insurance for drivers who cannot obtain such insurance in the standard market. Similar pools are required for workers compensation coverage in most states. **Fair Access to Insurance Requirements (FAIR) plans** are required by law in at least half of the states. These pools provide property insurance to qualified property owners who are unable to obtain coverage in the standard market.

Many states in the southeastern U.S., such as Florida, have pools that provide windstorm coverage for residents in storm-prone areas who cannot obtain coverage in the standard market. Similar statutory pools for other types of insurance are required by state law. The protection that these pools provide is underwritten by private insurers and not by state governments, although state and federal governments do act as insurers in some situations.

Fair Access to Insurance Requirements (FAIR) plans

An insurance pool through which private insurers collectively address an unmet need for property insurance on urban properties, especially those susceptible to loss by riot or civil commotion.

Despite the size and diversity of private insurers in the U.S., private insurers do not provide some types of insurance. Some loss exposures, such as catastrophic flooding, do not possess the characteristics that make them commercially insurable, but a significant need for protection against the potential losses still exists. Both the federal government and state governments have developed insurance programs to meet specific insurance needs of the public. Some federal government insurance programs serve the public in a manner that only the government can. For example, only the government has the ability to tax in order to provide the financial resources needed to insure some of the larger loss exposures.

The federal government offers several forms of insurance. One of the largest property insurance programs it offers is the National Flood Insurance Program (NFIP), which is administered by the Federal Insurance Administration under the Federal Emergency Management Agency (FEMA). Most property insurance policies exclude flood coverage because the catastrophic loss potential of floods would significantly raise property insurance premiums for all customers. Customers located in an area prone to flooding can obtain the needed coverage through the NFIP program.

The federal government provides a government "backstop" insurance program through the original Terrorism Risk Insurance Act (TRIA) of 2002.[1] TRIA ensures that commercial property owners can obtain reasonable and predictably priced terrorism coverage by specifying that the federal government will share the risk of loss from foreign terrorist acts. Without this backstop, financing for large commercial construction projects in high-population cities (terrorists' targets) would decline, stunting growth and hindering the economy. To qualify under TRIA, a terrorist act must be certified by the government. Federal assistance becomes available when such losses collectively exceed $5 million and when participating insurers pay a specified amount in related claims. Although originally designed to expire in three years, some form of the legislation has since been extended on each expiration date to provide continued backstop coverage.

All states offer some form of government insurance. For example, some states provide workers compensation insurance for some or all employers in the state. Most state workers compensation programs compete with private insurers. However, in some states, workers compensation insurance is offered exclusively by the state.

Residual market

The term referring collectively to insurers and other organizations that make insurance available through a shared risk mechanism to those who cannot obtain coverage in the admitted market.

Most states require motor vehicle owners to have auto liability insurance before registering their vehicles. However, drivers with poor driving records or with little driving experience may have difficulty obtaining insurance from private insurers. To make liability insurance available to almost all licensed drivers, all states have implemented automobile insurance plans through a **residual market**. The cost of operating such plans is spread among all private insurers selling auto insurance in the state.

In most states, FAIR plans make property insurance more readily available to property owners who have exposures to loss over which they have no control, such as being in a neighborhood with a high property crime rate. These state-run plans spread the cost of operating the plan among all private insurers selling property insurance in the state. Without such a program, individuals and business owners located in such areas who have exposures to loss over which they have no control would be unable to obtain property insurance for their buildings or contents.

Beachfront and windstorm insurance pools are residual market plans similar to FAIR plans. These plans, available in states along the Atlantic and Gulf Coasts, provide insurance to property owners who are unable to obtain this coverage from private insurers. The plans provide coverage for wind damage from hurricanes and other windstorms.

Place of Incorporation

The second classification of insurers is by place of incorporation and includes domestic insurers, foreign insurers, and alien insurers.

Insurance is regulated at the state level. Therefore, a domestic insurer is incorporated within a specific state or, if not incorporated, is formed under the laws of that state. An insurer is said to be operating in its own domiciled state when it is doing business in the state in which it is incorporated or was formed.

Reciprocal insurance exchanges are the only unincorporated insurers permitted in most states. Insurance exchanges and Lloyd's organizations are permitted under law in only a few states.

A foreign insurer is a domestic insurer that is licensed to do business in states other than its domiciled state. Alien insurers are incorporated or formed in another country.

Licensing Status

The third classification of insurers is by licensing status. An insurer's state license authorizes it to sell insurance in the state. A license indicates that the insurer has met the state's minimum standards for financial strength, competence, and integrity. If the insurer later fails to meet those standards or fails to comply with a state law, regulation, or rule, its license can be revoked.

A licensed insurer (admitted insurer) is an insurer that has been granted a license to operate in a particular state. An unlicensed insurer (nonadmitted insurer) has not been granted a license to operate in a given state.

Producers for primary insurance (except **surplus lines brokers**) are licensed to place business only with admitted insurers. Licensing status is also important for purposes of reinsurance.

Surplus lines broker

A person or firm that places business with insurers not licensed (nonadmitted) in the state in which the transaction occurs but that is permitted to write insurance because coverage is not available through standard market insurers.

Insurance Distribution Systems and Channels

The fourth classification of insurers is by their insurance distribution systems and distribution channels—that is, the method used to deliver insurance products to the marketplace. Insurers use many types of distribution systems and channels, designed to meet their particular marketing objectives. Most insurers use one or more of these insurance distribution systems:

- Independent agency and brokerage marketing system
- Direct writer marketing system
- Exclusive agency marketing system

Insurers also use these common **distribution channels** to promote products and services as well as to communicate with existing and prospective insureds: the Internet, call centers, direct response, group marketing, and financial institutions.

INSURER GOALS

Senior managers of insurers seek to meet the goals established by the insurer's owners. However, insurers' goals pose some challenges that other organizations do not face in meeting their goals.

An insurer's overall goals are similar to those of any other organization. The differences are how an insurer meets its goals and the conflicts that exist among competing goals.

Insurers have five major goals:

- Earn a profit
- Meet customer needs
- Comply with legal requirements
- Diversify risk
- Fulfill their duty to society

Earn a Profit

The profit goal is most commonly associated with proprietary, or for-profit, insurers. Cooperative insurers should also earn a profit, but doing so is not the primary goal for which they are formed.

Insurers earn money by charging insureds a "premium" for the insurance contract (policy). To be able to meet the contract terms through the payment of covered losses and to meet regulatory requirements, insurers invest the portion of premiums that is not needed to pay their operating expenses (called surplus). These investments produce income in the form of interest, dividends, and investment gains—when sold. The return on investments generates additional income to be further invested to pay future covered

Independent agency and brokerage marketing system

An insurance marketing system under which producers (agents or brokers), who are independent contractors, sell insurance, usually as representatives of several unrelated insurers.

Direct writer marketing system

An insurance marketing system that uses sales agents (or sales representatives) who are direct employees of the insurer.

Exclusive agency marketing system

An insurance marketing system under which agents contract to sell insurance exclusively for one insurer (or for an associated group of insurers).

Distribution channel

The channel used by the producer of a product or service to transfer that product or service to the ultimate customer.

losses, to expand the insurer's operations, or to be returned to the insurer's investors.

A proprietary insurer must earn a profit to provide a return on the investment made by the individuals and institutions that purchased the insurer's stock (stockholders). A proprietary insurer can attract capital only as long as its profits are comparable to or better than similar insurers. If investors do not believe that they will receive an acceptable rate of return on their investment, they will seek investment opportunities elsewhere. The insurer would then be unable to raise the capital needed to run the business.

Funds from policyholders (usually premiums) are one source of capital for cooperative insurers. Growth of surplus derived from underwriting operations is another. Funds in excess of those used to pay losses and operating expenses, generally considered profits, are contributed to surplus or returned to policyholders in the form of dividends. Surplus accumulation ensures continued solvency and protects against unforeseen catastrophic losses.

Under certain circumstances, a cooperative insurer can obtain additional capital by borrowing funds using surplus notes. These notes can usually be repaid only from profits, so funds from additional capital are also likely to depend on the insurer's anticipated profitability.

An insurer's premium volume can grow through increased policy sales, resulting from marketing efforts. Additionally, when an insurer's underwriting operation evaluates risks effectively—avoiding risks that will require excessive loss payments—and prices insurance products appropriately for the risk, premium volume also increases. Increased premium volume through marketing and underwriting performance provides greater profits for an insurer.

Meet Customer Needs

To attract customers, an insurer must provide the products and services those customers seek at a competitive price. This involves determining what customers need and what price is competitive and then finding the best way to satisfy those needs.

Insurance is an intangible product; the customer receives an insurance policy, but what the customer actually purchases is a transfer mechanism. The customer pays a premium to transfer some or all of the potential financial consequences of covered loss exposures to the insurer.

As in every retail or service organization, insurance customers expect prompt service and timely responses to inquiries. When insurance customers suffer a loss, they can be upset or under considerable stress. Consequently, the insurer must provide quick and professional assistance, which requires well-trained, customer-focused personnel and automated support systems.

Meeting customers' needs can often conflict with the profit goal. In some cases, offering high-quality insurance at a price that the customer can afford may not generate the profit that the insurer needs to attract and retain capital. This is particularly true in certain heavily populated areas where risk-based pricing would not be affordable for insureds.

Providing training, operating automated call centers, and maintaining current information technology can also become costly and can conflict with achieving the profit goal in the near term. However, the long-term benefits of these expenditures can reduce costs and help reduce premiums, and the improved customer service can create a competitive advantage by encouraging policy retention and new business.

Comply With Legal Requirements

Being a responsible corporate citizen dictates legal compliance. Additionally, legal compliance promotes the insurer's good reputation in the business community and the insurer's ability to attract capital and customers. Conversely, lack of compliance can lead to fines and penalties.

One of an insurer's greatest responsibilities is compliance with state regulations. The insurance industry is highly regulated, and the expenses associated with compliance can be substantial. Insurers incur expenses for filings, record-keeping and accounting, and legal activities. Additional expenses are incurred for participation in assigned risk plans, Fair Access to Insurance Requirements (FAIR) plans, and government-required insolvency funds. To the extent that these expenses increase the cost of insurance, they create a conflict between the profit goal and the customer needs goal.

Diversify Risk

Diversifying risk is an emerging goal for property-casualty insurers because of the increased catastrophe losses that have occurred over the past decade. The Insurance Information Institute has referred to the 2000s as "a decade of disaster." Catastrophes in the 2000s increased by 117 percent as compared to catastrophes in the 1990s. Florida accounted for 19 percent of all insured catastrophe losses in the United States from 1980 to 2008.[2] This high concentration of losses in a geographic area highlights individual insurers' need to spread risk over a wider geographic area and over multiple types of insurance business, such as property-casualty insurance. Meeting this goal complements the insurer's goals of earning a profit and fulfilling its duty to society.

Fulfill Their Duty to Society

All corporations are obligated to promote the well-being of society. At the minimum, this obligation demands that the insurer should avoid causing any public harm. Many insurers go well beyond the minimum as responsible corporate citizens.

Many insurers contribute funds, and sometimes they volunteer employees' time to medical, educational, and other public service organizations. Additionally, many insurers establish employee benefit plans that provide for the current and future well-being of their employees. Benefits such as medical insurance, disability insurance, retirement plans, employee assistance programs, and numerous other benefits help employees and retirees to use their personal resources to meet their needs and help to minimize the use of public resources. Insurers' participation in philanthropic activities and employee benefits improves employees' job satisfaction and emotional well-being. In addition, these activities help with employee retention and attract qualified candidates to these organizations.

While fulfilling their duty to society through philanthropic activities and employee benefit programs, insurers maintain a well-qualified, knowledgeable staff, which promotes the profit and customer needs goals. However, the required use of funds for such programs also competes with the customer needs and the profit goals. Insurers must balance the use of funds to best meet all of these goals.

CONSTRAINTS ON ACHIEVING INSURER GOALS

In achieving their major goals, insurers face numerous constraints.

Insurers must contend with numerous constraints that exist within the insurer's internal operation as well as in the external environment.

Internal Constraints

Several internal constraints might prevent an insurer from meeting all of its goals. Some of these constraints are imposed only in certain circumstances or only on certain types of insurers:

- Efficiency
- Expertise
- Size
- Financial resources
- Other internal constraints

Efficiency

Some insurers operate more efficiently than others. An insurer's lack of efficiency may be caused by poor management, insufficient capital, lack of information technology, an inability to adapt to change, or other causes.

Inefficient insurers are at a disadvantage when competing with efficient ones. This competitive weakness might prevent them from meeting their profit and service goals, which can lead, in turn, to the inability to meet humanitarian or societal goals.

Inefficiency, particularly in information technology and customer service, can prevent an insurer from adequately meeting its customers' needs. In extreme cases, inefficiency can lead to insolvency and a consequent failure to meet legal and regulatory goals.

The rapid pace of technology advances makes it difficult for insurers to integrate the latest technological trends into their business processes. The need for historic information on losses and insureds often creates a dependency on core legacy systems, which require ongoing maintenance in addition to integration with new technology. Modern United States culture demands information at the touch of a button, and insurer technology tends to lag behind that of other industries in meeting that demand. Technology demands can conflict with insurers' customer needs and profit goals.

Expertise

The insurance business is complex, and considerable expertise is required to successfully operate an insurer. This is particularly true as insurers move into niche or specialty markets, both of which require expertise in underwriting, pricing, and claim settlement for unusual losses.

Lack of expertise could prevent an insurer from making a profit or meeting customers' needs, or it could eventually cause the insurer to fail to attain any of its goals. As with efficiency, in extreme cases, lack of expertise could ultimately lead to insolvency.

The insurer should make sure that the current staff has the skills needed to perform their jobs adequately. If not, then the insurer should consider necessary training or hiring staff to better fulfill job requirements. The insurer's support of ongoing training initiatives can ensure that employees maintain the skills required to perform their jobs effectively.

Size

An insurer's size affects its ability to meet its goals. A small insurer has more challenges than a large insurer in terms of available resources. Large insurers can take advantage of economies of scale and may have more financial resources to update technology or reach additional markets. Large insurers can invest more in market research and product development than small insurers can. One advantage for a small insurer is that it can be more nimble, allowing it to respond quickly to an emerging trend or a change in the external insurance environment. However, the limited resources of a small insurer might still be a disadvantage.

Financial Resources

Insufficient financial resources can pose a serious threat to an insurer. When financial resources become strained, insurers are unable to effectively train staff, make new capital investments, or reach new markets. Management must make difficult decisions about allocating scarce resources among competing priorities.

The economic strain of the past decade, and especially the recession that began in late 2007, have caused some insurers to suffer reduced financial resources through underwriting losses, investment losses, or both. Financial constraints can further inhibit insurers' ability to achieve profit and/or societal goals.

Other Internal Constraints

Other internal constraints can interfere with achieving goals. Examples include lack of name or brand recognition, or a damaged reputation.

A newly established insurer might lack the name recognition necessary to achieve its profit goals even if it has the expertise and financial resources to do so. Many established banks experienced this difficulty when they entered the insurance industry. Banks are well known in the financial services area, but they lack the brand recognition of established insurers.

Another internal constraint is a reputation damaged by past problems. Even if past problems have been corrected and the insurer is operating flawlessly and ethically, overcoming a poor reputation requires work on the part of all employees within the organization. If the brand image has been damaged, the insurer may need to develop a concerted campaign to regain customer and public confidence as well as a plan to manage that image into the future. This plan should contain an ethics component, perhaps development or adoption of a code of ethics to be applied to all internal and external business practices, and training for all employees on ethical decision-making. While a damaged reputation is also an external constraint, the insurer must address internal issues as well to communicate appropriate information to staff and avoid morale issues or other negative outcomes, and to guide staff in handling related inquiries and promote a positive image within and outside the organization. An insurer that fails to address all internal issues could develop problems retaining and hiring high-caliber managers and other staff because of its damaged image. These factors could prevent the insurer from meeting customers' needs and could jeopardize profitability.

External Constraints

In addition to internal constraints, insurers contend with several external constraints that may prevent them from meeting their goals:

- Regulation
- Rating agencies
- Public opinion
- Competition
- Economic conditions

- Insurance marketing and distribution
- Other external constraints

Regulation

Insurance operations are closely regulated, extending from incorporation to liquidation and encompassing most activities in between. Insurance regulators monitor insurers' solvency to protect the insurers' policyholders and members of the public who benefit from the existence of insurance. Regulation can also extend to the insurance rates and forms insurers use. If filed rate increases are not approved by the applicable regulator, an insurer might not achieve its profit goals. Policy form approval and the time constraints related to the filing process might keep an insurer from fully meeting customers' needs.

Insurance regulation is complex and extensive. Regulation varies by state, and federal regulation adds another layer of complexity. Products that can be offered in one state may not be approved for use in another state. The variations in property-casualty laws in different states require a broader range of staff expertise. Consequently, regulation imposes a major constraint on insurers, requiring significant personnel and financial resources that can inhibit the insurer's ability to achieve its profit goals.

Rating Agencies

Financial rating agencies, such as A.M. Best Company, Standard & Poor's, and Moody's, rate insurers based on financial strength as an indication of an insurer's ability to meet policyholder obligations. To support their current ratings, well-managed and highly rated insurers typically must maintain capitalization levels in excess of the minimum amounts required. Because favorable financial ratings help to attract and retain customers, insurers try to conduct business to achieve the required capitalization levels in order to maintain or improve a favorable rating, but that also might constrain insurers from meeting their profit goals.

Rating agencies are also placing new demands when assessing insurers' financial health. While many other exposures can affect solvency, no single exposure can affect policyholder security more instantaneously than catastrophes. Catastrophic events are occurring more frequently and with greater loss potential because of significant increases in construction in heavily populated areas. To reflect this concern, rating agencies now require insurers to boost their capital to handle higher catastrophe risk. For example, A.M. Best subjects all insurers to a reduction in their reported surplus based on the greatest of a 100-year wind net **probable maximum loss (PML)**, a 250-year earthquake net PML, or a recent large loss within the calculation of Best's Capital Adequacy Ratio (BCAR)—an important financial benchmark that helps indicate whether an insurer has adequate capital to address its insurance and other risk exposures. While these boosts in capital to handle higher catastrophe risk and maintain or improve favorable ratings would help meet

Probable maximum loss (PML)

The largest loss that an insured is likely to sustain.

the insurer's customer needs and duty to society goals, they could impede the insurer's ability to achieve its profit goals.

An insurer's financial rating can also be a potential constraint for insurers whose rating has declined. Those insurers may find it very difficult to attract and retain customers, and a decrease in customers often causes financial ratings to decline further. Accordingly, a downgrade in a financial rating could adversely affect an insurer's position in the marketplace and could result in a reduction in the amount of business an insurer is able to write to achieve its profit goals.

Public Opinion

Public opinion about the insurance industry as a whole can act as a constraint for individual insurers in meeting goals. While many customers are satisfied with their insurers, several high-profile issues can lead to a negative perception of the insurance industry.

For example, highly publicized legal and ethical incidents involving some insurers over recent years have tended to decrease public trust in insurers in general. Negative media coverage on questions regarding insurer contingency commissions included ethics considerations and sometimes legal implications. Insurer marketing efforts and increased emphasis—and often expenditures—on customer service were required to regain public trust. Some insurers were criticized in the 2000s for their handling of claims in the aftermath of catastrophic hurricane damage. Decisions about whether damage was caused by windstorm (which was covered) or flooding (which was not covered) caused an emotional, public outcry. In some cases, insurers resolved to pay losses that were not covered to curtail damage to their reputations.

Matters of ethics are major components in managing an insurer's reputation; therefore, efforts to manage reputation should include ethics initiatives, including ongoing training of all staff in ethical decision-making. Managing expenses to repair or protect an insurer's image or the image of the industry conflicts with the profit goal but helps attain the customer needs goal.

Additionally, affordability and lack of availability of personal auto insurance in some states, such as California, have been highly publicized and overshadow overall customer satisfaction with insurers. Dissatisfaction with insurers can lead to the involvement of legislators and regulators. Corrective action, such as California's Proposition 103 mandating rate rollbacks, can seriously constrain individual insurers from achieving profit goals.

Ultimately, such issues can constrain insurers from attaining societal goals. When the insurance industry is viewed negatively by the public, it contradicts the idea of serving in the public's best interests.

Competition

Insurance industry underwriting cycles (or market cycles) are referred to as either hard cycles or soft cycles. The property-casualty insurance industry has exhibited various hard and soft cycles as far back as the 1920s. Hard cycles are characterized by periods of decreased competition and rising rates leading to increased profitability and high rates of return. After a hard cycle ends, the industry enters a low phase, a soft cycle, when prices moderate or decline as competition increases and, eventually, profitability diminishes.

The industry entered a protracted soft cycle in the late 1980s that continued throughout the 1990s. This soft cycle resulted in many mergers and the consolidation of major insurers because of decreasing premium levels. Many insurers that existed in 1990 either no longer existed in 2000 or had significantly changed their operations because of acquisitions or mergers with competitors. The industry encountered another hard cycle from 2000 through 2003 and then settled into a soft cycle leading into the 2007 recession.

Despite the decline in the number of insurers, so many insurers remain in the market that competition is great. Competition is further fueled in personal insurance by highly standardized products that customers view as commodities.

In soft cycles, competitive pressure to decrease prices makes it difficult for insurers to achieve their profit goals. Low profits can affect insurers' ability to achieve societal goals. Excessive competition can entice some insurers to bend the rules, making insurers unable to attain their legal and regulatory goals.

Economic Conditions

Insurers' investment operations can be affected severely by economic downturns. The investment income of most insurers grew substantially during the economic expansion throughout the 1990s. Investment gain increased beginning in 2003; however, the market experienced another downturn in 2007 with the economic recession that affected the U.S.

Insurers can be adversely affected during inflationary cycles as well. Inflation affects the cost of insurance losses through increased medical costs, construction costs, and other loss-related costs. A decline in the use of automobiles during the recent recession has resulted in an overall decline in frequency of auto collision losses; however, this appears to be offset by increasing loss severity resulting from inflated medical, vehicle repair, and litigation costs. Also, in no-fault states, marked increases in no-fault claim costs resulting from abuses, such as rampant fraud and inflated claims, have tended to increase loss severity.[3] Inflation and abuses ultimately affect insurance premiums, but the effect on losses is felt more quickly than the effect on premiums. This difference in timing makes it difficult for insurers to achieve their profit goals during periods of rapid inflation.

Insurance Marketing and Distribution

Insurance marketing and distribution systems that an insurer chooses to distribute its products can affect the insurer's ability to attain its goals. Insurers distribute their products through many types of distribution systems using different types of sales and service personnel and distribution channels to promote products and services as well as communicate with existing and prospective insureds.

Recent years have seen an increase in auto insurers experimenting with multiple distribution systems and channels. Several major companies use both insurance agents and direct sale methods to reach consumers, including Internet and telephone sales. Affinity sales, or selling through special interest groups, represent a growing distribution channel. Additionally, banks are increasingly selling property-casualty insurance to their bank clients. Each distribution system or channel meets the needs of some customers, and each fails to meet the needs of others.

Other External Constraints

Other external constraints can hinder an insurer's ability to reach its goals. Some of these constraints are natural or man-made catastrophe losses, which increased dramatically in the mid-2000s; disregard for law and order, particularly in some larger cities; and legal changes that affect liability claims.

MEASURING INSURER PERFORMANCE

Insurers use measurements that are specific to their industry to determine their success at meeting established goals.

Measuring the performance of an insurer involves determining how successful the insurer is at meeting established goals, including these:

- Meeting profitability goals
- Meeting customer needs
- Meeting legal requirements
- Meeting social responsibilities

As with any assessment, some measures are objective, while others may be subjective. Financial measurements are based on statistical evidence and are considered to be more objective. Measurements of legal requirements are also objective. Measurements of how well an insurer meets customer needs and social responsibilities are more subjective.

Meeting Profitability Goals

An understanding of how insurers make a profit is crucial to understanding how they meet their profitability goals. Like any business, an insurer generates income, or profits, when its revenue exceeds its expenses. The primary sources of revenue for insurers are insurance premiums (paid by insureds) and investment income. Insurers have investments because they receive premiums before they pay for losses and expenses. Insurers invest that money in the meantime and receive investment income as a result.

When determining expenses, insurers face a special challenge compared with other organizations. The largest portion of an insurer's expenses involves losses that will occur in the future and that are, by definition, more difficult to project than past or current expenses. Estimating these future expenses and setting aside the funds to pay for them is done through reserving.

Estimating insurer profitability is generally accomplished by examining premiums and either underwriting performance (underwriting gain or loss) or overall operating performance (gain or loss from operations). A review of these topics assists in understanding insurer profitability:

- Premiums and investment income
- Underwriting performance
- Overall operating performance
- Estimation of loss reserves

Premiums and Investment Income

An insurer's profits depend heavily on the premium revenue the insurer generates. Premiums are the amounts that insurers charge insureds for insurance coverages. Insurers use rates based on the insured's loss exposures to determine the premium to charge for insurance policies.

Insurers must charge premiums to have the funds necessary to make loss payments. In fact, an insurer's total revenue (premiums and investment income) must equal or exceed the amount needed to pay for losses and to cover its costs of doing business. For example, an insurer may use eighty cents of every premium dollar to pay for losses and twenty-five cents for other expenses. If the insurer can earn an amount equal to 5 percent of its premiums on its investments, it can break even. Consequently, an insurer's profitability must consider the volume of premium the insurer writes. Investment profit also depends, in part, on premium revenue that creates the funds used for investment.

Insurance operations generate substantial amounts of investable funds, primarily from loss reserves, loss adjustment expense reserves, and unearned premium reserves. Loss and loss expense reserves are especially significant for insurers that write liability insurance because the long delay inherent in the liability claim handling process generates very large loss reserves.

Measures of insurer profitability based on premiums consider premium growth issues and the rate of growth that is sustained over time. Premium growth is not always a positive indicator of an insurer's success. An insurer should achieve premium growth by writing new policies rather than depending solely on insurance rate increases or inflation. Premium growth, or the lack thereof, must be evaluated in light of current market conditions. During periods of intense competition, significant premium growth is difficult to achieve. However, rapid premium growth may be undesirable and could indicate lax underwriting standards or inadequate premium levels. Inappropriate premium growth can eventually lead to reduced profits as losses begin to exceed premiums collected for loss exposures. To determine profitability, an insurer should consider whether growth resulted from a competitive advantage, relaxed underwriting, inadequate insurance rates, or a combination of these factors.

Evaluating the rate of premium growth sustained over time helps determine insurer profitability. Establishing reasonable rules by which to measure the adequacy, inadequacy, or excessiveness of premium growth is difficult. Growth that is slower than the industry average usually indicates a problem. Likewise, a growth rate that is substantially higher than the industry average might indicate changes that could be unfavorable in the long term.

Underwriting Performance

An insurer's underwriting performance can be measured in terms of net underwriting gain or loss. This is determined as an insurer's earned premiums minus its incurred losses and underwriting expenses for a specific period. Incurred losses include loss adjustment expenses, and underwriting expenses include acquisition expenses, general expenses, taxes, and fees. Because net underwriting gain or loss ignores investment income (or investment losses) and investment expenses, it represents the extent of the insurer's profit or loss derived strictly from the sale of insurance products.

The formula for calculating net underwriting gain or loss can be expressed as: net underwriting gain or loss = earned premiums – (incurred losses + underwriting expenses).

Three specific ratios are used to measure an insurer's underwriting performance: the loss ratio, the expense ratio, and the combined ratio (trade basis). See the exhibit "Measuring an Insurer's Underwriting Performance."

Overall Operating Performance

An alternative way to measure an insurer's profits is through overall results from operations. An insurer's overall gain or loss from operations is its net underwriting gain or loss plus its net investment gain or loss for a specific period. This overall figure gives a more complete picture of an insurer's profitability because investment income generally helps to offset any underwriting losses. The formula for overall gain or loss from operations is expressed as: overall gain or loss from operations = net underwriting gain or loss + investment gain or loss.

Measuring an Insurer's Underwriting Performance

The loss ratio compares an insurer's incurred losses with its earned premiums for a specific period. The figure for incurred losses includes loss adjustment expenses. The loss ratio is calculated in this manner:

$$\text{Loss ratio} = \text{Incurred losses} \div \text{Earned premiums}$$

The expense ratio compares an insurer's underwriting expenses with its written premiums for a specific period. The expense ratio is calculated in this manner:

$$\text{Expense ratio} = \text{Incurred underwriting expenses} \div \text{Written premiums}$$

The combined ratio (trade basis) combines the loss ratio and the expense ratio to compare inflows and outflows from insurance underwriting. The combined ratio (trade basis) is calculated in this manner:

$$\text{Combined ratio (trade basis)} = \frac{\text{Incurred losses (including LAE)}}{\text{Earned premiums}} + \frac{\text{Incurred underwriting expenses}}{\text{Written premiums}}$$

This can be simplified in this manner:

$$\text{Combined ratio (trade basis)} = \text{Loss ratio} + \text{Expense ratio}$$

[DA02738]

After an insurer pays losses, expenses, and taxes, and reserves money to pay additional incurred losses, the remainder is net operating income, which belongs to the company's owners. The owners (stockholders or policyholders) may receive a portion of this remainder as dividends. The amount that is left after dividends are paid is added to the policyholders' surplus. The increase in policyholders' surplus enables the insurer to expand its operations in the future and provides a cushion against catastrophic losses.

To obtain an accurate picture of an insurer's profitability, it is important to analyze the overall gain or loss from operations for several years because any insurer might have a single unprofitable year that is offset by a pattern of profitability over a longer period.

Insurers may lose money on their underwriting activities (that is, when the combined ratio is more than 100 percent) and yet still generate a profit on investments. Ideally, the investment profit is more than enough to offset the underwriting loss so that the insurer has an overall gain from operations, and the policyholders' surplus grows through time and generates a suitable return on equity for the insurer's owners. See the exhibit "Measuring an Insurer's Overall Performance."

The investment income ratio, overall operating ratio, and return on equity are more specific measures of an insurer's operational performance.

Measuring an Insurer's Overall Performance

The investment income ratio compares the amount of net investment income (investment income minus investment expenses) with earned premiums over a specific period of time. The investment income ratio is calculated as shown:

$$\text{Investment income ratio} = \text{Net investment income} \div \text{Earned premiums}$$

The overall operating ratio, the trade basis combined ratio minus the investment income ratio, can be used to provide an overall measure of the insurer's financial performance for a specific period. Of all the commonly used ratios, the overall operating ratio is the most complete measure of an insurer's financial performance. The formula for overall operating ratio is as shown:

$$\text{Overall operating ratio} = \text{Combined ratio (trade basis)} - \text{Investment income ratio}$$

Return on equity, calculated by dividing the organization's net income by the average amount of owners' equity (policyholders' surplus) for a specific period, enables investors to compare the return that could have been obtained by investing in the insurer with the potential returns that could have been earned by investing their money elsewhere. In general, the owners' equity is invested in operations to generate income for the organization. For insurers, the policyholders' surplus is invested in underwriting activities. The formula for return on equity is as shown:

$$\text{Return on equity} = \text{Net income} \div \text{Owners' equity}$$

[DA02740]

Estimation of Loss Reserves

One of the biggest problems in measuring insurer profitability arises from errors in estimating loss reserves. Loss reserves are generally the largest liability in the insurer's balance sheet and can have a significant effect on the insurer's overall profitability. Insurers establish loss reserves not just for reported claims, but also for losses that have occurred but that have not yet been reported (known as incurred but not reported [IBNR] losses), for losses that have been reported but for which established case reserves are inadequate (known as incurred but not enough recorded [IBNER] reserves), and for claims that have been settled and then reopened.

Errors in estimating outstanding loss amounts, by either underestimating or overestimating the final cost of claims, can distort the insurer's reported profits. This is true for both the year in which inaccurate estimates were originally made and the year in which corrections are made to the estimates. For example, if reserves are initially underestimated and subsequently increased, then net income and policyholders' surplus will decrease when the understatement is recognized. Also, because the insurer's pricing relies on historical loss data, inadequate reserves can result in reduced premium revenues. Therefore, in the long term, if an insurer does not have adequate reserves, it may not have the funds necessary to pay claims. Conversely, if the loss reserves are overestimated (higher than the ultimate loss payments), based on the artificially inflated reserve estimates, the statutory limits on premiums that could be written may be less, and the premiums may be inflated for new and existing risks. Although the reserve estimates may be decreased later, in the interim, these artificial results can cause the insurer to be less competitive in pricing, its financial strength ratings could be lowered, and the insurer's profitability may suffer. A pattern of underreserving or overreserving may ultimately lead to the insurer's insolvency.

Meeting Customer Needs

Determining how well insurers meet customers' needs is difficult because insurers are more likely to hear from customers who believe they have not been treated fairly.

Complaints and Praise

All insurers receive complaints, and each complaint should be evaluated. In some instances, a real problem exists that the insurer should address. In other instances, customers hold expectations that the insurer had not intended to fulfill.

Insurance producers can also be a source of information for evaluating an insurer's success in this area, as they are in frequent contact with customers and hear their complaints about and praise of insurers. Producers seldom keep formal records of such customer reactions, so their evaluations are likely to be subjective.

Customer Satisfaction Data

Many insurers emphasize a customer focus to maintain and raise levels of customer satisfaction with the insurer's products and services. Insurers often use response cards and phone surveys to determine whether customers feel properly treated after a transaction, particularly following a claim. Insurers can also conduct customer focus groups or interviews to determine how well a new or an existing product meets customers' needs. Additionally, insurers can survey customers to obtain an overall satisfaction rating associated with their products and services.

Insurer's Retention Ratio and Lapse Ratio

Two particularly telling measurements of customer satisfaction are the retention ratio and the lapse ratio (sometimes called the cancellation ratio). The data for developing these ratios are found in internal statistical reports. The retention ratio is the percentage of expiring insurance policies that an insurer renews, and it can be measured by policy count, premium volume, or both.

The lapse ratio is calculated by dividing the number of policies that lapse during a period by the total number of policies written at the beginning of that period. A lapse in insurance is defined as a point in time when a policy has been canceled or terminated for failure to pay the premium, or when the policy contract is void for other reasons.

These ratios can indicate the number of policies a company is losing, whether because of a service or price issue or some other issue (such as loss to competition).

Insurer-Producer Relationships

Insurers that market products through independent agents and brokers usually view this network of producers as their customers, in addition to the ultimate insurance customer. These insurers recognize that many other insurers are available to producers and that a competitive marketplace exists within their industry. Being responsive to producer requests and permitting access to insurer policy data and information systems are examples of how insurers maintain and strengthen the insurer-producer relationship. As is the case for customers, insurers can survey or meet with producers to measure their satisfaction with the insurer or to reveal unserved needs the insurer might be able to meet.

State Insurance Department Statistics

Several state insurance departments tabulate complaints they receive and publish lists showing the number of complaints received for each insurer. The number of complaints might indicate one insurer's customer relations success or failure relative to other insurers in the industry.

Consumer Reports

Consumers Union periodically surveys its membership to determine its level of satisfaction with the performance of auto and homeowners insurers. The results are published in that organization's magazine, *Consumer Reports*, including a list of the most satisfactory and least satisfactory insurers as indicated by the survey responses. Only a few of the largest insurers are included in the list because smaller insurers are not mentioned in the responses with sufficient frequency to evaluate their performance fairly.

Meeting Legal Requirements

An insurer's success or failure in meeting legal requirements is indicated by the number of criminal, civil, and regulatory actions taken against the insurer. These actions are automatically brought to the attention of management and should be evaluated carefully to see whether they result from a consistent disregard of legal requirements.

State insurance departments monitor the treatment of insureds, applicants for insurance, and claimants, and they oversee four insurer operational areas: sales and advertising, underwriting, ratemaking, and claim settlement. This regulatory oversight, called market conduct regulation, exists in addition to the role of state insurance regulation in solvency surveillance.

Most states publish a listing of regulatory actions against insurers. This information can be useful in showing how one insurer's performance in this area compares to that of its competitors.

Financial rating agencies provide summary information about insurer financial strength in the form of a financial rating. These rating agencies review all financial information presented in an insurer's balance sheet and financial statements, including any outstanding legal actions involving the organization. The prospective outcome of such actions affects the ratings that these organizations assign to insurers and are another indicator of how well an insurer meets its legal requirements.

Meeting Social Responsibilities

Meeting social responsibilities is the most difficult of the major insurer goals to evaluate. No standards exist for judging an insurer's performance in this area, and little information on an individual insurer's performance is publicly available. Of course, an insurer can get information from its own records to show its own performance, but comparisons with competing insurers are difficult to make because of the lack of available information. Many insurers use their websites to indicate their participation in home and workplace safety programs, support of community projects, and involvement in other social programs.

Another possible indicator of social responsibility is the benefits that an insurer provides for its employees. Some insurers have begun to promote family-friendly policies within their organization to assist employees with balancing work and family responsibilities.

Comparative information for employee benefits is available from the United States Chamber of Commerce and from various insurer trade associations. Additionally, some periodicals provide feature articles in which they rank employers according to their employee benefit programs. Although generous employee benefit plans can be construed as merely another method of competing for good employees, they can also indicate an insurer's concern for the welfare of its employees.

Expenditures on loss control activities may also indicate an insurer's level of humanitarian concern; some insurers go beyond typical efforts in loss control to improve safety conditions for their insureds. Many insurers contribute to associations that do research and raise public concern for safety. Contributions to medical, welfare, and educational institutions and programs are another indication of humanitarian efforts and social responsibility.

Additionally, "green" initiatives are emerging for many insurers as they recognize their responsibility to preserve the environment. In addition to recycling and reusing materials used in the production of policies, handling claims, and reporting, insurers are increasingly interested in auto salvage programs. Salvage programs are better for the environment and more cost-effective for insureds.

FUNCTIONAL VIEW OF INSURANCE

The functional view of insurance examines the many and varied functions an insurer performs as it conducts its business operations.

To carry out the operations of an insurer, many people are needed, all of whom perform specific functions. A function generally describes a distinct type of work or an aspect of operations or management requiring special technical knowledge. An insurer's core functions are typically marketing and distribution, underwriting, and claims. These core functions represent the lifespan of the insurer's business operations, from getting the business (marketing and distribution), to pricing the business (underwriting), and then to administering the business (claims).

Insurers perform additional functions that are designed to support these three core functions. An insurer carries out these additional functions to facilitate risk transfer, to promote efficiency, and to meet its financial and nonfinancial goals.

This section provides an overview of these categories of insurer functions:

- Core functions
- Supporting functions
- Other common functional areas

All of the functions included in these categories interact to meet an insurer's goals. Some insurers may perform only some of these functions, some may combine or separate functions, and some may use different names for them. Specific types of products might also drive an insurer's functional needs— for example, an insurer that offers surety bonds might have a surety bond function, and an insurer that offers agricultural coverages might have an agricultural support function for unique underwriting and claim issues. Regardless of these differences, each function is closely linked to all the other functions, and none is performed in a vacuum. The interaction of these core and other functions is vital to an insurer's survival and success.

Core Functions

Although insurers may use varying organizational structures, three core functions exist within the structure of a typical insurer. These core functions—marketing and distribution, underwriting, and claims—form the basis of an insurer's business.

Marketing and Distribution

Marketing and distribution involves determining what products or services customers want and need, advertising the products (communicating their value to customers), and delivering them to customers. The marketing and distribution function contributes significantly to an insurer's goals of earning a profit and meeting customers' needs. The insurer cannot make a profit if it does not provide the products and services customers need.

The goals of the marketing and distribution function must be balanced with other insurer goals. For example, the objectives of the marketing and distribution function should support the insurer's overall growth and customer retention goals. If the insurer has targeted specific regions or lines of business as growth areas, the marketing and distribution function needs to align its efforts for overall growth and customer retention. An imbalance between the marketing and distribution function's goals and the goals of any other department within the organization may reduce the efficiency of the insurer.

Underwriting

Underwriting

The process of selecting insureds, pricing coverage, determining insurance policy terms and conditions, and then monitoring the underwriting decisions made.

Book of business

A group of policies with a common characteristic, such as territory or type of coverage, or all policies written by a particular insurer or agency.

Underwriting guidelines (underwriting guide)

A written manual that communicates an insurer's underwriting policy and that specifies the attributes of an account that an insurer is willing to insure.

Adverse selection

In general, the tendency for people with the greatest probability of loss to be the ones most likely to purchase insurance.

Once the marketing and distribution function has developed a relationship with potential customers, it is the job of the **underwriting** function to determine whether and under what conditions the insurer is willing to provide insurance products and services to the potential customers. The goal of underwriting is to write a profitable **book of business** for the insurer, which supports the insurer's profit goal. This is accomplished by developing appropriate **underwriting guidelines**, which underwriters use to evaluate risk. Underwriting serves both insurers and insurance buyers by helping the insurer avoid **adverse selection**. Avoiding adverse selection assists an insurer with remaining profitable and keeping premiums reasonable for insureds.

Claims

An insurance policy is a promise to make a payment to, or on behalf of, the insured if a covered event occurs. The purpose of the claims function is to fulfill the insurer's promise. To that end, the claims function is staffed by employees who are trained in the skills necessary to evaluate and settle claims and to negotiate or litigate the settlement of claims by or against insureds through the claim handling process.

The claim handling process is designed to achieve a fair settlement in accordance with the applicable insurance policy provisions. Claim settlements that exceed the amount payable under the policy increase the cost of insurance for all insureds. Settlements that are less than the coverage amount deprive the insured of benefits to which he or she is entitled under the insurance policy. Insurers have developed expertise in claim handling in all categories of loss exposures. Therefore, many insurance industry practitioners view claim handling as the primary service that insurers provide.

Supporting Functions

To support the core functions of marketing and distribution, underwriting, and claims, insurers provide a variety of supporting functions, including risk control, premium auditing, actuarial functions, reinsurance, and information technology. Although most insurers are able to provide these supporting functions in-house, many are available through third-party providers as well. These functions are not only necessary to the efficient operation of insurers, but are also used by a variety of other risk financing organizations, such as captives, pools, risk retention groups, and self-insurers:

- Risk control—An insurer's risk control function provides information to the underwriting function to assist in selecting and rating risks. The risk control function also works with commercial insureds to help prevent losses and to reduce the effects of losses that cannot be prevented. Insurers may also market their risk control services as a stand-alone product to third parties who have not purchased insurance policies from the insurer.

- Premium auditing—Although the premium for many types of insurance is known and guaranteed in advance, the premium is variable for some lines of insurance and cannot be precisely calculated until after the end of the policy period. For example, the premium for workers compensation insurance policies is calculated using wages paid during the policy period. Other commercial insurance policies may use rating variables such as sales or revenue to calculate the premium. Premium auditors ensure equitable treatment of insureds by reviewing the insureds' records to obtain accurate information on rating variables.

- Actuarial—Actuarial functions include calculating insurance rates, developing rating plans, estimating loss reserves, and providing predictive modeling services. The actuarial function also conducts sensitivity analysis to determine the financial security of the insurer. Furthermore, the actuarial function coordinates with the accounting and finance functions in developing reports for regulators to ensure that the insurer is adhering to all regulatory requirements.

- Reinsurance—When an insurer accepts a risk that is larger than it is willing or able to support, it can transfer all or part of that risk to other insurers through reinsurance transactions. Many insurers have a separate reinsurance department that arranges reinsurance and maintains reinsurance agreements.

- Information technology—The information technology function provides the infrastructure that supports all of an insurer's internal and external communications. Insurers use information technology to conduct their daily operations, manage marketing efforts, underwrite policies, track investments, and pay claims. Information systems are especially important to insurers because of the vast amounts of data associated with insurance operations.

Other Common Functional Areas

In addition to the core and supporting functions, insurers perform a host of other functions or outsource them to an external organization. Some common functions include investments, accounting and finance, customer service, legal and compliance, human resources, and special investigation units (SIUs).

- Investments—An insurer's investment operations enable it to earn investment income on the funds generated by its underwriting activities. This investment income enables the insurer to reduce the premium that it must charge in exchange for the risks it assumes. The nature of the insurance risks that an insurer assumes is a factor in determining the types of investments it acquires. For example, liability losses are paid out over a longer period than property losses. Therefore, liability policies can support more long-term investments, such as corporate bonds with long maturity periods, whereas property policies need to be supported by more liquid and short-term investments. An insurer that assumes only moderate underwriting risks might be able to assume greater investment risks with potentially higher investment yield, whereas an insurer that assumes high underwriting risks might need to be more conservative in its investment strategy.

- Accounting and finance—The primary responsibilities of the accounting and finance function are to ensure that the organization has funds to meet its obligations and to fairly and fully disclose the financial position of the insurer in conformance with generally accepted accounting principles (GAAP). Insurers, like all other types of businesses, use accounting to record, analyze, and summarize their financial activities and status. Once the information has been accumulated, an accountant must evaluate, interpret, and communicate the results to all stakeholders.

- Customer service—The customer service function can include an array of responsibilities that vary among insurers. Some insurers have customer service personnel assigned to specific work areas such as customer billing, claims services, underwriting support, agency relations or billing, agency technology support, customer Internet support, and information technology support services for internal users. The customer service function could apply to specific functions or to the entire organization. Customer service may be limited to telephone support, or it may include external support services, such as agency technology user support.

- Legal and compliance—The legal and compliance function provides legal counsel, support, and service to other functions within the insurer and ensures that statutory and administrative requirements are met. Large insurers may have legal counselors specifically assigned to their claim function. Activities of the legal and compliance function may include overseeing and managing litigation, managing corporate legal requirements, participating in legislative activities, and auditing all functions of the insurer for regulatory compliance and to ensure that organizational standards are met and procedures are followed.

- Human resources—The human resources function involves the selection, training, and dismissal of employees. The human resources area maintains employee records; supervises employee introduction to colleagues, performance reviews, and compensation management; conducts orientation and ongoing training; administers employee benefit programs; and performs related functions.

- Special investigation units (SIUs)—These units are established to combat insurance fraud, which includes any deliberate deception committed against an insurer or an insurance producer for the purpose of unwarranted financial gain. Fraud can occur during the process of buying, selling, or underwriting insurance, or making or paying a claim. Such fraud may be committed by applicants, insureds, claimants, medical and other service providers, and even by producers and the insurer's staff. SIU personnel investigate suspicious circumstances that affect claims such as underreporting payroll for a lower premium, overreporting square footage for the purpose of obtaining higher limits, or inflating the value on a proof of loss for a higher claim payment. SIUs collect evidence of possible fraud and may even withhold claim payments when fraud is suspected and likely.

These other functional areas may be separated into additional functions. For example, in some insurers, the human resources function is divided into human resources and training and development. Others insurers may group several of these other functional areas into one such area. For example, the actuarial, investment, and internal audit functions may be combined to form the accounting and finance function. See the exhibit "Insurance Fraud: Special Investigation Units (SIUs)."

Insurance Fraud: Special Investigation Units (SIUs)

Insurers are actively involved in the fight against insurance fraud and use various techniques, including predictive analytic tools, to detect and investigate fraudulent activity. Fraudulent activity increases insurance costs for both insurers and insureds.

According to industry estimates, fraud accounts for 10 percent of the property-casualty industry's losses.* Cases are referred to special investigation units (SIUs) based on criteria that vary by insurer. Some insurers refer every suspicious situation to SIUs; others refer cases based on the extent of the suspected fraud, the prospects of obtaining proof of the fraud, or other criteria.

Perpetrators of insurance fraud can suffer both civil and criminal prosecution. Both state and federal laws provide for the prosecution of insurance fraud and provide immunity to insurers who report information on suspected individuals. Statistics show that the number of criminal convictions and civil prosecutions continues to increase, offering evidence that SIUs have a positive effect on insurers' overall profitability.

*Insurance Information Institute, "Insurance Fraud," April 19, 2010, http://www.iii.org/issue-update/insurance-fraud (accessed July 23, 2010).

[DA06351]

SUMMARY

Insurers can be classified in several ways, including legal form of ownership, place of incorporation, licensing status, and the insurance distribution systems and channels the insurer uses to deliver its products and services to the marketplace.

An insurer's overall goals differ from those of other organizations in how an insurer meets its goals and in the conflicts that exist among competing goals. Insurers' major goals are to earn a profit, meet customer needs, comply with legal requirements, diversify risk, and fulfill their duty to society.

Insurers contend with numerous constraints in achieving their goals. These constraints exist within the insurer's internal operation (efficiency, expertise, size, financial resources, and other internal constraints) as well as in the external environment (regulation, rating agencies, public opinion, competition, economic conditions, insurance marketing and distribution, and other external constraints).

Measuring the performance of an insurer involves determining how successful the insurer is at meeting established goals. Measuring how well an insurer meets its profitability goals and legal requirements is more objective, while measuring how well an insurer meets customer needs and social responsibilities is more subjective.

An insurer's core functions are marketing and distribution, underwriting, and claims. Other supporting functions include risk control, premium auditing, actuarial functions, reinsurance, and information technology. Additional common functional areas in an insurer may include investments, accounting and finance, customer service, legal and compliance, human resources, and SIUs. While insurers vary regarding their structure and the exact role of each functional area, the interaction of the core functions and the other functions is vital to insurers' survival and success.

ASSIGNMENT NOTES

1. Each time the government extended the terrorism risk legislation, a new title (and acronym) for the act has been developed. "TRIA" is used here to represent each rendition collectively.

2. Robert P. Hartwig, "The P/C Insurance Industry at the Crossroads: Where We Are and Where We're Headed," March 22, 2010, http://www.iii.org/presentation/the-p-c-insurance-industry-at-the-crossroads-where-we-are-where-were-headed-032210(accessed April 10, 2010).

3. Hartwig, "The P/C Insurance Industry at the Crossroads: Where We Are and Where We're Headed."

Insurance Regulation

Educational Objectives

After learning the content of this assignment, you should be able to:

▷ Explain how insurance regulation protects consumers, contributes to maintaining insurer solvency, and assists in preventing destructive competition.

▷ Identify the regulatory activities of state insurance departments and the duties typically performed by state insurance commissioners.

▷ Describe the licensing requirements for insurers and insurance personnel.

▷ Describe the methods that regulators use to maintain the solvency of insurers and to manage insolvencies, and the reasons why insurers become insolvent.

▷ Describe the goals of insurance rate regulation, the major types of state rating laws, and the reasons supporting and opposing rate regulation.

▷ Explain how the contract language contained in insurance policies is regulated.

▷ Explain how the market conduct areas in insurance are regulated and how regulatory activities protect consumers.

▷ Explain how organizations that act as unofficial regulators affect insurance activities.

Insurance Regulation

REASONS FOR INSURANCE REGULATION

Because a well-functioning insurance market is essential to society, regulation is necessary to correct market imperfections, whether those imperfections result from externalities, incomplete information, costs, or other causes. However, the reasons for regulation can differ; each market participant, each regulator, and each observer may offer different reasons for regulating a particular market.

The insurance industry is regulated primarily for three reasons:

- To protect consumers
- To maintain insurer solvency
- To prevent destructive competition

Although these purposes clearly overlap, each is examined separately.

Consumers may not have complete information about the product of insurance, yet they need the product and often are required to purchase it. Because of consumers' incomplete information, insurance regulators must ensure that the products are beneficial to consumers and available at an equitable price. In addition, inadequate information, destructive competition, and mismanagement (among other things) can threaten the solvency of insurers. Implementation and enforcement of insurance regulation is necessary to correct each of these market imperfections. If regulation can correct or reduce the effect of the market imperfections, it can encourage insurer solvency.

Protect Consumers

The primary reason insurance is regulated is to protect consumers. When consumers buy electronics, clothing, or furniture, they can usually inspect the products before purchasing them to ensure that the products meet their needs. Even if consumers inspect the insurance policies they purchase, they might not be able to analyze and understand complex legal documents.

Regulators help to protect consumers by reviewing insurance policy forms to determine whether they benefit consumers and comply with state consumer protection laws. State legislatures can set coverage standards and specify policy language for certain insurance coverages. State insurance regulators can review policy language and disapprove policy forms and endorsements that are inconsistent with state consumer protection laws.

Insurance regulators also protect consumers against fraud and unethical market behavior. Departments of insurance receive complaints about these behaviors:

- Producers have intentionally sold unnecessary insurance.
- Producers have misrepresented the nature of coverage to make a sale.
- Producers have stolen or misused insured or insurer funds.
- Claim representatives have engaged in unfair claim practices, refusing to pay legitimate claims or unfairly reducing claim payments.
- Insurance managers have contributed to the insolvency of insurers through their dishonesty.

In addition to protecting consumers against such abuses, regulators also try to ensure that insurance is readily available, especially the insurance that is viewed as a necessity. For example, all states now try to ensure that continuous personal auto insurance coverage is available by restricting the rights of insurers to cancel or nonrenew personal auto insurance policies. At the same time, regulators recognize that insurers sometimes must break long-term relationships with insureds whose loss exposures no longer match those the insurer wants to cover. Cancellation restrictions aimed at promoting availability can therefore lead insurers to reject more new-business applications, which reduces insurance availability.

Insurance regulators also provide information about insurance matters so that consumers can make more informed decisions.

Maintain Insurer Solvency

Another reason insurance is regulated is to maintain insurer solvency. Solvency regulation protects insureds against the risk that insurers will be unable to meet their financial obligations. Consumers and even some sophisticated businesspeople may find it difficult to evaluate insurers' financial ability to keep their promises. Insurance regulators try to maintain a sound financial condition of private insurers for several reasons:

- Insurance provides future protection—Premiums are paid in advance, but the period of protection extends into the future. If insurers become insolvent, future claims may not be paid, and the insurance protection already paid for may become worthless.
- Regulation is needed to protect the public interest—Large numbers of individuals and the community at large are adversely affected when insurers become insolvent.
- Insurers have a responsibility to insureds—Insurers hold substantial funds for the ultimate benefit of insureds. Government regulation is necessary to safeguard such funds.
- Insurers have become insolvent despite regulatory reviews. The goal of regulation is not to eliminate all insolvencies but rather to minimize

the number of insolvencies. To eliminate insolvencies would mean that regulations must be set to allow the most inefficient insurer to continue to operate, which is not a desirable regulatory goal.

Prevent Destructive Competition

Insurance regulation also seeks to prevent destructive competition. Regulators are responsible for determining whether insurance rates are high enough to prevent destructive competition. At times, some insurers underprice their products to increase market share by attracting customers away from higher-priced competitors. This practice drives down price levels in the whole market. When insurance rate levels are inadequate, some insurers can become insolvent, and others might withdraw from the market or stop writing new business. An insurance shortage can then develop, and individuals and firms might be unable to obtain the coverage they need. Certain types of insurance can become unavailable at any price, such as when both products liability and directors and officers coverage became unavailable in the 1980s.

INSURANCE REGULATORS

Insurance professionals must be familiar with the entire regulatory framework for insurance, and state regulators and the National Association of Insurance Commissioners (NAIC) both play important roles in regulation.

Insurance is regulated primarily by state insurance departments. State regulators, in turn, are members of the NAIC, a nonprofit corporation that has no regulatory authority of its own but that plays an important coordinating role.

Insurers are also subject to federal regulations that affect noninsurance businesses as well. Although not discussed here, most of the state and local regulations that affect other businesses, such as zoning laws, also apply to insurers.

State Insurance Departments

Every state has three separate and equal branches of government:

- The legislative branch makes the laws.
- The judicial branch (the court system) interprets the laws.
- The executive branch implements the laws.

Day-to-day regulation of the insurance business is performed by state insurance departments, which fall within the executive branch of each state government. State insurance departments enforce insurance laws enacted by the legislature. These laws regulate the formation of insurers, capital and surplus requirements, licensing of producers, investment of funds, financial requirements for maintaining solvency, insurance rates that can be charged, marketing and claim practices, taxation of insurers, and the rehabilitation of financially impaired insurers or the liquidation of insolvent ones.

Under the insurance commissioner's direction, a state insurance department engages in a wide variety of regulatory activities that typically include these:

- Licensing insurers
- Licensing producers, claim representatives, and other insurance personnel
- Approving policy forms
- Holding rate hearings and reviewing rate filings
- Evaluating solvency information
- Performing market conduct examinations
- Investigating policyholder complaints
- Rehabilitating or liquidating insolvent insurers
- Issuing cease-and-desist orders
- Fining insurers that violate state law
- Publishing shoppers' guides and other consumer information (in some states)
- Preventing fraud

The Insurance Commissioner

Every state insurance department is headed by an insurance commissioner, superintendent, or director appointed by the governor or elected by the voting public.

The duties of a typical state insurance commissioner include these:

- Overseeing the state insurance department's operation
- Promulgating orders, rules, and regulations necessary to administer insurance laws
- Determining whether to issue business licenses to new insurers, producers, and other insurance entities
- Reviewing insurance pricing and coverage
- Conducting financial and market examinations of insurers
- Holding hearings on insurance issues
- Taking action when insurance laws are violated
- Issuing an annual report on the status of the state's insurance market and insurance department
- Maintaining records of insurance department activities

The commissioner does not personally handle most of these duties, but instead delegates them to others in the state insurance department.

Although most commissioners are appointed, some states elect their commissioners. Disagreement exists regarding which selection method better serves the public interest. Proponents of an elective system cite these reasons:

- An appointed insurance commissioner is subject to dismissal, while an elected commissioner is generally in office for a full term.
- An appointed commissioner might continue regulating in the same manner as his or her predecessor when a different approach is required, but an elected commissioner would more likely change the insurance department's stance.
- An appointed commissioner might not be aware of the public's concerns, but an elected commissioner would be keenly aware of the issues important to the public.
- An appointed commissioner might feel inclined to yield to the interests of those responsible for the appointment, while an elected commissioner is not obligated to any particular group or special interest.

Proponents of an appointing system cite these reasons:

- An appointed commissioner has no need to campaign or to be unduly influenced by political contributors.
- An appointed commissioner is less likely to be swayed by ill-informed public opinion than an elected one.
- An appointed commissioner is more likely to be perceived as a career government employee interested in regulation than as a politician interested in political advancement.

Many commissioners were employed in the insurance business before they entered public office, and many are employed by insurers or insurance-related organizations after leaving office. The expertise and understanding of insurance operations necessary to regulate effectively are most likely found in a person who has worked in the insurance business. However, some allege that such insurance commissioners have less than an objective relationship with the insurers they regulate.

In rebuttal, state insurance commissioners usually deny that they are overly responsive to insurers. Commissioners frequently issue cease-and-desist orders, fine or penalize insurers for infractions of the law, forbid insurers to engage in mass cancellations, limit insurance rate increases, and take numerous other actions that benefit policyholders at insurers' expense.

State Regulation Funding

State insurance departments are partly funded by state premium taxes, audit fees, filing fees, and licensing fees, but premium taxes are the major source of funding. Although state premium taxes are substantial, only a relatively small proportion is spent on insurance regulation. Premium taxes are designed primarily to raise revenues for the state as a whole.

The National Association of Insurance Commissioners (NAIC)

National Association of Insurance Commissioners (NAIC)

An association of insurance commissioners from the fifty U.S. states, the District of Columbia, and the five U.S. territories and possessions, whose purpose is to coordinate insurance regulation activities among the various state insurance departments.

The **National Association of Insurance Commissioners (NAIC)** coordinates insurance regulation activities among the insurance departments but has no direct regulatory authority. However, by providing a forum to develop uniform policy when appropriate, the NAIC has a profound effect on the nature and uniformity of state regulation.

The NAIC meets three times per year to discuss important problems and issues in insurance regulation. The NAIC developed uniform financial statement forms that all states require insurers to file. It collects and compiles financial information from insurers and warehouses the financial data for use by insurance regulators. It also assists state insurance departments by sharing financial information about insurers that are potentially insolvent and by developing model laws and regulations. The NAIC's Financial Analysis Working Group serves as both a coordinator and a fail safe mechanism for state insurance regulators as they oversee nationally significant insurers.

Model Laws and Regulations

The insurance laws and regulations of many states incorporate at least the primary concepts of NAIC model laws, resulting in some degree of uniformity among the states. Examples of model laws include model legislation on the regulation of risk retention groups, and a model property and liability insurance rating law.

Model law

A document drafted by the NAIC, in a style similar to a state statute, that reflects the NAIC's proposed solution to a given problem or issue and provides a common basis to the states for drafting laws that affect the insurance industry. Any state may choose to adopt the model bill or adopt it with modifications.

Model regulation

A draft regulation that may be implemented by a state insurance department if the model law is passed.

Laws are passed by the state legislature, while regulations are developed and enforced by a regulatory body such as the state insurance department. A **model law** is a draft bill that state legislatures consider; any state can choose to adopt or to adapt the model bill. A **model regulation** is a draft of a regulation that can be implemented by a state insurance department if the model law is passed.

Accreditation Program

In addition to developing model laws, the NAIC, in 1990, implemented an accreditation program to increase the uniformity of insurer solvency regulation across the states. To become accredited, a state insurance department must prove that it has satisfied the minimum solvency regulation standards required by the accreditation program.

State insurance departments must meet three criteria to satisfy the NAIC's Financial Regulation Standards and to be accredited:

- The state's insurance laws and regulations must meet basic standards of NAIC models.
- The state's regulatory methods must be acceptable to the NAIC.
- The state's insurance department practices must be adequate as defined by the NAIC.

As of June 2010, the insurance departments in fifty states and the District of Columbia had been accredited by the NAIC.[1]

Federal Regulation

The McCarran Act reverses the usual state-federal allocation of regulatory powers only for the business of insurance, and this does not include everything that insurers do. For example:

- As employers, insurers are subject to federal employment laws just like any other business.
- As businesses that sell their stock to the public to raise capital, stock insurers are subject to regulations like any other such business.

The Insurance Fraud Protection Act is part of a federal anti-crime bill titled "Violent Crime Control and Law Enforcement Act of 1994." [2]This broad legislation protects consumers and insurers against insolvencies resulting from insurance fraud.

The act prohibits anyone with a felony conviction involving trustworthiness from working in the business of insurance unless he or she secures the written consent of an insurance regulator. Moreover, it is illegal for insurers, reinsurers, producers, and others to employ a person who has a felony conviction involving breach of trust or dishonesty.

The act identifies these crimes involving the business of insurance:[3]

- Making false statements or reports to insurance regulators—including overvaluing assets—to influence regulatory decisions
- Making false entries in books, reports, or statements to deceive anyone about an insurer's financial condition or solvency
- Embezzling from anyone who is engaged in the business of insurance
- Using threats or force or "any threatening letter or communication to corruptly influence, obstruct, or impede" insurance regulatory proceedings

INSURANCE REGULATORY ACTIVITIES: LICENSING INSURERS AND INSURANCE PERSONNEL

At the beginning of any business development plan, insurers and insurance personnel should consider insurance regulation. By anticipating regulatory requirements and processes, they can reap strategic advantages. Knowledge of insurance regulation is also important to ensure that the insurer complies with regulatory requirements. Noncompliance can lead to impeded operations resulting from regulatory intervention and more frequent examinations. It can also lead to the loss of an insurer's license or damage an insurer's reputation in the marketplace.

From the time of their formation, insurers are subject to state insurance regulation. While the review processes for insurer licensing vary from state to state, all states require property-casualty insurers to receive approval before operating within the state.

Just as departments of insurance (DOIs) have the authority to regulate insurers and related entities, state laws also give them the authority to regulate insurance producers, claim representatives, and other insurance personnel.

Licensing Insurers

By issuing a license to an insurer, a state indicates that the insurer meets minimum standards of financial strength, competence, and integrity. If these standards change later, and if the insurer fails to meet the new standards, the insurer's license can be revoked. A license indicates that the insurer has complied with the state's insurance laws and is authorized to write certain types of insurance in the state. Once licensed, the insurer is subject to all applicable state laws, rules, and regulations.

In response to complaints about the length of time regulators took to license a new insurer, regulators developed the Uniform Certificate of Authority Application (UCAA) to streamline the process. All states and the District of Columbia participate in the UCAA. The UCAA process is designed to allow insurers to file copies of the same application for admission in numerous states. While each state still performs its own independent review of each application, the need to file different applications in different formats has been eliminated.

Licensing standards vary among admitted domestic, foreign, alien, and nonadmitted insurers. Risk retention groups face yet another set of standards.

Domestic insurer

An insurer doing business in the jurisdiction in which it is incorporated.

Domestic Insurers

An insurer licensed in its home state is called a **domestic insurer**. If a domestic insurer obtains licenses in states other than its state of domicile, it is a

foreign insurer in those other states. A domestic insurer's license generally has no expiration date. Licenses of foreign insurers and **alien insurers** generally must be renewed annually.

Domestic insurers usually must meet the conditions imposed on corporations engaged in noninsurance activities as well as some special conditions imposed on insurers. An applicant for an insurer license must apply for a charter. The applicant must provide the names and addresses of the incorporators, the name of the proposed corporation, the territories and types of insurance it plans to market, the total authorized capital stock (if any), and its surplus. The state insurance commissioner reviews the application to see whether the applicant also meets the state's licensing requirements.

An insurer must be financially sound. State laws require that domestic stock insurers satisfy certain minimum capital and surplus requirements before a license is granted. Domestic stock insurers must meet **capital stock** and **paid-in surplus** requirements. Minimum initial capital and paid-in surplus requirements vary widely by state and by amounts and types of insurance written. Minimum initial capital requirements range from as little as $100,000 to as much as $15 million.

For mutual or **reciprocal insurers**, the minimum financial requirement applies only to surplus because a mutual insurer does not have capital derived from the sale of stock. When a mutual insurer is forming, its initial surplus can be derived from premium deposits paid by prospective policyholders. Also, a portion of the initial surplus can be borrowed. Most states require mutuals to have an initial surplus equal to the minimum capital and paid-in surplus requirement for stock insurers writing the same type of insurance. However, some states have set a minimum surplus requirement for mutuals that is lower than the minimum capital and paid-in surplus requirement for stock insurers. In most states, minimum surplus requirements for mutual insurers and reciprocals are the same.

Many states require the organizers of a mutual insurer to have a minimum number of applications with deposit premiums for a minimum number of separate loss exposures and aggregate premium exceeding a specific amount. These requirements help to guarantee that the insurer has a minimum book of business and hence some stability before it officially begins operations.

In addition to financial requirements, states impose other requirements on new insurers. For example, the proposed name for a new mutual insurer must include the word "mutual," and the proposed name of a new insurer must not be so similar to that of any existing insurer that it would be misleading. The commissioner might have the authority to refuse a license if he or she believes the insurer's incorporators or directors are not trustworthy.

Some states even permit the commissioner to deny a license to an otherwise worthy applicant if the commissioner believes that no additional insurers are needed in the state. Once the license has been issued, it can be revoked if the insurer operates in a manner that is clearly detrimental to the welfare of

Foreign insurer

An insurer licensed to operate in a state but incorporated in another state.

Alien insurer

An insurer domiciled in a country other than the United States.

Capital stock

A balance sheet value that represents the amount of funds that a corporation's stockholders have contributed through the purchase of stock.

Paid-in surplus

The amount stockholders paid in excess of the par value of the stock.

Reciprocal insurer

An insurer owned by its policyholders, formed as an unincorporated association for the purpose of providing insurance coverage to its members (called subscribers), and managed by an attorney-in-fact. Members agree to mutually insure each other, and they share profits and losses in the same proportion as the amount of insurance purchased from the exchange by that member.

its policyholders (for example, consistent failure to pay legitimate claims or fraudulent business conduct).

Foreign Insurers

To be licensed in an additional state (in other words, as a foreign insurer), an insurer first must show that it has satisfied the requirements imposed by its home state (its state of domicile, or the state where it is a domestic insurer). Second, a foreign insurer must generally satisfy the minimum capital, surplus, and other requirements imposed on the state's domestic insurers.

Alien Insurers

Alien insurers (insurers domiciled outside the United States) must satisfy the requirements imposed on domestic insurers by the state in which they want to be licensed. Additionally, they must usually establish a branch office in any state and have funds on deposit in the U.S. equal to the minimum capital and surplus required.

Nonadmitted Insurers

An admitted insurer is licensed by a state insurance department to do business in the insured's home state. A nonadmitted insurer is not licensed (not authorized) in the insured's home state; it may be an admitted insurer in other states, and it may even be an alien insurer.

A nonadmitted insurer is typically a surplus lines insurer. The surplus lines insurance mechanism allows U.S. consumers to buy property-casualty insurance from nonadmitted insurers when consumers are unable to purchase the insurance they need from admitted insurers. Surplus lines insurers provide a positive and legal supplement to the admitted insurance market. The business that surplus lines insurers generally accept includes distressed risks (those that have underwriting problems), unique risks (those that are difficult to evaluate), and high-capacity risks (those that require very high coverage limits). Surplus lines coverages commonly include products liability, professional liability, employment practices liability, special events, and excess and umbrella policies.

Under surplus lines laws, a nonadmitted insurer might be permitted to transact business through a specially licensed surplus lines producer if (1) the insurance is not readily available from admitted insurers, (2) the nonadmitted insurer is "acceptable," and (3) the producer has a special license authorizing him or her to place such insurance. The surplus lines producer usually must be a resident of the state.

An "acceptable" nonadmitted insurer generally must file a financial statement that the insurance commissioner finds satisfactory; supply documentation of transactions to state regulators; obtain a certificate of compliance from its home state or country; and, if an alien insurer, maintain a trust fund in the

U.S. Some states leave the determination of acceptability to the producer. A few states permit producers to use other nonadmitted insurers if the desired insurance cannot be obtained from either admitted or "acceptable" nonadmitted insurers.

The National Association of Insurance Commissioners (NAIC) maintains an International Insurers Department that helps insurance regulators evaluate the financial status of alien insurers. The International Insurers Department prepares and disseminates a quarterly listing (Non-Admitted Insurers Quarterly Listing) of alien nonadmitted insurers to assist state insurance regulators, surplus lines brokers, and the public in evaluating whether to do business with one of the insurers on the listing. An insurer that would like to be included on the quarterly listing must file an application for listing. The insurer must also agree to provide pertinent financial information to allow the International Insurers Department to determine whether the insurer meets certain capital requirements, has established the applicable U.S. trust accounts, and meets the requisite character traits such as trustworthiness and integrity. The minimum capital and surplus required is $15 million. The minimum requirements for the trust account are $100 million or an amount established by a risk-based formula, but in no event should it be less than $5.4 million. The requirement for the trust account has long been a source of discontent for alien surplus lines insurers and reinsurers.

A nonadmitted insurer writing business in the surplus lines market does not face regulatory constraints on insurance rates and forms. From the insured's perspective, a distinct disadvantage of surplus lines insurance is that it is not usually protected by the state's guaranty fund. Thus, the requirements for capital and trust accounts provide assurance for insureds that nonadmitted insurers will be able to pay their claims.

Risk Retention Groups

A risk retention group is a special type of assessable mutual insurer enabled by the 1986 Liability Risk Retention Act. Risk retention groups are often formed under state captive laws, which generally maintain lower capital and surplus requirements for captives than for traditional property-casualty insurers. Once licensed as a commercial liability insurer under the laws of at least one state, a risk retention group can write insurance in other states without a license by filing the appropriate notice and registration forms with the nonchartering state. A risk retention group can write only commercial liability insurance for its members and may not write other lines of business. However, in a nonchartering state, a risk retention group might be subject to some state laws, such as unfair claim settlement practice laws, and to premium taxes. The risk retention group might also be required to become a member of a joint underwriting association (JUA) or a similar association with which insurers share losses in such areas as assigned-risk auto insurance.

Some state regulators have expressed concerns about the financial security of risk retention groups, particularly when the group providing the insurance is licensed in another state. Congress assisted with addressing these concerns by allowing the licensing state to request and, if necessary, mandate an examination of a group's financial condition—even when the commissioner has no reason to believe that the group is financially impaired. However, some state regulators still fear abuses under the act, while some advocates of risk retention groups remain concerned about the possibility of overregulation.

Licensing Insurance Personnel

In addition to licensing insurers, state regulators also license some categories of insurance personnel. States license many of the people who sell insurance, give insurance advice, or represent insurers, including producers, claim representatives, and insurance consultants.

Producers

Producers must be licensed in each state where they do business. To obtain a license to sell a particular type of insurance, a producer must pass a written examination. Insurance producers operating without a license are subject to civil, and sometimes criminal, penalties.

Traditionally, lack of uniformity among the states' licensing requirements has been a source of frustration and an expense for producers licensed in more than one state. Provisions in the Gramm-Leach-Bliley (GLB) Act have led to greater licensing reciprocity among states. Regulators' ultimate goal is to move beyond reciprocity and to resolve issues related to uniformity in producer licensing. Meeting this goal will streamline the licensing process while retaining state regulatory authority over it.

Much progress has been made in recent years to address producer concerns about the lack of uniformity. The development of the National Insurance Producer Registry (NIPR) has eliminated many of the inconveniences that arise from a multi-state regulatory system. The NIPR is a unique public-private partnership that supports the work of the states and the NAIC in making the producer licensing process more cost effective, streamlined, and uniform for the benefit of regulators, insurance producers, insurers, and consumers. The NIPR vision is to provide one place for producers to go to meet all aspects of the producer licensing and appointment process using an electronic communication network. The NIPR developed and implemented the Producer Database (PDB) and the NIPR Gateway.

- The PDB is an electronic database consisting of information relating to insurance producers that links participating state regulatory licensing systems into one common repository of producer information. The PDB also includes data from the NAIC Regulatory Information Retrieval System to provide a more comprehensive producer profile. Some of the key benefits of PDB are increased productivity, lower cost, reduction of paper, access to real-time information, and the ability to conduct national verification of the license and status of a producer.

- The NIPR Gateway is a communication network that links state insurance regulators with the entities they regulate to facilitate the electronic exchange of producer information. Data standards have been developed for the exchange of license application, license renewal, appointment, and termination information.

Claim Representatives

Some states require claim representatives to be licensed so that those who make claim decisions for insurers are aware of prohibited claim practices, have a minimum level of technical knowledge and skill, and understand how to handle insureds' claims fairly. Licensing of claim representatives in most states includes an examination, which is important because of the complex and technical nature of insurance policies and the claim process. The licensing process also typically involves a background check, as well as ethics requirements, to help protect consumers who file claims from unfair, unethical, and dishonest claim practices.

Public adjusters, who represent insureds for a fee, are generally required to be licensed to ensure technical competence and to protect the public.

Insurance Consultants

Insurance consultants give advice, counsel, or opinions about insurance policies. Some states require insurance consultants to be licensed, and requirements for a consultant's license vary by state. Separate examinations are usually required to be an insurance consultant in both life-health insurance and property-casualty insurance.

INSURANCE REGULATORY ACTIVITIES: MONITORING INSURER SOLVENCY

Individual consumers and most businesses do not have the skills or resources to analyze claim-paying ability when selecting an insurer. However, because insurers hold large sums of money paid by consumers for long periods of time, their financial strength must be carefully monitored to ensure their continued ability to pay covered claims, both in the present and in the future. The United States regulatory framework helps to maintain insurers' solvency and thus protect consumers.

Monitoring solvency protects insureds and the public by accomplishing two broad goals:

- Reducing the insolvency risk
- Protecting the public against loss when insurers fail

A delicate balance exists between achieving these goals and reducing the total cost of risk for society as a whole. Insurers' costs are raised by requirements that increase the amount of capital they must hold in reserve. Whether directly or indirectly, insurance consumers pay for the costs of regulation, including regulators' salaries and the costs of collecting and maintaining financial data. Other insurers must pay for the losses of an insolvent insurer, and these additional costs are passed on to insureds. Insurance regulators recognize it is important both for regulation to be efficient and for inefficient insurers to cease to operate. As a result, regulators do not regulate to completely eliminate insolvencies, but rather to effectively use their regulatory resources to keep insolvencies infrequent and manageable.

Methods to Maintain Solvency

The U.S. regulatory framework is a national system of state-based regulation where the regulatory responsibility for insurer solvency monitoring rests with the state insurance regulator. The state insurance regulators are assisted by the National Association of Insurance Commissioners (NAIC), an organization of the chief insurance regulatory official in each state, the District of Columbia, and five U.S. territories. The NAIC provides financial, actuarial, legal, technology, research, and economic expertise to state regulators to assist them in meeting regulatory goals.

The mission or purpose of U.S. insurance regulation is to protect the interests of the insured and those who rely on the insurance coverage provided to the insured, while also facilitating an effective and efficient marketplace for insurance products. To accomplish this mission, insurance regulators must have appropriate regulatory authority and be able to operate independent of undue influence from insurers or other groups. The commissioner needs to maintain adequate staffing levels of sufficiently trained personnel and be able, by law, to treat confidential information appropriately.

The U.S. regulatory framework relies on an extensive system of peer review, featuring frequent communication and collaboration to provide the necessary checks and balances needed to make the system work. Much of this collaboration occurs through the NAIC where the diverse perspectives of its members are reflected in solutions embodied in model laws and regulations. These solutions have resulted in a risk-focused approach that is constantly evolving to meet changing local, national, and international developments.

Uniformity of approach to financial regulation has been facilitated by the NAIC accreditation program. As part of the peer review process, the accreditation program subjects state insurance regulators to a thorough and comprehensive review to determine if the state has met minimum, baseline standards of solvency regulation. To become accredited, the state must submit to a full on-site accreditation review. Depending on the results of the review, the state is accredited or it is not (that is, a pass/fail system is used). To remain accredited, an accreditation review must be performed at least once every five years with interim annual reviews. The evaluation looks at these factors:

- The adequacy of the state's solvency laws and regulations to protect consumers

- The ability of the regulator to meet standards regarding effective and efficient financial analysis and examination processes based on the priority status of insurers

- The ability and willingness of the state regulator to cooperate and share pertinent information with other state, federal, or foreign regulatory officials

- The ability of a state to take timely and effective action when an insurer is identified as financially troubled or potentially troubled

- The quality of the state regulator's organizational and personnel practices

- The effectiveness of the state's processes for company licensing and review of proposed changes in control

At the present time, all fifty states and the District of Columbia are accredited. However, accreditation is not automatic. There have been several occasions when not all states have been accredited. See the exhibit "Financial Solvency Core Principles."

The U.S. regulatory framework has evolved over time into the risk-focused approach used by regulators today. There is not a single U.S. market, but rather a variety of state-based, regional, or even intrastate insurance markets that collectively are referred to as the U.S. market. A wide variety of insurers, ranging from the very small to large-sized insurer groups and some financial conglomerates, serve these markets. This wide range of regulated entities calls for a flexible and collegial approach to regulation that focuses on the risks undertaken by each regulated entity.

Financial Solvency Core Principles

Core Principle 1	Regulatory reporting, disclosure, and transparency	• Insurers are required to file standardized reports annually and quarterly to assess the insurer's risk and financial condition. • These reports contain both qualitative and quantitative information, and are updated as necessary to incorporate significant common insurer risks.
Core Principle 2	Off-site monitoring and analysis	• Assess on an ongoing basis the financial condition of the insurer as of the valuation date and to identify and assess current and prospective risks through risk-focused surveillance. • The results of the off-site analysis are included in an insurer profile for continual solvency monitoring. • Many off-site monitoring tools are maintained by the NAIC (such as the NAIC Financial Analysis Solvency Tools—FAST).
Core Principle 3	On-site, risk-focused examinations	• U.S. regulators carry out risk-focused, on-site examinations in which an insurer's corporate governance, management oversight, and financial strength are evaluated, including the system of risk identification and mitigation both on a current and prospective basis. • The reported financial results are assessed through the financial examination process and a determination is made of the insurer's compliance with legal requirements.
Core Principle 4	Reserves, capital adequacy, and solvency	• Insurers are required to maintain reserves and capital at all times and in such forms so as to provide an adequate margin of safety. • The most visible measure of capital adequacy requirements is associated with the risk-based capital (RBC) system. The RBC calculation uses a standardized formula to benchmark specified level of regulatory actions for weakly capitalized insurers.
Core Principle 5	Regulatory control of significant, broad-based, risk-related transactions/ activities	The transactions/activities encompass these: • Licensing requirements • Change of control • The amount of dividends paid • Transactions with affiliates • Reinsurance
Core Principle 6	Preventive and corrective measures, including enforcement	• The regulatory authority takes preventive and corrective measures that are timely, suitable, and necessary to reduce the impact of risks identified during on-site and off-site regulatory monitoring. • These regulatory actions are enforced as necessary.
Core Principle 7	Exiting the market and receivership	• The legal and regulatory framework defines a range of options for the orderly exit of insurers from the marketplace. • Solvency is defined and a receivership scheme established to ensure the payment of insured obligations of insolvent insurers subject to appropriate restrictions and limitations.

"The United States Insurance Financial Solvency Framework," National Association of Insurance Commissioners, February 19, 2010, pp. 3-5, http://www.naic.org/documents/committees_e_us_solvency_framework.pdf (accessed July 14, 2010). [DA06398]

The U.S. regulatory framework is built on a set of solvency requirements for insurers. States are evaluated during the accreditation process to measure the extent to which the state requires the insurer to comply with the provisions. These are examples of solvency requirements:

- Insurers must submit annual and quarterly financial statements to the domestic regulator and the NAIC using a prescribed format called the "annual statement" or the "blank." The NAIC data captures the financial statements, performs some data quality checks, and maintains a data warehouse for use by state financial regulators.

- Insurers are required to use the NAIC's Accounting Practices and Procedures Manual and the Annual Statement Blank and Instructions for consistency of accounting treatment and financial reporting.

- The accounting practices have been codified, and an insurer using a state approved permitted practice must disclose the differences so that anyone using the financial statement can make the appropriate adjustments to remove the effect of the permitted practice.

- Most insurers (excepting the very small) must submit their financial statement to a Certified Public Accountant (CPA) for audit.

- Most insurers must have their reserves evaluated by an actuary and have the actuary attest to the accuracy of the reserve estimates.

- Insurers must perform a risk-based capital (RBC) calculation and report the results to regulators. The RBC calculation uses a standardized formula to benchmark specified level of regulatory actions for weakly capitalized insurers. The RBC amount, based on industry experience, explicitly considers the size and risk profile of the insurer. The RBC calculation provides for higher RBC charges for riskier assets or for riskier lines of business so that more capital is required as a result. Although risk-based capital results indicate when an insurer's capital position is weak or deteriorating, a ladder of intervention levels exists within the RBC system. Thus, regulators have the authority to require insurers to take some action, or the regulator may have the authority to take action with respect to an insurer when the capital level falls within certain threshold amounts that are above the minimum capital requirement. The degree of action depends upon the relative capital weakness as determined by the RBC result and the existence of any mitigating or compounding issues.

- Insurers are required to adhere to state minimum capital and surplus requirements.

- State investment laws limit the types and quantity of investments an insurer may make, encouraging insurers to maintain a conservative and diversified investment portfolio. Invested assets outside the scope are not allowed to be counted in solvency calculations.

- Insurers are required to report investment values to the NAIC Securities Valuation Office. These results are made available to regulators and used for valuing assets reported in financial statement filings. State insurance regulators are able to look up a particular CUSIP (Committee on

Uniform Securities Identification Procedures) number and determine if an insurer owns a particular security and, if so, how much. Instructions are contained in the NAIC Securities Valuation Office's (SVO) Purposes and Procedures Manual.

- State laws specify limitations on the amount on any single insured risk a property-casualty insurer may underwrite.

- Treatment of reinsurance is governed by the NAIC Credit for Reinsurance Model Law, which imposes standards on credits allowed to the reporting insurer.

Liquidation of Insolvent Insurers

Insolvency

A situation in which an entity's current liabilities (as opposed to its total liabilities) exceed its current assets.

If an insurer falls into **insolvency**, the insurance commissioner places it in receivership. With proper management, successful rehabilitation might be possible. If the insurer cannot be rehabilitated, it is liquidated according to the state's insurance code. Many states now liquidate insolvent insurers according to the Uniform Insurers Liquidation Act drafted by the NAIC. This model act promotes uniformity in liquidating assets and paying claims of a failed insurer. Under this act, creditors in each state in which the insolvent insurer has conducted business are treated equally; creditors in the state where the insurer is domiciled do not receive preferential treatment. Some states prioritize claimants who are entitled to the failed insurer's assets. In 2005, NAIC members adopted the Insurer Receivership Model Act to replace the earlier model. The new model was amended in 2007 and has been adopted in only a few states at the time of this writing.

State Guaranty Funds

Guaranty fund

A state-established fund that provides a system for the payment of some of the unpaid claims of insolvent insurers licensed in that state, generally funded by assessments collected from all insurers licensed in the state.

Guaranty funds do not prevent insurer insolvency, but they mitigate its effects. All states have property-casualty insurance guaranty funds that pay some of the unpaid claims of insolvent insurers licensed in the particular state. With the exception of New York, where a pre-assessment system maintains a permanent fund, a post-insolvency assessment method is used to raise the necessary funds to pay claims. Insurers doing business in the state are assessed their share of the unpaid covered claims of the insolvent insurer. Although the amounts involved are not trivial—over the last 40 years, the state guaranty funds have paid more than $24 billion in claims.[4]—they still represent a very small percentage of total premiums. Insurers can recoup all or part of the assessments by insurance rate increases, special premium tax credits, and refunds from the state guaranty fund.

State guaranty funds vary by state. However, these characteristics are common:[5]

- Assessments are made only when an insurer fails (except in New York)—The definition of "failure" varies by state. Some states regard an insolvency order from a state court as evidence of failure. Others require a liquidation order from the state. All states limit the amounts that insurers can be assessed in one year.

- Policies usually terminate within thirty days after the failure date—Unpaid claims before termination, however, are still valid and paid from the guaranty fund of the insured's state of residence if the insolvent insurer is licensed in the state. Under the NAIC's model act, if the failed insurer is not licensed in the state, an insured or claimant cannot file a claim with the guaranty fund but must seek payment by filing a claim against the failed insurer's assets that are handled by the liquidator.

- Claim coverage varies by state—No state guaranty fund covers reinsurance or surplus lines insurance (except New Jersey).

- Claims are subject to maximum limits—The maximum limit is usually the lesser of $300,000 or the policy limit. Some states have limits under $300,000, and a small number of states have higher limits, such as $500,000 or $1 million.

- Most states provide for a refund of unearned premiums—A few states have no unearned premiums claim provision. In these states, an insured with a failed insurer is not entitled to a refund of the unearned premiums from the guaranty fund.

- Most states apply a $100 deductible to unpaid claims—Many states exempt workers compensation claims from a deductible.

- Most states divide their guaranty funds into separate accounts, usually auto, workers compensation, and other types of insurance—Auto or workers compensation assessments can be limited to insurers that write only that line of insurance.

- Assessment recovery varies by state—Thirty-two states permit insurers to recover assessments by an insurance rate increase. The remaining states generally reduce annual state premium taxes, usually over a period of five years. Consequently, taxpayers and the general public, as well as insureds, subsidize the unpaid claims of insolvent insurers.

Homeowners and auto insurance claims are covered by all state funds, but some types of insurance, such as annuities, life, disability, accident and health, surety, ocean marine, mortgage guaranty, and title insurance often are not covered. Self-insured groups are not protected by guaranty funds. Risk retention groups are prohibited by federal law from participating in the state guaranty fund system. Only one state has established a special guaranty fund for surplus lines.

Reasons for Insolvency

It is difficult to state the exact reasons for an insurer's failure. Usually, there isn't a single event or mistake that causes an insurer to become insolvent; rather, poor management and adverse events combine to cause insolvencies. Increased competition among insurers, leading to lower premium prices during soft phases of the underwriting cycle, often contributes to an increase in insurer insolvencies. Some insolvencies occur when an insurer is overexposed to losses resulting from a major insured catastrophe, especially during periods when intense competition causes lower insurance prices.

Experts have identified these factors that frequently contribute to an insurer's insolvency:

- Rapid premium growth
- Inadequate insurance rates
- Inadequate reserves
- Excessive expenses
- Lax controls over managing general agents
- Uncollectible reinsurance
- Fraud

Poor management is at the root of most of these factors. A combination of inadequate insurance rates and lax underwriting standards can start deterioration in a book of business. If these problems are not detected and corrected promptly, the decay in the quality of the business accelerates.

Rapid premium growth precedes nearly all major insolvencies. Rapid growth by itself is not harmful, but it reduces the margin for error in insurers' operations. Moreover, it usually indicates lowered rates and lax underwriting standards. If insurance rates are inadequate and losses understated, net losses and capital deterioration rise more quickly than management can effectively respond to.

INSURANCE REGULATORY ACTIVITIES: REGULATING INSURANCE RATES

Insurers must comply with rate regulatory laws in each state in which they write insurance. Additionally, insurers are often required to satisfy social concerns that are not included in state statutes. The primary goal of rate regulation is insurer financial stability and, as a result, consumer protection.

Of the types of insurance regulation, rate regulation may well receive the most public attention. When consumers complain about lack of fairness, equity, or affordability in insurance, policymakers search for remedies through regulation.

In seeking to ensure the financial stability of insurers and protect consumers, states use a variety of approaches to rate regulation, but they all have the same broad goals relating to fairness. The proponents of different types of rate regulation present reasons to support either prior-approval systems or competitive market systems.

Insurance Rate Regulation Goals

The three major goals of rate regulation are to ensure that rates are adequate, not excessive, and not unfairly discriminatory.

Adequate

Rates for a specific type of insurance should be high enough to pay all claims and expenses for that type of insurance. This requirement helps maintain insurer solvency. If an insurer fails because its rates are inadequate, it cannot pay for losses of its insureds and third-party claimants, who would consequently be financially harmed.

Several factors complicate the regulatory goal of rate adequacy:

- An insurer usually does not know what its actual expenses will be when a policy is sold. Premiums are paid in advance, but they might be insufficient to pay all related claims and expenses that occur later. An unexpected increase in claim frequency or severity can make the rate inadequate.

- Insurers might charge inadequate rates in response to strong price competition in order not to lose business.

- State rate approval systems may not approve insurers' requests for adequate rates for public policy reasons or because of disagreement over the level of requested rates.

- Unanticipated events could lead to higher losses than those projected when rates were set.

- Regulatory actuaries and insurer actuaries may disagree about the assumptions used to determine trends or account for socioeconomic components of a proposed rate change.

Although insurance rate adequacy is a goal of insurance regulation, no method of rate regulation guarantees that rates will be adequate.

Not Excessive

Although rates should be adequate, they should not be excessive. Insurers should not earn excessive or unreasonable profits. Regulators have considerable latitude and discretion in determining whether rates are excessive for a given type of insurance, and they consider factors, such as these:

- Number of insurers selling a specific coverage in the rating territory
- Relative market share of competing insurers
- Degree of rate variation among the competing insurers
- Past and prospective loss experience for a given type of insurance
- Possibility of catastrophe losses
- Margin for underwriting profit and contingencies

- Marketing expenses for a given type of insurance
- Special judgment factors that might apply to a given type of insurance

Regulators sometimes use the fair rate of return approach in determining whether an insurer's rates are adequate or excessive. This approach is based on the premise that an insurer should expect at least some minimum rate of return on the equity invested in its insurance operations and that a fair rate of return should be similar to the rate of return of other types of businesses—especially if insurers are to attract investment capital. Regulators, insurers, and investors often disagree as to what constitutes a fair rate of return for insurers.

Not Unfairly Discriminatory

Rates that are adequate and are not excessive must also not be unfairly discriminatory. The word "discrimination" carries negative connotations, but the word itself is neutral, implying only the ability to differentiate among things. Discrimination, in the neutral sense, is essential to insurance rating. However, insurers' discrimination must be fair and consistent. This means that insureds with loss exposures that are roughly similar regarding expected losses and expenses should be charged substantially similar rates. For example, two drivers age twenty-five operating similar vehicles in the same rating territory who buy the same type and amount of auto insurance from the same insurer should be charged the same rates.

The use of sophisticated computer simulation modeling for catastrophes and the use of innovative risk classification systems, such as credit-based insurance scores, have greatly complicated regulatory evaluation of whether rates are unfairly discriminatory.

Regulation seeks to prohibit only unfair discrimination, not fair discrimination. If loss exposures are substantially different in terms of expected losses and expenses, then different rates can be charged. For example, if a woman age twenty-five and another age sixty-five are in good health and purchase the same type and amount of life insurance from the same insurer, it is not unfair rate discrimination to charge the older woman a higher rate. The higher probability of death for a woman at age sixty-five clearly and fairly justifies a higher rate.

Types of Rating Laws

A state's rating laws influence how it achieves its three major rate regulation goals and the rates property-casualty insurers can charge. Rating laws apply not only to rates for a new type of insurance, but also to rate changes. The major types of state rating laws are these:

- Prior-approval laws require rates and supporting rules to be approved by the state insurance department before they can be used. In some cases, a prior-approval law contains a deemer provision stating that filing is deemed approved if the insurer has not heard from the regulator within a given time (usually thirty to ninety days).

- File-and-use laws allow the insurer to use the new rates immediately after filing with the state insurance department. The department has the authority to disapprove the rates if they cannot be justified or if they violate state law.

- Use-and-file laws, a variation of file-and-use laws, allow insurers to use the new rates and later submit filing information that is subject to regulatory review.

- No filing laws (information filing or open competition), do not require insurers to file rates with the state insurance department. Market prices driven by the economic laws of supply and demand, rather than the discretionary acts of regulators, determine the rates and availability. However, insurers might be required to furnish rate schedules and supporting statistical data to regulatory officials, and the state insurance department has the authority to monitor competition and to disapprove rates if necessary. The goals of adequate, nonexcessive, and equitable rates still apply.

- Flex rating laws require prior approval only if the new rates exceed a certain percentage above (and sometimes below) the rates filed previously. Insurers can increase or decrease their rates within the established range without prior approval. Typically, a range of five to ten percent is permitted. Flex rating permits insurers to make rate adjustments quickly in response to changing market conditions and loss experience, but it prohibits wide swings within a short period of time. Flex rating also can restrict insurers from drastically reducing rates to increase market share. The result should be smoother insurance pricing cycles.

Variations of these filing approaches exist. For example, open competition might apply as long as insurers meet certain tests, such as evidence of competitive markets or keeping rate increases to less than 25 percent per year. Insurers that fail to meet these criteria would be subject to prior approval or another type of regulatory review.

Controversy regarding regulation of insurance rates is ongoing. Most consumer advocacy groups and regulatory agencies support prior-approval systems allowing regulators to determine the adequacy and fairness of rates. However, most insurers and economists favor competitive rating systems where the

Prior-Approval Systems Versus Competitive Rating Systems

Arguments for Prior-Approval Systems	Arguments for Competitive Rating Systems
• Prior-approval systems require insurers to justify requests for rate increases with supporting actuarial data.	• Prior-approval systems may cause rates to be inadequate for writing profitable business by the time they are approved because of the time required for the regulatory review and approval process. Inadequate rates may cause insurers to reduce the amount of new business written or leave a state or a market, leading to a problem with insurance availability.
• Prior-approval systems help maintain insurer solvency through regulatory review of data to analyze the adequacy of rates for reported losses.	• Competitive rating systems are less expensive to administer and allow regulators to focus their resources on other areas, such as solvency regulation and consumer affairs.
• Prior-approval systems help keep rates reasonable and fair.	• Competitive rating systems are more flexible, allowing rates to be adjusted quickly in response to changing economic and market conditions.
• Prior-approval proponents believe that without regulatory approval, insurers would raise rates unfairly to earn excessive profits.	• Competitive-rating proponents believe that free market forces, rather than government regulation, lead to reasonable and fair rates.

[DA06392]

market determines rates. See the exhibit "Prior-Approval Systems Versus Competitive Rating Systems."

INSURANCE REGULATORY ACTIVITIES: REGULATING INSURANCE POLICIES

Insurance policies are complex documents. Regulation of insurance policies helps to protect insurance consumers, who often may not understand their policies. Also, insurance policies are usually drafted by insurers, who sell them to the public on a take-it-or-leave-it basis. Regulation can protect insureds from policies that are narrow, restrictive, deceptive, or that fail to comply with state laws and regulations.

Contract language contained in insurance policies is regulated through legislation and insurance departments' rules, regulations, and guidelines. Regulation may require certain forms, provisions, or standards, or it may prohibit certain provisions. Court decisions may arise from legal disputes regarding the language in insurance contracts and can also result in changes to policy language and forms.

Legislation

Insurance policy regulation starts with a state legislature passing laws that control the structure and content of insurance policies sold in the state. Legislative policy regulation affects these five areas: standard forms, mandatory provisions, prohibited provisions, forms approval, or readability standards.

Legislation might require insurers to use a standard policy to insure property or liability loss exposures. A standard policy is one policy all insurers must use if a coverage is sold in the state.

Legislation might also require that certain standard mandatory policy provisions appear in certain types of insurance policies. The required and optional provisions might be based on a model bill developed by the National Association of Insurance Commissioners (NAIC). For example, states usually require that workers compensation insurance, no-fault auto coverage, and often uninsured motorists coverage contain mandated policy provisions. State laws and regulations might require that the mandated policy provisions meet certain minimum standards, providing at least a basic level of protection.

State laws and regulations might list certain provisions that are prohibited in insurance contracts. For example, some states, such as South Dakota and Maryland, prohibit binding arbitration clauses in insurance contracts.

Legislation might mandate that policies be filed and/or approved by the state to protect policyholders against ambiguous, misleading, or deceptive policies. Many states require that a policy be submitted for approval before it is used. However, if a specified period elapses and the policy has not been disapproved, the policy is considered approved. (Some states permit the state insurance department to extend the review period.) The purpose of such approval is to encourage a prompt review of the policy. However, it can cause a perfunctory review.

In recent years, speed to market for insurance products has become increasingly important to insurance regulators and regulated entities. The NAIC has implemented a series of operational efficiencies along with the System for Electronic Rate and Form Filings (SERFF). SERFF has dramatically improved the timeliness of product filings. The SERFF system is designed to enable insurers to send and states to receive, comment on, and approve or reject rate and form filings. Filing volume has risen from just over 3,000 filings in 2001 to more than 500,000 filings in 2009. SERFF facilitates communication, management, analysis, and electronic storage of documents and supporting information. The system is designed to improve the efficiency of the rate and form filing and approval process and to reduce the time and cost involved in making regulatory filings. It also provides up-to-date filing requirements when they are needed.

Finally, legislation might require that insurance policies meet a readability test. Legislation may specify policy style and form as well as the size of print. Readability legislation has influenced the drafting of both personal and commercial insurance policies, but readability tests do not necessarily measure how well the policies can be understood.

Policy Rules, Regulations, and Guidelines

State insurance departments implement specific directives from the legislature or exercise the general authority they have to regulate insurance policies. Administrative rules, regulations, and guidelines can be stated in (1) regulations communicated by the state insurance department to insurers, (2) informal circulars or bulletins from the same source, and (3) precedents set during the approval process. For example, the state insurance department might require specific wording in certain policy provisions or might notify insurers that certain types of policy provisions will be disapproved.

Courts

Although the courts do not directly regulate insurers, they do influence them by determining whether insurance laws are constitutional and whether administrative rulings and regulations are consistent with state law. The courts also interpret ambiguous and confusing policy provisions, determine whether certain losses are covered by the policy, and resolve other disputes between insurers and insureds over policy coverages and provisions.

Court decisions often lead insurers to redraft their policy language and to modify provisions. For example, based on the legal doctrine of concurrent causation, certain courts ruled that if a loss under a risk of direct physical loss (formerly "all-risks") policy is caused by two causes of loss, one of which is excluded, the entire loss is covered. As a result of this doctrine, insurers were required to pay certain flood and earthquake claims they had believed were excluded by their property insurance policies. Subsequent revision of the language in many such property policies explicitly excluded coverage for flood and earthquake losses in cases in which a nonexcluded cause of loss contributed to the loss.

INSURANCE REGULATORY ACTIVITIES: MARKET CONDUCT AND CONSUMER PROTECTION

Regulation of the insurance industry's market conduct is concerned with consumer protection. By overseeing producers, sales and advertising, underwriting, ratemaking, and claim settlement procedures and activities, state departments of insurance help protect insurance consumers from such practices as unfair discrimination, insurer fraud, and excessive rates. Additionally, market conduct regulation promotes competition within the insurance marketplace.

Regulators have traditionally monitored three key areas of market conduct:

- Producer practices
- Underwriting practices
- Claim practices

While maintaining their focus on these practices, regulators are moving away from traditional market conduct examinations and toward market analysis. In addition to monitoring insurers, state insurance departments also provide information and assistance directly to insurance consumers.

Monitoring Market Conduct

Laws regarding unfair trade practices prohibit abusive practices. Currently, all United States jurisdictions except American Samoa and Guam have laws against unfair trade practices. Unfair trade practices acts at the state level regulate the trade practices of the business of insurance as required under the McCarran Act.

Unfair trade practices cases can be decided by the commissioner of the state in which the activity occurred. If an insurer is found to be in violation of the unfair trade practices act, the insurer is subject to one or both of two penalties:

- Fine per violation—The fine is often increased significantly if the activity is considered flagrant, with conscious disregard for the law.
- Suspension or revocation of license—This may occur if the practice occurred frequently and if the insurer's management knew or should have known of the unfair trade practice.

If an insurer disagrees with the commissioner's findings, generally it can file for judicial review. If the court agrees with the commissioner, the insurer must obey the commissioner's orders.

The National Association of Insurance Commissioners (NAIC) Model Unfair Trade Practices Act prohibits insurers from any activity that would restrain trade or competition in the business of insurance. The act also prohibits an insurer from misrepresenting its own or another insurer's financial status. Additionally, there are numerous provisions in the Model Act to protect insurance consumers.

The key insurer market conduct areas that are regulated by the Model Act and state-level unfair trade practices acts include producer practices, underwriting practices, and claim practices.

Producer Practices

Producers are subject to fines, penalties, or license revocation if they engage in certain illegal and unethical activities. A producer might be penalized for engaging in practices that violate the state's unfair trade practices act, such as these:

- Dishonesty or fraud—A producer might embezzle premiums paid by insureds or misappropriate some claim funds.

- Misrepresentation—A producer might misrepresent the losses that are covered by an insurance policy, which might induce a client to purchase that policy under false pretenses.

- Twisting—A producer might induce an insured to replace one policy with another, to the insured's detriment. This is a special form of misrepresentation called "twisting."

- Unfair discrimination—A producer might engage in any number of acts that favor one insured unfairly over another.

- Rebating—A producer might engage in rebating, the practice of giving a portion of the producer's commission or some other financial advantage to an individual as an inducement to purchase a policy. Rebating is currently illegal in almost all states.

Underwriting Practices

Insurance regulators attempt to prevent improper underwriting that could result in insurer insolvency or unfair discrimination against an insurance consumer. See the exhibit "Examples of Unfair Trade Practices With Respect to Underwriting."

Examples of Unfair Trade Practices With Respect to Underwriting

- Discriminating unfairly when selecting loss exposures
- Misclassifying loss exposures
- Canceling or nonrenewing policies contrary to statutes, rules, and policy provisions
- Using underwriting rules or rates that are not on file with or approved by the insurance departments in the states in which the insurer does business
- Failing to apply newly implemented underwriting and rating factors to renewals
- Failing to use correct policy forms and insurance rates
- Failing to use rules that are state specific

[DA02905]

To protect consumers, insurance regulators take actions such as these:

- Constrain insurers' ability to accept, modify, or decline applications for insurance—To increase insurance availability, states often require insurers to provide coverage for some loss exposures they might prefer not to cover.

- Establish allowable classifications—Regulators limit the ways in which insurers can divide consumers into rating classifications. For example, unisex rating is required in some states for personal auto insurance. This promotes social equity rather than actuarial equity.

- Restrict the timing of cancellations and nonrenewals—All states require insurers to provide insureds with adequate advance notice of policy cancellation or nonrenewal so that insureds can obtain replacement coverage. Insurers are typically allowed to cancel or nonrenew only for specific reasons.

Claim Practices

Regulatory controls on claim practices are intended to protect insureds and maintain public confidence in the promise of insurance to pay valid claims promptly and fairly. All states prohibit certain claim practices by law. Apart from regulatory penalties, failure to practice **good-faith claims handling** can lead to claims for damages that allege **bad faith** on the insurer's part. Unfair claim practices laws prohibit unethical and illegal claim practices. The laws generally are patterned after the NAIC Model Unfair Claims Settlement Practices Act. See the exhibit "Examples of Unfair Claims Settlement Practices."

In some cases, courts have ruled that an insurer's improper claims handling constitutes not only a breach of contract or a violation of regulations, but also an independent tort—the tort of bad faith. Legal remedies for bad-faith

Good-faith claims handling

The manner of handling claims that requires an insurer to give consideration to the insured's interests that is at least equal to the consideration it gives its own interests.

Bad faith (outrage)

A breach of the duty of good faith and fair dealing.

Examples of Unfair Claims Settlement Practices

- Knowingly misrepresenting important facts or policy provisions

- Failing to properly investigate and settle claims

- Failing to make a good-faith effort to pay claims when liability is reasonably clear

- Attempting to settle a claim for an amount less than the amount that a reasonable person believes he or she is entitled to receive based on advertising material that accompanies or is part of the application

- Failing to approve or deny coverage of a claim within a reasonable period after a proof-of-loss statement has been completed

---

[DA02906]

actions can lead both to first-party actions (involving the insured) and to third-party actions (involving a claimant). An insurer that violates good-faith standards can be required to honor the policy's intent (paying the claim) and pay extracontractual damages (damages above the amount payable under the terms of the insurance policy), such as emotional distress and attorney fees.

Market Analysis

Insurance regulators are moving away from traditional market conduct examinations and toward market analysis. Market analysis allows regulators to identify general market disruptions, promotes uniform analysis by applying consistent measurements between insurers, and facilitates communication and collaboration among regulators from different states. One of the fundamental components of market analysis is the collection of regulatory information from insurers using the Market Conduct Annual Statement (MCAS). In 2009, twenty-nine states participated in the MCAS project and began to assemble some baseline statistics that are used to benchmark insurer performance. As a work in progress at the time of this writing, regulators are engaged in these activities:

- Defining the scope of the market analysis program
- Determining minimum required skills and essential education necessary for market analysis professionals
- Developing, prioritizing, and coordinating data collection and analysis techniques
- Making recommendations regarding the expansion of the data elements for MCAS
- Developing analysis techniques to ensure states expand their focus from company-specific issues to general market problems

Ensuring Consumer Protection

In a sense, all insurance regulatory activities protect insurance consumers. However, certain activities are designed specifically to support consumers. For example, state insurance departments respond to consumer complaints, and they also provide information and education to consumers.

State insurance departments often assist with complaints about rates or policy cancellations or with consumers' difficulty in finding insurance. Although state insurance departments usually have no direct authority to order insurers to pay claims when facts are disputed (such disputes are typically resolved through the courts), most state insurance departments can investigate and follow up on a consumer complaint, at least to the extent of getting a response from the insurer involved.

Many states compute complaint ratios, and some make them readily available to consumers through the Internet. To help make consumers more knowledgeable about the cost of insurance, some states publish shoppers' guides and other forms of consumer information, and much of this information can be found on the Internet. Consumers can obtain information provided by state insurance departments by linking to each state insurance department's website from the NAIC website at www.naic.org.

UNOFFICIAL REGULATORS IN INSURANCE

Insurance regulation involves numerous entities that interact to influence insurer activities.

Only state and federal governments have the legal authority to regulate insurers. However, the National Association of Insurance Commissioners (NAIC) plays an influential role in insurance regulation, although it has no direct regulatory authority. Other entities—"unofficial regulators"—also affect insurer activities, including these four types of organizations:

- Financial rating organizations
- Insurance advisory organizations
- Insurance industry professional and trade associations
- Consumer groups

Financial Rating Organizations

Because good financial ratings help attract and retain customers—and vice versa—insurers try to conduct business in ways that maintain good ratings. Several financial rating agencies provide insurer financial ratings, including these:

- A.M. Best Company
- Duff and Phelps

- Moody's
- Standard & Poor's
- Weiss Ratings, Inc.

Generally, these organizations provide summary information about insurer financial strength in the form of a financial rating, typically a letter grade similar to those appearing on a student's report card. Corporate risk managers, independent insurance producers, consumers, and others consult these ratings when choosing an insurer. Many corporate and public entity risk managers purchase insurance only from insurers whose financial ratings meet or exceed a specific rating. Contractors and other organizations are often required to furnish a certificate of insurance in various business transactions, such as bidding on projects or applying for financing, from an insurer with a specified minimum financial rating. Banks and other lending institutions typically require **mortgagors** to provide evidence of insurance from an insurer with a specified minimum financial rating.

Insurers whose financial ratings have declined can find it difficult to attract and retain customers, and a decrease in customers can cause a financial rating to decline further. Insurers pay close attention to the factors financial rating agencies consider and endeavor to avoid an adverse rating. An insurer whose financial rating is threatened can implement remedial measures, such as purchasing more reinsurance; limiting new business; selling a portion of its book of business; selling stock to raise additional capital; or merging with another, more financially secure, insurer.

Poor financial ratings are not a widespread problem in the insurance industry. In addition, a "poor" rating does not mean an insurer will become insolvent, and a "good" rating does not guarantee that the insurer will never become insolvent. Some large insurers that have failed in recent years received high financial ratings until a year or two before they were declared insolvent. The value of financial ratings is limited because they are based on past performance. Despite this limitation, the ratings are widely used to evaluate insurers' financial strength, and insurers strive to maintain sound financial ratings.

Insurance Advisory Organizations

Insurance **advisory organizations** are companies that work with, and on behalf of, insurers. They provide services to member insurers and insurers that purchase or subscribe to their services. Advisory organizations develop standard insurance policy forms and provide data regarding rates or **prospective loss costs**. They may also file loss costs and policy forms with the state on behalf of their member and subscribing insurers. They may provide other

Mortgagor

The person or organization that borrows money from a mortgagee to finance the purchase of real property.

Advisory organization

An independent organization that works with and on behalf of insurers that purchase or subscribe to its services.

Prospective loss costs

Loss data that are modified by loss development, trending, and credibility processes, but without considerations for profit and expenses.

valuable services, such as these, to participants in the insurance market and insurance regulators:

- Developing rating systems
- Collecting and tabulating statistics
- Researching important insurance topics
- Providing a forum for discussing important issues
- Educating members, the industry, insurance regulators, and the public about relevant issues
- Monitoring regulatory issues of concern to members

Insurers pay a fee for the services of insurance advisory organizations. Well-known insurance advisory organizations include Insurance Services Office (ISO), the American Association of Insurance Services (AAIS), and the National Council on Compensation Insurance (NCCI).

By developing rate information and standard insurance forms, advisory organizations provide a degree of uniformity that can benefit consumers and regulators as well as serve insurers. Relatively few insurers have the resources to independently develop the statistical data on which to base their own insurance rates or to develop policy forms, endorsements, and rating systems for many different coverages that also comply with regulations from many different states. Insurance consumers benefit from competition among insurers who base their rates on sound statistical data. Uniformity in insurance policy forms also makes it easier for consumers to compare proposals from different insurers.

Insurance Industry Professional and Trade Associations

Several national property-casualty industry professional associations and trade associations provide services to their member insurance professionals, insurers, and producers. Professional organizations' members are individuals who share a common profession; whereas the trade associations' members are companies that share a common industry. However, some professional associations also accept corporate members, and some trade associations may permit individual members. Trade and professional associations have similar activities, and their main purpose is to advance the success of members as well as uphold ethical standards.

Professional associations in the property-casualty insurance industry provide educational, leadership, and ethical development for individual members and their employers. These associations provide services either industry-wide or to specialized professional groups (such as claim representatives or actuaries), offering education and information about continuing trends and developments in the industry or a particular field. Associations may also be active in recommending or supporting industry practices or legislative initiatives. See the exhibit "Insurance Industry Professional and Trade Associations."

Trade associations serve an important function for property-casualty insurers, reinsurers, and producers. For a fee, members have timely access to legislative developments on the national level and can use association personnel to help them lobby on behalf of the industry group. Trade association members can also participate on trade association committees to help draft new legislation or to influence pending legislation. Participation in one or more major trade associations can provide insurers with information that would otherwise require a large internal staff to obtain. Individual insurers would find it difficult to match the prompt dissemination of information and the scope of coverage that the trade associations provide.

Trade associations operate not only on the national level but also at state and local levels. They report on new regulations issued by state insurance departments in response to new or modified state insurance laws. Many state and local associations focus on local issues important to their members. For insurers and producers doing business only in one or two states, membership in state or local associations may be more cost-effective than membership in a national trade association that may provide many more services than the insurer or producer needs.

Trade associations at the national, state, and local levels influence the NAIC, state and federal legislators, and state insurance regulators. Each trade association has the collective power of its membership behind it. One person speaking on behalf of a major segment of insurers affected by a proposed piece of legislation can have far more influence than the representative of a single insurer expressing the same opinion.

Proposed legislation or regulation may be based on incorrect market assumptions and misinformation or may be introduced in reaction to a crisis. Trade associations can provide accurate information to legislators and regulators about critical issues in time to influence the development of legislation, regulations, and rules. Trade associations can sometimes persuade legislators and regulators that the insurance industry can solve a problem without legislation. This type of intervention provides an important service to association members.

Consumer Groups

Consumers, through consumer groups, have had a major influence on state insurance departments, state and federal legislators, the NAIC, and insurance consumers themselves. Some consumer groups focus solely on insurance issues, while others tackle a variety of public interest issues. Some have adopted a watchdog approach, carefully monitoring insurers and their actions. Others take a more activist approach to confront issues and to work for change.

Insurance Industry Professional and Trade Associations

Name	Year Founded	Members	Interests
American Insurance Association (AIA), www.aiadc.org	1964, with roots in the National Board of Fire Underwriters established in 1866	Property-casualty insurers	Provides safety and legislative services
Casualty Actuarial Society www.casact.org	1914	Insurance actuaries	Advances the knowledge of actuarial science applied to property and casualty insurance
CPCU Society www.cpcusociety.org	1944	Insurance industry professionals	Promotes excellence through ethical behavior and continuing education
Council of Insurance Agents and Brokers, www.ciab.com	1913	Commercial property-casualty insurance agencies and brokerage firms	Takes an active leadership role in crafting the commercial insurance industry's response to issues that affect members and their customers
Independent Insurance Agents & Brokers of America (IIABA), www.iiaba.net	1896	Independent insurance agencies handling property, fire, casualty, and surety insurance	Promotes education of agents and promotes regulatory and legislative issues of agents
Inland Marine Underwriters Association (IMUA), www.imua.org	1930	Member companies representing inland marine insurers	Provides its members with education, research, and communications services that support the inland marine underwriting discipline
National Association of Mutual Insurance Companies (NAMIC), www.namic.org	1895	Property-casualty insurers	Promotes governmental affairs representation; compiles and analyzes pertinent information
National Association of Professional Insurance Agents, www.pianet.com	1931	Insurance agents	Provides educational, representative, and service-oriented activities
National Association of Professional Surplus Lines Offices (NAPSLO), www.napslo.org	1975	Associate and wholesale brokers and agents	Sets standards for surplus lines industry and provides educational seminars and workshops and internships

Name	Year Founded	Members	Interests
Property Casualty Insurers Association of America (PCI), www.pciaa.net	2004, by the merger of the National Association of Independent Insurers and the Alliance of American Insurers	Property-casualty insurers	Provides a voice on public policy issues affecting property-casualty insurers before state and federal regulatory agencies and in the courts; serves as an information and education clearinghouse for consumers and the media
Reinsurance Association of America (RAA), www.reinsurance.org	1968	Property-casualty reinsurers	Promotes the interests of the property-casualty reinsurance industry to federal and state legislators, regulators, and the public
Risk and Insurance Management Society (RIMS), www.rims.org	1950	Individuals representing more than 4,000 member companies	Promotes the practice of risk management

Sources: Encyclopedia of Associations, 2000, 36th ed., vol. 1, part 1, Tara E. Sheets, ed. (Detroit, Mich.: Gale Research, Inc., 2000); The Fact Book 2001 (New York: Insurance Information Institute, 2001); and organizations' websites listed above. [DA02907]

One such group, the Consumer Federation of America (CFA), is headquartered in Washington, D.C. CFA is an advocacy organization that provides information to consumers about auto insurance and works to improve the safety of household products. Another well-known consumer group that monitors the insurance industry, Public Citizen, has contributed to substantive reforms in automobile safety and seat belt laws.

Consumer complaints made to state insurance departments can trigger market conduct examinations that may lead to actions ranging from insurer warnings to revocation of an insurer's license. Additionally, regulators view multiple complaints about an insurer as a sign of potential financial trouble that may trigger a financial examination. Consumers and consumer groups often influence state insurance commissioners to hold hearings on specific issues. Such hearings can lead insurers to take corrective action or lead regulators to develop legislative proposals.

SUMMARY

Insurance regulation is considered necessary to protect consumers, to maintain insurer solvency, and to avoid destructive competition.

Every state has an insurance department, headed by a commissioner that is responsible for regulating insurance in that state. Insurance regulators belong to a nonprofit association, the NAIC, which has no regulatory authority of its own but has substantial influence in coordinating the activities of various state regulators and developing model acts and regulations, as well as sharing financial information.

Federal regulation takes many forms, including the Insurance Fraud Protection Act, and a variety of regulations that affect insurers and other organizations alike.

Insurance regulators govern the formation and licensing of insurers and the licensing of insurance personnel. By issuing a license to an insurer, a state indicates that the insurer meets minimum standards of financial strength, competence, and integrity. States also license many of the people who sell insurance, give insurance advice, or represent insurers, including producers, claim representatives, and insurance consultants.

Regulators in the U.S. have a framework to prevent insurer insolvencies and to manage those that do occur despite preventive efforts. The NAIC provides tools for uniformity and a risk-based approach in solvency regulation founded on seven core solvency principles. The NAIC has also drafted a model act for uniform procedures to liquidate insolvent insurers. State guaranty funds, financed through assessments of insurers operating in the insolvent insurer's state, provide payments for that insurer's valid claims after the insolvency. Most insurer insolvencies occur because of poor management practices.

States regulate insurance rates to help maintain insurer solvency and protect consumers. Three major goals of rate regulation are that rates be adequate, not excessive, and not unfairly discriminatory. State rating laws influence the rates property-casualty insurers can charge. The major types of state rating laws are: prior-approval laws, file-and-use laws, use-and-file laws, no filing laws, and flex rating laws. Proponents of rate regulation offer reasons to support prior-approval systems versus proponents of a competitive market system who offer reasons to oppose prior-approval systems.

Regulating contract language contained in insurance policies is necessary because insurance policies are complex documents, and they are almost always drafted by insurers, who sell them to the public on a take-it-or-leave-it basis. Insurance policy regulation starts with a state legislature passing laws regarding insurance policy form and content. State insurance departments implement specific directives from the legislature or exercise their general authority to regulate insurance policies through administrative rules, regulations, and guidelines. Courts influence insurers by determining whether insurance laws are constitutional and by interpreting insurance policy provisions.

Insurance regulators have traditionally monitored insurers' compliance with the provisions of unfair trade practices acts through market conduct examinations that focus on producers' practices, underwriting practices, and claim practices. The primary purpose of unfair trade practices laws and regulations is to protect consumers. Additionally, these laws are also intended to help maintain insurers' solvency while encouraging competition.

Regulators are moving away from the traditional market conduct examinations and toward market analysis, an approach that will allow the practices of an entire market, consisting of multiple insurers, to be reviewed.

In addition to their monitoring of insurers' conduct, regulators also protect those who purchase insurance by providing information and assistance directly to consumers.

Various types of organizations serve as unofficial insurance regulators. Financial rating organizations encourage insurers to maintain or improve their financial strength ratings. Insurance advisory organizations develop standard policy forms and provide loss cost data. Insurance industry professional and trade associations, in addition to other services, provide education, training, and information to members and act as lobbyists on issues important to their members. Consumer groups serve as watchdogs and activists.

ASSIGNMENT NOTES

1. "Financial Regulation Standards and Accreditation Program," National Association of Insurance Commissioners, March 2010, www.naic.org (accessed June 28, 2010).

2. 18 USC Sec. 1033.

3. Ann Monaco Warren, Esq., and John William Simon, Esq., "Dishonesty or Breach of Trust" in 18 U.S.C. Section 1033: "Are You Criminally Liable on the Basis of an Associate's Record?" FORC *Quarterly Journal of Insurance Law and Regulation*, vol. X, edition III, September 12, 1998.

4. "After 40 Years the P/C Guaranty Fund System Thrives," The National Conference of Insurance Guaranty Funds, p.1, www.ncigf.org (accessed July 4, 2010)

5. www.ncigf.org (accessed July 14, 2010).

Insurance Marketing and Distribution

Educational Objectives

After learning the content of this assignment, you should be able to:

▷ Describe the following attributes of the competitive property-casualty insurance marketplace: distinguishing characteristics of insurance customers, insurer marketing differentiations, and unique factors in the insurance marketplace.

▷ Explain how typical insurer marketing activities are performed and why they are performed.

▷ Describe the main types of insurance distribution systems and channels, including the principal characteristics that distinguish one distribution system from another.

▷ Describe the functions performed by insurance producers.

▷ Describe the key factors an insurer should evaluate during the distribution-system and distribution-channel selection process.

Insurance Marketing and Distribution

3

PROPERTY-CASUALTY INSURANCE MARKETPLACE

The property-casualty insurance marketplace is the highly competitive meeting point between customers' needs and insurers' abilities to meet those needs. Competition is an important dynamic in the marketplace to provide reasonable premiums to insureds. However, the environment that influences the transactions and the price of those transactions renders the marketplace dynamic and continuously evolving.

Competition between property-casualty insurers for customers is a dynamic function of the insurance marketplace. The drivers of that competition arise from the needs and characteristics of the insurance customers. Property-casualty insurers have differentiated marketing characteristics to meet the needs of one or more customer groups.

Insurers and customers interact in an environment with factors that are unique to the insurance marketplace. These numerous factors, predictable and unpredictable, affect competition and insurers' profitability. See the exhibit "The Property-Casualty Insurance Marketplace."

Characteristics of Property-Casualty Insurance Customers

Each type of insurance customer can be distinguished in terms of insurance needs, knowledge of the insurance markets, methods of accessing the insurance market, negotiating ability, and access to alternative risk financing measures. These five distinguishing characteristics are significant to customers because they drive the demand for insurance products and services. Customers' characteristics are significant to insurers because they directly affect the products and services they supply to each type of customer group: individuals, small business, middle markets, and national accounts.

Individuals

From an insurance perspective, individuals generally share the same needs for property coverage to protect real and personal property and liability coverage for losses arising out of their personal actions and their ownership and use of property. Because so many individuals have the same insurance needs, insurers

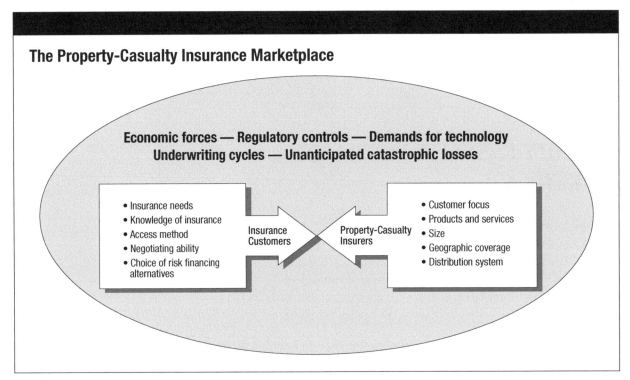

The Property-Casualty Insurance Marketplace

Economic forces — Regulatory controls — Demands for technology
Underwriting cycles — Unanticipated catastrophic losses

Insurance Customers
- Insurance needs
- Knowledge of insurance
- Access method
- Negotiating ability
- Choice of risk financing alternatives

Property-Casualty Insurers
- Customer focus
- Products and services
- Size
- Geographic coverage
- Distribution system

[DA06182]

are able to pool individual insureds' loss exposures based on relevant underwriting factors to determine the appropriate premiums for their policies.

Individuals are typically the least knowledgeable about insurance markets and the insurance mechanism. Therefore, they often need to rely on the expertise of a **producer** to help them decide which types of coverages, policy limits, and deductible levels are most appropriate for their individual circumstances. Individuals may also use direct access to insurers through websites or call centers to purchase their insurance products.

Producer

Any of several kinds of insurance personnel who place insurance and surety business with insurers and who represent either insurers or insureds, or both.

Individuals have few risk financing alternatives available besides retention and insurance. In addition, they are often required to purchase insurance by mortgagees and lenders. Individuals must also purchase auto liability coverage to meet state requirements because retention alternatives are financially unfeasible.

Individuals have little negotiating power in insurance transactions. Most personal lines insurance contracts are offered on an as-written basis by the insurer; therefore, very little negotiation occurs. If the individual customer is not satisfied with the policy's terms or price, typically his or her only option is to look to other insurers for coverage.

Small Business

In general, "small business" describes organizations with few employees and limited revenue. Small businesses do not usually have any employees with full-time risk management responsibilities. Often it is the owner, or a designated partner or manager with a limited knowledge of insurance markets, who is responsible for making risk management decisions—including the risk financing decision to purchase insurance. This decision is often made with the help of a local agent or a small local broker. Small businesses are not the typical target market for regional or national brokers because such businesses often do not generate sufficient commissions.

The insurance needs of small businesses can usually be covered by a limited number of commercial insurance policies, such as a businessowners policy, a workers compensation policy, and commercial auto policies.

Small businesses have little negotiation power with insurers and a limited number of choices when it comes to risk financing alternatives. Some small businesses have been able to join with similar organizations to form small risk retention groups or purchasing groups as alternatives to the standard commercial insurance market.

Middle Markets

Organizations that can be classified as middle markets are larger organizations with insurance needs that vary considerably according to the products or services they provide. For example, a company that manufactures airplane components will have significantly higher products liability insurance needs than a company that manufactures greeting cards.

Middle-market organizations are often large enough that their loss histories provide credible statistics for use in projecting future losses. These organizations may have a risk manager (or a small risk management department) to assist with coverage decisions. The risk managers typically use brokers to access the insurance markets and may be targeted by small (local), regional, or national brokers. They typically have some negotiating power with insurers because they have a more credible loss history, generate more premium income for the insurer, and have broker representation that can assist in their presentations to insurers.

Middle-market organizations have increasing access to risk financing alternatives such as **captive insurers** and **risk retention groups**.

National Accounts

The national accounts segment contains the largest organizations seeking insurance coverage. These organizations, such as Fortune 500 companies, chemical and other manufacturing organizations, and large municipalities, have the most complex insurance needs, the most comprehensive knowledge of the insurance market (with a large risk management department and regional or national broker representation), and the widest variety of risk financing alternatives.

Captive insurer, or captive

A subsidiary formed to insure the loss exposures of its parent company and the parent's affiliates.

Risk retention group

A group captive formed under the requirements of the Liability Risk Retention Act of 1986 to insure the parent organizations.

National accounts often generate millions of dollars in premiums annually, giving national account brokers the most negotiating power with insurers. This power can be used to negotiate broader coverages, lower deductibles, higher limits, or premium reductions.

National account organizations are likely to have complex insurance programs that combine commercial insurance coverages with sophisticated retention plans and captive insurers. The use of captives by large organizations provides them with additional flexibility to bypass the standard commercial insurance market and access reinsurance markets directly. Furthermore, unique loss exposures that require extremely high limits or highly specialized underwriting consideration are often insured by a consortium of insurers that work together to provide the necessary insurance program. See the exhibit "Comparison of Insurance Consumers."

Comparison of Insurance Consumers

	Individuals	Small Business	Middle Markets	National Accounts
Insurance Needs	Least complex	Somewhat complex	Complex	Highly complex
Knowledge of the Insurance Market	Least knowledgeable	Some knowledge	Risk manager on staff—more knowledgeable	Full-time risk management department—most knowledgeable
Access Method	Direct access/agents	Agents/small brokers	Brokers—small/regional/national	Brokers—regional/national
Negotiating Ability	Little, if any, negotiating ability	Little, if any, negotiating ability	Some negotiating ability	Most negotiating ability
Choice of Risk Financing Alternatives	Retention only alternative	Retention/few other alternatives	Some alternatives—rent-a-captives, risk retention groups	Wide variety of alternatives

[DA02712]

Property-Casualty Insurer Marketing Differentiations

Insurers differentiate themselves within the insurance market in various ways to meet the coverage and service needs of one or more customer groups or segments within customer groups. The level of competition for insurance customers is high. Competition is an important aspect of the functioning of insurance markets because it ensures that customers will receive competitive prices and services to meet their insurance needs.

An insurer's marketing differentiations uniquely match the characteristics of the customer groups or segments of those groups that they target for sales.

Customer Focus

To be customer focused, an insurer must understand the characteristics of specific customer groups and provide products and services that respond to those characteristics.

Customer focus is improved through **market intelligence**, which provides information that is relevant to understanding customers' current and future needs, preferences, attitudes, and behaviors. This depth of understanding leads to better customer interaction through an intensified customer-market view. Through market intelligence, the insurer understands where its insurance offer fits and discovers untapped or underserved potential markets.

Market intelligence
Information gathered and analyzed regarding a company's markets to improve competitive decision-making.

The purpose of increasing the quantity and quality of market intelligence is to accurately and confidently make decisions regarding opportunities, strategies, and market development and to assess changes in the environment that may affect the nature of the market in the future.

Products and Services

Property-casualty insurers can be further differentiated by line, for example, personal or commercial lines. Personal or commercial lines insurers may focus on property or liability insurance, package policies, or specialty lines but often sell a range of insurance products that meet the needs of their customers. Services are also tailored to respond to customers' needs identified through market intelligence.

Size

An important driver of competition is the size of the organizations in an industry. For a given number of organizations, the level of competition is usually greater if all organizations are approximately the same size than if there are two or three large organizations and many small ones. The larger companies may dominate the market, reducing competition.

An insurer's size influences its decision in the market it enters and the customer groups to which it chooses to market. If a market is dominated by a large organization, a smaller insurer might select a subsection of the market or niche market to target and tailor its product to better meet the closely defined needs of that group.

Similarly, a small insurer might avoid the national accounts market, where large written premiums must be reinsured or offset by significant reserve levels, reducing an insurer's ability to write a substantial number of other accounts.

For a small insurer that relies on a single large account, the risk of losing that account can be disproportionate to the benefits of serving a single account.

Geographic Area

Property-casualty insurers are differentiated by the geographic area they serve. Although thousands of insurers may compete in the United States, not all of them compete nationally. Many insurers are small organizations that compete in only one or a limited number of states.

An insurer's decision regarding geographic area is based on its size, its level of expertise in writing coverage in broader geographic areas, the level of competition in those areas, and its customer focus. An insurer that chooses a regional area for operation can more narrowly focus its marketing intelligence to address customers' insurance needs in the smaller area. In contrast, writing insurance nationally or internationally requires substantially more marketing intelligence to understand customers and successfully meet a wider range of insurance needs.

Distribution System

An insurer's choice of marketing system(s) is influenced by its customers' knowledge of insurance products and the risk financing alternatives available. For example, individuals generally have limited knowledge of insurance products and limited risk financing alternatives that are usually in the form of deductible selections. Insurers focused on mature customers with homes, autos, and valuable personal property may choose a distribution system based on exclusive agents or independent agents, who can assist them with coverage, limits, and deductible selections. Alternatively, an insurer targeting sales of personal auto insurance to young drivers who have a high probability of selecting the lowest-priced coverage might choose an Internet-based distribution system, which allows buyers to comparison shop in a medium in which they are comfortable.

Similar decisions regarding the selection of marketing systems are made for small-business, middle-market, and national accounts. Small businesses lack sufficient personnel to dedicate to risk management and insurance placement tasks; therefore an independent-agent distribution system is appropriate to provide that assistance. As accounts grow larger and have risk management staff to make selection decisions or work with brokers for coverage selection, broker-based distribution systems might be the selected option.

Unique Factors in the Insurance Marketplace

All marketplaces are influenced by changes in the economy, such as business cycles, interest rates, and rates of unemployment as well as changing consumer demographics and social pressures, which gradually require shifts in operations, products, and distribution systems.

The property-casualty insurance marketplace is also shaped by unique economic forces, regulatory controls, and technology demands that set the parameters within which insurers must operate. Underwriting cycles, as well as the financial shock of unanticipated catastrophic losses, further shape the marketplace. Within this changing environment, insurers adjust to maintain the competitive dynamic required for the functioning of the marketplace.

Economic Forces

Property-casualty insurers manage a narrow margin of underwriting profitability to remain competitive. Inflation is a factor in increasing the costs of losses and the costs of an insurer's operations. Similarly, the availability of reinsurance influences the price and the cost of insurer operations. Investment earnings frequently offset high losses and rising costs. When investment earnings are diminished or the prospect of catastrophe losses increase, insurers must raise premiums to sustain risk-appropriate rates of return.

Many companies invest reserve funds to gain investment earnings. The importance of investment earnings to a property-casualty insurer's profitability is a key feature of the industry. Insurers operations are frequently dependant on investment earnings because premiums are held competitively low to attract customers.

Regulatory Controls

State-based insurance regulations stipulate the financial requirements that insurers must sustain to operate within a state and the marketing conduct to which insurers must adhere. In this way, insurance regulation is a stabilizing control that ensures the sustainability of insurance companies and their ability to reliably provide compensation for insureds' losses and fair treatment to insureds in business practices.

Insurance regulatory controls are a marketplace feature unique to the insurance industry creating an environment where a minimum standard of practice is required by all competitors.

Demands for Technology

The demand for technology is a powerful factor in the insurance marketplace because of the computer networks that interconnect insurers and producers as well as the technological connections between insurers and customers through the Internet. Producers complete applications and access insureds' information through computer networks to facilitate service. Customers obtain coverage information and compare premium quotations through insurers' websites or sites that provide quotes from multiple insurers.

The primary demand for technology in these marketing applications is ease of use. Both producers and customers are drawn to user interfaces that are easy to understand and navigate. This requires significant engineering to provide point-of-use instruction and easy user operation.

Underwriting Cycles

Underwriting cycle

A cyclical pattern of insurance pricing in which a soft market (low rates, relaxed underwriting, and underwriting losses) is eventually followed by a hard market (high rates, restrictive underwriting, and underwriting gains) before the pattern again repeats itself.

Underwriting cycles, a key feature in the insurance marketplace, create additional competitive shifts to which insurers continuously adapt. Because underwriting cycles have numerous causes, they have varying duration and depth. As a result, insurers must also adapt as the cycle patterns reveal themselves to remain competitive.

Approaches vary among companies, but insurers are collectively challenged when books of business are shuffled as competitors' premiums rise and fall. Insurers may decide to change insurance prices with the cycles or maintain a more consistent pricing philosophy throughout the cycle. In response to either decision, the underwriting cycles create dynamic balancing challenges to maintain profitability.

Unanticipated Catastrophic Losses

Insurers maintain reserves and reinsurance to pay catastrophe losses. However, catastrophes of unanticipated severity can cause losses that exceed maximum anticipated losses. These exceptional losses can result from disasters such as record-breaking hurricane losses, terrorist attacks, and oil spills, or extraordinary tort awards and class action lawsuits. Unplanned losses can result in insurer insolvencies, withdrawal of insurers from geographic markets, and reinsurance shortages.

In any year, an insurer is challenged to price a product for which the loss-cost can only be estimated. In years of extraordinary catastrophes, the market must respond with improved catastrophe ratemaking and forecasting that anticipates even greater unforeseen events.

INSURER MARKETING ACTIVITIES

Marketing is an insurer's information portal to insurance customers. Through this portal, insurers gather information about customers, make decisions about segments of customers whose needs they can address, and disseminate information to existing and prospective customers.

An insurer's marketing activities are focused on information gathering, synthesis, and dissemination. The goal is the development of products for groups of customers with results that meet the insurer's strategies and objectives.

Activities performed by marketing can be divided into these categories:

- Marketing research
- Market development
- Marketing information

- Marketing planning
- Product development
- Advertising and promotion
- Customer and public relations
- Sales fulfillment

Marketing Research

Marketing research is the systematic gathering and analyzing of data to assist in making decisions. Marketing research cannot guarantee success, but it can improve an insurer's chances of making correct decisions.

Marketing research is typically done on a project basis with a stated objective, research design, data collection, analysis, and formal report. Effective marketing research results include conclusions and implications or recommendations. Ideally, cost-benefit measures are used to track the value of information developed from the various studies. Decisions based on the research are then implemented and evaluated on a cost-benefit basis. See the exhibit "Market Research Project Examples."

Market Research Project Examples

- Test prospecting sources through wholesale clubs to determine whether the concept is worthy of prototype development and pilot testing on a larger scale

- Determine why policies lapse or are terminated by policyholders and the cost-benefit of implementing a conservation program to retain those policyholders

- Examine the insurance purchase behaviors of first-time car owners to determine what actions are needed to attract those customers

- Identify the relationship between a policyholder's claim experience and retention of the policyholder through subsequent renewals

- Use secondary data from the U.S. Government's Standard Industrial Classification (SIC) coding system combined with Metropolitan Statistical Areas (MSAs) to identify businesses within the insurer's preferred business types and geographic areas for targeted advertising

[DA06195]

Insurers use increasingly sophisticated marketing research methods to gather meaningful information, such as customer profiles, product preferences, and refinements to improve distribution channels. One important result of this research is the development of market segments in which the insurer will compete for customers.

Market Research Methods

The best marketing research is conducted as scientifically as possible. A researcher should strive for objectivity, eliminating preconceptions and bias to the extent possible. The research may consist of qualitative studies, such as **focus groups** and observer impressions, and quantitative studies that use survey research techniques and statistical analysis of the data included in corporate databases.

Focus group
A small group of customers or potential customers brought together to provide opinions about a specific product, service, need, or other issue.

The two broad categories of market data are secondary data and primary data. Research typically begins with secondary data, which is data collected by other parties, because it is immediately available at little or no cost. Many research questions can be answered at minimal expense from secondary data before the more costly primary data research is conducted, requiring the collection of data first-hand by the insurer. Primary data collection is more expensive, but it addresses issues specific to the marketing research project.

Predictive analytics
Statistical and analytical techniques used to develop models that predict future events or behaviors.

Increasingly, insurers are applying **predictive analytics** to improve the outcome of market research. The forms of predictive models applied in analytics vary depending on the behavior or event they are predicting.

Most predictive models generate a score, with the higher score indicating a higher likelihood that the given behavior or event will occur. Predictive scores are typically used to measure the risk or opportunity associated with a specific customer or transaction. These evaluations assess the relationships between many variables to estimate risk or response.

Predictive analytics models are used in many aspects of marketing. For example, insurers can use models to examine the purchasing patterns of insurance customers and can use the resulting information to increase the marketing function's hit ratio and retention ratio. An insurer could also use models to answer specific questions, such as, "What characteristics of small businesses result in the most profitable commercial insurance accounts?" Variables such as premium size, geography, business type, years in business, and form of ownership could affect the profitability of an account. A predictive model would weigh the importance of each relevant variable to provide an estimate of the likely profitability of each characteristic.

Insurers can take advantage of additional applications for predictive analytics in marketing:

- Cross-selling—identifying existing policyholder groups to whom efforts to sell additional policies will be most successful
- Target marketing—defining and refining marketing efforts on a specific group of customers
- Individualized customer support—tailoring customer support to specific customers' needs

- New agent contracting—determining which characteristics of exclusive and independent agents result in the most successful market penetration
- Designing and evaluating marketing campaigns—defining aspects of advertising efforts that result in the highest response rates from prospective customers

Market Segmentation

Insurers use **market segmentation** to differentiate themselves from other insurance providers to meet the needs of customer groups. **Target marketing** is a practice of more closely defining a group of customers within a market segment. **Niche marketing** is a well-defined, often small marketing segment of the population that has specific needs. For example, a market segmentation of small businesses can include a target market of retailers with a niche market of jewelry stores.

By identifying the characteristics of the various market segments, target market groups, and niches, insurers build a competitive advantage through designing specific marketing strategies to address their needs and characteristics. The more closely a group of customers is defined, the more closely an insurer can develop expertise regarding the customers' needs and tailor products and services to meet those needs. As groups are more closely defined, insurers are less likely to encounter competition for that group than in the open market.

- Behavioristic segmentation—the division of a total consumer market by purchase behavior
- Geographic segmentation—the division of markets by geographic units
- Demographic segmentation—the division of markets based on demographic variables, such as age, gender, education, occupation, ethnicity, income, family size, and family life cycle
- Psychographic segmentation—the division of markets by individuals' values, personalities, attitudes, and lifestyles

Marketing management defines logical market segments that provide an opportunity for success. Criteria regarding the segments, as well as the external environment and the insurer's internal environment, are considered in the market segment selection. See the exhibit "Market Segment Selection Considerations."

Market Development

Market development activities provide leadership when an insurer enters a new market. The new market may be a new territory, a new customer type, or a new product. Other examples of major projects managed might include new approaches to selling the insurer's products or delivering web-based applications for insurance policies.

Market segmentation
The process of identifying and dividing the groups within a market that share needs and characteristics and that will respond similarly to a marketing action.

Target marketing
Focusing marketing efforts on a specific group of consumers.

Niche marketing
A type of marketing that focuses on specific types of buyers who are a subset of a larger market.

Market Segment Selection Considerations

Each marketing segment should be:

- Accessible—Segments should be able to be effectively reached and served.

- Substantial—Size and purchasing power should suggest potential profitability.

- Responsive—Actions taken by the insurer should produce satisfactory results.

Internal marketing environment:

- Technical resources—What technical resources are needed to support the customers and products sold?

- Type of products sold—Do the products available meet the specific segment's needs, or do they address homogeneous needs of a larger group? What is the product fit to the market segment?

- Age of product—Do the products available meet current customer needs?

- Product mix—Do the products we will sell to this market segment help us achieve our optimum product mix?

- Distribution channels—Are our distribution channels appropriate to the characteristics of this market segment?

- Corporate ownership—Does our ownership affect our ability to obtain the sources of funds needed for growth, expansion, or financial stability to market successfully to this market segment?

- Company size and resources—Are we limited by our company size and resources to compete for customers in this market segment?

External marketing environment:

- Market segment competition—How significant is the competition within this market segment? What are the characteristics of competing insurers in this market segment (such as customer focus, size, distribution systems, and technological capabilities)?

- Economic environment—Are there issues in the current economic environment (such as inflation, investment earnings, customers' spending habits, availability and cost of employees) that affect our chances of success in this market segment?

- Social environment—What behaviors or beliefs in the population of this market segment will increase or decrease our chances of success in offering our products and services?

- Regulatory environment—Are the products and services we are proposing for this marketing segment permitted under applicable laws and regulations?

[DA06196]

Market development involves actions required to ensure the success of the venture, including development and implementation of a broad range of activities:

- Training programs
- Problem resolution

- Process documentation
- Funding assistance
- Technical assistance
- Public relations campaigns

The market development staff includes project managers who generate and screen ideas. Project managers are also skilled in developing project scope documents, decision grids, task outlines, progress reports, and project reports. The project manager usually handles only one or two projects at a time because of the high level of effort and responsibility involved in each project.

Marketing Information

Marketing information activities develop and maintain information needed in market planning to support management at all levels in answering specific questions concerning markets, customers, producers, and competitors. The marketing information function serves the company best when it can deliver timely and cost-effective information essential to decision making.

Marketing information is divided into two major systems: internal accounting and market monitoring.

- The internal accounting system provides report and analysis capability based on transactions associated with sales activity. Much of the essential information on production, retention, and policies in force is available as a byproduct of the systems that keep track of commissions and billings.
- The market monitoring system provides intelligence about the external environment to inform senior management about important develop- ments and changing conditions. The market monitor should provide current, unfiltered, and unbiased information about customers, producers, and competitors. Customers and producers are monitored to determine their satisfaction levels with the service they receive from the insurer, and the resulting information helps the insurer shape decisions related to growth and profitability strategies. The market monitor also maintains up-to-date competitive intelligence about the strategies and actions of key competitors. Competitor monitoring also includes benchmark studies of competitors that excel in success factors crucial to a property-casualty insurer. Benchmark information helps management develop strategies for closing the gap between company performance and key competition.

Marketing Planning

Marketing planning provides the tools and facilitation skills to assist manage- ment in developing fact-based marketing plans. This activity also assists in the development and updating of the company's strategic plans.

Before introducing a new insurance product or service, the insurer completes a comprehensive marketing plan. The plan identifies the product or service to be promoted and the customers to be targeted, and it details the resources and strategies that will be used to create, price, promote, and sell the product or service. Because marketing plans affect many other insurer functions, representatives from other departments often participate in the creation or review of marketing plans.

Marketing plans are as varied as the products and services they promote. However, all plans serve the same fundamental purpose: they provide the "roadmaps" necessary to profitably and effectively acquaint sellers with potential buyers.

A marketing plan for a typical insurance product or service might include, but is not limited to, these items:

- Product proposal and sales goals—A summary of the new product's operation, a description of the unmet need the product is designed to fulfill, and summarized sales projections.
- Situational analysis—A SWOT (strengths, weaknesses, opportunities, threats) analysis of the current marketplace, including analyses of the competition; critical factors required for success; resource, technology, and training requirements; and an assessment of the existing legal and regulatory environment.
- Marketing goals—An outline of the proposed target market, including detailed sales projections and specifics as to how success will be measured.
- Marketing strategies—Plans and proposals for how the product will be developed, priced, promoted, and sold. These strategies include determining the appropriate distribution channels for products and services.
- Projected outcome—The pure loss ratio and ultimate loss ratio over a five-year period.

Product Development

An insurer's management team must decide which insurance products and services will be sold to which markets. There are many product decisions to be made, ranging from what product lines to offer to what coverages, limits, and deductibles will be included in the policy.

Insurers usually follow a series of steps in product development. See the exhibit "Product Development Steps."

Advertising and Promotion

The advertising function is responsible for managing the company's communications through mass media with its chosen target markets. The advertising program is developed to be consistent with strategic direction and marketing plans and supportive of distribution system efforts. Advertising is intended to build and reinforce the company's image as an acceptable choice in the minds of target customers.

Product Development Steps

1. Opportunity assessment

- Monitor market
- Identify opportunity
- Relate opportunities to business strategy
- Develop specifications
- Secure senior management approval to proceed

In the first step, market monitoring results in the identification of an opportunity for a new product. Marketing personnel evaluate the opportunity against the insurer's business strategies and continue the process if there is a successful match by developing specifications for the product and obtaining approval.

2. Development of contract, underwriting, and pricing

- Develop coverage and policy forms
- Develop guidelines for underwriting and claims
- Develop classifications
- Develop pricing structure
- Secure approval from functional managers to proceed

The second step is to develop the policy forms, guidelines, classifications, and prices in a cooperative effort across the insurer functions of underwriting, actuarial, claims, reinsurance, premium audit, and risk control. This step concludes with a tangible product plan.

3. Business forecast

- Review the product plan with profit center management
- Identify requirements for statistics
- Develop business forecast
- Secure senior management approval to proceed

In the third step, the product is submitted to an assessment of sales potential. The business forecast establishes benchmarks for evaluating the success of the product including expected premium volume, producers' participation, loss ratio, and methods of gathering data that can be used to analyze the product success or failure.

4. Regulatory requirements

- File with regulators
- Develop statistical information systems
- Communicate regulatory approval

The fourth step moves the development process to the regulatory arena. At a minimum, state regulators require notification of new policy forms, rating plans, and policy writing rules. Some states require regulatory approval of new products and changes in existing products to protect policyholder interests.

5. Distribution requirements

- Develop advertising and sales promotional information
- Develop sales training
- Plan roll-out strategy

In the fifth step, the insurer determines distribution requirements, which include the overall plan for effectively advertising and distributing the new product to targeted customers.

6. Introduction

- Implement sales training and promotion
- Measure and compare results to plan

The sixth step is the introduction of the product in one or more states with advertising and sales promotions. The results are monitored, and marketing management takes actions to improve the product performance or eliminates weak products in this step if the actual results do not achieve profitability objectives.

Advertising is expensive. Insurers face a dilemma when trying to decide how much advertising is enough to communicate effectively with customers while staying within a reasonable budget. The effectiveness of marketing communications can be measured in several ways. For example, an insurer might pilot test advertising to determine its effectiveness or might also show proposed advertising to a focus group to obtain feedback.

Sales promotion reinforces the image and positioning created by the insurer's advertising efforts when carried down to the agency level. Sales promotion includes brochures used in the sales process, giveaway items promoting the insurer and the producer, and awards merchandise. Regular communications with producers and sales management, such as newsletters, may be part of the sales promotion function.

Customer and Public Relations

The customer relations function manages communications with individual customers from the home office. This functional area ensures that all written communications seen by customers are understandable and consistent in quality and tone.

The customer relations function also provides a forum for communications to the insurer initiated by customers, including complaints, suggestions, and questions. Insurers are often asked to respond to state insurance departments, which themselves are responding to consumer complaints about the insurer. Typically, a complaint is addressed to an insurer's CEO and must be addressed within a specified period, often ten working days.

The customer relations function also provides management with low-cost, high-value information about the evolving wants and needs of policyholders.

Public relations activities include communications with the public on behalf of the insurer to ensure a strong public image. Individuals performing these activities may also be called communications or media specialists. They design and implement a consistent description of the organization and its actions.

The public relations staff provides periodic information to the insurer's community about the organization's activities. They may communicate with employees to request their participation in media or educational events, such as conferences or public speaking engagements, to ensure that the insurer's messages are included and a positive image provided. In times of crisis, the public relations staff coordinates a consolidated message to the media to provide consistent communication as well as to respond to negative publicity, if necessary.

Sales Fulfillment

Sales fulfillment is the satisfactory delivery of the products and services that result from the product development activity. Fulfillment of a product plan affects many of an insurer's functional areas. For example, the introduction of policies and services to target high-net-worth individuals as a market segment must include participation by customer service, underwriting, claims, and other functional areas. The senior management team must communicate the goals, strategies, and action plans to all areas of the organization. Each functional area must determine the impact of the plan on operations, budget, and performance standards.

Milestones should be established for the functional areas with metrics to periodically check the results of the marketing plan and take action in any area where goals are not met. If sales results do not meet projections, marketing analysis can help determine why and recommend improvements.

INSURANCE DISTRIBUTION SYSTEMS AND CHANNELS

Insurers are driven by competition to address customer preferences. In this environment, insurers examine the efficiency of their distribution systems and channels.

No single approach to distribution meets the needs of all insurers and all insurance customers. Insurers select one or a combination based on overall business plans and their core products and services.

Insurers use many types of **distribution systems** based on their organizational structure, business and marketing plans, growth goals, technological capabilities, staffing, and other resources necessary to support the selected system(s). The principal characteristics that distinguish one distribution system from another include the relationship to the insurer and customers, ownership of expirations, compensation methods, and functions performed. These are the main insurance distribution systems:

Distribution system
The necessary people and physical facilities to support the sale of insurance products and services.

- Independent agency and brokerage marketing systems
- Exclusive agency marketing system
- Direct writer marketing system

Insurers use these common distribution channels to promote products and services as well as to communicate with existing and prospective insureds:

- Internet
- Call centers
- Direct response
- Group marketing
- Financial institutions

Mixed marketing systems include more than one distribution system or channel.

Independent Agency and Brokerage Marketing Systems

The independent agency and brokerage marketing system uses agents and brokers who are independent contractors rather than employees of insurers. These independent agents and brokers are usually free to represent as many or as few insurers as they want.

Independent Agents and Brokers

An independent agency is a business, operated for the benefit of its owner (or owners), that sells insurance, usually as a representative of several unrelated insurers. An insurance broker is an independent business owner or firm that sells insurance by representing customers rather than insurers. Brokers shop among insurers to find the best coverage and value for their clients. Because they are not legal representatives of the insurer, brokers are not likely to have authority to commit an insurer to write a policy by binding coverage, unlike agents, who generally have binding authority. See the exhibit "Similarities and Differences Between Brokers and Agents."

Similarities and Differences Between Brokers and Agents

In practice, despite the technical distinctions between brokers and independent agents, the differences are minimal. Both brokers and independent agents are intermediaries between insurers and insurance buyers, and both collect premiums from insureds and remit them to insurers. Both are in the business of finding people with insurance needs and selling insurance appropriate to those needs. In fact, the same person can act as an agent in one transaction and as a broker in another. A person acts as an agent when placing insurance with an insurer for which he or she is licensed as an agent but may act as a broker when placing insurance with other agents or insurers.

[DA06205]

The independent agency or brokerage can be organized as a sole proprietorship, a partnership, or a corporation.

Agency expiration list

The record of an insurance agency's present policyholders and the dates their policies expire.

One of the main distinguishing features between independent agents and brokers and other distribution systems is the ownership of the **agency expiration list**. If an insurer ceases to do business with an agency, the agency has the right to continue doing business with its existing customers by selling them insurance with another insurer. The ownership of expiration lists is an agency's most valuable asset. An independent agency has the right to sell its expiration lists to another independent agent.

Compensation for independent agents and brokers is typically in two forms:

- A flat percent commission on all new and renewal business submitted
- A contingent or profit-sharing commission based on volume or loss ratio goals

Disclosure of the commission paid to agents or brokers enhances the transparency of the transaction for prospective insureds.

The independent agents and brokers distribution system is flexible; it can meet the needs of many different insurance customers, and it is spread geographically across the United States. In addition to insurance placement, agents and brokers may also assist their customers in establishing and managing self-insurance programs, implementing risk control measures, and determining alternatives or supplements to insurance. Some have draft authority from insurers to settle small first-party losses.

National and Regional Brokers

National and regional brokers generally represent commercial insurance accounts that often require sophisticated knowledge and service. In addition to insurance sales, large brokerage firms may provide extensive risk control, appraisal, actuarial, risk management, claim administration, and other insurance-related services that large businesses need. These brokers are often equipped to provide services that are supported by offices in multiple states.

Large insurance brokerage firms operate regionally and nationally, and some even operate internationally. They can tailor insurance programs for customers or groups of customers who require a particular type of coverage for multiple locations. Examples of such programs are insurance marketed to attorneys, which might include professional liability coverage, and an insurance program for daycare centers that includes coverages for exposures related to child care.

The brokers receive negotiated fees for the services they provide, or they receive fees in addition to commissions, subject to state regulation.

Independent Agent Networks

Independent agent networks, also known as agent groups, agent clusters, or agent alliances, consist of independent agencies and brokerages that join together to gain advantages normally available only to large national and regional brokers. Agent networks operate nationally, regionally, or locally and, in the majority of cases, allow their agent-members to retain individual agency ownership and independence.

By combining individual agency forces into a single selling, negotiating, and servicing unit, an agent network can offer many benefits to its agent members, including these:

- Obtaining access to an increased number of insurers
- Meeting **countersignature law** requirements for businesses in multiple states
- Combining premium volume to meet insurer requirements for profit-sharing

Countersignature laws
Laws that require all policies covering subjects of insurance within a state to be signed by a resident producer licensed in that state.

- Generating additional sales income
- Receiving preferred agency contracts
- Facilitating agency succession planning
- Providing expertise in risk management services
- Offering expertise in financial planning services
- Enabling resource sharing and expense reduction
- Increasing market share

Managing General Agents

Managing general agent (MGA)

An authorized agent of the primary insurer that manages all or part of the primary insurer's insurance activities, usually in a specific geographic area.

Managing general agents (MGAs), also referred to as management general underwriters (MGUs), serve as intermediaries between insurers and the agents and brokers who sell insurance directly to the customer, similar to wholesalers in the marketing system for tangible goods.

The exact duties and responsibilities of an MGA depend on its contracts with the insurers it represents. MGAs can represent a single insurer, although they more commonly represent several insurers. Some MGAs can be strictly sales operations, appointing and supervising subagents or dealing with brokers within their contractual jurisdiction. That jurisdiction can be specified in terms of geographic boundaries, types of insurance, or both. A few MGAs cover large multistate territories, although frequently only for specialty insurance.

An insurer operating through an MGA reaps several advantages:

- A low fixed cost—An insurer who writes business through an MGA does not have to staff and support a branch office. The MGA is usually compensated by a commission override on business its subagents sell. The MGA, by writing relatively small amounts of business for each of several insurers, generates enough commissions to cover its expenses and earn a profit. The MGA might also receive a contingent commission based on the profitability or the volume of business it writes.

- Specialty expertise—MGAs develop expertise in particular markets and design insurance programs in collaboration with the insurers they represent. Specialty insurance programs offered by MGAs include those for such diverse risks as petroleum distributors, fire departments, horse farms, employment practices liability, and directors and officers liability.

- Assumption of insurer activities—Full-service MGAs can provide an array of benefits to their subagents and brokers, including claim administration, information management, risk control and risk management services, underwriting and marketing services, policy issuance, and premium collection. Insurers must supervise the MGAs that represent them, and most states regulate the MGAs' activities and contracts.

Surplus Lines Brokers

Most agents and brokers are limited to placing business with licensed (or admitted) insurers. The circumstances under which business can be placed with an unlicensed (or nonadmitted) insurer through a surplus lines broker vary by state. Normally, a reasonable effort to place the coverage with a licensed insurer is required.

The agents and brokers, who must be licensed to place surplus lines business in that state, might be required to certify that a specified number (often two or three) of licensed insurers have refused to provide the coverage. In some states, agents and brokers must provide letters from the insurers rejecting the coverage. Some state insurance departments maintain lists of coverages that are eligible for surplus lines treatment without first being rejected by licensed insurers. Some states also maintain lists of eligible surplus lines insurers, requiring producers to place business only with financially sound insurers.

Surplus lines brokers have access to insurers that have the capacity to provide the needed insurance, which might not be available from insurers licensed to do business in the state. This provides a system for insuring specific customers or exposures:

- A customer that requires high limits of insurance
- A customer that requires unusually broad or specialized coverage
- An unusual or a unique loss exposure
- Loss exposures requiring a tailored insurance program
- An unfavorable loss exposure, such as a poor claim history or difficult-to-treat exposures

Surplus lines brokers work to ensure that 1) coverage is placed only with eligible nonadmitted insurers, 2) the customer's unique or unusual requirements can be met by the prospective surplus lines insurer, and 3) the financial security of the surplus lines insurer is properly evaluated.

Surplus lines brokers, like national or regional brokers, maintain their independence, can represent multiple insurers, and are compensated based on a portion of the commissions generated by the business they write.

Exclusive Agency Marketing System

The exclusive agency marketing system uses independent contractors called exclusive agents (or captive agents), who are not employees of insurers. Exclusive agents are usually restricted by contract to representing a single insurer. Consequently, insurer management can exercise greater control over exclusive agents than over independent agents. However, some exclusive agency companies allow their agents to place business with other insurers if the exclusive agency insurer does not offer the product or service needed.

Exclusive agents are usually compensated by commissions. During initial training, some of them might receive a salary, a guaranteed minimum income, or income from a drawing account. In terms of overall compensation, insurers in the exclusive agency system commonly pay one commission rate for new business and another, lower rate for renewal business. For exclusive agents, the focus is on new-business production, and a reduced renewal commission rate encourages sales and supports growth.

Exclusive agents typically do not own expirations as independent producers do. However, some insurers that market through the exclusive agency system do grant agents limited ownership of expirations. Usually, such ownership of expirations applies only while the agency contract is in force. When the agency contract is terminated, the ownership of expirations reverts to the insurer. The insurer might be obligated to compensate the agent for the expirations upon termination of the agency contract; however, the agent does not have the option of selling the expirations to anyone other than the insurer.

The exclusive agency insurer handles many administrative functions for the exclusive agent, including policy issuance, premium collection, and claim processing. Exclusive agents might offer loss adjustment services similar to those offered by independent agents and brokers; however, these agents might be restricted in their ability to offer some risk management services to their customers.

Direct Writer Marketing System

The direct writer marketing system uses sales agents (also known as sales representatives) who are employees of the insurers they represent. The sales agents sell insurance for the insurer at office locations provided by the direct writer insurer. Sales agents in the direct writer system may be compensated by salary, by commission, or by both salary and a portion of the commission generated.

Because sales agents are employees of the insurers they represent, they usually do not have any ownership of expirations and, like exclusive agents, are usually restricted to representing a single insurer or a group of insurers under common ownership and management.

Sometimes a customer needs a type of policy not available from the direct writer insurer that the sales agent represents. When this happens, the sales agent may act as a broker by contacting an agent who represents another insurer and apply for insurance through that agent, who usually shares the commission with the direct writer sales agent. Insurance sold in this manner is referred to as brokered business.

Sales agents are largely relieved of administrative functions by their employers. These insurer-assumed functions include policy issuance, premium collections, and claim functions. One key ingredient in direct writer insurer relationships with their sales agents is active encouragement to develop new business. Relieving the producer of nonselling activities and compensating at a lower renewal rate help accomplish this goal.

Distribution Channels

The distribution channels used by insurers and their representatives are conduits for contacting and establishing communication with their customers and prospective customers. Insurers' increasing use of multiple distribution channels has been driven by technology and customer preference. Customers who are familiar with the prompt, efficient delivery and service they obtain from other product providers expect the same type of response from their insurers.

Insurers and their representatives are constantly searching for ways to quote and issue policies more quickly, while keeping costs reasonable. At the same time, customers desire competitive pricing, customized insurance products, and high-quality service.

Internet

As a distribution channel, the Internet can be used to varying degrees by all parties to the insurance transaction: the insurer, its representatives, and the customer. Interactions range from exchanges of email to multiple-policy quoting, billing, and policy issuance. See the exhibit "Internet Benefits and Challenges for Insurers."

The customers' ability to access information has increased dramatically, as has the speed of the insurance transaction itself. Customers also interact with insurers on the Internet via web-based insurance distributors, also called insurance portals or aggregators. These portals deliver leads to the insurers whose products they offer through their websites. Portals benefit customers by offering the products and services of many insurance providers on one Internet site, in a form of cyberspace one-stop shopping. Although the leads that portals generate must subsequently be screened and fully underwritten by the insurers accepting the coverage, those leads can increase market share and brand awareness.

Call Centers

Call centers sell insurance products and services through telemarketing. Call centers operate with customer service representatives, touch-tone service, or speech-enabled (voice response) service.

The best-equipped call centers can replicate many of the activities of producers. In addition to making product sales, call center staff can (1) respond to general inquiries, (2) handle claim reporting, (3) answer billing inquiries, and (4) process policy endorsements. In some cases, a customer can begin an inquiry or a transaction on the Internet, then have a customer service representative at the insurer's call center access the Internet activity and answer the inquiry or conclude the transaction.

Internet Benefits and Challenges for Insurers

Insurers and their representatives derive a number of benefits from having an Internet presence:

- Reduced costs for underwriting and claims-processing services because of lower overhead arising from automated operations
- Streamlined business practices—the need for fewer employees to conduct direct sales
- Increased brand awareness
- Broadened marketing potential
- Lead-generation and cross-selling opportunities for all products, not just property-casualty insurance

However, Internet sales present challenges for insurers:

- Regulation requirements—Purchases transacted completely via the Internet may not meet regulatory compliance requirements that a licensed agent consummate the sale.
- Assumed cost advantage—Consumers perceive that a product bought over the Internet will be less expensive than the same product bought from a producer. These assumptions are not necessarily valid.
- Competitors are only a click away—If customers do not like what they see, they are likely to click to another, more favorable, website.
- Quoting capabilities—An insurer's ability to quote easily and quickly is critical, because about 50 percent of users will simply move to another website if the quoting mechanism is too complicated.
- Availability of information—Many customers do not fully understand insurance products; the Internet largely eliminates intermediaries who would otherwise provide explanations and advice. Therefore, a website should maintain a frequently asked questions (FAQ) section and/or a "live contact."
- Extent of services provided—The insurer or producer must determine whether its Internet presence will be sales-only or a combination of sales and service.
- The informed consumer—Information about many insurance products and their prices is available to customers, shifting the customer's focus toward price rather than service.
- Security concerns—Some customers are unwilling to transmit personal and financial information over the Internet.
- Website content—Information posted on the website must be kept fresh, interesting, and accessible.

[DA06206]

Direct response distribution channel

An insurance distribution channel that markets directly to the customer through such distribution channels as mail, telephone, or the Internet.

Direct Response

The **direct response distribution channel** markets directly to customers. No agent is involved; rather the direct response relies primarily on mail, phone, and/or Internet sales. Although this distribution channel is also called direct mail, customers can also contact insurers via telephone and the Internet. Direct response relies heavily on advertising and targeting specific groups of affiliated customers.

With direct response, commission costs, if any, are greatly reduced. However, a disadvantage is that advertising costs are typically higher. The customer can sometimes "opt out" and speak with a call-center customer service representative or be assigned to a local servicing office.

Group Marketing

Group marketing sells insurance products and services through call centers, the Internet, direct mail response, or a producer to individuals or businesses that are all members of the same organization. Distributing insurance to specifically targeted groups is known by a number of terms, including these:

- **Affinity marketing**—Insurers target various customer groups based on profession, interests, hobbies, or attitudes. For example, the insurer, agent, or broker might decide to market personal insurance products to university alumni groups, chambers of commerce, bar associations, or users of a particular credit card. Coverage is sometimes offered at a discounted premium.

> **Affinity marketing**
> A type of group marketing that targets various groups based on profession, association, interests, hobbies, and attitudes.

- Mass marketing or mass merchandising—Insurers design an offer for their policies to large numbers of targeted individuals or groups. Coverage is frequently offered at a discounted premium, and the insurer retains the right to underwrite each applicant, with guaranteed policy issuance available as an option.

- Worksite marketing or payroll deduction—Employers can contract directly with an insurer or through a producer to offer voluntary insurance coverage as a benefit to their employees. Worksite marketing (or "franchise marketing") of insurance is used frequently to offer personal insurance coverages or optional life, health, and disability coverage to employees. Premiums for employees are usually discounted and are deducted (after tax) from employees' paychecks, with an option available for employees to pay for the coverage in another way.

- Sponsorship marketing—A trade group sponsors an insurer in approaching a customer group. The sponsor participates in the profitability of the program. For example, a wholesale club sponsors an insurer to market to club members for a fee based on the success of the program.

The success of any marketing group program depends on the support of the sponsoring organization or employer, offering discounted premiums, treating the employees as a preferred group for underwriting purposes, and facilitating program operation, particularly from the employer's administrative perspective.

Financial Institutions

Insurers and producers can elect to market their products and services through a bank or another financial services institution, either exclusively or through using additional distribution channels. Marketing arrangements can range from simple to complex. For example, a small insurance agency may place an agent at a desk in a local bank, or a large insurer may form a strategic alliance with a regional or national financial holding company to solicit customers.

The prospect of diversifying into new markets appeals to many financial institutions. In fact, some financial institutions have expanded into insurance by participating in renewal rights arrangements by which they purchase only a book of business and not the liabilities of an agency or insurer.

Insurers view financial institutions as beneficial strategic partners because of these qualities:

- Strong customer base
- Predisposition to product cross-selling
- Strength at processing transactions
- Efficient use of technology for database mining geared to specific products and services

To sustain distribution relationships with financial institutions, insurers must focus on providing saleable products and efficient administration and support while also protecting their professional presence in financial institutions from competitors.

Mixed Marketing System

The term "mixed marketing system" refers to an insurer's use of more than one distribution system or channel to attract a wider range of customers. For example, some insurers that traditionally sold insurance only through independent agents are now also using direct response. Conversely, some direct writing insurers, seeking to expand their business, have entered into agency agreements with independent agents in some areas.

Similarly, insurers are using multiple distribution channels to more effectively communicate with customers.

Combining insurance distribution systems and channels requires consideration of several issues:

- Maintaining consistent customer communications—An insurer must send customers the same clear, consistent message about its products and services. In addition, the insurer's internal communications must be consistent across marketing systems and distribution channels, and workflows, data management, and underwriting standards must be communicated.
- Providing a consistent customer experience—The experience a customer has when interacting with an insurer must be consistent across

all marketing distribution systems and channels. Customers' access to the Internet and its wealth of information has created knowledgeable, demanding insurance customers with distinct preferences and expectations.

- Matching the type of insurance with an appropriate distribution system and channel—Some marketing systems are more suitable than others based on the product being sold. Personal insurance and commercial insurance vary in terms of the products' levels of complexity and in terms of the expertise insurers, agents, and brokers need in order to properly sell the products to consumers and service them after the sale. The combination of systems and channels selected depends on the particular type of insurance to be sold.

FUNCTIONS OF INSURANCE PRODUCERS

The functions insurance producers perform vary widely from one marketing system to another and from one producer to another within a given marketing system. Generally, producers are the initial contact with insurance customers and provide expertise and ongoing services.

Insurance producers represent one or more insurance companies. As a source of insurance knowledge for their customers, producers provide risk management advice, solicit or sell insurance, and provide follow-up services as customers' loss exposures or concerns change.

Insurance producers typically perform these functions:

- Prospecting
- Risk management review
- Sales
- Policy issuance
- Premium collection
- Customer service
- Claim handling
- Consulting

Prospecting

Virtually all producers prospect. Prospecting involves locating persons, businesses, and other entities that may be interested in purchasing the insurance products and services offered by the producer's principals. Prospects can be located using several methods:

- Referrals from present clients
- Referrals from strategic partners, such as financial institutions and real estate brokers

- Advertising in multimedia and direct mail
- Interactive websites
- Telephone solicitations
- **Cold canvass**

Cold canvass

Contacting a prospect without an appointment.

Large agencies and brokerages may have employees who specialize in locating prospective clients. However, a producer is typically responsible for his or her own prospecting. Insurers might also participate in prospecting, especially in the exclusive agent and direct writer marketing systems.

Risk Management Review

Risk management review is the principal method of determining a prospect's insurance needs. The extent of the review varies based on customers and their characteristics.

Individual or Family

For an individual or a family, the risk management review process might be relatively simple, requiring an interview or completion of a questionnaire that assists in identifying the prospect's loss exposures, which are often associated with property ownership and activities. Using the results of the interview or questionnaire, the producer suggests methods of risk control, retention of loss exposures, and insurance.

Businesses

The risk management review process for businesses is likely to be more complex because they have property ownership, products, services, employees, and liabilities that are unique to the size and type of organization. Substantial time is required to develop and analyze loss exposure information for a large firm with diversified operations.

Loss run

A report detailing an insured's history of claims that have occurred over a specific period, valued as of a specific date.

A **loss run** report can guide the producer in helping the business owner develop risk management plans, track the results of current risk management efforts, identify problem areas, and project costs. Loss runs include, at a minimum, lists of losses and their total cost. More comprehensive loss runs provide details that can lead to additional questions and suggest areas of risk management improvement. For example, comprehensive workers compensation loss runs reveal lag times in reporting, creating potentially higher costs. These reports can also indicate litigation rate; a high rate can be an indication of poor communication between employers and employees or overall employee dissatisfaction.

Sales

Selling insurance products and services is one of the most important activities of an insurance producer because it is essential to sustaining the livelihood of the agency or brokerage. Commission on business sold is the principal source of income for producers, and the ownership of policy expirations applicable to the business sold is the principal asset of an insurance agency.

Steps in the sales process include contacting the prospective client, determining the prospect's needs, preparing and presenting a proposal, and closing the sale.

Policy Issuance

At the producer's request, insurers issue policies and their associated forms, either mailing them directly to policyholders or sending them to the producer for delivery. In paperless environments, the policies and forms may be produced on a compact disk or placed in an Internet filing cabinet along with endorsements, bills, and loss history information.

Some producers use their own agency management systems to generate computer-issued policies on-site.

Premium Collection

Producers who issue policies may also prepare policy invoices and collect premiums. After deducting their commissions, they send the net premiums to the insurers, a procedure known as the **agency bill** process. For business that is agency billed, there are three widely used methods of transmitting premiums to the insurer:

- Item basis—The premium (less commission) is forwarded to the insurer when the producer collects it or when it becomes due. This is the least complex of the three methods. The producer is usually not required to pay the insurer until the premium has been collected.

- Statement basis—The insurer sends a statement to the producer showing the premiums that are due. The producer is obligated to pay the premiums indicated as due or to show that the statement is in error.

- Account current basis—The producer periodically prepares a statement showing the premiums due to the insurer, after deducting appropriate commissions, and transmits that amount to the insurer. The agency contract indicates how often the producer must submit the account current statement. The most common interval is monthly. The producer must pay the insurer when the premium is due, even if the policyholders have not paid the producer.

To give the producer some protection against policyholders' late payments, premiums are usually not due to the insurer until thirty or forty-five days after the policy's effective date. This delay also permits the producer to invest the premiums collected until they are due to the insurer. The resulting investment income can be a significant part of the producer's remuneration.

Agency bill

A payment procedure in which a producer sends premium bills to the insured, collects the premium, and sends the premium to the insurer, less any applicable commission.

Agency billing may be used for personal insurance policies, but it is more commonly used with large commercial accounts. For small commercial accounts and the vast majority of personal insurance, the customer is usually directed to send premium payments to the insurer, bypassing the producer in a procedure known as the **direct bill** process.

Customer Service

Most producers are involved to some degree in customer service. For independent agents and brokers, value-added services and the personalization of insurance packages are what differentiate them in the marketplace. For the producer of a direct writer, service might consist of providing advice, taking an endorsement request over the phone, providing coverage quotes, or transferring a policyholder who has had a loss to the claim department.

Producers are expected to facilitate contacts between policyholders and the insurer, including these:

- Responding to billing inquiries
- Performing customer account reviews
- Engaging in field underwriting, such as obtaining loss reports, insurance credit scores, and motor vehicle reports
- Answering questions regarding existing coverage and additional coverage requirements
- Corresponding with premium auditors and risk control representatives

Claim Handling

All producers are likely to be involved to some extent in handling claims filed by their policyholders. Because the producer is the policyholder's principal contact with the insurer, the policyholder naturally contacts the producer first when a claim occurs.

In some cases, the producer might simply give the policyholder the telephone number of the claim department and possibly the name of a person to speak with. Alternatively, the producer might obtain some basic information about the claim from the policyholder, relay it to the insurer, and arrange for a claim representative to contact the policyholder. Frequently, insurers issue their policies with a "claim kit" that informs their policyholders about the proper procedures and contacts.

Some producers are authorized by their insurers to adjust some types of claims. Most often, the authorization is limited to small first-party property claims. However, a few large agencies or brokerages that employ skilled claim personnel might be authorized to settle large, more complex claims. The limitations on the producer's claim-handling authority should be specified in the agency contract.

Direct bill

A payment procedure in which the insurer assumes all responsibility for sending premium bills to the insured, collecting the premium, and sending any commission payable on the premium collected to the producer.

Claim handling by qualified producers offers two major advantages: quicker service to policyholders and lower loss adjustment expenses to the insurer. Conversely, if the producer is not properly trained in how to handle claims, overpayment of claims can offset the savings.

Consulting

Many producers offer consulting services, for which they are paid on a fee basis. Such services are usually performed for insureds, but they may also be performed for noninsureds or for prospects. Services might be provided for a fee only, or the producer might set a maximum fee to be reduced by any commissions received on insurance written because of the consulting contract.

Laws in some states prohibit agents from receiving both commission and a fee from the same client. Fees are billed separately from any insurance premiums due, whereas commissions are included in the premium totals billed.

DISTRIBUTION SYSTEM AND CHANNEL SELECTION FOR INSURANCE MARKETING

Any firm that sells a product has a distribution system to carry out some of its marketing functions. Distribution systems for intangible products, such as insurance, are more flexible and adaptable than those for tangible products because they are not constrained by large investments in physical facilities. This intangibility gives insurers options to meet a wide array of customers' needs as well as their own operational needs. Distribution channels provide even more options for communicating with existing and potential customers.

Insurance distribution systems and channels provide the necessary people, physical facilities, and conduits for communication between insurers and customers.

An insurer usually selects a distribution system before it begins writing business. Changing distribution systems for existing business can be difficult and possibly expensive because of existing agency contracts and possible ownership of expirations. However, an insurer that has previously chosen one distribution system might decide to use a different one when entering a new territory or launching a new insurance product. In contrast, distribution channels selected by insurers and their representatives are more readily changeable.

The key factors in selecting distribution systems and channels are based on customers' needs and characteristics as well as the insurer's profile. See the exhibit "Distribution Systems and Conduits for Insurance Marketing."

Distribution Systems and Conduits for Insurance Marketing

Distribution systems consist of the necessary people and physical facilities to support the sale of the insurance product and services.	Independent agency and brokerage marketing system • Independent agents and brokers • National and regional brokers • Independent agent networks • Managing general agents (MGAs) • Surplus lines brokers Exclusive agency marketing system Direct writer marketing system
Distribution channels are communication conduits for promoting and servicing products as well as communicating with existing and prospective insureds.	• Internet • Call centers • Direct response • Group marketing • Financial institutions

[DA06250]

Customers' Needs and Characteristics

The needs and characteristics of customers—both existing and those in target markets—are key factors in an insurer's selection of distribution systems and channels because their satisfaction drives their purchase decisions. These are examples of customer needs and characteristics:

- Products and services—What are customers' expectations regarding coverage, accessibility, price, and service? Customers with low service expectations, such as purchasers of minimum-coverage personal auto insurance, may be satisfied with the ease of comparison shopping over the Internet for direct writers' policies. Conversely, a large commercial account's risk manager will seek the expertise of an agent or broker to provide advice, assist in coverage placement, and respond to changing needs as the organization's internal and external environments change.

- Price—To what degree is the price of products and services a factor for customers? Some consumers' paramount concern is the price of insurance. Others are concerned with price to a degree, but are unlikely to make changes if they are satisfied with a product. Still others seek risk management alternatives, including insurance that will minimize the adverse effects of losses for the organization over the long term.

- Response time—How quickly can inquiries and transactions be processed? Customers routinely experience speedy financial services transactions and increasingly expect the same response from their insurance providers.

For those customers whose inquiries and transactions can be addressed by telephone or via the Internet, a variety of distribution systems and channels can meet those needs. However, speed can be an issue in attracting commercial accounts that demand extensive services if producers are not in the territory of the businesses' facilities.

Insurer's Profile

An insurer's profile—including its strategies and goals, strengths, existing and target markets, geographic location, and the degree of control over producers it requires or desires—frames the business and marketing environments within which it operates. The insurer must evaluate these key factors in selecting distribution systems and channels.

Insurer Strategies and Goals

An insurer's strategies, defined by high-level organizational goals, provide purposeful direction for the organization. These strategies and goals often address issues regarding market share size, sales, service, and the markets in which the insurer competes. They may also relate to acquisitions, strategic alliances, or mergers.

Changes in market strategies or aggressive goals can be a catalyst for an insurer to reexamine its distribution systems and channels if current approaches are inadequate to achieve required results. For example, a regional personal lines insurer that contracts independent agents as a distribution system may adopt a strategy to expand to the national market. Rather than contracting additional independent agents in the expanded geographic territory, the insurer assumes the role of a direct writer and uses the Internet as a distribution channel to reach customers through Web-based insurance distributors. This approach can reduce long-term costs and accelerate the insurer's market-share growth.

Insurer Strengths

Organizations evaluate their internal and external environments to assess their strengths and weaknesses compared to external opportunities and threats. Determining where its strengths lie, an insurer selects those distribution systems and channels that maximize its opportunities to capture market share and minimize its weaknesses. In doing so, the insurer may analyze these factors:

- Financial resources—The initial fixed cost of entering the market through the exclusive agency system or direct writer system is greater than doing so through the independent agency system. The insurer must hire, train, and financially support the direct writer and exclusive agency producers at substantial cost before they become productive. Similarly, Internet-based distribution channels have high start-up costs for supporting information systems. In comparison, the cost of conducting a direct response campaign can be much lower. Consequently, insurers with the financial resources to initiate distribution systems and channels with high start-up costs have the option of competing in markets that are best served by those marketing methods. Insurers that lack the financial resources to cover those start-up costs may be limited in the target markets they enter.

- Core capabilities—Core capabilities include the abilities of an organization's staff, processes, and technology. An insurer whose strength is successfully servicing large, complex commercial accounts can capitalize on the firm's core capabilities. Complex commercial accounts require personalized service and are well served by agents and brokers, who can provide advice and ongoing service to expand the types of businesses to which the insurer markets or its geographic market.

- Expertise and reputation of producers—Because agents and brokers are the point of contact with customers, their expertise and reputation can be a crucial strength or weakness for the insurer. The level of expertise required of a producer depends on the lines of insurance written. Specialty target markets, such as international manufacturing, high-net-worth individuals, and large public entities require knowledgeable and prominent producers to advise them. Having producers with those attributes in a direct writer distribution system allows the insurer to expand into similar or secondary markets. An insurer attempting to enter specialty markets without the skill base on staff must compete for agents and brokers who can provide the needed expertise and reputation.

Existing and Target Markets

The characteristics of an insurer's existing book of business should be considered in any change in distribution system or channel. If agents or brokers own the expirations for current accounts, the insurer must either give up that business and start over or purchase the expirations from producers. Either option might be expensive, depending on the quality of the existing business.

Disruptions in communication channels can also cause changes in communication patterns that can result in policyholder dissatisfaction and lost accounts. As a result, insurers change market systems and channels for existing customers with great caution. However, some catalysts are sufficiently threatening to cause an insurer to change marketing approaches. For example, an insurer that is losing market share to an aggressive new competitor has ample incentive to change its approach to better address customers' needs and characteristics.

Customers' needs and characteristics are driving factors for an insurer that is considering changing its marketing approach or adopting a mixed marketing approach for a new target market. If an insurer's existing distribution systems and channels do not adequately address the customers' profiles as determined through marketing research, the insurer is less likely to gain market share. To make an optimum choice, the insurer carefully balances the cost of changing its distribution systems and channels with expected benefits resulting from the new accounts it will write.

Geographic Location

The geographic location of existing policyholders or target markets is a key concern in selecting a distribution system and channels because the insurer's fixed costs of establishing an exclusive agent or direct-writer agent in a territory are substantial. Exclusive agent or direct writer marketing systems can be successful only when a sufficient number of prospects exist within a relatively small geographic area.

Because the cost of appointing an independent agent or using the direct response system is generally lower than the cost of appointing an exclusive or direct-writer agent, those systems can be used in sparsely populated areas or when the target market customers are widely dispersed. Some insurers that traditionally used either the exclusive agency system or the direct writer system have elected to use the independent agency system in rural areas and small towns because of the lower startup costs.

Degree of Control Required

The extent of control the insurer wants to exercise over its marketing operations may influence its choice of a distribution system:

- An insurer can exercise the greatest control over producers in the direct writer system. Under that system, the producer is an employee of the company, and the company can exercise control over both the results achieved and the methods used to achieve them. For example, an insurer can specify the number and type of new applications the producer must submit each month (results) as well as the marketing approaches the producer can use (methods).

- Under both the agency and brokerage system and the exclusive agency system, the producers are independent contractors; therefore, the insurer can control only the results they produce, not the methods by which they produce them. For example, an insurer can specify the number and type of new applications the producer must submit each month (results). However, the agent or broker can engage in any advertising or marketing campaign to achieve those results that does not violate insurance regulations or contractual agreements with the insurer.

- Producers are not involved in the direct response system. Consequently, the insurer has complete control of its distribution system.

Degree of control becomes important in meeting the needs of some customers. For example, pharmaceutical manufacturers require specialized risk management advice that includes a risk control recovery plan following the release of a tainted drug or defective medical device to the public. The insurer may wish to control the nature of the risk management alternatives recommended to those insureds that foster transparency and immediate response following products liability losses.

Other insurers value discretion in the producers who represent them. For example, an insurer that specializes in church insurance or distributes insurance through religious affinity groups will expect to have some control over the producers' use of social media (web-based sites used to exchange content with selected or broad audiences through the Internet). A producer's indiscretions posted in public forums can cause an insurer to lose accounts. Therefore, the insurer might choose a direct writer distribution system under which producers are employees and subject to the insurer's guidelines for media use.

SUMMARY

The property-casualty insurance marketplace is the unique environment where insurance customers' needs and characteristics are addressed by insurers. Key features of the insurance marketplace include these:

- Insurance customers who come to the market with varying insurance needs, knowledge of insurance, access methods, negotiating ability, and choice of risk financing alternatives
- Insurers that compete in the market for customers based on differentiations in customer focus, products and services, size, geographic area, and distribution system
- Marketplace features that are unique to the industry, such as economic forces, regulatory control, demands for technology, underwriting cycles, and unanticipated catastrophic losses

An insurer's marketing activities collectively gather and analyze information so that the organization can make optimal and informed choices in market segmentation, efficient product development, and effective communication to customers to promote product sales. Marketing activities include these examples:

- Marketing research
- Market development
- Marketing information
- Marketing planning
- Product development
- Advertising and promotion
- Customer and public relations
- Sales fulfillment

Insurance distribution systems consist of the necessary people and physical facilities to support the sale of insurance products and services. The main insurance distribution systems are these:

- Independent agency and brokerage marketing system
- Exclusive agency marketing system
- Direct writer marketing system

Insurers use distribution channels to promote products and services as well as to communicate with existing and prospective insureds. These are common insurance distribution channels:

- Internet
- Call centers
- Direct response
- Group marketing
- Financial institutions

No one distribution system or channel is best; insurers may select a mixed marketing system based on their marketing and business needs.

Insurance producers represent one or more insurance companies and perform these typical functions:

- Prospecting
- Risk management review
- Sales
- Policy issuance
- Premium collection
- Customer service
- Claim handling
- Consulting

Insurers should evaluate various factors when selecting distribution systems and channels. These factors include customers' needs and characteristics, such as the products and services they require, the price they are willing to pay, and the response time they require.

Insurers' profiles serve as guidelines that affect their choice of distribution systems and channels. Insurers' profiles include their strategies and goals, strengths, existing and target markets, geographic location, and the degree of control required.

The Underwriting Function

Educational Objectives

After learning the content of this assignment, you should be able to:

▷ Describe the purpose of underwriting.

▷ Describe the underwriting activities typically performed by line and staff underwriters.

▷ Describe the importance of compliance with underwriting authority in individual account selection.

▷ Describe the constraining factors considered in the establishment of underwriting policy.

▷ Describe the purposes that underwriting guidelines and underwriting audits serve.

▷ Summarize the steps in the underwriting process and the purpose of each.

▷ Explain how an insurer's underwriting results are measured and how financial measures can be distorted.

The Underwriting Function

PURPOSE OF UNDERWRITING

Insurance companies assume billions of dollars in financial risk annually, risk that is transferred to them from individuals and businesses via the insurance transaction. Insurance underwriters, using the underwriting process and various supporting underwriting tools, are employed by insurers to assess both their new and current business. An insurance company's overall profitability can depend significantly on the quality of its underwriting.

Underwriting has multiple purposes. The overarching purpose is to develop and maintain a profitable book of business for the insurer. Underwriting is crucial to an insurer's success; underwriting goals flow directly from the insurer's corporate strategies and objectives. Favorable underwriting results are necessary for an insurer's ability to sustain profitable growth.

To achieve profitability, the underwriting function serves additional purposes:

- Guarding against adverse selection
- Ensuring adequate policyholders' surplus
- Enforcing underwriting guidelines

Guarding Against Adverse Selection

Underwriters are an insurer's guard against adverse selection. These are examples of adverse selection:

- Some property owners in areas prone to coastal storms purchase windstorm coverage or increase their limits only before a hurricane season, when they expect severe losses.
- A disproportionate percentage of property owners in an earthquake-prone zone purchase earthquake insurance, as compared to property owners in areas less prone to earthquakes.

Underwriters minimize the effects of adverse selection by carefully selecting the applicants whose loss exposures they are willing to insure, charging appropriate premiums for the applicants that they do accept with premiums that accurately reflect the loss exposures, and monitoring applications and books of business for unusual patterns of policy growth or loss.

Ensuring Adequate Policyholders' Surplus

Policyholders' surplus

Under statutory accounting principles (SAP), an insurer's total admitted assets minus its total liabilities.

Capacity

The amount of business an insurer is able to write, usually based on a comparison of the insurer's written premiums to its policyholders' surplus.

An insurance company must have adequate **policyholders' surplus** if it wishes to increase its written premium volume. An insurer's **capacity** is limited by regulatory guidelines and often by its own voluntary constraints, which are frequently more conservative than those imposed by regulators. If an insurer's underwriting practices generate policy premiums that exceed losses and expenses, the policyholders' surplus will increase, thereby increasing capacity.

Underwriters ensure the adequacy of policyholders' surplus by adhering to underwriting guidelines, making certain that all loss exposures are correctly identified, and charging adequate premiums for the applications that are accepted.

Enforcing Underwriting Guidelines

Underwriting authority

The scope of decisions that an underwriter can make without receiving approval from someone at a higher level.

Underwriting guidelines reflect the levels of **underwriting authority** that are granted to varying levels of underwriters, producers, and managing general agents (MGAs). Exactly who has what level of underwriting authority varies considerably by insurer and by type of insurance.

Underwriting ensures that applicants accepted adhere to underwriting guidelines. If loss exposures, risks, or policy limits on an application exceed an underwriter's authority, he or she will seek approval through supervisory and management ranks within the underwriting department.

UNDERWRITING ACTIVITIES

In insurance organizations, underwriting responsibilities are delegated by members of senior management to line and staff underwriters who coordinate the day-to-day risk selection decisions and the management-level underwriting activities. This coordinated effort is crucial to the achievement of the insurer's profitability goals.

Line underwriter

Underwriter who is primarily responsible for implementing the steps in the underwriting process.

Staff underwriter

Underwriter who is usually located in the home office and who assists underwriting management with making and implementing underwriting policy.

There is no standard method to organize insurer underwriting activities. However, insurers commonly distinguish between **line underwriters** and **staff underwriters**. The focus of line underwriters is evaluating new submissions and renewal underwriting. Line underwriters work directly with insurance producers and applicants. The focus of staff underwriters is managing the risk selection process. Staff underwriters work with line underwriters and coordinate decisions with other departments to manage the insurance product, pricing, and guidelines. See the exhibit "Underwriting Activities Performed by Line and Staff Underwriters."

Line Underwriting Activities

Line underwriters evaluate individual accounts for acceptability and execute underwriting policy by following practices and procedures outlined by staff

Underwriting Activities Performed by Line and Staff Underwriters

Line underwriters

- Select insureds
- Classify and price accounts
- Recommend or provide coverage
- Manage a book of business
- Support producers and insureds
- Coordinate with marketing efforts

Staff underwriters

- Research the market
- Formulate underwriting policy
- Revise underwriting guidelines
- Evaluate loss experience
- Research and develop coverage forms
- Review and revise pricing plans
- Arrange treaty reinsurance
- Assist others with complex accounts
- Conduct underwriting audits
- Participate in industry associations
- Conduct education and training

[DA06264]

underwriters. The specific tasks line underwriters perform may vary by insurer; however, most line underwriters are responsible for these major activities.

Select Insureds

Line underwriters select new and renewal accounts that meet the criteria established in underwriting guidelines. Underwriters' effective account selection is essential to attaining these goals:

- Avoiding adverse selection
- Charging adequate premiums for accounts with a higher-than-average chance of loss
- Selecting better-than-average accounts for which the premium charged will be more than adequate
- Rationing an insurer's available capacity to obtain an optimum spread of loss exposures by location, class, size of risk, and line of business

Line underwriting selection activities are continuous. Line underwriters monitor accounts to ensure that they continue to be acceptable. A line underwriter may cancel or nonrenew an account if risk control recommendations made at the policy's inception are not implemented or if the insured fails to take corrective action to control loss frequency.

Classify and Price Accounts

Account classification is the process of grouping accounts with similar attributes so that they can be priced appropriately. Line underwriters are responsible for ensuring that all the information needed for classification is obtained and that accounts are priced properly. In many insurance companies, line underwriters do not personally perform either the classification or the pricing task. However, they are accountable for the correct accomplishment of these activities.

The price charged must not only be adequate to permit the insurer to continue to write profitable business, but also it must be competitive. A consequence of misclassification is that the premium charged is not commensurate with the risk transferred. Accounts that are misclassified and priced too low are a bargain for the policyholder, but the insurer receives premiums that are inadequate for the loss exposures they assume. In contrast, policyholders may move accounts that are overcharged, because of a misclassification, to another insurer once the policyholder discovers a better price.

Insurers submit classification plans to state insurance regulators; those who do not implement their classification plan as filed are subject to possible fines. For some lines of business and in some states, line underwriters may not have any discretionary latitude in policy pricing. In other lines of insurance, the line underwriter can use individual rating plans to apply debits and credits to the account that will adjust the premium to reflect the characteristics of the individual insured. The line underwriter must be sure that the account characteristics justify the adjustment and must document that it complies with the insurer's individual rating plan filed with regulatory authorities.

Recommend or Provide Coverage

Determining an applicant's coverage needs is generally the responsibility of the insurance agent or broker or the insured's risk manager. However, some applicants select alternative risk treatment for some exposures but choose to use insurance for other exposures. Line underwriters support the producers and policyholders by inquiring about an insured's risk management program to ensure that they are using other risk management techniques to address gaps in insurance coverage. For example, an applicant requests a Building and Personal Property Coverage Form (BPP) with the Causes of Loss—Broad Form to insure the loss exposures of a manufacturing location. While reviewing the applicant's operations as described in the inspection report, the underwriter discovers that the applicant has a loss exposure to property in transit that would not be covered adequately by these coverage forms. The underwriter discusses this loss exposure with the producer and offers to provide the coverage in an inland marine policy, thereby broadening the insured's coverage.

Sometimes an underwriter must narrow an insured's coverage. Producers often request broader coverage for the loss exposures of a particular applicant than the insurer is willing to provide. Rather than decline the application, the underwriter may offer a more limited form of coverage involving higher deductibles or covering fewer causes of loss. The producer has an opportunity to provide reduced coverage that may be acceptable to the applicant rather than reject the applicant altogether.

Line underwriters also have a role in ensuring that applicants obtain the coverage they request. The task of providing requested coverage often involves collaboration with the producer. Because each account is unique, producers and applicants often want to know how coverage will respond to a specific type of loss. Line underwriters respond to these requests by explaining the types of losses the coverage forms are designed to cover and the endorsements that must be added to provide the coverage desired.

For some complex or unique accounts, the line underwriter will draft a **manuscript policy** or endorsement that is worded to address the specific coverage needs of the insured. For most accounts, however, the line underwriter simply ensures that the policy is being issued with the appropriate forms and endorsements that provide the requested coverage.

Manuscript policy
An insurance policy that is specifically drafted according to terms negotiated between a specific insured (or group of insureds) and an insurer.

Manage a Book of Business

Frequently, line underwriters are expected to manage a book of business. Underwriting management usually reinforces departmental goals through individual line underwriters. An insurer, for example, may want to limit the number of workers compensation policies it sells that are not accompanied by an account's other insurance. The line underwriters are expected to help achieve that goal by writing workers compensation without supporting business only on a selective basis.

Some insurers also make line underwriters responsible for the profitability of a book of business accepted from a producer, or written in a territory or line of business. The line underwriter works to ensure that each book of business achieves established goals such as product mix, loss ratio, and written premium.

Support Producers and Insureds

The services that line underwriters are expected to provide to producers and insureds vary by insurer. Some insurers rely on customer service departments to respond to routine inquiries and requests. Insurers operating through independent agents often rely on their sales force to perform many policy service functions. Because customer service activities and underwriting are often interwoven, line underwriters have an active interest in ensuring that producers' and insureds' needs are met.

Line underwriters are usually directly involved with producers in preparing policy quotations. Producers devote significant time and expense to prospecting new accounts. This effort is lost if the insurer develops a quote that will not "win" the account.

Coordinate With Marketing Efforts

Insurer marketing efforts should conform with the insurer's underwriting policy. Producers are discouraged from submitting accounts that are clearly outside the insurer's underwriting guidelines. Likewise, line underwriters should not reject applications that meet insurer underwriting guidelines simply because of an underwriter's bias against a particular class of business.

Supporting the insurer's marketing objectives can have broader implications for the line underwriter. Some insurers rely on special agents or field representatives to market the insurer and its products to agents and brokers. Some insurers have blended the responsibilities of special agents and line underwriters into the position of production underwriter. Production underwriters usually confer personally with producers and assist them with developing accounts that are acceptable to the insurer.

Staff Underwriting Activities

Staff underwriters work closely with underwriting management to perform activities essential for profitable risk selection. These major activities are common to staff underwriters.

Research the Market

Insurers must continually research fundamental issues such as which markets the insurer should target. Staff underwriters typically share these research responsibilities with actuarial and marketing departments. Research includes an ongoing evaluation of these items:

- Effect of adding or deleting entire types of business
- Effect of expanding into additional states or retiring from states presently serviced
- Optimal product mix in the book of business
- Premium volume goals

Formulate Underwriting Policy

Underwriting policy (underwriting philosophy)

A guide to individual and aggregate policy selection that supports an insurer's mission statement.

Staff underwriters formulate and implement underwriting policy. An insurer's **underwriting policy**, also referred to as underwriting philosophy, guides individual and aggregate decision making. For most insurers, underwriting policy translates an insurer's mission and goals into specific strategies that, in turn, determine the composition of the insurer's book of business. Underwriting policy is communicated through underwriting guidelines.

Staff underwriters work with employees from other departments to formulate underwriting policy. Actuarial, claim, risk control, and marketing departments each have responsibilities so closely tied to those of the underwriting department that their involvement is needed to make most changes to underwriting policy.

No single underwriting policy is appropriate for all insurers. Insurers often develop their underwriting policy within the context of these markets they serve:

- Standard market—Average to better-than-average accounts for which the standard premium is at least adequate
- Nonstandard market—Higher-risk applicants who are charged a higher-than-average premium
- Specialty market—Accounts that have unique needs, such as professional liability, that are not adequately addressed in the standard market

Beyond these broad market selections, the goals for an insurer's book of business and resulting underwriting policy may be established by types of insurance and classes of business to be written; territories to be developed; or forms, insurance rates (such as filed rates and surplus lines pricing), and rating plans to be used.

Revise Underwriting Guidelines

Staff underwriters are usually responsible for revising underwriting guidelines so that they accurately reflect changes in underwriting policy. The underwriting guides identify the major elements that line underwriters should evaluate for each type of insurance.

Some underwriting guides include systematic instructions for handling particular classes of commercial accounts. Such guides may identify specific hazards to evaluate, alternatives to consider, criteria to use when making the final decision, ways to implement the decision, and methods to monitor the decision. The guides may also provide pricing instructions and reinsurance-related information. Other insurers use underwriting guides that are less comprehensive. For example, they may list all classes of business and indicate their acceptability by type of insurance. Codes are then assigned to indicate the desirability of the loss exposure and the level of authority required to write the class of business.

Texas Underwriting Guidelines

The Texas Administrative Code Section 5.9342 requires insurers writing personal automobile, residential property, or workers compensation insurance to file a full copy of their underwriting guidelines with the Texas Department of Insurance every three years.

The Texas Insurance Code Sections 38.002 and 2053.031 define underwriting guidelines as "rules, standards, guidelines, or practices, whether written, oral, or electronic, that are used by insurers or their agents to decide whether to accept or reject an application for coverage or to determine how to classify those risks that are accepted for purposes of determining a rate."

Evaluate Loss Experience

Staff underwriters evaluate an insurer's loss experience to determine whether changes should be made in underwriting guidelines. Insurance products that have losses greater than those anticipated are usually targeted for analysis. Staff underwriters research loss data to determine the specific source of the excess losses. Part of this research includes an analysis of insurance industry loss experience that may reveal trends affecting the insurer's products. Based on their evaluation, staff underwriters, usually with the agreement of other key departments, adjust the insurer's underwriting guidelines.

Research and Develop Coverage Forms

Insurance advisory organizations have a significant role in the development of commonly used coverage forms. Insurance advisory organization-developed coverage forms are usually developed by coverage experts who consider the scope of coverage being provided, coverage provided by other policies, and legal restrictions that apply to coverage-form development.

Staff underwriters work cooperatively with the actuarial and legal departments to develop new coverages and modify existing coverage forms developed by advisory organizations. As in other businesses, insurers develop new coverages to meet changing consumer needs and competitive pressures. Additionally, insurers modify existing coverages so that the coverage being provided by the insurer will respond as anticipated. An unfavorable court decision, for example, may cause an insurer to rewrite a coverage form to limit the coverage being provided.

Review and Revise Pricing Plans

Staff underwriters review and update rates and rating plans continually, subject to regulatory constraints, to respond to changes in loss experience, competition, and inflation.

Historical loss data are gathered by the insurer or by advisory organizations to develop prospective loss costs. Then, each insurer examines its own operational profit and expense requirements. Staff underwriters combine prospective loss costs with an insurer-developed profit and expense loading to create a final rate used in policy pricing. Production efficiencies or a superior account-selection process is reflected in lower expense loadings, which can lead to a pricing plan that provides the insurer with a competitive advantage.

For those coverages for which advisory organizations do not develop loss costs, the insurer must develop its own rates. In such situations, reviewing and revising rating plans become even more crucial to ensure that the loss costs adequately reflect **loss development** and **trending**.

Arrange Treaty Reinsurance

Staff underwriters are responsible for securing and maintaining **treaty reinsurance**. Their responsibility includes determining the insurer's needs for reinsurance, selecting reinsurers, negotiating the terms and conditions of reinsurance treaties, and maintaining the insurer's relations with its treaty reinsurers.

For many insurers, treaty reinsurance limitations are directly reflected in their underwriting guidelines. For example, staff underwriters specify in the underwriting guidelines the maximum coverage limits that can be offered because higher limits of treaty reinsurance were not purchased. Additionally, some types of accounts cannot be insured because the insurer's treaty reinsurance agreements specifically exclude the account's classification. For commercial property accounts, many staff underwriters maintain a line authorization guide, which serves as a control on the property limits accepted based on the treaty reinsurance agreement.

Assist Others With Complex Accounts

Staff underwriters often serve as consultants to other underwriters. Generally, staff underwriters have significant first-hand line underwriting experience. They regularly see complex and atypical accounts, unlike most line underwriters. Staff underwriters also function as "referral underwriters"—that is, when an application exceeds a line underwriter's authority, a referral underwriter can review and approve the risk.

Conduct Underwriting Audits

Staff underwriters are often responsible for monitoring line underwriter activities and adherence to underwriting authority by conducting **underwriting audits**. The audits focus on proper documentation; adherence to procedure, classification, and rating practices; and conformity of selection decisions to the underwriting guide and bulletins.

Staff underwriters also monitor underwriting activity by analyzing statistical results by type of insurance, class of business, size of loss exposure, and territory. Statistical data show the extent to which underwriting goals are met, but they do not conclusively demonstrate whether the results are a product of implementing the insurer's underwriting guidelines.

Trending
A statistical technique for analyzing environmental changes and projecting such changes into the future.

Loss development
The increase or decrease of incurred losses over time.

Treaty reinsurance
A reinsurance agreement that covers an entire class or portfolio of loss exposures and provides that the primary insurer's individual loss exposures that fall within the treaty are automatically reinsured.

Underwriting audit
A review of underwriting files to ensure that individual underwriters are adhering to underwriting guidelines.

Participate in Industry Associations

Many insurers are members of national and state associations that address insurance industry concerns. Additionally, insurers often share in the operating of residual market mechanisms, such as automobile joint underwriting associations and windstorm pools. Staff underwriters typically represent the insurer as a member of these organizations. Staff underwriters may also serve on an advisory organization's committees that study standard policy forms and recommend changes.

Conduct Education and Training

Staff underwriters are usually responsible for determining the education and training needs of line underwriters. Sometimes, these training needs are addressed through a formal training program that all newly hired underwriters must complete. At other times, the training need is transitory and is provided through classes that address a specific underwriting issue or procedure.

Some training needs are met through programs provided by the insurer's human resources department. However, staff underwriters often develop courses and serve as instructors in technical insurance subjects.

UNDERWRITING AUTHORITY

The levels of underwriting authority granted to underwriters reflect their experience and knowledge in risk selection decisions. Authority may also be granted to producers and managing general agencies. Compliance with levels of authority is crucial to maintaining the appropriate controls over risk selection.

Underwriters have different levels of authority. As their levels of underwriting authority increase, the responsibility for accurately applying experience and judgment also increases. Compliance with levels of authority ensures that the insurer accepts applicants within its underwriting policy.

Before accepting an applicant, a line underwriter must determine whether he or she has the necessary underwriting authority to make the decision. The underwriting authority granted typically varies by position, grade level, and experience.

Underwriting authority requirements are usually communicated to an underwriter through the insurer's underwriting guidelines. A notation next to a specific classification in the underwriting guide, for example, might indicate that a senior underwriter must review and approve an application from that classification before it is processed further. Depending on the concerns that underwriting management places on a classification, underwriting approval might be required from the line underwriter's branch manager or a staff underwriter at the home office. Another approach to controlling underwriting authority is to specify in the underwriting guidelines the policy limits at which the accounts must be submitted to a higher authority.

In addition, some rating plans, such as composite rating, might require higher underwriting authority to review the merits of the account. Similarly, certain endorsements or coverage forms named in the underwriting guidelines might require specific levels of authority for approval.

Compliance with levels of underwriting authority ensures that the individuals making application-selection decisions have the experience necessary to evaluate which risks are acceptable and the unique knowledge required to judge risk for specialized lines of insurance.

To place controls on levels of underwriting authority, insurers generally grant authority in these ways:

- Underwriters gain underwriting authority with experience and positive results.

- Producers may gain underwriting authority based on experience, profitability, and contractual arrangements. Authority, if granted, may be only for certain types of insurance within specific limits of coverage.

- Managing general agents (MGA), when appointed, assume decentralized underwriting authority, which capitalizes on an MGA's familiarity with local conditions.

Insurers with conservative internal underwriting philosophies may not grant underwriting authority to any entities beyond their own internal underwriters. Specialty insurers, such as those offering surety bonds, aviation insurance, and livestock mortality insurance, also usually centralize underwriting authority. See the exhibit "Managing Underwriting Authority."

Managing Underwriting Authority

Some insurers centralize their line underwriters and, consequently, their underwriting authority. Others insurers extend underwriting authority to producers, believing it to be more expeditious to empower their producers to exercise underwriting authority, as well as to pay claims, within a defined range. Normally, not all of an insurer's producers are granted underwriting authority, but those who are usually receive additional commission to compensate for the additional expenses incurred.

The primary responsibility of producers is to sell insurance. Many insurers, however, rely on their producers to "field underwrite" accounts. This means that the producer knows the types of accounts the insurer is interested in writing and submits those that are of the quality the insurer is usually willing to accept. Producers who can perform account selection before submitting the account to the insurer are often referred to as front-line underwriters. These producers save insurers from having to evaluate accounts that the insurer's underwriters will ultimately reject.

Even those producers who do not have underwriting authority know the types of accounts the insurer is actively seeking. Special agents or production underwriters, as well as periodic communication with the insurer, keep producers informed of the products the insurer wants to sell. Some insurers provide their producers with their underwriting guidelines so that issues regarding account acceptability can be determined before submission.

Many insurers use information systems to manage underwriting authority. Rather than physically submit an account for others to review, insurer information systems are able to provide those people who have approval responsibility with sufficient information to approve or disapprove the referred account. Information systems can also make it possible to identify those classifications that the insurer is making exceptions to write, despite restrictions in the underwriting guidelines, and who is requesting them. Depending on the type of insurance, insurers use automated underwriting systems to encode underwriting guidelines. This is especially common for personal lines insurance, such as auto and homeowners insurance.

[DA06261]

CONSTRAINTS IN ESTABLISHING UNDERWRITING POLICY

An insurer's underwriting policy promotes the type of insurance anticipated to produce a growing and profitable book of business. However, various factors constrain what an underwriting policy can accomplish.

An insurer's senior management formulates an underwriting policy that guides individual and aggregate underwriting decisions. Underwriting policy determines the composition of the insurer's book of business, including the lines and classes of business that the insurer will offer, the amount of business the insurer is willing to write, the rating philosophy and forms the insurer will apply, and the territories to be developed. See the exhibit "Lines of Business."

Lines of Business

The National Association of Insurance Commissioners (NAIC) Annual Statement, which is prescribed for financial reporting in all states, divides property and liability coverages into thirty-three separate lines of business. Examples of these statutory prescribed lines of business are fire, allied lines, workers compensation, commercial multiperil, and ocean marine. A complete listing appears in the NAIC Annual Statement. Insurers must report premiums, losses, and expenses by the lines of business, but related lines of business are combined to create insurance products. For example, an insurer who markets commercial auto insurance will have to offer the following NAIC Annual Statement lines of business: commercial auto no-fault (personal injury protection), other commercial auto liability, and commercial auto physical damage. When they use the term "line of business," underwriters are mentally combining several related NAIC Annual Statement lines into a single reference, such as "commercial auto."

[DA06262]

All insurers would like to obtain profitable results, and most insurers would like to expand premium writings or increase market share. However, when these changes involve the insurer's underwriting policy, major constraining factors must be considered. See the exhibit "Constraints of Underwriting Policy."

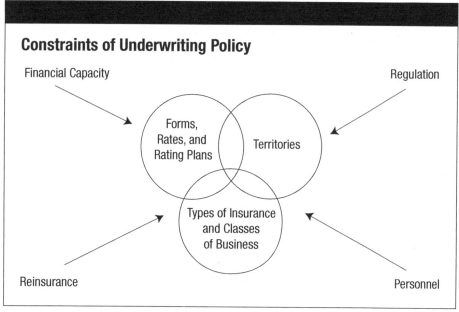

[DA06270]

Financial Capacity

An insurer's financial capacity refers to the relationship between premiums written and the size of the policyholders' surplus, which is an insurer's

Premium-to-surplus ratio, or capacity ratio

A capacity ratio that indicates an insurer's financial strength by relating net written premiums to policyholders' surplus.

Statutory accounting principles (SAP)

The accounting principles and practices that are prescribed or permitted by an insurer's domiciliary state and that insurers must follow.

net worth. That relationship is crucial in evaluating insurer solvency. The National Association of Insurance Commissioners (NAIC) has developed a series of financial ratios that it uses in conjunction with analytical evaluations to identify insurers that should receive additional solvency surveillance from regulators. The **premium-to-surplus ratio** is one of those key ratios, and it is considered too high when it exceeds 300 percent, or 3-to-1.

Insurers may exceed the premiums-to-surplus ratio through the rapid growth of premiums written. Because of conservative **statutory accounting principles** used in insurance, rapid growth results in a reduction in policyholders' surplus to pay for expenses generated by that growth. This constraint often precludes premium expansion unless the insurer purchases reinsurance or obtains more capital. See the exhibit "Statutory Accounting Rules."

Statutory Accounting Rules

Since the beginning of state oversight of insurance, insurance regulators have been primarily concerned with insurer solvency. The National Association of Insurance Commissioners (NAIC) was formed in 1871 to reduce the inconsistencies and confusion caused by multiple state financial reporting requirements. The accounting system that evolved to satisfy insurance regulations is called statutory accounting principles (SAP). SAP are conservative accounting rules designed to determine whether an insurer can meet its obligations to policyholders. Most other businesses use generally accepted accounting principles (GAAP), which focus on the organization as an ongoing enterprise, for financial reporting.

[DA06271]

Return on equity (ROE)

A profitability ratio expressed as a percentage by dividing a company's net income by its net worth (book value). Depending on the context, net worth is sometimes called shareholders' equity, owners' equity, or policyholders' surplus.

Insurers recognize the limitations of their capacity and seek to write those lines of business or accounts that maximize **return on equity**. These activities help realize maximization:

- Setting return thresholds—Insurers typically establish a return-on-equity threshold against which capacity allocation proposals are evaluated. If, for example, the insurer wants a 10 percent return on equity and the sale of workers compensation insurance in a specific state is expected to generate a 12 percent return on equity, then the insurer should expand into this territory and line of business if no better opportunity is present.

- Redirecting focus on target business classes—An insurer may decide to stop pursuing one class of business and, instead, use capacity elsewhere. For example, an insurer may stop pursuing a class of general liability accounts whose losses exceed expectations and develop a marketing campaign for accounts that offer more promising returns.

- Adjusting underwriting policy based on jurisdiction—Jurisdiction can be relevant in this process. For example, inadequate rate levels and rising benefit levels for claimants in many states led some insurers to develop restrictive acceptance criteria for workers compensation submissions.

Effective account selection allows insurers to be commercially viable by rationing their available capacity to obtain an optimum spread of loss exposures by territory, business class, size of risk, and line of business. See the exhibit "Return on Equity."

Return on Equity

Return on equity is not only a benchmark for employing capacity but also a fundamental measure of insurer profitability. This financial ratio relates net operating gain (after taxes) as a percentage of prior-year capital and surplus.

The SAP and GAAP approaches to calculating return on equity differ, as shown below:

$$\text{Return on equity (SAP basis)} = \frac{\text{Net income}}{\text{Average policyholders' surplus}}$$

$$\text{Return on equity (GAAP basis)} = \frac{\text{Net income}}{\text{Average owners' equity}}$$

Stock insurers calculate both ratios since they report their financial performance using both SAP and GAAP bases. Mutual insurers calculate return on equity using only the SAP basis.

Return on equity is also a key financial ratio used by insurance regulators for solvency surveillance. An acceptable value for return on equity falls between 5 and 15 percent.

[DA06272]

Regulation

States promulgate insurance regulations that take the form of statutes enacted by state legislatures and regulations adopted by the state insurance department. Insurance is a highly regulated industry, and regulations directly and indirectly affect most insurer activities.

Regulation affects underwriting policy in several ways:

- Insurers must be licensed to write insurance in each state in which they write insurance.

- Rates, rules, and forms must be filed with state regulators.

- Some states specifically require underwriting guidelines to be filed.

- If consumer groups believe that the insurance industry has not adequately served certain geographic areas, regulatory focus on insurance availability can lead to requirements to extend coverage to loss exposures that an insurer might otherwise not write.

State regulators perform **market conduct examinations** to ensure that insurers adhere to the classification and rating plans they have filed. When a

Market conduct examination

An analysis of an insurer's practices in four operational areas: sales and advertising, underwriting, ratemaking, and claim handling.

market conduct examination discloses deviations from filed forms and rates or improper conduct, the insurer is subject to penalties.

Insurance regulation is not applied uniformly across states. In some jurisdictions, insurers may be unable to get rate filings approved, or approval may be granted so slowly that rate levels are inadequate relative to rising claim costs. Some insurers have chosen to withdraw from states that impose regulations they consider too restrictive.

Personnel

Insurers require the talent of specialists to market their products effectively, underwrite specific lines of business, service their accounts, and pay claims for losses that occur. An insurer must have a sufficient number of properly trained underwriters to implement its underwriting policy. No prudent insurer, for example, would pursue the highly technical lines of aviation, surety, or ocean marine insurance without a sufficient number of experienced underwriting specialists in those lines of business.

In addition to having personnel with the necessary skills, the insurer must have the personnel where they are needed. As a general practice, an insurer should obtain premiums from a broad range of insureds to create the widest possible distribution of loss exposures. However, regulatory expenses and policyholder service requirements make it difficult for small insurers to efficiently handle a small volume of business in many widespread territories. Insurers must have a sufficient volume of premium to operate efficiently in an area. Information systems are especially important; many growth plans have been abandoned because computer support was not available.

Reinsurance

The availability and cost of adequate reinsurance can influence underwriting policy. Reinsurance treaties may exclude certain types of insurance or classes of business, or the cost of reinsurance may be prohibitive.

Reinsurers are also concerned about the underlying policy forms offered by the insurer. A reinsurer may not have any reservations about an insurer's use of forms developed by advisory organizations. However, it may expressly exclude reinsurance coverage for loss exposures covered by manuscript forms developed for a particular insured or covered by forms developed independently of an advisory organization.

IMPLEMENTING UNDERWRITING POLICY

Staff underwriters develop underwriting guidelines, which distill underwriting policies into directions for line underwriters' policy selection. Underwriting audits ensure that established underwriting standards are reasonably consistent.

Insurers convey underwriting policy through their underwriting guidelines. The guidelines describe the parameters of acceptable applicants for insurance for which the insurer has priced its insurance products.

Underwriting audits are the insurer's quality control check for uniform application of the underwriting guidelines and for continuous improvement.

Purposes of Underwriting Guidelines

An insurer's underwriting policy is communicated to underwriters through underwriting guidelines, which are continually updated to reflect changes in policy. Underwriting guidelines identify the major elements that underwriters should evaluate for each type of insurance, as well as boundaries, such as maximum coverage limits, for application selection.

Some underwriting guides include step-by-step instructions for handling particular classes of insureds. Such guides might identify specific hazards to evaluate, alternatives to consider, criteria to use when making the final decision, ways to implement the decision, and methods to monitor the decision. Some guidelines also provide pricing instructions and reinsurance-related information. Other insurers use underwriting guides that are less comprehensive. For example, they may list all classes of business and indicate their acceptability by type of insurance. Codes are then assigned to indicate the desirability of the loss exposure and the level of authority required to write the class of business.

Because underwriting guidelines usually specify the attributes of accounts that insurers are willing to insure, insurers consider them trade secrets. Disclosure of this proprietary information might cause an insurer to lose its competitive advantage over others. See the exhibit "Sample Commercial Underwriting Guidelines."

Underwriting guidelines serve these purposes:

- Provide for structured decisions
- Ensure uniformity and consistency
- Synthesize insights and experience
- Distinguish between routine and nonroutine decisions
- Avoid duplication of effort
- Ensure adherence to reinsurance treaties and planned rate levels
- Support policy preparation and compliance
- Provide a basis for predictive models

Provide for Structured Decisions

Underwriting guidelines provide a structure for underwriting decisions by identifying the major considerations underwriters should evaluate for each type of insurance the insurer writes. For example, the section of an insurer's

Sample Commercial Underwriting Guidelines

I. GENERAL:

The Risk Selection Guide is a comprehensive alphabetical listing by class of business showing what the Midley Insurance Companies believe to be the desirability of insuring an average risk in the class. The Guide grades each class for Property, Commercial Automobile, Workers Compensation, Burglary and Robbery, Fidelity, Premises/Operations Liability, and Products/Completed Operations Liability. In addition, the final column titled "Form" indicates whether the General Liability coverage must be written on a Claims-Made Form (indicated by a "CM"), or whether the Occurrence Form is available (indicated by an "O"). Please remember the risk selection guide is only a guide. The company retains final authority regarding the acceptance or rejection of any specific risk.

II. CLASSIFICATION ACCEPTABILITY RATINGS:

The Risk Selection Guide is being published as a section of this agent's manual to answer this question: "Are risks within a particular class likely to be accepted by the Midley Insurance Companies?" In light of this question, the risk grades as found in the Risk Selection Guide are defined as follows:

E—Excellent

This class of business is considered to have excellent profit potential. Unless a specific risk in this class has unusual hazards or exposures, it will rarely present any underwriting problems. Risks graded as "E" may be bound by the agent without prior underwriting consent.

G—Good

This class of business is considered to have good profit potential. Normally this risk may be written before obtaining an inspection or developing additional underwriting information other than that present on the application. The agent may bind risks graded as "G" without prior underwriting consent.

A—Average

Potential for profit is marginal because of high variability of risks within the class. It is understood that the underwriter might think it is necessary to inspect the risk before authorizing binding. In all instances, it is recommended that the agent call the underwriter and discuss the risk before binding.

S—Submit

The account presents little potential for profit. These risks will require a complete written submission before binding. The underwriter must obtain a complete inspection and evaluate any other underwriting information deemed necessary before authorizing the binding of this risk.

D—Decline

Due to the lack of potential for profit, this class of risk is prohibited and will not be considered. Under no circumstances may a risk classified as "D" be bound without the prior written approval of the Vice President of Commercial Underwriting.

III. FOOTNOTES:

Footnotes sometimes are indicated as applying to an individual classification for a specific line of insurance. These footnotes are displayed at the bottom of each page and are designed to make you aware of certain hazards or exposures that are unacceptable or need to be addressed in an acceptable manner.

We hope the Risk Selection Guide will be valuable in understanding the types of business our companies want to be writing. However, please do not hesitate to call your underwriter if you are unsure as to how to classify a particular risk, or if you feel the factors associated with a specific risk make it considerably better or worse than the grading assigned by this guide.

Description	Property	Auto	Workers Compensation	Burglary and Robbery	Fidelity	Premises and Operations	Products and Completed Operations	Form
Painting—exterior—buildings or structures—three stories or less in height	A[1]	G	A	A	A	G[2]	G	0
Painting—interior—buildings or structures	A[1]	G	G	A	A	G[2]	G	0
Painting—oil or gasoline tanks	A[1]	G	D	A	A	D	D	0
Painting—ship hulls	A[1]	G	D	A	A	D	D	0
Painting—shop only	S[1,3]	G	S	A	A	G	G	0
Painting, picture, or frame stores	G	G	G	G	G	E	G	0
Paper coating or finishing	D	A	D	A	A	G	A	0
Paper corrugating or laminating—workers compensation only			D					
Paper crepeing—workers compensation only			D					
Paper goods manufacturing	D	A	D	A	A	G[4]	G[4]	0
Paper manufacturing	D	A	D	A	A	G[4]	G[4]	0
Paper products distributors	S	A	A	A	A	G[4]	G[4]	0
Paper, rag, or rubber stock dealers and distributors—secondhand	D	D	D	D	D	D	D	0
Paperhanging	G	G	G	G	G	G	G	0
Parachute manufacturing	D	A	D	D	D	D	D	0
Parades	D	D	D	D	D	D	D	0
Parking—private	A	A	S	S	S	A	A	0
Parking—public—open air	A	A	S	S	S	A	A	0
Parking—public—operated in conjunction with other enterprises	A	A	S	S	S	A	A	0
Parking—public—not open air	A	A	S	S	S	S	A	0
Parking—public shopping centers—(lessor's risk only)	G	G	S	G	G	G	G	0
Parks or playgrounds	A[5]	A	A	A	A	S[5]	S[5]	0
Paste, ink, or mucilage manufacturing—workers compensation only			S					

[1] Flammable liquid storage must be minimal and controlled.

[2] A minimum property damage deductible of $250 on premises and operations coverage is mandatory.

[3] The risk is unacceptable if any painting or finishing is done inside without an approved spray booth.

[4] Acceptability will depend on the specific nature of the operation and specific types and uses of the products.

[5] This risk is unacceptable unless this classification constitutes only a small part of other properties or operations.

[DA06292]

underwriting guidelines addressing contractors' equipment might indicate that equipment use is of paramount importance in determining acceptability and pricing. Contractors' equipment used in mountainous areas is more likely to be subject to upset and overturn and therefore requires more scrutiny and premium than contractors' equipment used on flat terrain.

By identifying the principal hazards associated with a particular class of business, underwriting guidelines ensure that underwriters consider the primary hazard traits of the exposures they evaluate.

Ensure Uniformity and Consistency

Underwriting guidelines help ensure that selection decisions are made uniformly and consistently by all of the insurer's underwriters. Ideally, submissions that are identical in every respect should elicit the same response from different underwriters. Guidelines facilitate uniformity because they include acceptable approaches to evaluating applicants and the overall desirability of a particular type of risk or class of business.

Synthesize Insights and Experience

Underwriting guidelines synthesize the insights and experience of seasoned underwriters. Staff underwriters, who assist with the insurer's unique or challenging accounts on a referral basis, often are able to include the approaches they have taken in underwriting particular classifications and lines of business. For many insurers, underwriting guidelines serve as a repository for an insurer's cumulative expertise.

Distinguish Between Routine and Nonroutine Decisions

Underwriting guidelines help line underwriters distinguish between routine and nonroutine decisions:

- Routine decisions are those for which the line underwriter clearly has decision-making authority according to the underwriting guidelines.
- Nonroutine decisions involve submissions that fall outside the underwriter's authority.

Underwriting guides usually indicate that the classifications and lines of business must be either declined or submitted to a higher level of authority for approval.

Avoid Duplication of Effort

Many underwriting situations recur. If the problems inherent in a particular situation have been identified and solved, the solution should apply to all similar situations that might arise in the future. Underwriting guidelines contain the information necessary to avoid costly duplication of effort.

Ensure Adherence to Reinsurance Treaties and Planned Rate Levels

Compliance with underwriting guidelines ensures that coverage limits and accepted loss exposures will not exceed the insurer's treaty reinsurance, because staff underwriters reflect those treaty limitations in the guidelines.

Compliance with underwriting guidelines also ensures selection of loss exposures in an overall book of business commensurate with the planned rate levels for those policies. The importance of compliance with underwriting guidelines as it affects the profitability of a book of business is illustrated by an example of the outcome when compliance with guidelines fails. Many homeowners policy underwriting guidelines require property to be insured to within a percentage (such as 100 percent) of the replacement cost of the dwelling. Because most property losses are partial losses, rates are developed with the expectation that total losses will be rare. If property insured in a portfolio is significantly undervalued, average losses will equal a larger percentage of the average dwelling-coverage limits. The portfolio might also experience a greater number of losses equal to the total dwelling-coverage limit. Overall, the profitability of the book of business will decline as losses exceed expectations.

In resolving this profitability problem, one alternative is to increase the rates charged. However, that does not resolve the underlying problem of undervaluing the property insured, and the increased rates might not be competitive in the market. A better alternative is to enforce compliance with underwriting guidelines, ensure adequate coverage to replacement cost at the time of the initial application, and implement a program to increase dwelling coverage to keep pace with inflation and building cost increases. See the exhibit "Undervalued Homes Statistics."

This illustration can be applied to other situations in which the failure to comply with underwriting guidelines results in inadequate premiums for loss exposures accepted that are not anticipated in the insurer's planned rate levels.

Support Policy Preparation and Compliance

Underwriting guides provide information to assist underwriters and support staff in policy preparation. Rules and eligibility requirements for various rating plans are also included. Specialized information, such as eligibility for experience and retrospective rating together with appropriate rating formulas, often appears in the underwriting guide. Underwriting guidelines also support compliance with state regulatory requirements, as staff underwriters incorporate applicable regulations in the guidelines.

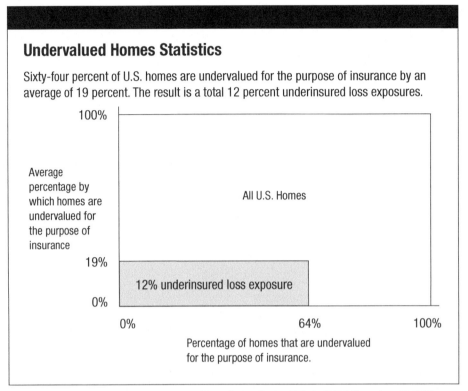

Undervalued Homes Statistics

Sixty-four percent of U.S. homes are undervalued for the purpose of insurance by an average of 19 percent. The result is a total 12 percent underinsured loss exposures.

Adapted from Marshall & Swift/Boeckh, "Degree of Home Undervaluation Shifts in 2008," News, June 17, 2009, www.msbinfo.com/Company/News/17 (accessed July 2, 2010). [DA06293]

Provide a Basis for Predictive Models

Predictive modeling

A process in which historical data based on behaviors and events are blended with multiple variables and used to construct models of anticipated future outcomes.

Underwriters use **predictive modeling** to identify applications that present lower underwriting risk. Predictive modeling incorporates underwriting thought processes with underwriting guidelines by assigning a rank or score to all of the variables presented by an account and its loss exposures. Predictive models function in this way:

- Multiple data variables of individual risks are developed to rank the relative likelihood of insurance loss.

- Data variables are based on underwriting guidelines along with the insurer's loss experience, loss data collected from external sources, and underwriting expertise.

- The ranking or score developed from the data variables is a predictive measure of future profit potential based upon the account's characteristics.

Predictive modeling can provide a consistent way to review individual applications that improves the overall profitability of a book of business. It can also help in managing a large book of business for which conducting an in-depth underwriting review on every account would be too costly.

Purposes of Underwriting Audits

Staff underwriters conduct periodic audits to monitor line underwriters' adherence to the practices and procedures outlined in the underwriting guidelines. Audits are a management tool used to achieve uniformity and consistency in the application of underwriting standards.

Underwriting audits are typically conducted on-site at the branch or regional office being audited. A typical underwriting audit may involve selecting accounts at random or reviewing files that had experienced notable claims. These accounts are then scrutinized to determine whether prescribed procedures were followed and whether the underwriter acted in accord with the insurer's underwriting policy. Feedback from the audit of individual files provides individual line underwriters with strategies to improve future underwriting decisions.

Underwriting audits can also be used to monitor statistics for books of business. This can provide indications of applications written in excess of underwriting guidelines. For example, an excessive number of workers compensation applications accepted with hazardous classification codes in one territory could indicate an imbalance of product mix. It can also indicate inconsistent adherence to underwriting guidelines.

An underwriting audit provides staff underwriters with information on the effectiveness of the underwriting guidelines. Underwriting guidelines that are not being followed may be either outdated or considered unrealistic. This could indicate that a critical review for updates is required. Line underwriters, for example, might ignore the underwriting guidelines when changes in the insurance marketplace have occurred without corresponding changes having been made to the underwriting guidelines. As a result, staff underwriters might learn that producers are not receptive to complying with the insurer's underwriting guidelines. If compliance with underwriting guidelines is not leading to the desired results, such information is valuable in the ongoing effort of developing or revising effective underwriting guidelines.

STEPS IN THE UNDERWRITING PROCESS

Whether relying on independent judgment or the guidance of expert systems, underwriters engage in a series of steps and tasks designed to ensure that, ultimately, insurers are able to reach their business goals.

After a producer submits an **application** for insurance to an insurer, the application must be qualified for acceptance. **Underwriters** qualify an application through following the steps in the underwriting process. The underwriting process is also applied to renewal policies and certain policy changes, such as requests to add new locations to a property policy. For ease of discussion, applications, renewals, and policy changes to which the underwriting process is applied are referred to as **underwriting submissions**.

Application

A legal document that provides information obtained directly from an applicant requesting insurance and that an insurer can use for underwriting and claim handling purposes.

Underwriter

An insurer employee who evaluates applicants for insurance, selects those that are acceptable to the insurer, prices coverage, and determines policy terms and conditions.

Underwriting submission

Underwriting information for an initial application, or a substantive policy midterm or renewal change.

The underwriting process is a series of steps to determine which submissions will be accepted, for what amount of insurance, at what price, and under what conditions. In addition to considering the merits of an individual submission, underwriters consider how a submission fits into the insurer's business portfolio mix and whether a submission provides opportunity for profitability.

These general steps in the underwriting process provide a sound framework within which underwriters can make decisions:

- Evaluate the submission
- Develop underwriting alternatives
- Select an underwriting alternative
- Determine an appropriate premium
- Implement the underwriting decision
- Monitor underwriting decisions

Evaluate the Submission

Loss exposure

Any condition or situation that presents a possibility of loss, whether or not an actual loss occurs.

Hazard

A condition that increases the frequency or severity of a loss.

The first step in the underwriting process is evaluating a submission's **loss exposures** and associated **hazards.** See the exhibit "The Role of Expert Underwriting Systems."

The Role of Expert Underwriting Systems

Typically, an underwriter evaluates submissions for commercial lines, while insurers often use expert systems to evaluate personal lines submissions (as well as some small commercial lines submissions). Expert systems, also known as knowledge- or rules-based systems, help insurers improve efficiency and make more consistent underwriting decisions by asking for all the information necessary to make an underwriting decision. They are widely used, particularly for submissions that tend to be similar and with which variations are limited, but their ability to handle larger commercial accounts is growing. Ultimately, even expert systems still rely on underwriters both to monitor the parameters applied by the system and to make decisions regarding submissions that do not fall within those parameters.

[DA_10556]

Underwriters must understand the activities, operations, and character of each applicant. To do so, they determine the information needed to make decisions regarding acceptance, coverage amounts, conditions, and price. However, trade-offs are necessary to control underwriting expenses and to handle a reasonable number of submissions.

Information efficiency

The balance that underwriters must maintain between the hazards presented by the account and the information needed to underwrite it.

Before gathering the information necessary to evaluate a submission, underwriters must determine what information is essential and what information may be desirable or available, but not essential. Underwriters seek to achieve **information efficiency** by weighing the need for information against the cost to obtain it. For example, an underwriter is likely to investigate a chemical manufacturer extensively but may require much less information to underwrite a gift shop. Sometimes a submission's premium size drives the decision regarding the amount of information gathered or the resources used to gather it. A submission with a small premium volume may not justify expensive research.

Underwriters can use various sources to obtain the information needed to evaluate a submission. These are the principal sources of underwriting information:

- Producers—The producer usually prequalifies, or field-underwrites, applicants and often has firsthand knowledge of the applicant's business operations and reputation.

- Applications—Insurance applications provide general information required to process, rate, and underwrite loss exposures of the applicant and specific information necessary to evaluate the acceptability of an applicant's loss exposures for a particular type of insurance. In addition, insurers often use supplemental applications or questionnaires for certain coverages or classes of business to obtain more pertinent information in evaluating the submissions.

- Inspection reports—Inspections or risk control reports provide useful information about the property's physical condition, the business operations' safety record, and the applicant's management.

- Government records—Motor vehicle reports; criminal court records; civil court records, including records of suits, mortgages and liens; business licenses; property tax records; Securities and Exchange Commission (SEC) filings; and bankruptcy filings may all provide relevant underwriting information.

- Financial rating services—An applicant's financial status provides important underwriting information. Dun & Bradstreet, Standard & Poor's, and Experian are examples of services that can provide an overall picture of the applicant's financial status.

- Loss data—The applicant's loss history may provide information on loss frequency and severity, types of losses, and trends in loss experience and reporting. Loss data analysis is a significant tool for predicting future losses and is also important for policy pricing.

- Premium audit reports—A **premium audit** report can provide useful information about the insured's operations that may have underwriting implications.

- Claim files—Underwriters can obtain insights into renewal policies by reviewing insured claim files. Claim representatives typically accumulate and document a significant amount of underwriting information during their investigations.

Many evaluation tools are available to help underwriters evaluate, select, and price submissions. Choosing the right tools requires a holistic understanding

Premium audit

Methodical examination of a policyholder's operations, records, and books of account to determine the actual exposure units and premium for insurance coverages already provided.

of the information available and of the usefulness of that information in predicting which submissions are likely to provide an **underwriting profit**. See the exhibit "Underwriting Evaluation Tools."

Underwriting profit

Income an insurer earns from premiums paid by policyholders minus incurred losses and underwriting expenses.

Counteroffer

A proposal an offeree makes to an offeror that varies in some material way from the original offer, resulting in rejection of the original offer and constituting a new offer.

Rating plan

A set of directions that specify criteria of the exposure base, the exposure unit, and rate per exposure unit to determine premiums for a particular line of insurance.

Experience rating

A rating plan that adjusts the premium for the current policy period to recognize the loss experience of the insured organization during past policy periods.

Schedule rating

A rating plan that awards debits and credits based on specific categories, such as the care and condition of the premises or the training and selection of employees, to modify the final premium to reflect factors that the class rate does not include.

Retrospective rating

A ratemaking technique that adjusts the insured's premium for the current policy period based on the insured's loss experience during the current period; paid losses or incurred losses may be used to determine loss experience.

Underwriting Evaluation Tools

- Telematics—the use of Global Positioning System (GPS) tracking to collect and analyze data regarding driver behavior and vehicle use

- Predictive analytics—statistical and analytical techniques used to develop models that predict future events or behaviors

- Predictive modeling—a process in which historical data based on behaviors and events are blended with multiple variables and used to construct models of anticipated future outcomes

- Catastrophe (CAT) modeling—a type of computer program that estimates losses from future potential catastrophic events

[DA06331]

Develop Underwriting Alternatives

The second step in the underwriting process is developing underwriting alternatives. Such alternatives include accepting a submission as is, rejecting the submission, or making a **counteroffer** to accept the submission subject to certain modifications.

The underwriter typically makes a counteroffer to accept a submission from among these major types of modifications:

- Require risk control measures—A counteroffer may require the applicant to implement additional risk control measures. Measures such as installing an automatic fire-extinguishing sprinkler system, adding guard service, and improving housekeeping and maintenance can reduce physical hazards. Installing machinery guards can reduce the frequency of employee bodily injuries. If the applicant accepts the counteroffer, the insurer generally establishes controls to verify that the required risk control measures have been implemented.

- Change insurance rates, **rating plans**, or policy limits—A rate modification could either increase or decrease the premium. Using a different rating plan can provide pricing flexibility; the underwriter can properly price a submission based on its loss exposures. Examples of rating plans for commercial applicants include **experience rating**, **schedule rating**, and **retrospective rating**. An underwriter may also counteroffer with different policy limits. The insurer's underwriting guidelines usually specify the maximum limits of insurance that an underwriter can approve; these limits generally reflect reinsurance limitations or reinsurance availability and possible catastrophic loss from a single loss exposure. If high policy limits are requested, the underwriter may suggest lower limits or use **facultative reinsurance**.

- Amend policy terms and conditions—When the requested coverage cannot be provided, the underwriter might counteroffer to amend policy terms and conditions by modifying the policy to exclude certain causes of loss, add or increase a deductible, or make another coverage change. For example, an insurer may be unwilling to provide replacement cost coverage on a poorly maintained building but may be willing to provide a more limited coverage form. Increasing a deductible might make coverage more viable for a small commercial account in which a large number of small losses have caused unsatisfactory loss experience in the past. The underwriter's flexibility varies by type of insurance. Coverage modification is not always permitted on policies that have been approved by state regulators.

- Use facultative reinsurance—If an applicant is in a class of business or has atypical loss exposures that are excluded from the insurer's treaty reinsurance agreement, or if the amount of insurance needed exceeds the limits of the treaty reinsurance agreement, the underwriter may be able to transfer a portion of the liability for the applicant's loss exposures to a facultative reinsurer. An alternative to purchasing facultative reinsurance is for the producer to divide the insurance among several insurers—an approach sometimes called "agency reinsurance."

> **Facultative reinsurance**
> Reinsurance of individual loss exposures in which the primary insurer chooses which loss exposures to submit to the reinsurer, and the reinsurer can accept or reject any loss exposures submitted.

Select an Underwriting Alternative

The underwriter must evaluate each underwriting alternative carefully and select the optimal one under the circumstances. In some cases, the underwriter has no choice but to reject a submission; however, rejections produce neither premium nor commission, only expense. Therefore, underwriters try to make submissions acceptable whenever possible.

Selecting an alternative involves weighing a submission's positive and negative features, including loss exposures contemplated in the insurance rate, risk control measures, and management's commitment to loss prevention. These factors also should be considered before selecting an underwriting alternative:

- Underwriting authority—Before accepting a submission, an underwriter must determine whether he or she has the necessary underwriting authority or whether the submission must be referred to an individual with higher underwriting authority.

- Supporting business—A submission that is marginal by itself might be acceptable if the applicant has desirable supporting business. The **account underwriting** approach evaluates all lines together, as a whole.

- **Mix of business**—The underwriter must consider whether accepting the submission supports the insurer's goals for mix of business.

> **Account underwriting**
> A method of underwriting in which all of the business from a particular applicant is evaluated as a whole.
>
> **Mix of business**
> The distribution of individual policies that compose the book of business of a producer, territory, state, or region among the various lines and classifications.

- Producer relationships—The relationship between underwriters and producers should be based on mutual trust and respect. Underwriters should consider the opinions and recommendations of the producer before determining an underwriting alternative. While differences of opinion are common, collaboration and a willingness to see the other's viewpoint are essential to building a satisfactory working relationship.
- Regulatory restrictions—State regulations restrict underwriters' ability to accept or renew business. Many states also establish timeframes within which a submission must be declined or a policy nonrenewed, with notice of refusal to renew provided. Underwriters must know these restrictions and make timely decisions to avoid mandatory acceptance or renewal of an otherwise unacceptable submission.

Determine an Appropriate Premium

Loss costs

The portion of the rate that covers projected claim payments and loss adjusting expenses.

Underwriters must ensure that each loss exposure is accurately classified so that it is properly rated, with the appropriate premium charged. Insurance **loss costs** are typically based on a classification system that combines similar loss exposures into the same rating classification. Rating classifications enable the insurer to match potential loss costs with an applicant's particular loss exposures. Consequently, the insurer can develop an adequate premium to pay losses and operating expenses and to produce a profit.

Accurate classification ensures a pooling of loss exposures with similar expected loss frequencies and loss severity. Misclassification can produce adverse results, including insufficient premium to cover losses and expenses, and the inability to sell policies because prices are higher than competitors' prices. For most types of personal insurance, workers compensation, and some other commercial insurance, proper classification automatically determines the premium. For major types of commercial insurance, such as general liability, the underwriter might have the option of adjusting the premium based on the characteristics of the submission's loss exposures.

Implement the Underwriting Decision

Once an underwriter has evaluated a submission, selected and applied any appropriate modifications, and determined the premium, the next step is to implement the underwriting decision. Implementing underwriting decisions generally involves three tasks.

First, the underwriting decision is communicated to the producer. If the decision is to accept the submission with modifications, the reasons must be clearly communicated to the producer and applicant, and the applicant must agree to accept or implement any modifications made as a counteroffer. If the submission is rejected, the underwriter must provide a clear explanation of why that applicant does not meet the insurer's underwriting requirements. Effective communication of both positive and negative decisions clarifies the insurer's standards and helps the producer understand what kinds of business the insurer wants to write.

The second task is issuance of any required documents. For example, in accepting a submission, the underwriter may need to issue a **binder** or prepare **certificates of insurance**.

The third task is to record data about the applicant and the policy for policy issuance, accounting, statistical, and monitoring purposes. Data may include location, limits, coverages, price modifications, and class of business. These data are coded so that the insurer and the industry can accumulate and aggregate information on all accounts for ratemaking, statutory reporting, financial accounting, and book-of-business evaluations. Such information is also used to monitor the account, trigger renewals, and flag situations requiring special attention.

Binder

A temporary written or oral agreement to provide insurance coverage until a formal written policy is issued.

Certificate of insurance

A brief description of insurance coverage prepared by an insurer or its agent and commonly used by policyholders to provide evidence of insurance.

Monitor Underwriting Decisions

The final, and ongoing, step in the underwriting process is monitoring underwriting decisions. After an underwriting decision has been made on a new-business submission or a renewal, the underwriter is tasked with monitoring both individual policies and books of business to ensure that satisfactory results are achieved.

When monitoring individual policies, underwriters must be alert to changes in insureds' loss exposures. Changes in the nature of an insured's business operation, for example, could significantly raise or lower the insured's loss potential. Underwriters do not have the resources necessary for constant monitoring of all individual policies, so monitoring of existing policies usually occurs in response to one or more of these triggering events that may indicate a change in the account:

- Substantive policy change requests
- Significant and unique loss occurrences
- Risk control and safety inspection reports
- Premium audit results

Policy monitoring also frequently occurs on renewal. As a policy's expiration date approaches, the underwriter may need to repeat the underwriting process before agreeing to renew the policy for another term. Renewal underwriting, however, can generally be accomplished more quickly than new-business underwriting because the insured is already known to the insurer and more information might be available if claim reports or risk control reports have been added to the file.

In addition to monitoring individual policies, underwriters must monitor books of business. Monitoring a book of business means evaluating the quality and profitability of all the business written for any group of policies. The evaluation should identify specific problems for each type of insurance, which can be subdivided into class of business, territory, producer, and other policy subgroups. Monitoring a book of business is also necessary to ensure that premium volume covers fixed costs and overhead expenses for each book of business.

Underwriters use premium and loss statistics to identify aggregate problems in a deteriorating book of business. Reviewing the book of business can also help determine compliance with underwriting policy and may detect changes in the type, volume, and quality of policies that may require corrective action.

MEASURING UNDERWRITING RESULTS

An insurer's underwriting results are a key indicator of its profitability. Without a clear understanding of their underwriting performance, insurers may not be able to respond to conditions that adversely affect them or recognize opportunities to improve their performance.

Insurers typically track their underwriting results through the use of financial and nonfinancial measures. The most common financial measure of underwriting results over a specific time period—typically one year—is the insurer's combined ratio. Proper underwriting should produce an underwriting profit or perhaps a small underwriting loss that is more than offset by investment profits. However, financial measures are not always reliable indicators of underwriting success in the short term.

Nonfinancial measures can be used to evaluate the actions of individual underwriters and underwriting departments, rather than their results.

Financial Measures

Combined ratio

A profitability ratio that indicates whether an insurer has made an underwriting loss or gain.

Many insurers use the **combined ratio** (or combined loss and expense ratio) to measure the success of underwriting activities. See the exhibit "Combined Ratio."

From an insurer's perspective, the lower the combined ratio, the better. For example, a combined ratio of 95 percent means that an insurer has an outflow of $0.95 for every premium dollar, while a combined ratio of 115 percent means that the insurer has an outflow of $1.15 for every premium dollar. Therefore, a lower combined ratio reflects a higher level of profitability for an insurer.

Although the combined ratio is the most often cited measure of underwriting success, the results that it produces are generally subject to an additional analysis of its components. For example, individual categories of insurer expenses may be compared to those of other insurers or to industry norms, or the specific lines of business that exceeded anticipated losses may be examined. An in-depth analysis permits an insurer to make changes to its underwriting guidelines that yield desired results in the future. See the exhibit

Combined Ratio

$$\text{Combined ratio (or trade-basis combined ratio)} = \frac{\text{Loss and loss adjustment expenses incurred}}{\text{Premiums earned}} + \frac{\text{Underwriting expenses incurred}}{\text{Premiums written}}$$

When the combined ratio is:

Exactly 100 percent	Every premium dollar is being used to pay claims and cover operating costs, with nothing remaining for insurer profit.
Greater than 100 percent	An underwriting loss occurs: more dollars are being paid out than are being taken in as premiums.
Less than 100 percent	An underwriting profit occurs because not all premium dollars taken in are being used for claims and expenses.

Most insurers consider any combined ratio under 100 percent to be acceptable because it indicates a profit from underwriting results, even before income from an insurer's investment activity is considered in its overall financial performance.

[DA06399]

"Property-Liability Insurance Combined Ratio—All Lines Combined for the United States."

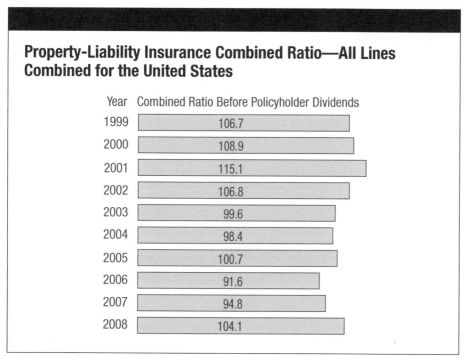

Property-Liability Insurance Combined Ratio—All Lines Combined for the United States

Year	Combined Ratio Before Policyholder Dividends
1999	106.7
2000	108.9
2001	115.1
2002	106.8
2003	99.6
2004	98.4
2005	100.7
2006	91.6
2007	94.8
2008	104.1

Changes in premium volume, major catastrophic losses, and delays in loss reporting can distort the combined ratio, making it difficult to evaluate the effectiveness of underwriting. Additionally, any discussion of insurer underwriting profitability needs to be considered within the context of the underwriting cycle.

Distortions Created by Changes in Premium Volume

An insurer's combined ratio must be evaluated, taking into consideration fluctuations in premium volume and the distortions that they can create. Premium volume and underwriting policy are related. Restrictive underwriting policy usually reduces premium volume. Conversely, a less restrictive underwriting policy generally increases premium volume.

Changes in underwriting policy, however, often do not have the immediate effect desired. For example, an insurer that becomes more restrictive in its underwriting criteria will usually see a reduction in premiums written. Because incurred losses remain outstanding from the prior period that had a less restrictive underwriting policy, the loss ratio component of the combined ratio will likely deteriorate. With this reduction in premiums written, the expense ratio will increase, even though the insurer's underwriting expenses might have remained relatively unchanged. Similarly, a significant relaxation of underwriting standards, at least in the short term, can make an insurer appear profitable and even cost conscious when its book of business is underpriced.

Distortions Created by Major Catastrophic Losses

Underwriting results are usually evaluated annually. However, major hurricanes, major earthquakes, and other natural catastrophes occur too irregularly to be predicted annually. Floods, for example, are typically predicted over a hundred-year period. Certain flood plains are predicted to have a flood, on average, once every one hundred years or, in lower-elevation areas, once every ten or twenty years.

Catastrophes such as industrial explosions, airplane crashes, nuclear reactor breakdowns, or terrorist activities likewise occur with too little regularity to create a predictable pattern. Ideally, insurance rates allow for unpredicted losses. Still, a major catastrophe is likely to cause an underwriting loss for that year for most if not all affected insurers. However, failure to predict the unpredictable does not necessarily indicate inadequate underwriting.

Distortions Created by Delays in Loss Reporting and Loss Development

Delays in loss reporting reduce the value of the information provided by the combined ratio. If premiums and losses could be readily matched, an insurer could determine whether its book of business was underpriced and then make corrections in its pricing structure. This information is valuable to insurance regulators as well, because an inadequately priced book of business is a significant threat to an insurer's solvency.

Insurers establish a loss reserve amount when a claim is reported. Reserved losses are included in incurred losses and reflected in the combined ratio. The type of loss usually determines how quickly the insurer is notified of a claim and how quickly the reserve is replaced with the amount of final payment. With certain types of insurance, particularly liability insurance, a considerable amount of time can elapse between when a loss is reported and when a claim is settled. Reserves are established as soon as the loss is reported, but significant inaccuracy exists in estimating ultimate loss costs that will be paid at some future date. The longer the time between the estimate and the ultimate claim settlement, the greater the inaccuracy is likely to be.

These delays in loss reporting and loss settlement can result in an understatement of losses in one year and an overstatement in another year that appear in the combined ratio. However, these misstatements do not reflect changes in actual underwriting results.

Distortions Created by Underwriting Cycle

Historically, insurance industry underwriting cycles have consisted of a period of underwriting profits followed by a period of underwriting losses, as measured by the combined ratio. When insurers earn underwriting profits, they may use those profits to reduce their premium rates and offer broader coverage to increase their market share.

At times of underwriting losses, insurers may need to increase premium rates and restrict the availability of coverage to increase underwriting profits. These tactics may be necessary for the insurer to maintain the policyholders' surplus it needs to support its level of business.

Because insurance premium levels, capital allocation strategies, investment strategies, and insurer profitability are affected by this market phenomenon, insurers have tried to better understand what factors cause the underwriting cycle to shift to a different phase. Insurers essentially want to be able to maintain their competitive advantage and market share regardless of the cycle phase.

In addition, insurance regulators are concerned about the effects of the underwriting cycle on insurance availability and affordability. Although most of the factors affecting the underwriting cycle have been identified through examination of past cycles, changes in the insurance marketplace have reduced the predictive value of these factors. This increases the difficulty of determining when the next cycle phase will begin.

Individual insurers cannot change the underwriting cycle. However, effective underwriting and financial management can enable an insurer to periodically reposition itself through changes in its underwriting guidelines and allocation of capital to underwriting. This allows the insurer to maximize profits and market share growth during the cycle phases. See the exhibit "Phases of the Underwriting Cycle."

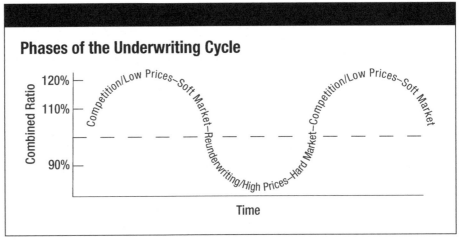

Phases of the Underwriting Cycle

[DA02639]

Nonfinancial Measures

The success of an insurer depends on the ability of every underwriter to attain and maintain profitable results over the long term. This profitability goal is accomplished in part by using nonfinancial measures to assess performance.

Nonfinancial measures link an organization's business strategy and its outputs to its performance. These measures evaluate individual underwriters and underwriting departments based on their actions rather than on their results. If underwriters adhere strictly to underwriting guidelines, underwriting should produce favorable financial results over the long term, barring uncontrollable variables. Underwriting performance standards include these areas of underwriting:

- Selection
- Product or line of business mix
- Pricing
- Accommodated accounts
- Retention ratio
- Hit ratio
- Service to producers
- Premium to underwriter

Expert systems, or knowledge-based systems

Computer software programs that supplement the underwriting decision-making process. These systems ask for the information necessary to make an underwriting decision, ensuring that no information is overlooked.

Some of these nonfinancial measures apply only to commercial lines underwriting departments. Others apply to both personal and commercial lines. Portions of both types may be automated using **expert systems**. Some measures can be evaluated during an underwriting audit. Insurer management and underwriting staff typically work together to agree on the nonfinancial measures or standards that constitute underwriting goals.

Selection

Insurers often establish selection goals for underwriters in order to ensure that the quality of the underwriter's book of business does not deteriorate. For example, an underwriter might be required to have specific percentages of its book of business be considered "highly desirable," "average," and "below average." For this type of performance standard to be effective, the insurer's underwriting guidelines need to clearly delineate among account categories. Selection standards for individual underwriters usually support overall underwriting goals and are evaluated during an underwriting audit.

Product or Line of Business Mix

Measuring product or line of business mix is one way to evaluate an underwriter's contribution to a profitable book of business. Building a proper mix in a book of business requires that underwriters have a thorough knowledge of the insurer's business goals, including the types of products it prefers to write and the "appetite" the insurer has for certain types of risks. For example, if product liability losses are causing an adverse effect on the insurer's entire book of business, the product mix standard might require a reduction in manufacturing classes and a concerted effort to increase the writing in the contractor, service, and mercantile classes.

This performance measure requires a statement in the insurer's underwriting guidelines of the desired product or line of business mix for new and renewal business. Underwriters are often held accountable for supporting product or line of business mix goals, provided the goals are clearly stated in the insurer's underwriting guidelines.

Pricing

Insurers generally establish pricing standards as a nonfinancial measure. Pricing standards enable insurers to determine levels of premium adequacy by comparing premiums charged to the established pricing standards. For example, in commercial insurance, underwriters typically modify rates for each account being underwritten to reflect specific features of that account. Pricing standards indicate the extent to which these modifications depart from the insurer's regular or "standard" pricing. If one or more underwriters continually apply excessive premium credits to accounts to obtain new business or to retain it on renewal, an underwriting audit might reveal that profitability is being sacrificed in return for short-term growth.

Insurers also track through information systems the extent to which their underwriters deviate from the insurer's established pricing for specific classifications. This information might be useful in determining the extent to which the underwriter's book of business is underpriced or overpriced and where pricing adjustments might be made, should market conditions change.

Accommodated Accounts

Making an underwriting accommodation usually means accepting substandard exposures in return for other, more profitable accounts. Some insurers require that underwriters note the accommodation in the file for the account. Other insurers require underwriters to keep a log in which all accommodated risks are entered, along with the reasons for the accommodations. Evaluating the accommodation notes in the files or the log as part of underwriting audits and reviews can reveal whether the underwriter is making excessive accommodations and can ensure that the producer has increased volume or has fulfilled some other promise in exchange for the accommodations.

Retention Ratio

The retention ratio is the percentage of expiring policies that an insurer renews. Retention can be measured by policy count, premium volume, or both. Because most, if not all, of the underwriting investigation work has been completed for existing policies, retaining those policies offers more profit potential than acquiring new business, which involves acquisition costs.

A low retention rate might indicate serious deficiencies in the way insurers do business, including poor service to producers, noncompetitive pricing, or unfavorable claim service. This standard of performance requires careful monitoring of the renewal rate and evaluation of any trends detected.

Hit Ratio

Production underwriting
Performing underwriting functions in an insurer's office as well as traveling to visit and maintain rapport with agents and sometimes clients.

Hit ratio
The ratio of insurance policies written to those that have been quoted to applicants for insurance.

Increasingly, underwriters have dual responsibilities. They are responsible not only for underwriting a profitable book of business, but also for meeting any new business sales goals the insurer makes applicable to their book of business, which is often referred to as **production underwriting**. The **hit ratio**, sometimes called the "success ratio," is a nonfinancial measure used to determine how well underwriters (or the insurer as a whole) are meeting their sales goals.

Underwriting management usually monitors this performance measure more closely than the other standards of performance because the hit ratio provides information about the insurer's competitiveness in the current insurance market. Ratios that are either inordinately high or low might require further investigation. A high hit ratio might indicate any of these conditions:

- Competition is easing.
- Rates are inadequate or lower than other insurers' rates.
- Coverage is broader than other insurers'.
- The underwriter has the skill set for production underwriting.

- Underwriting selection criteria are deteriorating.
- An extremely good relationship exists between the insurer and the producer.

A low hit ratio might indicate one of more of these conditions:

- Competition is increasing.
- Rates are higher than other insurer's rates.
- Coverages or forms are too restrictive.
- The underwriter does not have the skill set for production underwriting.
- Selection criteria are too stringent.
- Service is poor.
- A poor relationship exists between the insurer and the producer.

Service to Producers

Producers work most frequently with insurers who work most cooperatively with them. Because producers usually rank insurers on the basis of service received, an insurer must be able to evaluate its own performance.

This standard requires establishing a set of minimum acceptable standards for certain types of service to producers. The actual performance of each underwriter, branch, or region being evaluated is then compared with the targeted level of performance. See the exhibit "Example of Service to Producers Underwriting Standards."

Example of Service to Producers Underwriting Standards

	Category	Minimum Acceptable Standard
1.	Quotations	3 working days
2.	New policies	3 working days
3.	Replies to correspondence	2 working days
4.	Cancellations, endorsements, certificates	5 working days
5.	Direct cancellation notices	Same-day service
6.	Renewals	No later than 10 days before expiration

[DA06401]

Premium to Underwriter

The volume of premium an underwriter is able to handle is an often-used measure of performance. Underwriting management uses this measure to determine whether individual underwriters are assuming their share of work compared with other underwriters in the same company handling similar accounts.

SUMMARY

The overarching purpose of underwriting is to develop and maintain a profitable book of business for the insurer. To accomplish this, underwriting serves additional purposes:

- Guarding against adverse selection
- Ensuring adequate policyholders' surplus
- Enforcing underwriting guidelines

Line underwriters are primarily responsible for making day-to-day risk selection decisions, which include these activities:

- Select insureds
- Classify and price accounts
- Recommend or provide coverage
- Manage a book of business
- Support producers and insureds
- Coordinate with marketing efforts

Staff underwriters assist underwriting management with making and implementing underwriting policy, which includes these activities:

- Research the market
- Formulate underwriting policy
- Revise underwriting guidelines
- Evaluate loss experience
- Research and develop coverage forms
- Review and revise pricing plans
- Arrange treaty reinsurance
- Assist others with complex accounts
- Conduct underwriting audits
- Participate in industry associations
- Conduct education and training

Underwriting authority reflects an insurer's underwriting policy. Compliance with levels of underwriting authority is important because it ensures that people with the proper experience and knowledge are making risk selection decisions.

An insurer's senior management formulates an underwriting policy to guide underwriting and the composition of the insurer's book of business. These major constraining factors are considered in establishing an underwriting policy:

- Financial capacity
- Regulation
- Personnel
- Reinsurance

Underwriting guidelines describe the parameters of acceptable applicants for insurance for which the insurer has priced its insurance products. Underwriting guidelines serve these purposes:

- Provide for structured decisions
- Ensure uniformity and consistency
- Synthesize insights and experience
- Distinguish between routine and nonroutine decisions
- Avoid duplication of effort
- Ensure adherence to reinsurance treaties and planned rate levels
- Support policy preparation and compliance
- Provide a basis for predictive models

Underwriting audits are a quality control check for uniform application of underwriting guidelines. Continuous improvement results from audits in the form of feedback to underwriters and from enhancements to the underwriting guidelines.

The underwriting process is a series of steps with related tasks applied to determine which submissions will be insured and for what amount of insurance, at what price, and under what conditions. The underwriting process consists of these general decision-making steps:

- Evaluate the submission
- Develop underwriting alternatives
- Select an underwriting alternative
- Determine an appropriate premium
- Implement the underwriting decision
- Monitor underwriting decisions

An insurer's underwriting results are a key indicator of its profitability. However, the combined ratio, a widely used measurement, can be distorted by these factors:

- Changes in premium volume
- Major catastrophic losses
- Delays in loss reporting and loss development
- Underwriting cycles

Nonfinancial measures are useful in evaluating individual underwriters' and underwriting departments' performance. Such measurements include these:

- Selection
- Product or line of business mix
- Pricing
- Accommodated accounts
- Retention ratio
- Hit ratio
- Service to producers
- Premium to underwriter

Risk Control and Premium Auditing

Educational Objectives

After learning the content of this assignment, you should be able to:

▷ Describe the goals of insurer risk control activities.

▷ Describe the risk control services provided by insurers.

▷ Explain how risk control cooperates with other insurer functions.

▷ Explain why premium audits are conducted.

▷ Describe the premium auditing process.

▷ Explain why premium audits must be accurate.

▷ Explain how premium auditing contributes to other insurer functions.

Risk Control and Premium Auditing

INSURER RISK CONTROL GOALS

The primary purpose of an insurer's risk control function is to evaluate loss exposures to assist with underwriting decisions. Another important risk control function is to recommend strategies to customers to prevent or mitigate losses.

Insurers conduct risk control activities to achieve several goals:

- Earn a profit
- Meet customer needs
- Comply with legal requirements
- Fulfill duty to society

Earn a Profit

Risk control activities can help insurers reach their profit goals in several ways:

- Improving underwriting decisions—By inspecting the premises and operations of insurance applicants, risk control representatives can improve the information on which the underwriting department bases its decisions about which applicants to accept and how to price coverage. Better underwriting information enables the insurer to do a better job of selecting insureds and pricing its coverage at a competitive level to produce an underwriting profit.

- Improving premium volume—Risk control personnel often recommend risk control measures that can change a marginal account to an acceptable account, thereby increasing the insurer's premium volume while meeting underwriting guidelines. In addition, risk control personnel and the services they offer can be instrumental in winning new business by helping producers demonstrate added value to their prospective clients.

- Encouraging insureds to improve risk control—Risk control representatives can influence insureds to implement more effective risk control initiatives by working with them to identify risk control opportunities and safety improvements.

- Reducing insureds' losses—Risk control representatives can continue to monitor insureds and suggest appropriate risk control measures as the nature or extent of the insureds' loss exposures change. Consequently, risk control representatives can reduce losses that the insurer must pay, thereby helping to keep the insurer's book of business profitable.

- Providing an additional revenue source—Traditionally, insurers provided risk control services only to their insureds and did not charge a fee in addition to the policy premium. Now, many insurers also sell unbundled risk control services to firms that have chosen to retain, or self-insure, their losses. Some insurers also provide their insureds with supplemental risk control services for a fee in addition to the policy premium. Several major insurers offer access to a variety of experts, such as nurses, ergonomic specialists, industrial hygiene specialists, engineers, attorneys, and chemists.

- Reducing errors and omissions claims against the insurer—Competent risk control service reduces the possibility of errors and omissions claims by insureds or others alleging injury because of the insurer's negligence. In addition, the errors and omissions liability loss exposure can influence an insurer's decision about what types or levels of risk control services to provide.

Meet Customer Needs

Some insurers offer risk control activities in response to the needs of insurance customers—usually their commercial and industrial customers.

These needs have resulted partly from the pressures of legislation such as the Occupational Safety and Health Act, the Consumer Products Safety Act, the Comprehensive Environmental Response Compensation and Liability Act, and the Americans with Disabilities Act. The threat of large liability judgments in certain areas has also contributed to the demand for risk control services.

By exercising sound risk control, organizations make their accounts more attractive to underwriters (especially during a hard market); help control their insurance premiums and possibly even lower them; reduce disruption to operations following accidents; remain socially responsible; comply with occupational safety and health standards; comply with local, state, and federal laws; and improve their financial performance.

Insurers who rely on the independent agency system to market their products often provide risk control services to help agents develop their relationships with insureds and potential accounts. By providing risk control services, the insurer can also experience these additional benefits:

- Enhance its relationship with the producers, staff, and customers of the independent agency
- Increase its own market share as well as that of the agency
- Attract and retain higher-quality accounts
- Help the agency and its customers accomplish their goals

By satisfying customer needs for risk control services, insurers can attract new customers, retain satisfied customers, and gain a competitive advantage over insurers that do not provide these services.

Comply With Legal Requirements

Some states require insurers to provide a minimum level of risk control service to commercial insureds. This requirement applies most often to workers compensation insurance but may also exist for other lines of coverage. Some insurers charge an additional fee for providing risk control services that exceed what the law requires. Charges for services often depend on the premium volume associated with the account. Insurers comply with these laws to not only meet the state's legal requirements and avoid financial penalties, but also to minimize the possibility of errors and omissions claims by insureds.

Fulfill Duty to Society

Insurers benefit society by providing financial resources to help individuals and businesses recover from accidental losses. However, preventing accidental losses is clearly preferable. An occupational injury can cause pain, suffering, and loss of income for an individual and his or her family. A fire at a large factory can cause loss of business income, employee layoffs, and contingent business income losses for the firm's suppliers. Accidental losses collectively have a profound adverse effect on society.

Insurers have an ethical obligation to use their expertise wisely. By assisting insureds in preventing or reducing accidental losses, insurers pursue humanitarian goals and benefit society. This is true even when the insurer derives no direct financial benefit from its risk control services.

RISK CONTROL SERVICES PROVIDED BY INSURERS

Many insurers employ individuals who specialize in risk control. Insurance personnel who perform risk control activities have varying titles, such as safety specialist, risk control specialist, loss control representative, or loss control engineer. The term "risk control representative" refers to all risk control personnel, regardless of job title. Risk control representatives are often members of an insurer's risk control department, which might be centralized in the home office or decentralized in field offices.

Insurers provide three types of risk control services:

- Conducting physical surveys
- Performing risk analysis and improvement
- Developing safety management programs

An insurer with the necessary resources might provide services in all three categories for some of its insureds. Insurers' decisions regarding the risk control services they provide to their insureds are influenced by several factors, including line of insurance, commercial insured size, types of loss exposures insured, and potential legal liability.

Some insurers employ a limited number of risk control staff, or none at all. These insurers often choose to contract with private firms to provide risk control services on an as-needed basis. An insurer that has its own risk control department might also contract with private firms to provide services in geographically remote areas, for highly specialized risks, or to augment its in-house staff during busy times or major underwriting initiatives.

Conducting Physical Surveys

Conducting physical surveys consists mainly of collecting underwriting information on a customer's loss exposures, such as building construction type(s), worker occupations, site diagrams, and fire protection systems.

On a typical survey, a risk control representative inspects the customer's premises on a walking tour and interviews the customer's management to discover details that might not be apparent from the tour. The risk control representative evaluates loss exposures and associated hazards relating to these factors:

- Fire, windstorm, water damage, burglary, and other causes of property loss
- Legal liability arising out of premises, operations, products, completed operations, automobile, mobile equipment, environmental impairment, and other sources of liability
- Employee injuries relative to working conditions, machinery hazards, and employee safety practices

In addition to evaluating loss exposures and physical hazards, the risk control representative evaluates management's ability to control exposures effectively. Their ability to control exposures depends on the experience of the management team, the consistent use of rules and procedures, the use of engineering controls and protective clothing, and the use of safety systems such as safety committees and job safety analysis. Two key components of the success of risk control measures are management's commitment to risk control and employee attitudes about safety. By carefully evaluating management's approach to accident prevention, the risk control representative can obtain important insight into the possibility and extent of **moral hazards** and **morale hazards**.

At the tour's conclusion, the risk control representative meets with management to ask questions, discuss loss exposures and hazards, and provide recommendations for controlling hazards identified during the survey. After leaving the customer's premises, the risk control representative organizes the information in a formal report, which is sent to the insured along with any applicable resource information to help implement the recommendations. Resource information might include training materials, an example of

Moral hazard

A condition that increases the likelihood that a person will intentionally cause or exaggerate a loss.

Morale hazard (attitudinal hazard)

A condition of carelessness or indifference that increases the frequency or severity of loss.

a written safety program, a self-inspection checklist template, or regulatory compliance information. Risk control correspondence is typically shared with underwriting and with the producer, and it might also be shared with claims and other insurer departments. See the exhibit "Sample Risk Control Report."

The written recommendations made by the risk control representative can help the customer eliminate or control loss exposures. They also help the underwriting department and the producer to follow up on the customer's progress in addressing the identified hazards. Typically, recommendations are generated when a risk control representative identifies a loss exposure that falls below a satisfactory level. With mercantile loss exposures, for example, a common recommendation is to control slip-and-fall hazards by improving the maintenance program for aisles, steps, and stairwells.

Recommendations should be as practical as possible, conform to industry and regulatory standards, and be explained in enough detail to allow successful implementation by the insured. The potential cost of addressing a particular hazard should be considered when a recommendation is made but should not determine whether the recommendation is actually made. When the cost of addressing a hazard in the traditional manner is high or even prohibitive, alternatives should be offered to accomplish risk control in a more cost-effective manner. A simple cost-benefit analysis can be done to help ensure that recommendations are not unnecessarily burdensome. Too often, recommendations are limited to fixing what is broken or upgrading the item in question to meet regulatory standards. It is in the best interest of the insured and the insurer to offer recommendations that are not merely minimum requirements but "best practices."

A survey report might also include information about a property valuation (appraisal) that has been done by others. This can be important if the actual values differ from the coverage limits requested by the customer. For example, if a customer has requested $500,000 insurance coverage (actual cash basis) on an older building, and a professional appraisal then values that building at $750,000 (functional replacement cost basis), a coverage gap can be avoided. The underwriter, and even the producer, might determine the current estimated value of a property using commercially available software. However, most insurers choose to avoid making an official determination of property values for policy-limit purposes, as doing so can subject them to errors and omissions claims. Risk control representatives generally do not participate in determining actual property values, but their observations and experience can help to identify situations in which the stated values or requested policy limits should be examined more closely. By accurately determining a building's actual cash value, functional value, or full replacement cost, the correct limit of insurance can be determined and the most appropriate basis of coverage used.

Sample Risk Control Report

Insurance Company
429 Smithtown Rd., Anywhere, PA 22484

INSURED
Terry's Casual Wear

MAILING ADDRESS
4814 Hwy. 17 South, N. Myrtle Beach, S.C.

LOCATION SURVEYED
SAME

PERSON INTERVIEWED
Theresa M.

SURVEY DATE
6/28/X3

RISK CONTROL REPRESENTATIVE
John H.

POLICY NUMBER
CR07234525

EXPLAIN OR MAKE RECOMMENDATIONS FOR ALL CIRCLE O ANSWERS

A. RISK OVERVIEW

OVERALL RISK	LOSS CONTROL	PREMISES CONDITION	HOUSEKEEPING	PRIOR LOSS	OPINION OF RISK
☐ Low	☑ Good	☑ Good	☑ Good	○ Yes	☑ Good
☑ Medium	☐ Fair	☐ Fair	☐ Fair	☑ No	☐ Fair
○ High	○ Poor	○ Poor	○ Poor		○ Poor

B. DESCRIPTION OF OPERATIONS

1. Description of business and/or operations:
   Retail clothing store

C. GENERAL DATA

1. Insured is: ☑ Owner ☐ Tenant ☐ Lessee
2. Insured is: ☑ Corporation ☐ Partnership ☐ Individual
3. Yrs. in business: _5_ At this location _3_
4. Business hours: _10_ to _11_
5. Estimated gross annual sales: $225,000
6. Neighborhood is: ☑ Commercial ☐ Rural ☐ Residential ☐ Industrial

7. Neighborhood is: ☑ Stable ○ Other
8. Does business appear successful? ☑ Yes ○ No
9. Management attitude satisfactory? ☑ Yes ○ No
10. Other occupants in building? ☐ Yes ⊘ No
    If YES, describe: _____

BUILDING

1. Year built: __20X0__

2. Building height (stories & ft./story): __1__

3. Exterior wall construction: Frame __Wood__ Cover: __Wood shingle__

4. Floor construction: __Wood__

5. Roof const.: Support: __Wood__ Deck: __Metal__ Cover: __Metal__

6. Area (include basement only if finished); sq. ft. __1,320__

7. ☐ Fire Resistive ☐ Ordinary
   ☐ Non-Combustible ☑ Frame

8. Vertical openings:
   Stairways protected? ☐ Yes ○ No ☑ None
   Elevators protected? ☐ Yes ○ No ☑ None
   Elevators: # of passengers: _____ # of freight: _____

9. Int. finish: Walls: __Wood__ Ceiling: __S/R__

10. Building condition satisfactory? ☑ Yes ○ No

11. Basement in building? ○ Yes ☑ No
    If YES, ☐ Full ☐ Partial _____ %
    ○ Finished ☐ Unfinished

HAZARDS

1. Heating type: __FA central loc elsewhere__
   A. Fuel ☐ Gas ☑ Electric ☐ Wood/Coal ☐ LP Gas ☐ Oil
   B. Appears safely arranged? __not seen__ ☐ Yes ○ No

2. Air conditioning? ☐ Yes ○ No
   Type: ☑ Central ☐ Package ☐ Portable ○ Other

3. Electrical type: ☐ Conduit ☑ Romex ☐
   A. Overcurrent Protection: ☑ Cir. Brkrs. ☐ Fuses
   B. Appear safely arranged? ☑ Yes ○ No

4. Are the following satisfactory?
   A. Housekeeping ☑ Yes ○ No
   B. Maintenance ☑ Yes ○ No
   C. Trash Removal ☑ Yes ○ No
   D. Smoking Control ☑ Yes ○ No
   E. Flam./Combust. liquids ☐ Yes ○ No ☑ None noted
   F. Welding/hot work ☐ Yes ○ No ☑ None noted
   G. Other special hazards ☐ Yes ○ No ☑ None noted

FIRE PROTECTION

1. Risk within city limits? ☑ Yes ○ No

2. Fire department: ☐ None ☑ Paid ☐ Volunteer

3. Distance to fire dept.: __1/3__ Miles

4. Number of hydrants and distance: __1 at 50'; 1 at 370'__

5. Adequate fire extinguishers? ☑ Yes ○ No
   Size and type: __2A__

6. Extinguishers properly tagged and serviced? ☑ Yes ○ No

7. Sprinkler system? ☑ Yes ○ No
   A. Coverage: ○ Full ○ Partial _____ %
   B. Alarm: ☐ Full ☐ Local ☐ Central Station

8. Fire detection/alarm system? ☑ Yes ☐ No

9. Watchman service? ☑ Yes ☐ No

10. Fire dept. name and class: __N. Myrtle Beach__

Operations

Your insured is a corporation that has been in business for five years. It has been in business at the present location since the shopping mall was constructed three years ago. The mall has numerous small shops and restaurants built up on a boardwalk over a small inlet, approximately 3,000 feet from the Atlantic Ocean. Insured leases this space for a clothing store, selling moderately priced ladies' casual wear and a few accessories, such as purses, belts, and so forth. Also, a small line of costume jewelry is in one case at the counter.

Building

The building is three years old, of wood frame construction, and found to be in good condition and well maintained. The building is on wood pylons, and a portion of the building is above the water (see diagram).

Heating and Air Conditioning

Heat and air conditioning are ducted from elsewhere in the mall and are said to be water controlled and thought to be electric; however, the unit was not located. The insured said she believes the units are near Hwy. 17, several hundred feet from the building.

Wiring

Wiring is Romex with breaker protection. This appears to be in good condition and is three years old.

Protection

Insured is located in North Myrtle Beach, and the North Myrtle Beach fire department will respond there. No unusual fire department obstructions were noted.

Portable extinguishers were posted all around the mall area, and these were properly tagged and serviced. Also, a Z100 Moose digital alarm system protects the shop. This has heat detectors as well as infrared motion detectors, and insured states she believes these are directly monitored by the fire department. The alarm system was installed by the owners of the mall, and apparently these are present in every location.

Much of the mall is sprinklered, and there is a PIV valve fifty feet outside the insured's location; however, this particular shop is not sprinklered.

Security guards are employed by the mall, and the insured said that they patrol this area twenty-four hours a day.

Liability

The shop was in good condition from a liability standpoint. Stock is neatly stored and arranged in a clutter-free manner. Floor covering, lighting, and egress are good, and there are marked exits. All parking is controlled by the mall.

Losses

Contact states no losses have occurred under these coverages. They did have one business interruption loss during Hurricane Hugo in 1989.

Comments

Because of premises and building conditions, as well as good controls and the nature of insured's operation, this risk rates "good" for all coverages surveyed.

Note

Initially, we visited insured on 6/20; however, the contact was not in. We phoned back on several occasions before she contacted us on 6/28 to obtain loss and other information.

Recommendations

None are deemed necessary at this time.

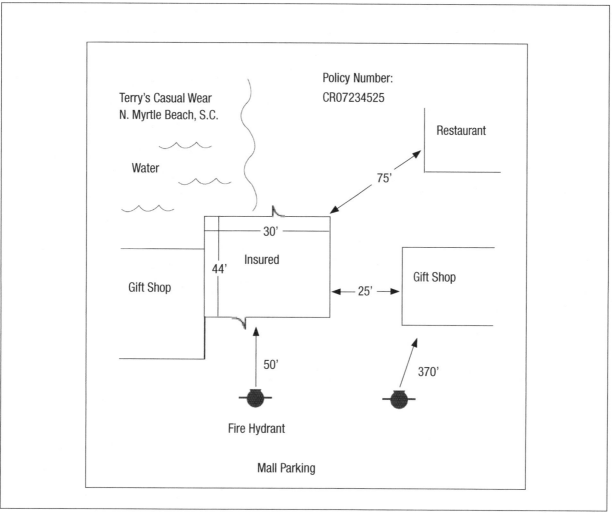

[DA03354]

Physical surveys provide benefits to both the underwriter and the insured:

- The survey report helps the underwriter gain a better understanding of the loss exposures being insured. Underwriters often provide an insurance quotation with the condition that various risk control recommendations in the survey report be implemented.

- The insured can gain a better understanding of its loss exposures and the steps that could be taken to prevent or reduce losses, comply with applicable laws and regulations, and provide a better working environment for employees, all of which can increase employee morale and productivity.

- If a property valuation is part of the survey, the insured can be more confident of an adequate recovery in the event of a total loss and less likely to incur a coinsurance penalty in the event of a partial loss.

Performing Risk Analysis and Improvement

In addition to completing a physical survey and loss exposure and hazard evaluation, the insurer's risk control representative might analyze the customer's loss history (risk analysis) and submit written recommendations (improvements) to the business owner or manager about how to reduce hazards that have led to previous losses. A risk control representative or the producer usually contacts the insured within sixty to ninety days to follow up on the insured's progress in complying with the recommendations. Some insurers' risk control departments follow up on all recommendations on a scheduled basis—for example, sixty to ninety days from when the recommendations were made. Depending on the procedures of the particular insurer, follow-up might occur at intervals or as part of the renewal process. Some insurers require that the producer conduct the follow-up. Ideally, underwriting will have written confirmation from the insured that the recommendations have been implemented.

To support the risk analysis and improvement effort, the insurer's risk control representatives can provide training, information, or counseling services, such as these:

- Coordinated safety programs
- Technical risk-control information resources
- Workers compensation risk management strategies
- Fire protection systems testing and evaluation
- Preconstruction counseling

A safety training program includes a series of presentations on safety-related subjects to raise workers' awareness of loss exposures and appropriate safety behaviors. Typical subjects are fire safety, driver safety, and machine operation safety. Subjects are selected based on an analysis of the insured's loss exposures or trends in loss experience. Priority is given to subjects that could significantly improve the insured's loss experience. Films, slide shows, and videotapes can be shown in conjunction with training programs or can be loaned to insureds as requested.

Safety programs can help to develop positive safety attitudes among all workers, improve workers' understanding of safety-related matters, and help workers accept responsibility for their role in the organization's safety program. To prepare the insured's managers for assuming a leadership role in risk control, the insurer might also conduct supervisory safety training sessions.

A written safety program is a collection of policies and procedures the insured uses in its operations to facilitate risk control. Written safety programs generally include information on awareness and training, life safety, accident reporting and investigation, reporting of safety concerns, employee responsibilities, supervisory responsibilities, and regulatory compliance.

Many insurers also serve as a source of technical risk control information. Information sought by the insured might relate to specific hazards and appropriate controls, the interpretation of standards, or particular safety management products or suppliers. By providing this information, the insurer helps the insured save time and effort in obtaining information needed to make informed risk control decisions. The insurer also builds a working relationship with the insured that can help to retain the account in the future.

The risk control departments of some larger insurers enter into service contracts with their insureds or other clients to provide periodic testing and maintenance for fire protection and detection systems. The insurer's concerns include whether the system will respond in an emergency and whether the system is designed properly for the insured's current loss exposures. However, most insurers rely on the insured property owner to contract for these services directly with outside service providers.

When business owners expand existing facilities or build new structures, they often overlook the connection between construction features and insurance rates. Generally, rating credits can be given for noncombustible or fire-resistive construction, sprinkler systems, smoke detectors, burglar alarms, security hardware, and other features. A pre-construction review by the insurer of the drawings and specifications allows the insured to see how insurance rates and underwriting acceptability will be affected by the new construction. Any plan alterations can be made more cost effectively before construction begins.

Developing Safety Management Programs

The development of safety management programs is often coordinated by senior risk control staff, who generally have the advanced technical and communication skills needed for more in-depth consultation work.

Developing safety management programs begins with a complete evaluation of the insured's operations, just as in risk analysis and improvement risk control services. After reviewing the evaluation, the more experienced risk control representative or risk control consultant assists the insured in establishing risk control goals, selecting appropriate risk control measures, organizing the resources necessary to implement the chosen risk control measures, and establishing procedures to monitor the program.

Because of several concerns, the insured is ordinarily responsible for implementing the program on a daily basis without direct assistance from the risk control consultant. These concerns include errors and omissions liability, lack of authority to exercise a management role in the insured's business, and the need for management to have program ownership.

After being implemented, the program must be monitored to determine whether adjustments are needed. The risk control consultant can provide a great deal of technical assistance in the monitoring phase of the program.

The consultation process normally requires several visits to the insured's premises to gather initial information, plan the review with management, and follow up to monitor the program. Depending on the needs, abilities, and preferences of the insured, ongoing risk control visits may occur on a semi-annual, quarterly, or monthly basis.

Factors Affecting Service Levels

Every insurer must decide what levels of risk control service to provide and to which insureds. Several factors influence insurers' decisions.

Line of Insurance

One of the factors that will influence an insurer's decision about the level and type of risk control service to provide is the line of insurance. An insurer that writes only personal insurance is unlikely to provide extensive risk control services. The relatively small premium for a typical personal auto or home-owners account does not justify the expense necessary to conduct on-site safety inspections.

During personal insurance underwriting, insurers sometimes request that their agents or salespeople photograph a house or an auto (the latter to verify a car's vehicle identification number). Insurers might provide producers with checklists to ensure that certain items are either requested specifically of the applicant or identified during the producer's drive-by inspection. See the exhibit "Personal Insurance Property Report."

Producers can effectively implement risk control programs when insurers provide explicit instructions. When insuring exceptionally high-valued property, such as a mansion or a yacht, the insurer might use specifically trained risk control representatives to develop underwriting information or recommendations for reducing physical hazards.

In addition to conducting on-site inspections, an insurer can promote risk control among its personal lines insureds by publishing educational bulletins or by offering rate discounts for home security systems, deadbolt locks, automobile anti-theft devices, driver education, or other risk control measures. An insurer might also support industry associations that disseminate information, conduct research, lobby legislators, or otherwise support risk control efforts to benefit society. Fire safety and highway safety are two major areas addressed by such associations.

Commercial Insured Size

The large premiums generated by commercial insureds and the increased values at risk often make it economically feasible to provide such insureds with risk control services. The level of service rendered to a commercial insured can depend on the size of the account. Typically, an insurer devotes more resources to accounts that generate a substantial premium. Some

Personal Insurance Property Report

PERSONAL INSURANCE PROPERTY REPORT

DATE   November 1, 20XX
POLICY NUMBER   PCA 123 4579
NAME   Willis B.
MAILING   Providence Road
ADDRESS   Malvern, PA 19355
PROPERTY
LOCATION
(IF OTHER THAN ABOVE)

PHOTOS
☑ ATTACHED

  # PHOTOS _____
  (IF MORE THAN ONE)
☐ NOT AVAILABLE

AMT. OF COVERAGE $ 194,000

OBSERVATIONS	VALUES

OBSERVATIONS

1. Apprx. Year Built: ___1977___   OTHER:

2. Number of Stories: ☐1 ☑2 ☐3   ☐_____

3. Occupancy:
    ☑Single Family   ☐Two Family   ☐_____

4. Predominant Constr. Material:

    A. Dwg. ☑Frame ☐Brick ☐Solid ☐_____
          Veneer   or Stone   Brick

    B. Roof ☑Comp. ☐Tar & ☐Wood ☐_____
          Shingle   Gravel   Shingle

    C. Outbuildings ☐None ☑Frame
          ☐Masonry ☐Metal ☐_____

5. Condition:
    A. Dwg.   ☑Good ☐_____
    B. Roof   ☑Good ☐_____
    C. Outbuildings ☐None ☑Good ☐_____

6. Neighborhood:
    A. Type ☑Residential ☐Commercial
          ☐Rural   ☐_____
    B. Status ☐Improving ☑Stable ☐_____

7. Protection:
    Approximate Distance in Feet to Nearest Hydrant   100 ft
    Approximate Distance in Miles to Nearest
    Responding Fire Department   1-1/2 mi

8. Liability Hazards:
    ☑Outside Pool   ☑Fenced   _____
    ☐Horses   ☐Unfenced
    ☐Large Dogs   ☐Business use

9. Hazards Noted: ☐None
    ☐Vacant or   ☐Isolated or   ☐Difficult Access
    Seasonal   Hidden   for Fire
    Property   ☐Wood Stove   Department
    ☐Dead Trees   ☐Combustible   ☐Open
    or Limbs   Brush or Debris   Foundation
    ☐Adjacent   ☐Flooding or
    Property   High Water   ☐Other

VALUES

DIAGRAM—SHOW DIMENSIONS

Utility shed

Deck

Covered porch

Two-car garage

Estimated replacement cost using:

☑ Room count method

☐ Square foot method

$ 210,000

CUSTOM HOME FEATURES:
_____
_____
_____
_____

Date of Report   9/1/20XX
Agency: F.A. Smith, West Chester
Inspector: Bill S.

REMARKS—RECOMMENDATIONS
FOR IMPROVEMENT _____
_____
_____
_____
_____
_____

[DA03355]

insurers make some or all of their risk control services available to smaller accounts who request them.

Sometimes, insureds might not want a higher level of service than the insurer normally provides with its insurance. Insurers may provide options for insureds to purchase supplemental risk control services. By not including the cost for such supplemental services in the premium, insurers allow insureds who do not want or need these additional services to avoid subsidizing the costs associated with them.

Types of Loss Exposures Insured

The risk control services an insurer provides depend to some degree on the types of loss exposures the insurer is willing to cover. An insurer that covers large and complex industrial firms needs skilled personnel and sophisticated equipment to meet the risk control requirements of such firms, including these examples:

- Testing and evaluating the effects of noise levels on employees
- Assessing the hazards to employees from solvents, toxic metals, radioactive isotopes, and other substances
- Assisting in the design of explosion suppression systems or fire extinguishing systems for dangerous substances or easily damaged equipment
- Evaluating products liability loss exposures and preparing programs to minimize such loss exposures
- Consulting on complex and specialized risk control problems

An insurer that deals primarily with habitational, mercantile, and small manufacturing loss exposures might be able to maintain a less-sophisticated risk control department.

Potential Legal Liability

Making recommendations to existing insureds is an important risk management tool for insurers. However, the threat of being named in a lawsuit for negligence in providing risk control services may lead some insurers to choose not to offer risk control services at all or to limit their risk control activities in order to avoid or minimize their exposure.

Some states have enacted statutes that protect insurers by preventing insureds, their employees, and third parties (including applicants) from bringing suit against an insurer for injuries or damages sustained as a result of providing, or failing to provide, risk control services. Although relatively infrequent, negligent inspection claims do occur. If an insurer's underwriting department chooses to require certain controls as a prerequisite to providing coverage, such controls should be expressed as conditions of the insurance quote and the subsequent insurance agreement rather than as risk control recommendations, in order to avoid unnecessary exposure to potential legal liability.

COOPERATION BETWEEN RISK CONTROL AND OTHER INSURER FUNCTIONS

An insurer's risk control efforts are most effective when they complement the activities of its other departments and various external organizations.

Cooperation between risk control representatives and the representatives of other insurer functions can improve the quality of information available to an insurer and the services it offers. Insurers and insureds can also benefit from cooperative relationships between the risk control function and various external organizations, particularly producers. Other external organizations include reinsurers; trade associations that engage in risk control activities; the Occupational Safety and Health Administration (OSHA) and other regulatory agencies; law enforcement and codes enforcement agencies; and public safety entities such as fire departments.

These are the principal opportunities for risk control cooperation:

- Underwriting
- Marketing and sales
- Premium auditing
- Claims
- Producers

Underwriting

The risk control function provides information to underwriters that enables them to make better underwriting decisions. This information consists primarily of field inspection reports on the premises and operations of new applicants and existing insureds renewing their policies. Inspection reports should provide a clear profile of the applicant's loss exposures and related hazards. Additionally, an insurer's risk control department can provide technical support to its underwriting department in many areas, such as fire hazards of new building materials, health hazards of materials or production processes, and new techniques or equipment for materials handling.

The risk control function can also help underwriters modify a new applicant's loss exposures to meet eligibility requirements. After an applicant has been accepted, risk control can help the insured to remain within underwriting guidelines and qualify for policy renewal. Risk control can even help "rehabilitate" a marginal account that underwriting has accepted because of competitive considerations.

Risk control representatives also play an important role in communicating effectively with insureds. Often, a risk control representative is the main communications link between the underwriter and the insured.

Marketing and Sales

The risk control function also can be instrumental in helping the insurer's marketing and sales staff meet its goals. By evaluating an applicant's premises and operations, interviewing management staff, and evaluating the nature of historical losses, risk control representatives can help determine if an applicant's current risk controls are acceptable or if there are ways to improve an accepted applicant's risk controls. The risk control representative's evaluation can make the difference between an applicant's acceptance or rejection.

By making marginal accounts acceptable, risk control helps marketing reach its sales goals. Risk control can also help marketing by proving to applicants and insureds that the insurer understands their business operations and associated hazards, and is prepared to help them protect their interests. The risk control representative can offer crucial advice on improving safety.

After applicants become insureds, risk control can play a key role in retaining them as customers. In fact, a commercial insured might have more regular contact with the insurer's risk control representatives than with any other employee of the insurer. By providing professional and courteous service, risk control personnel can create customer goodwill.

Finally, through their direct contact with insureds, risk control representatives can learn the insurance coverages or services insureds need or want. By conveying this information to the appropriate marketing or sales personnel, risk control representatives can assist the marketing department in either meeting an insured's specific needs or developing product enhancements that will appeal to many insureds.

For example, a risk control survey might reveal that the insured has acquired new property that is not adequately covered under their existing policy. If conveyed to the appropriate marketing staff, this information might lead to the sale of additional coverage to that insured. If several insureds experience the same problem, that information could lead to a decision to revise the insurer's policy forms to provide better coverage for newly acquired property.

Premium Auditing

In one respect, the roles of risk control representatives and premium auditors are similar, because both visit the insured's premises and have direct insured contact. However, risk control representatives typically visit the insured at the beginning of the policy period and as needed throughout the policy period, while premium auditors visit at the end of the policy period. Premium auditors often visit the insured after the point at which recordkeeping deficiencies resulting from the insured's lack of knowledge or misunderstanding can be corrected. Risk control personnel can use the opportunity provided by their own inspections, as well as information from recent premium audits, to help improve insured documentation and the accuracy of premium audits. During the premium auditing process, a new exposure or an increase in exposure that is discovered by an auditor can prompt risk control involvement.

To take advantage of this opportunity, however, premium auditors must communicate their needs to risk control representatives so that they can, for example, note the location of the accounting records and the name of the person to contact at audit time. They can also record the names, titles, and duties of executive officers.

The risk control representative's description of operations could be a starting point for the auditor's classification of loss exposures. They might help estimate the payroll by classification or at least the number of employees per department. They can report the existence of any new operations. If properly informed, they can also advise the insured about recordkeeping requirements and the need for good risk transfer practices, including certificates of insurance with additional insured-specific language and written contracts that include hold-harmless language.

Finally, risk control representatives can offer the assistance of the insurer's premium auditors to deal with any complex questions about an audit. Problems such as a gap in coverage, a burdensome charge for additional premium at the end of a policy year, or a significant return of premium can be prevented.

Claims

A partnership between risk control and claims can be just as valuable to an insurer as the partnership between risk control and underwriting, marketing, or premium auditing. The risk control department needs claim experience information to direct risk control resources and efforts to crucial areas. The claims department relies on risk control for loss exposure data and background information that can support the loss adjusting process. Claims and risk control personnel should discuss common concerns and review loss cases regularly. The claim experience information that can be useful to the risk control function includes frequency and severity of losses by type of insurance, by cause of loss, by the kind of business the insured engages in, and by worker occupation.

Regarding individual accidents, particularly in the workers compensation area, risk control can also benefit from information about the type of accident, the body part injured, how the accident occurred, and perhaps other details from the adjuster's report. Risk control staff can use this information for these purposes:

- Identifying areas for research
- Targeting loss exposures for additional attention
- Identifying characteristics associated with particular types of losses
- Developing alternatives to control losses

Risk control representatives are usually well informed in engineering, mechanical, and technological areas with which claims personnel might be unfamiliar. Therefore, the risk control department can provide codes, standards, technical advice, laboratory analyses, valuable insight based on experience, and other assistance to the claims department when investigating and settling claims. A risk control specialist can design product recall procedures to assist claims personnel and insureds in controlling specific product losses. Risk control representatives can also support the claims function by reviewing and emphasizing the importance of thorough loss documentation and proper claim reporting procedures.

Producers

Traditionally, producers encouraged the insured's risk control activities and coordinated the efforts of the insurer's risk control representatives with the insured. Producers still perform this role. However, many large agencies and brokerages maintain their own risk control departments, and some can furnish services equivalent to those offered by insurers. If an insured is receiving risk control services from both the insurer and its producer, the risk control entities of both organizations should strive to coordinate their efforts for the mutual benefit of all parties involved, particularly the insured.

REASONS FOR PREMIUM AUDITING

The premium auditing function plays a vital role in the insurance mechanism. With knowledge of insurance principles, accounting procedures, and particular state regulations, premium auditors can obtain the information needed to calculate premiums accurately and collect the data used to establish future insurance rates. By safeguarding the accuracy of information on which insurance premiums are based, premium auditing helps make the insurance mechanism work as intended and support the insurer's profit goal by ensuring that appropriate premiums are charged for policies provided.

Insurers conduct premium audits for these reasons:

- To determine correct premiums
- To collect ratemaking data
- To meet regulatory requirements
- To deter and detect fraud
- To reinforce confidence of insureds
- To obtain additional information

The need for a premium audit arises because some insurance policies have adjustable premiums. For these kinds of insurance policies, loss exposure varies substantially by individual insured. A standard premium rate might be far from reflecting an insured's actual exposure to loss. When entering an adjustable premium contract, the insured pays a standard premium, which is adjusted the following year based on the actual loss exposure. Adjustable premium policies include a clause that allows the insurer to perform premium audits to determine the actual amount of **exposure units** on which the premium will be based.

For many commercial insurance policies, the premium paid at the beginning of the policy period is a provisional premium based on an estimate of the extent of operations to be insured. At the end of the policy period, typically one year, the insured's records are examined, or audited, by a premium auditor to determine the exposure units. After the auditor reports the data, the audit processors apply the rates and various factors, such as experience modification and premium discounts, to determine the final earned premium. If the insured's operations were more extensive than estimated, an additional premium is charged. If less extensive, the insured receives a partial refund.

Premium auditing is performed for many coverages, including workers compensation, which is rated per $100 of payroll, and general liability, which is rated per $1,000 of payroll or sales. Commercial auto policies for large fleets are rated based on the vehicles that are exposed to loss during the policy period. Although premium auditing most often involves liability insurance, some property insurance policies, such as those covering fluctuating inventory values, are also subject to premium audit. These premium bases are also called exposure units. An exposure unit is the fundamental measure that is used to calculate the policy premium.

Exposure unit (unit of exposure)

The unit of measure (for example, area, gross receipts, payroll) used to determine an insurance policy premium.

Determine Correct Premiums

The primary reason for premium auditing is to determine the correct premium for the policy period. The insurer bears a responsibility to determine the premium correctly. Unless premiums are sufficient for the loss exposures covered, the insurer cannot operate profitably. If, however, the insurer overcharges the insured, it will certainly encounter negative reactions when the error is discovered and will probably lose the business. The insurer's interest and obligation, therefore, require as much certainty and precision in the premium determination as possible. A premium audit provides that accuracy.

When a policy is written subject to audit, the actual premium can be calculated only after the end of the policy period when the exact exposure units or premium bases during the policy period are known. In most cases, the applicable manual for the type of insurance involved has rules that strictly define the procedure to be followed, specifying inclusions and exclusions in the premium base and defining distinct rating classifications. For example, for workers compensation coverage, manual rules specifically indicate how to assign payroll for clerical or construction employees. Mastering these rules requires considerable effort and practice.

Insureds have the accounting information or other data that are used to determine the premium base, but they rarely understand insurance manual rules well enough to present the information in the necessary form. A skilled premium auditor, employed by the insurer, usually assembles the information and determines the actual earned premium. Even if the insured can provide the necessary premium data, having a premium auditor inspect the original books of account makes the insurer more confident that the data are accurate. However, because of staff shortages, heavy workloads, expenses, or company policies, some insurers do not have their own premium auditors and may rely on voluntary audit reports or external premium auditing consultants.

A premium audit is also important to provide the insurer with current and accurate information to determine whether the renewal premium estimate is in line with the audited exposures. This allows the insurer to collect sufficient premium in advance in the event that the insured experiences financial problems during the policy period, which could make collection of a retrospective premium adjustment difficult.

Collect Ratemaking Data

Insurance advisory organizations collect ratemaking data and, in most cases, project the costs of future losses, or loss costs. To these loss costs, insurers add their own expense component to determine a final insurance rate.

Calculating actuarially credible rates begins with data about claim payments, earned premiums, and insured exposure units for each rating classification. Although claim reports provide the necessary information on claims for a given period, the premium volume and total insured loss exposures by class cannot be determined with any degree of certainty without compiling data from premium audits.

A detailed classification breakdown of exposure units obtained by a premium audit is necessary for the insurer's statistical report to the advisory rating organizations (rating bureaus), as well as for billing purposes. When an advisory organization has credible statistics showing premium volume, loss experience, and total insured exposure units for each rating class, its actuaries can calculate appropriate loss costs that are used to establish rates. These data usually must be filed with state regulators to support rate increases or other rate filings.

Meet Regulatory Requirements

Although requirements vary by state, premium audits are often required to meet workers compensation insurance regulations. Compared with other types of insurance, workers compensation regulation tends to be more restrictive because of the compulsory nature of its coverage. It can be argued that in requiring such insurance coverage, the state has also assumed an obligation to guarantee its availability and to administer the coverage equitably. Therefore, uniform workers compensation rules and rates are usually prescribed even in states allowing open competition on other types of insurance. As an added protection for insureds, the rules prevailing in some states stipulate that the insurer must audit the records of insureds that meet certain criteria, usually related to premium size or type of business, within specific time frames, such as every three years.

Deter and Detect Fraud

Premium auditing tends to deter fraud. Insureds are less likely to submit false or misleading information to an insurer when they know the information might be checked and independently verified by a premium auditor. Although uncovering fraud is not the primary purpose of premium auditing, premium auditors have often uncovered deceptive business practices during routine audits. Such discoveries can lead to a maze of falsified or missing records. The insurer's usual recourse is not to renew the policy; however, any such decision depends on accurate and precise information from the auditor. Therefore, even when performed randomly, premium audits are an effective control on the integrity of the premium computation and collection process.

Reinforce Confidence of Insureds

Most insureds want to deal fairly with insurers and to be dealt with fairly by insurers. Competent premium audits can contribute to insureds' confidence that they are receiving fair treatment. A premium computed from a meticulous audit has credibility when the insured knows the auditor exercised due care in collecting and verifying the data. Observing the audit process counters the notion that premium adjustments are arbitrary and conveys the impression that all insureds are, and in fact must be, treated according to uniform and equitable standards. A good premium auditor also explains the audit procedure to the insured so that any premium adjustment does not surprise the insured.

The benefits of a competent audit extend beyond the premium audit itself. An insured with a favorable impression of the insurer is less likely to look for another insurer at renewal time or when the need for additional coverage arises. Having gained from the audit procedure a greater understanding of how the premium is determined, an insured might improve record keeping, especially when having properly organized records reduces the premium charges. The insured might also be more receptive to risk control advice or other services the insurer can provide after a well-conducted premium audit.

Obtain Additional Information

A premium audit might generate additional underwriting information about the insured, such as an incorrect classification or a new loss exposure that the underwriter had not previously identified. A premium audit can also identify all named insureds on the policy to make sure all exposures from additional entities are included in the exposure. Such information can be extremely useful to the underwriter in determining whether to renew a policy. Premium audit information can also identify marketing opportunities and assist the claim department in adjusting certain types of losses. Finally, a premium audit is a source of feedback on the insurer's image and effectiveness.

PREMIUM AUDITING PROCESS

Premium auditors follow a systematic process for each audit to ensure that their information is accurate and complete and that others can rely on their work.

At each stage of the auditing process, premium auditors make judgments and decide how to proceed. Sometimes they need more information about the insured's operations, additional records, or an explanation of an apparent discrepancy. These judgments are necessary because premium auditors must be satisfied that the information they receive is reasonable and reliable.

These stages in the premium auditing process provide a framework for organizing the many decisions premium auditors must make:

- Planning
- Reviewing operations
- Determining employment relationships
- Finding and evaluating books and records
- Auditing the books and records
- Analyzing and verifying premium-related data
- Reporting the findings

As with many other processes, each stage of the premium auditing process is not necessarily a clearly defined step. The process is a continuum, and many of the stages blend.

Planning

Because insurers cannot afford the expense of auditing every auditable policy every year, they must decide which policies to audit. In some cases, an insurer might determine that an audit is not worth the cost and elect to waive it, if permissible by regulators, after considering the policy and its endorsements, prior audit reports, and the potential reliability of a voluntary report from the insured.

A voluntary report (also called a policyholder's report) is a form the insured completes and returns to the insurer's premium audit department. The insurer includes instructions to assist the insured in compiling the exposure unit information required to adjust the premium for the expired policy period. Once the insurer receives the voluntary report, it might choose to accept it (to perform a two-year audit at the end of the next policy period) or to

Voluntary (Policyholder's) Report

POLICYHOLDER'S REPORT

Your Insurance Policy was issued on an **estimate** of the premium bases listed below. We now need the **actual amounts** so we can figure the premium. Please fill in the amounts for the period of time shown in the section called **Reporting Period**. If you have any questions, **please contact your agent**. We will appreciate your response by the **due date**. Thank you.

NAME AND ADDRESS OF AGENT		NAME AND ADDRESS OF COMPANY	
Arnold Agency P. O. Box 1224 Atlanta, GA 30301	AGENCY CODE 3207	Midley Insurance Company P. O. Box 1000 Springton, PA 19809	

NAME AND ADDRESS OF INSURED	POLICY NUMBER	KIND OF POLICY

NAME AND ADDRESS OF INSURED	POLICY NUMBER WC 1234	KIND OF POLICY Workers Compensation	
John's Sporting Goods, Inc. 1972 Olympic St. Atlanta, GA 30301	POLICY PERIOD MONTH–DAY–YEAR TO MONTH–DAY–YEAR 6-6-X5 TO 6-6-X6		DATE 6-7-X6
	REPORTING PERIOD 6-6-X5 TO 6-6-X6		DUE DATE 7-6-X6

CODE	DESCRIPTION/LOCATION	PREMIUM BASE	AMOUNT	RATE	PREMIUM
8017	Retail Stores N.O.C.	Remu- neration		3.73 per $100	

☐ COMPLETE   ☐ DO NOT COMPLETE THIS SECTION   EXECUTIVE OFFICERS/PARTNERS/PROPRIETORS

TITLE	NAME	SPECIFIC DUTIES	EARNINGS
			DO NOT INCLUDE IN UPPER SECTION

Who keeps your records? David S.
 NAME

Signature *David S.*   Title Treasurer

Where are they kept? 178 Trimmings Ct.
 ADDRESS

Phone Number 522-3054   Date 7-1-X6

RETURN TO   ☒ COMPANY   ☐ PRODUCER

[DA03359]

initiate an immediate field audit to confirm the voluntary report. See the exhibit "Voluntary (Policyholder's) Report."

Field audits (also called physical audits) consist of examinations of the insured's books and records at the insured's premises. Field auditors must judge how long each audit will take and decide how to schedule audit appointments efficiently. For each audit, auditors must anticipate the classification and loss exposure concerns and must determine the premium base and any necessary allocations. They must then plan how to approach the audit, what records to use, where to locate the records, whom to contact, and which questions to ask. Planning greatly improves the efficiency and quality of the premium audit.

The decision about whether to conduct a field audit is influenced by legal requirements, premium size, the insured's operations, prior audit experience, nature of the policy, cost of auditing, geographical factors, and staffing requirements. For example, a workers compensation audit might be legally required. Advisory organization rules usually require audits of all policies involving a premium above a certain amount and might restrict audit waivers to no more than two in a row. Advisory organization rules also restrict classification changes, except under specific circumstances.

Some audit teams use predictive modeling in planning both mandatory and discretionary audits. The model can help with strategies for mandatory audits by scheduling the order of audits within contract terms to achieve the optimal effect on the insurer's earned premium. A wider variety of strategies is available for discretionary audits, including determining which insureds to audit and whether to conduct a survey, telephone, or field audit.[1]

Reviewing Operations

Before they look at the books, skilled premium auditors determine the nature of the operations insured; observe the nature of the operation and compare it to similar businesses, looking for classifications that might not be shown on the policy; assess management quality and cooperation to determine how to proceed with the audit; and report any significant information to the underwriting department. Additionally, auditors note organizational changes and are always alert to other clues about the nature and direction of the insured's business.

The process the premium auditor uses is also known as auditing the risk, rather than auditing the policy. By reviewing the operations, organization, and business processes, the premium auditor notes what exposures exist and reports any changes or additional exposures, both new and not previously identified, to the underwriter. The underwriter may request additional information from the insured or have a risk control representative inspect the operations and make recommendations. Newly identified exposures could result in the underwriter's deciding to cancel or not to renew the policy or to propose additional coverage options.

The insured often does not communicate changes or new operations to the producer or the insurer. Even if such information is reported, it might be incomplete, faulty, or otherwise insufficient for underwriting purposes. A premium auditor should supply the underwriting department with details about ownership and operations that are sufficient for rating purposes.

The auditor should also indicate the proper classifications for any new loss exposures. Other items of interest to the underwriting department include the experience of a new operation's management, the financing of the operation, the marketing of its product(s), the derivation of its income, and any information about unusual hazards.

The Insurance Services Office, Inc. (ISO) Premium Audit Advisory Service (PAAS) offers numerous guides and publications to assist premium auditors as they review insureds' operations. Classification guides, which are available in electronic format, provide detailed descriptions of all ISO general liability classifications and National Council on Compensation Insurance (NCCI) workers compensation classifications, as well as state exceptions to these classifications. PAAS also publishes a series of electronically distributed bulletins to provide current information and updates for premium auditors.

Determining Employment Relationships

After analyzing the insured's operations, premium auditors must determine those employees covered by the types of insurance for which premiums are based on payroll. These determinations are not always simple. Employees' payroll might constitute the premium base for both workers compensation and general liability policies, but the definition of "employee" is not necessarily the same for both coverages.

The premium basis of workers compensation policies includes the payroll of every person considered an employee under workers compensation laws. Therefore, the premium auditor must distinguish between employees and independent contractors (who are not covered under workers compensation). Moreover, applicable workers compensation laws vary by state. Many insureds do not realize that they must obtain certificates of insurance from their subcontractors; otherwise, premium auditors must include the subcontractors' payroll in the premium base.

Each state also has regulations regarding workers compensation for corporate officers, sole proprietors, and partners. Most states exclude sole proprietors and partners from workers compensation coverage, although coverage may be extended to them under the voluntary compensation endorsement. Some states allow exclusion of corporate officers, and all states have rules regarding the payroll amount to be used in determining premium for the corporate officers listed in the corporate charter.

Many of the state workers compensation **Test Audit** programs also review the claims filed under workers compensation policies to verify that the injured

Test Audit
An audit conducted by an insurance advisory organization or bureau to check the accuracy of insurers' premium audits.

employees were valid employees or under the insured's direction and control, subject to coverage, and that the employee's class assignment is proper. This process was developed to substantiate the ratemaking process as well as the experience modification calculation. As a result, many insurers require their premium auditors to review and verify the claims for each workers compensation audit.

Finding and Evaluating Books or Records

Premium auditors can examine all books or records of the insured related to insurance premiums. Auditors must decide, however, which records provide the necessary information most efficiently and reliably. They must evaluate the accounting system to determine record accuracy and to identify any alternative sources to confirm the data. The quality of the insured's accounting system and records can reflect the quality of the management. Poor quality of the accounting records will reduce the auditor's confidence in their reliability and accuracy, and the auditor should take special care to verify the information obtained from those records.

Premium pay (shift differential)

A payroll system that increases the regular hourly wage rate for the night shift or other special conditions.

In addition to meeting accounting standards, insureds should set up their records to take full advantage of insurance rules and requirements. Producers can assist in this process. For example, insureds should separate their payroll records by classification and arrange their records so that auditors can easily identify previously unreported classifications. Payroll records should identify the overtime **premium pay**, which is not typically included in the premium basis. Severance and per diem pay are excludable in all states. The basis of premium includes other forms of remuneration, such as vacation pay, tool allowances, bonuses, commissions, sick pay, the value of board and lodging, and other types of nonmonetary compensation.

The premium auditor's role includes determining what benefits and compensation are included or excluded in the workers compensation premium base for each, as well as what is included for the general liability premium base. The PAAS Chart of State Exceptions can assist the premium auditor in making these determinations. See the exhibit "Example of Premium Auditor's Determination of Excludable Benefits."

Example of Premium Auditor's Determination of Excludable Benefits

For nonunion construction companies that are required to pay prevailing wage rates, fringe benefits (additional benefits paid by employers in addition to wages), that are usually paid to the union at union companies, may be deducted for workers compensation premium calculation. These fringe benefits, however, would not be deducted for general liability premium calculations.

[DA06137]

For large accounts, auditors frequently visit a prospective insured before the insurer accepts the account or shortly after acceptance. During this pre-audit survey, the premium auditor confirms the information on the application. The auditor can also assist in setting up appropriate bookkeeping procedures.

Auditing the Books and Records

The auditor's job involves not only counting the loss exposures but also classifying them correctly. Classifying an account properly can be a complex task. Rating manuals contain numerous rules and exceptions, and insureds' operations change over time. Particularly when a policy does not generate premium sufficient to justify an on-site inspection or a risk control report, a premium audit can uncover any classification changes necessary to revise coverage.

The premium auditor's expertise with classification questions can help underwriters maintain the proper classifications of the insured's operations and align the **deposit premium** with the loss exposures covered by the policy. Proper classifications are important for two reasons:

Deposit premium
The amount the primary insurer pays the reinsurer pending the determination of the actual reinsurance premium owed.

- If the classification is incorrect and the rate on the policy is too high, the insured is being overcharged and consequently might be placed at a competitive disadvantage when bidding for jobs or pricing products. Such a situation could have serious legal ramifications if the insurer has acted negligently.

- If the classification is incorrect and the rate on the policy is too low, an account is less likely to be profitable for the insurer. Premiums might decrease, but claims and expenses do not decrease when an insured is classified incorrectly.

When premium auditors examine the insured's accounting records, they must decide how much evidence is sufficient to determine the loss exposures and classifications with a reasonable degree of confidence. If evidence is not readily available, they must balance the time and expense of obtaining it against its potential effect on the audit.

When the insured uses an automated accounting system, the premium auditor must evaluate the system's capabilities and the accounting process's reliability and must decide what output to accept for premium determination purposes and what additional data to request. If the output does not include all the necessary information, the premium auditor must determine the steps to take to obtain the information. Time spent at the beginning of the audit arranging for the computer to produce the necessary data can save significant overall auditing time.

Analyzing and Verifying Premium-Related Data

Once premium auditors have obtained the data necessary for calculating the premium, they must decide whether the data are reasonable. These are some of the questions the premium auditor might ask:

- Are the data logical?
- Do the data seem complete?
- Do the data reflect enough detail for the insured's operations?
- Are the data consistent with industry averages? For example, are the ratios of payroll to sales or labor to materials reasonable considering the nature of the insured's operation?
- Can deviations from expected amounts be explained?

Premium auditors should verify premium-related data against the general accounting records and reconcile any discrepancies. If a risk is misclassified, the auditor should attempt to correct the error and notify the underwriter as soon as possible when the error involves a lower-rated class. The NCCI *Basic Manual* rules require an insurer to add or change a classification at the audit or during the policy period if the addition or change results in a premium decrease. If the appropriate class is higher rated, the correction may not be applied until the next renewal. There are exceptions in some states, such as Delaware and Pennsylvania, which are independent from NCCI and use only authorized classes regardless of the effect on rate.

Usually, the rates for workers compensation policies are based on an exposure unit of $100 of payroll. However, there are other premium bases, such as per capita for domestic workers, "upset payroll" (factors based on wood production) for loggers, and per shift for taxi drivers. General liability policies may use a number of different premium bases, such as units, area, frontage, payroll, sales, costs, or gallons. Sales and payroll are usually based on exposure units of $1,000 or gallons of 10,000. Because they are not regulated by any bureaus, general liability policies may also be written on a composite-rated basis, using whatever was agreed when the policy was written. The most important fact is that all parties should understand the premium basis being used for all policies and how records should be maintained to develop the final premium.

Verification and analysis ensure that the audit is appropriate in relation to the insured's actual loss exposures and should confirm expectations developed in the audit planning and operations review. Considerable judgment is required of auditors when analyzing and verifying premium-related data to ensure the validity of the audit findings.

Reporting the Findings

No premium audit is complete until the results are submitted. The premium-related data should be recorded and the billing information clearly summarized so that the audit can be processed and billed immediately. In addition, premium auditors must show in their reports how they obtained the data to enable others to retrace their audit steps.

The premium auditor should succinctly describe the insured's operations and explain any deviations from the usual operations for that type of business. Premium auditors must also identify other significant information obtained during the audit and communicate it effectively to the appropriate people, such as underwriters.

IMPORTANCE OF ACCURATE PREMIUM AUDITS

A premium audit error can have lasting and far-reaching effects. It is important that premium audits be accurate for the sake of the insured, the insurer, and insurance rates.

The insurance mechanism relies on each insurer to measure and classify loss exposures correctly. Premium audit errors can distort the insurer's rating structure and cause significant problems for both the insured and the insurer.

Importance for the Insured

If audit errors slip past insurers and insureds undetected, insureds may end up paying the wrong premium for their insurance. Some insureds may pay more than their proportional share for the loss exposures covered; others may pay less than their share. Insureds who pay excessive insurance premiums are placed at a competitive disadvantage and can experience financial problems. Other insureds are placed at a competitive advantage; they might continue to operate despite unusually hazardous working conditions because audit errors can lead to a subsidy in the form of underpriced insurance coverage. Insureds can also experience problems if their financial planning decisions are based on erroneous past audits. A recent, more accurate audit can result in a substantial difference in premium.

Errors in audits also result in incorrect **experience modifications**. Experience rating bases an insured's current premium on the insured's past experience (exposure units and losses). If those exposure units and losses are incorrect, the experience modification is incorrect, and so are any future premiums. In addition, if an error in an audit is detected, the rating bureau cannot calculate the correct experience modification until it receives the correct audit data. Depending on whether the modification is higher or lower than the current premium, the insured is either overpaying or underpaying for insurance until the rating bureau calculates the final, correct modification.

Experience modification
A rate multiplier derived from the experience rating computation.

Errors in premium can also reduce insureds' confidence in premium auditors, in the insurer, and in the insurance mechanism in general. This loss of confidence can reduce insureds' cooperation with the insurer and their perception of insurance as an appropriate risk management option.

Importance for the Insurer

Incorrect or incomplete premium audits negatively affect the insurer in a variety of ways. Each audit error impairs the efficiency of an insurer's operations even when the errors are corrected. Timely and correct premium audits can significantly benefit the insurer's financial position, customer relations, operational efficiency, and collections.

Financial Position

The premium audit function significantly affects the insurer's balance sheet. A prompt and accurate premium audit can benefit the insurer's financial position in three ways:

- Accurate classification of loss exposures is important to ensure equitable and accurate insurance rates. Misclassifying hazardous business into a lower-rated classification results in loss of premium volume, which might make an otherwise profitable policy unprofitable. Similarly, the insurer could unintentionally insure additional loss exposures because of errors in a premium audit.

- Timely premium audits directly affect an insurer's cash flow management. The premium audit is the foundation of the premium collection process for auditable commercial businesses. Delay in audits and the resulting billing delay can have a negative effect on the insurer's cash flow. Even more important is the effect of increasing the deposit premium for a renewal policy based on the premium audit. Keeping the deposit premium at a realistic level provides additional cash at policy inception and prevents any later collection problems.

- Premium that has been developed by audit is fully earned and, consequently, has an immediate effect on profit and policyholders' surplus. Policyholders' surplus determines the insurer's ability to write new business.

The accuracy of premium audits is critical to an insurer's financial position. Repeated premium auditing errors can undermine the profitability of an insurer.

Customer Retention

Undetected premium audit errors can cause some insureds that are overcharged to switch to another insurer to obtain coverage at a lower premium. Insureds that are undercharged are likely to remain with their insurers. Consequently, the insurer loses premium volume, and underwriting results deteriorate.

Goodwill

When insureds are informed of errors in the premium audit, the insurer's image suffers. Insureds could lose confidence in the insurer's competence and might consider switching to another insurer. Insureds who continue their coverage with the insurer despite an incorrect premium audit might be less cooperative in claim investigations or in implementing risk control recommendations. Perhaps the biggest cost, however, is the marketing and underwriting effort expended to replace business that is lost because of premium audit errors.

Efficiency

In addition to the extra work required to replace lost business, incorrect or incomplete audits can cause extra work for several insurer departments. Redoing the audit drains the resources of the premium audit department. Other departments may become involved in attempting to explain the error and reassure the insured. Underwriters may have to correct records and may be drawn into controversy. The accounting department may have to adjust entries and issue a corrected bill. The marketing department may also have additional work to try to regain the insured's confidence.

Collections

Insureds are less likely to pay premium bills they suspect to be incorrect. For example, suppose that a prompt audit of a policy expiring December 31 leads to a January 23 billing for an additional premium of $14,000, payable within forty-five days. On March 25, the producer reports significant errors in the premium audit, requiring a re-audit of the insured's records. The insured refuses to pay until the errors are corrected. The re-audit, conducted on April 2, reveals a correct additional premium of $11,000. That amount is billed on April 20. The insured expresses doubts about the accuracy of the re-audit. Because the initial audit was incorrect, the insured has no confidence in the revised premium and continues to refuse to pay the bill. The insurer's premium collection department has to spend a great deal of time and effort with the producer and the insured before the billing issues are resolved.

Importance for Insurance Rates

An equitable insurance premium requires that similar loss exposures be priced similarly. Therefore, all insureds presenting similar loss exposures belong in the same rate classification. Lack of consistency in audit classification of loss exposures causes inequity not only in the level of the current premium paid but also in the resulting distortion of the classification loss results, which determine the future insurance rates.

Particularly in workers compensation insurance, in which a large volume of the business is audited, the results of premium audits substantially affect insurance rate equity and accuracy. No matter what ratemaking method is used to develop the rates for the various workers compensation classifications, the accuracy of the underlying classification rate can be no better than the data provided by the premium audits.

Premium audits affect the equity and accuracy of rates in two ways:

- Consistency and accuracy of classification determinations—If premium auditors in one area of a state consider a particular industrial class to be in classification X, while the premium auditors in another part of the state consider it to be in class Y, then the inconsistency distorts the resulting loss data from both classes and leads to inequitable rates for all insureds in the state for those two classes. Equally important in the ratemaking procedure is accurately classifying claims. By notifying the claim department when additional classifications are assigned and by reviewing the classification of past claims at the time of an audit, premium auditors can assist the claim department in accurately classifying losses as well as loss exposures.
- Measurement of the exposure unit base—An audit error, not in classification but in determining the exposure units, also distorts the rate structure. However, rate distortions resulting from misreporting of exposure units are likely to be minor relative to distortions resulting from misclassification. Either underreporting or overreporting the exposure units affects the rate for that class.

PREMIUM AUDITING CONTRIBUTIONS

Effective insurer management capitalizes on the opportunities for premium auditing to contribute to other insurer functions.

Premium auditors may be the only insurer representatives to meet insureds, see their operations, and review their financial records. This direct contact not only significantly influences the insured's impression of the insurer, but also provides a channel to communicate relevant information to other insurer functions, including these:

- Underwriting
- Marketing and sales
- Claims
- Risk control

Underwriting

Premium auditing contributes most directly to underwriting. Premium audit reports constitute a valuable source of information for underwriters, and effective cooperation between underwriters and premium auditors is essential to ensuring that existing accounts remain profitable. Premium auditing can contribute significant information to many areas of underwriting. These examples are some of the more important and common ones. The premium auditor should develop an underwriter's perspective of an account and use the premium auditor's report, or an acceptable substitute, to communicate the desired information.

A crucial responsibility of the premium auditing function is to classify insured exposures correctly. Often, the audit is the only source of information for proper classifications. Although underwriting must establish the classifications when the policy is issued, the information submitted is occasionally incomplete or inaccurate. Properly classifying an account can be complex, and the operations of insureds can change. The premium audit, conducted at the end of the policy period, can reveal any classification changes necessary to update the policy. Premium auditors notify underwriting of any discrepancies between the classifications on the policy and those classifications that are proper for the operation.

Another important contribution of the premium auditing function to underwriting is the identification of inadequate exposure estimates. When the insured exposure has been underestimated or incorrectly classified, an inadequate deposit premium for a renewal will result. Although the premium audit will help to develop the proper exposure, it is possible that additional premium charged after the end of the policy period will never be collected.

A premium audit report can also provide a comparison of anticipated loss exposures to actual loss exposures. In a well-managed insurance operation, anticipated loss exposures should not differ significantly from actual loss exposures. Unless the insured has changed its business operations, the premium audit assessment at the end of the policy period should correspond with the underwriting assessment at the beginning of the policy period.

For large accounts, advance audits—or pre-audit surveys—can be used to support underwriting decisions by ensuring that insurers issue policies based on correct business classifications and exposure bases. During these advance audits, the premium auditor can classify the operation, verify the estimated premium base, and observe the operation. These visits can also contribute to greater efficiency in conducting the audit at the end of the policy period.

New exposures are another important area in which underwriting information might be deficient. New exposures can result from a change in operations or a new venture. The insured often does not communicate such changes or new operations to the producer or the insurer, and, even if reported, the information might not be sufficient for underwriting purposes. Premium auditing can assist underwriting by identifying new exposures during review of the insured's operations. The premium auditor can also indicate the proper classifications for the new exposures.

Premium auditors are also in a position to provide underwriting with information on the desirability of an account. Premium auditors visit the insured's premises, meet with management, review business records, and observe the employees and operations. These activities provide valuable insight that can assist the underwriter in determining an account's desirability and can help guide underwriting decisions about the most appropriate coverage options and amounts.

While on the insured's premises, a premium auditor can become aware of physical, moral, and morale hazards. Examples of physical hazards include construction, hazardous materials, and poor safety or hygiene practices. Moral hazards can be indicated by questionable business practices or a failing business. Indicators of morale hazards include indifference to proper maintenance or poor financial records. Any of these hazards noted in the premium auditing process should be promptly communicated to underwriting.

Premium audits can also assist in underwriters' evaluation of producers. Comparing premium audit reports with producers' applications might reveal inaccurate or deficient information, which, when corrected, can improve future underwriting decisions.

Marketing and Sales

Premium auditing can also play a significant role in the area of marketing and sales. It is important that premium audits be conducted in a timely manner. A delay of a return premium due to an insured could adversely affect the insurer's future marketing efforts. The auditor's professional conduct and skill are also important factors in retaining an account. Auditors must often be able to convince an insured of the accuracy of an audit when the audit results in additional premium owed by the insured. This additional premium might significantly affect the profit margin and thus the insurer's decision about retaining the account.

During a premium audit, insureds may mention plans to expand operations or erect new buildings. They may be considering an employee benefits plan or business interruption insurance, or they may have gaps in present coverage observed during the audit. All of these situations may present new marketing opportunities for the insurer, and the auditor can benefit both the insured and insurer by referring the insured to marketing or sales.

Advance audits or pre-audit surveys can have significant public relations value. Insureds appreciate visits prior to the actual audit, especially if the auditor can help the insured with recordkeeping to take advantage of manual rules that might save the insured money.

Claims

Claims information can be valuable to premium auditing in the verification of employment classifications. However, premium auditing provides an even more valuable contribution to the claims function by verifying or correcting the classification codes assigned to an insured's claims. Various insurance regulators have emphasized the importance of improving claims-coding accuracy. This review also ensures that claims and premiums are matched in the same classifications, thus improving the credibility of rates.

Premium auditors can also verify that injured employees in workers compensation claims were employees of the insured when their injuries occurred. The premium audit can assist in verifying the earnings of injured employees. If there are any discrepancies in employment dates or wages, the premium auditor can notify claims.

Additionally, premium auditors can provide values of inventories, contractors' equipment lists and values, automotive equipment values, and other facts that are important to the claims function. For example, the claims department might request that the auditor review crime and fidelity losses during the premium audit. Although this line does not usually have auditable exposures, the premium audit can help determine that the amount claimed was accurately calculated from the insured's books and records.

Risk Control

Risk control also has an interest in the premium auditor's observations. Since risk control representatives cannot visit every insured, the premium auditor can serve as a source of information for risk control. The premium auditing process can contribute information about unsafe procedures or working conditions, observations of insureds' vehicles, and any hazards that provide opportunities for further risk control investigation and recommendations.

SUMMARY

The primary purpose of an insurer's risk control function is to evaluate loss exposures to assist with underwriting decisions and to help the insured prevent losses or reduce their effect. Insurers conduct risk control activities to achieve several goals: earn a profit, meet customer needs, comply with legal requirements, and fulfill their duty to society.

Insurers provide three types of risk control services: conducting physical surveys, performing risk analysis and improvement, and developing safety management programs.

Every insurer must decide what levels of risk control services to provide to which insureds. Several factors that influence insurers' decisions regarding the type and extent of risk control services they provide to insureds include the line of insurance, the size of commercial insureds, the types of loss exposures insured, and potential legal liability.

An insurer's risk control function is most effective when performed in cooperation with other insurer functions, such as underwriting, marketing and sales, premium auditing, and claims. Additionally, both insurers and insureds can benefit from risk control cooperation with external organizations, such as producers, reinsurers, OSHA and other regulatory agencies, law enforcement and codes enforcement agencies, and public safety entities.

Premium auditing plays an important role in the insurance mechanism because of the number and size of policies now written with a variable premium base. Premium audits are used to determine correct policy premiums; to meet regulatory requirements; to collect ratemaking data; to deter and detect fraud; to reinforce confidence of insureds; and to obtain additional information about the insured that may be useful to other insurer functional areas such as underwriting, marketing, and claims.

A systematic process for conducting premium audits is important to provide complete, accurate reports and to effectively use premium audit resources. The stages in the premium auditing process include planning, reviewing operations, determining employment relationships, finding and evaluating books or records, auditing the books and records, analyzing and verifying premium-related data, and reporting the findings.

Accurate premium audits are important for the financial positions of both the insured and the insurer, and the accuracy of audits has a significant effect on the insurer-insured relationship. It is also essential that premium audits be accurate for the insurance ratemaking process to determine equitable insurance rates.

Because premium auditors are often the only insurer representatives with direct insured contact, premium auditing can provide important contributions to other insurer functions, such as underwriting, marketing and sales, claims, and risk control.

ASSIGNMENT NOTE

1.   Sharon Carney, "Using Predictive Analytics to Optimize the Premium Audit Process," *ISO Review*, December 2009.

Direct Your Learning ▶▶

6

The Claim Function

Educational Objectives

After learning the content of this assignment, you should be able to:

▷ Explain how an insurer's claim function achieves its primary goals, provides valuable information to other departments, and interacts effectively with its outside contacts.

▷ Describe claims departments in terms of the following:

- How they can be structured
- The types and functions of claims personnel
- How their performance can be measured

▷ Explain how the following measures are used to ensure regulatory compliance:

- Claims guidelines, policies, and procedures
- Controls
- Supervisor and manager reviews
- Claims audits

▷ Summarize the activities performed in the claim handling process and the purpose of each.

▷ Describe the framework for coverage analysis and the information obtained by following it.

▷ Given a claim scenario, demonstrate how a claim representative can use the claim handling process and the framework for coverage analysis to resolve a claim.

The Claim Function

OVERVIEW OF THE CLAIM FUNCTION

An insurer's claim function must fulfill its responsibility to the insured and pay covered claims, while also supporting an insurer's financial goals.

Proper, efficient performance of the claim function greatly influences the insurer's success. When the two goals of the claim function are attained, success results. An outcome of the claim function is a vast amount of information that is essential to an insurer's marketing, underwriting, and actuarial departments. From the perspectives of the insured and the public, claim personnel are among the most visible of insurer employees; consequently, they must be able to interact effectively with individuals within and outside the insurance organization.

Claim Function Goals

When establishing goals for the claim function, senior management should recognize the effect the claim function has on both the insurance customer and the insurer itself. The claim function has these two primary goals:

- Complying with the contractual promise
- Supporting the insurer's financial goals

Complying With the Contractual Promise

The first goal of the claim function is to satisfy the insurer's obligations to the insured as set forth in the insurance policy. Following a loss, the promise of the insuring agreement to pay, defend, or indemnify in the event of a covered loss is fulfilled.

The insurer fulfills this promise by providing fair, prompt, and equitable service to the insured, either (1) directly, when the loss involves a first-party claim made by the insured against the insurer, or (2) indirectly, by handling a third-party claim made by someone against the insured to whom the insured might be liable.

From the insurer's perspective, claims are expected, and claim representatives must deal with them routinely. For the individuals involved, the loss occurrence and its consequences are not routine and can be overwhelming. Claim representatives, therefore, routinely deal with insureds and claimants in stressful situations. A claim representative should handle a claim in a way that treats all parties involved fairly and equitably, and do so in a timely manner. Were it not for insurance, administered through the claim handling process, recovery would be slow, inefficient, and difficult.

Supporting the Insurer's Financial Goals

The second goal of the claim function is supporting the insurer's financial goal. Achieving this goal is generally the responsibility of the marketing and underwriting departments. However, it would be shortsighted not to recognize the role of the claim function in helping insurers achieve an underwriting profit by controlling expenses and paying only legitimate claims.

By managing all claim function expenses, setting appropriate spending policies, and using appropriately priced providers and services, claim managers can help maintain an insurer's underwriting profit. Similarly, claim staff can avoid overspending on costs of handling claims, claim operations, or other expenses. Finally, by ensuring fair claim settlement, claim representatives prevent any unnecessary increase in the cost of insurance and subsequent reduction in the insurer's underwriting profit.

Insureds and other claimants are entitled to a fair claim settlement. By overcompensating an insured or a claimant, the insurer unnecessarily raises the cost of insurance for all of its insureds. Overpaid claims can lower insurer profits and result in higher policy premiums.

Conversely, underpaid claims can result in dissatisfied insureds, litigation, or regulatory oversight. Insureds and claimants who believe they are being treated fairly are likely to accept the claim representative's settlement offer, but if insureds and claimants are treated unfairly, they might sue the insurer or file a complaint with their state insurance department. Mishandled claims can lead to litigation or regulatory oversight, both of which erode goodwill and generate increased insurer expenses, thereby reducing the insurer's profitability.

An insurer's success in achieving its financial goal is reflected in its reputation for providing the service promised. A reputation for resisting legitimate claims can undermine the effectiveness of insurer advertisements or its goodwill earned over the years. Consequently, the two goals of the claim function work together to help bring about a profitable insurance operation.

Claim Information Users

The claim function provides valuable information to other insurer departments. The three primary recipients of claim information are the marketing, underwriting, and actuarial departments.

Marketing

The marketing department needs information about customer satisfaction, timeliness of settlements, and other variables that assist in marketing the insurance product. The marketing department recognizes that the other services the insurer performs for the insured are forgotten quickly if the insurer fails to perform well after a loss occurrence.

Many insurers that market commercial policies have developed "niche" products to address the needs of specific types of insureds. The intent of these insurers is to become the recognized expert in certain business classes, providing a product and service that cannot easily be equaled elsewhere. The claim handling process can be a source of new coverage ideas and product innovations for niche marketers.

Producers must be prepared to explain any premium changes and changes to policy provisions to their insureds. Producers must have insured loss information to prepare renewal policies properly because many commercial policies are subject to rating plans that affect the policy premium, based partly on the insured's loss experience. In personal insurance, personal auto policies might be surcharged when property damage claims are paid during the policy year. Additionally, claim personnel often inform producers of court rulings that affect the insurer's loss exposures or pricing, such as interpretations of policy exclusions or application of limits.

Underwriting

The insurance business operates effectively if underwriters accept loss exposures that are likely to experience only the types and amounts of losses anticipated in the insurance rates. If underwriters accept loss exposures that experience more losses than anticipated, the rates charged by the insurer will be inadequate, and the insurer could become financially insolvent. Claim personnel help underwriters in this regard by ensuring that claims are paid fairly and according to the policy. Proper, consistent, and efficient claim handling enables underwriters to evaluate, select, and appropriately price loss exposures based on consistent claim costs.

When claim representatives inspect accident scenes in homes or at work sites as part of the claim investigation, they sometimes notice loss exposure characteristics, either negative or positive, that were not readily apparent in the insurance application. When claim representatives report such findings to the underwriter, the underwriter may adjust the premium or take other actions to accommodate the difference in the exposure. For example, based on information from the claim representative, the underwriter may cancel coverage or renew it only if the insured implements corrective measures. Alternatively, the underwriter may grant a premium credit based on a claim representative's report of an above-average loss exposure.

A number of similar claims may also alert underwriting management to a problem for a particular type or class of insured. These claims might be the result of new processes or technologies being used by the class of insureds as a whole. For example, some roofing contractors might have tried to speed the process of replacing composite roofs by moving the tar smelter to the roof of the structure being repaired. This practice might have caused a number of fire losses. An adverse court ruling could also cause the loss experience of a class of business to deteriorate or could increase the number of claims presented.

Claim representatives' interaction with underwriters is not limited to providing loss information. Although claim personnel are typically the final authority on coverage interpretation, underwriters can provide insight into the intentions of the two parties to the insurance policy using the insurance application and producer's notes, which may affect coverage interpretation. When claim representatives explain their interpretations of coverage to underwriters, the underwriters can reassess coverage forms and endorsements and make any needed changes to clarify the coverages.

Actuarial

Actuaries need accurate information not only on losses that have been paid but also on losses that have occurred and are reserved for payment, collectively called incurred losses. Loss reserves can be increased or decreased as the claim develops, and reserve change reports help actuaries more accurately predict loss development. Incurred loss information helps actuaries establish reserves for incurred but not reported (IBNR) losses and project the development of open claims for which the reserves might change substantially before the claim is finally settled.

In addition to incurred loss information, actuaries need accurate information on loss adjusting expenses and recoverable amounts associated with claims, such as salvage and subrogation, any ceded reinsurance recoverable, and deductibles (when the insurer pays an entire claim and then asks the insured to reimburse the deductible amount).

All of the claim information that actuaries collect from claim personnel must be accurately represented through appropriate reserving methods in the insurer's financial statements. Actuaries must update these statements for reporting at various times during the year. When claim payments are recorded accurately and realistic reserves are set in the insurer's claim processing system, then the raw data that actuaries use to develop rates will be accurate and the rates will reflect the insurer's loss experience.

Claim Department Contacts

Other than the producer, claim department personnel are the contacts within the insurer who are most visible to the public. Therefore, the claim department must interact effectively with outside contacts, such as the public, lawyers, and state regulators.

The Public

Although many insurers have a public relations department that handles advertising, the insurer's public image is determined largely by the claim department's behavior.

Because the claim representative is an insured's and a claimant's primary contact with the insurer, claim service significantly affects an insured's or a claimant's (referred to as "claimant" through the remainder of this section) satisfaction with an insurer. The claim representative's skill at communicating directly with claimants influences their satisfaction with the insurer.

Claim representatives' first contact with a claimant occurs after the claimant has sustained a loss. Most claimants suffer some type of emotional reaction to a loss, which may include anger, depression, frustration, or hopelessness. Claim representatives must empathize with claimants to interact effectively with them.

Most claimants' knowledge of insurance is less sophisticated than that of an insurance professional. Claim representatives must be prepared to explain the policy's claim provisions to the claimant as those provisions apply to the claimant's property damage or injury. A well-prepared, professional claim representative who empathizes with the claimant will gain the claimant's confidence and increase the likelihood of reaching a mutually agreeable settlement.

Claim representatives must recognize that claim handling requires a high degree of integrity, involving honesty and diplomacy. If the claim representative is concerned that coverage will not apply to the damage or injury, he or she must explain those concerns to the claimant and preserve the insurer's right to deny a claim that is not covered. Even when a claim is denied, a claim representative who carefully explains the issues and empathizes with the claimant might be able to avoid costly litigation.

Technological improvements have allowed many insurers to improve the quality and speed of their claim service. Starting with the growth of cell phones and the Internet and progressing to improvements in wireless technologies, claim departments have found new ways to streamline the claim process and improve customer satisfaction.

Technology facilitates communications among field personnel, regional or local claim offices, claimants, vendors, and service providers. In catastrophe losses, floods, tornadoes, hurricanes, and earthquakes can cause significant damage to the infrastructure used for traditional communication systems. Satellite transmissions and other modern communication devices used in wireless technology may overcome these problems to enable continued electronic communications for claim personnel and, ultimately, faster and better customer service for claimants when they need it most.

Lawyers

For some types of claims and in certain areas of the United States, claimants are more likely to hire lawyers, often leading to costly litigation. Although legal representation can result in a higher payment by the insurer, representation does not necessarily result in higher settlements for claimants, because claimants must pay expenses and legal fees from settlements. Legal representation also does not guarantee a faster settlement. Even if litigation ensues, claim representatives should continue to interact in a cordial, professional manner with claimants' lawyers.

When an insurer needs a lawyer either to defend the insured or to defend itself, it will typically hire a lawyer from the jurisdiction in which the claim is submitted. The lawyer will provide advice regarding specific losses and legal issues. Claim representatives will assist the insurer's lawyers as needed by sharing claim details and assembling information that supports the insurer's legal position.

State Regulators

State insurance regulators monitor insurers' activities in the claim handling process. Regulators exercise controls by licensing claim representatives, investigating consumer complaints, and performing market conduct investigations. Enforcement is usually handled through the Unfair Claims Settlement Practices Act or similar legislation.

Not all states currently license claim representatives, and no standard procedure or uniform regulation exists for those that do. Some states require licensure only for independent adjusters, who work for many insurers, or for public adjusters, who represent insureds in first-party claims against insurers. Other states require staff claim representatives to be licensed.

State insurance regulators also handle customer complaints made against an insurer. Most states have a specific time limit within which the insurer must answer or act on inquiries from the insurance department. Failure to respond can result in expensive fines and even in the loss of the claim representative's—or his or her employer's—license.

Insurance regulators periodically perform market conduct investigations either as part of their normal audit of insurer activities or in response to specific complaints. The typical market conduct audit includes more than just claim practices; it audits all departments that interact directly with insureds and claimants.

CLAIMS DEPARTMENT STRUCTURE, PERSONNEL, AND PERFORMANCE

Because the claim function is crucial to an insurer's promise to pay covered losses, an insurer's claim department must operate efficiently.

The loss payments, expenses, and other information generated by the claim department are essential to marketing, underwriting, and pricing insurance products. Claims personnel are among the most visible of insurer employees to insureds and the public and therefore must be able to interact well with a variety of people. Examining the structure, personnel, and performance of an insurer's claim department helps explain how it operates.

Claims Department Structure

An insurer's claims department can be organized in several different ways. A sample departmental structure can illustrate the various claim positions within the department. See the exhibit "Claims Department Organization Chart."

Usually, a senior claim officer heads the claims department and reports to the chief executive officer, the chief financial officer, or the chief underwriting officer. The senior claim officer may have a staff located in the same office. This staff is often called the home-office claims department. Within the home-office claims department, any number of technical and management specialists can provide advice and assistance to any remote claim offices and claim representatives.

The senior claims officer may have several claim offices or branches country-wide or worldwide. Staff from remote claim offices can all report directly to the home-office claims department, or regional/divisional claims officers may oversee the territory. Regional claims officers may have one or more branch offices reporting to them. Each branch office may have a claims manager, one or more claims supervisors, and a staff of claims representatives. Similar department structures are adopted by **third-party administrators (TPAs)**.

Claims Personnel

A claims representative (a generic title that refers to all who adjust claims, except for public adjusters) fulfills the promise to pay the insured or to pay on behalf of the insured by handling a claim when a loss occurs. People who handle claims may be staff claim representatives, independent adjusters, employees of TPAs, or producers who sell policies to insureds. In addition, public adjusters also handle claims by representing the interests of insureds to the insurer.

Third-party administrator (TPA)
An organization that provides administrative services associated with risk financing and insurance.

Claims Department Organization Chart

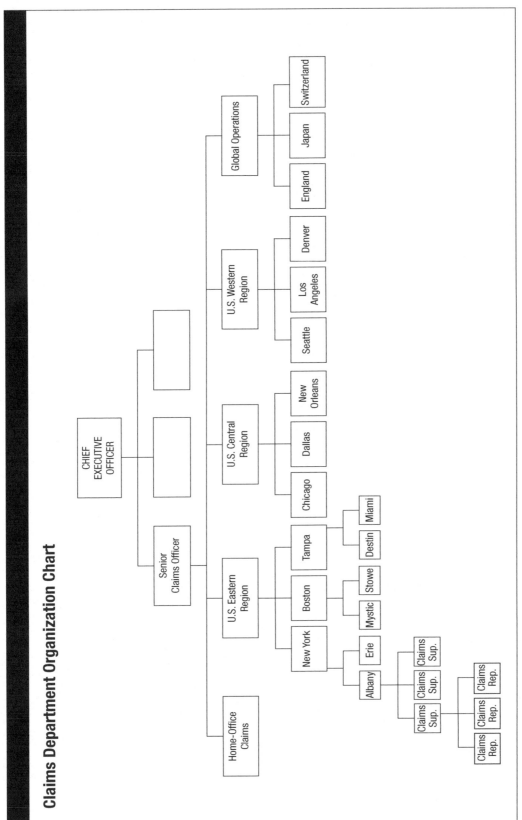

[DA02262]

Staff Claims Representatives

Staff claims representatives are employees of an insurer and handle most claims. They may include inside claims representatives, who handle claims exclusively from the insurer's office, and field claims representatives, who handle claims both inside and outside the office. Field claims representatives, also called outside claims representatives, handle claims that require such tasks as investigating the scene of the loss; meeting with insureds, claimants, lawyers, and others involved in the loss; and inspecting damage. Staff claims representatives usually work from branch or regional offices rather than at the insurer's home office. If the branch or region covers a large territory, the insurer may set up claims offices in areas away from the branch office to enable the claim representative to serve insureds efficiently.

Independent Adjusters

Certain insurers may not find it economically feasible to set up claim offices in every state in which insureds are located. Insurers may contract with **independent adjusters** to handle claims in strategic locations.

Some insurers use independent adjusters for all field claims work. These insurers employ claims personnel in their home office or branch offices to monitor claims progress and settle claims but use independent adjusters to handle all the field work.

Some insurers hire independent adjusters when their staff claims representatives are too busy to handle all claims themselves. For example, staff claims representatives may need assistance when a disaster strikes to handle the large number of claims quickly enough to satisfy the insurer and its insureds. Insurers may also use independent adjusters to meet desired service levels or when special skills are needed. For example, some independent adjusters are experts in highly specialized fields, such as investigating aircraft accidents.

Some independent adjusters are self-employed, but many work for adjusting firms that range in size from one small office with a few adjusters to national firms with many offices employing hundreds of adjusters.

Independent adjuster
An independent claims representative who handles claims for insurers for a fee.

Third-Party Administrators

Businesses that choose to self-insure do not use agents, underwriters, or other typical insurer personnel. However, they do need personnel to handle the losses that arise. Self-insured businesses can employ their own claims representatives or contract with TPAs, who handle claims, keep claims records, and perform statistical analyses. TPAs are often associated with large independent adjusting firms or with subsidiaries of insurance companies. Many property-casualty insurers have established subsidiary companies that serve as TPAs.

Producers

The term "producer" is used to describe anyone who sells insurance. This can include agents, brokers, insurer employees, or intermediaries. Insurers may give some producers the authority to pay claims up to a certain amount, such as $2,500. Those producers can issue claims payments, called drafts, directly to insureds for covered claims, thus reducing the time an insured waits for payment. In this capacity, producers function much like inside claims representatives.

Public Adjusters

Public adjuster

An outside organization or person hired by an insured to represent the insured in a claim in exchange for a fee.

If a claim is complex, or if settlement negotiations are not progressing satisfactorily with the insurer, the insured may hire a **public adjuster** to protect his or her interests. Some states have statutes that govern the services public adjusters can provide. In general, the public adjuster prepares the insured's claim and negotiates the settlement with the staff claims representative or independent adjuster. The insured, in turn, pays the public adjuster's fee, which is usually a percentage of the settlement.

Claims Performance Measures

Because a claims department staff can be diverse and may be spread over a wide geographic area, insurers face special issues in evaluating and measuring their performance. Insurers are businesses and, as such, must make a profit to survive. Claims departments play a crucial role in insurer profitability by paying fair amounts for legitimate claims and by providing accurate, reliable, and consistent ratemaking data. Because fair claims payment does not conflict with insurer profit goals, an insurer measures its claim and underwriting departments' performance using a loss ratio, which is a profitability measure. The quality of a claims department's performance can be measured using best practices, claims audits, and customer satisfaction.

Profitability Measures

A loss ratio is one of the most commonly used measures for evaluating an insurer's financial well-being. It measures losses and loss adjustment expenses against earned premiums and reflects the percentage of premiums being consumed by losses. An increasing loss ratio could indicate that the insurer is improperly performing the claims function. Increasing losses could also mean that underwriting failed to select above-average loss exposures or that the actuarial department failed to price the insurer's products correctly.

When an insurer's loss ratio increases, the claims department, along with other insurer functions, is pressured to reduce expenses. Claim representatives could quickly reduce loss adjusting expenses in the short term by offering insureds and claimants the settlement demanded rather than the settlement deserved. However, to reduce loss adjusting expenses in the long term, inflated settlement demands should be resisted; researched; negotiated; and, if necessary, litigated. Loss adjustment expenses can also be reduced by following claims procedures. By managing losses and controlling expenses associated with handling losses, the claims department plays an important role in an insurer's profitability.

Apply Your Knowledge

An insurer's chief executive officer is analyzing the organization's profitability. He observes that in 20X0, the insurer's loss ratio was 0.67, while, in 20X1, the insurer's loss ratio was 0.70. In 20X2, the loss ratio was 0.75. Further analysis indicates that the actuarial department is pricing the insurer's products correctly and that the underwriting department was selecting above-average loss exposures. This leads the CEO to focus on the claims department as potentially undermining the organization's profitability. Which of the following are measures that the claims department could employ in an attempt to reduce loss adjusting expenses in the long term?

a. Resisting; researching; negotiating; and, if necessary, litigating inflated settlement demands.

b. Following claims procedures.

c. Offering insureds and claimants the settlement demanded rather than the settlement deserved.

d. None of these measures will reduce loss adjusting expenses.

Feedback: a. and b. Offering insureds and claimants the settlement demanded rather than the settlement deserved reduces loss adjusting expenses in the short term, while the first two choices reduce adjusting expenses in the long term.

Quality Measures

Three of the more frequently used methods of evaluating a claims department's performance are best practices, claim audits, and customer satisfaction.

In the context of a claims department, the term "best practices" usually refers to a system of identified internal practices that produce superior performance. Best practices are usually shared with every claim representative. An insurer can create best practices by studying its own performance or the performance of similar successful insurers.

Claims department best practices are often based on legal requirements specified by regulators, legislators, and courts. For example, a claims department may have a best practice that states "Every claim will be acknowledged within twenty-four hours." This time frame may have been selected because of a regulation, law, or court decision that requires insurers to acknowledge a claim within twenty-four hours of receipt.

Insurers use claims audits to ensure compliance with best practices and to gather statistical information on claims. A claims audit is performed by evaluating the information in a number of open and closed claim files. Claims audits can be performed by the claims staff who work on the files (called a self-audit), or they can be performed by claims representatives from other offices or by a team from the home office. Claims audits usually evaluate both quantitative and qualitative factors. See the exhibit "Quantitative and Qualitative Audit Factors."

Quantitative and Qualitative Audit Factors

Quantitative	Qualitative
Timeliness of reports	Realistic reserving
Timeliness of reserving	Accurate evaluation of insured's liability
Timeliness of payments	Follow-up on subrogation opportunity
Number of files opened each month	Litigation cost management
Number of files closed each month	Proper releases taken
Number of files reopened each month	Correct coverage evaluation
Percentage of recovery from subrogation	Good negotiation skills
Average claim settlement value by claims type	Thorough investigations
Percentage of claims entering litigation	
Percentage of cases going to trial	
Accuracy of data entry	

[DA02267]

The quality of a claims department's performance is also measured by customer satisfaction. Claims supervisors and managers monitor correspondence they receive about the performance of individual claim representatives. While compliments are usually acknowledged, supervisors or managers must respond to complaints, and most claim departments have procedures for doing so. Complaints may come directly from the insured, claimant, or vendor, or they can be submitted by a state insurance department on behalf of an insured, a claimant, or a vendor.

However received, the complaint must be investigated by management and responded to in a timely manner. Complaints about issues such as not receiving a return phone call may indicate legitimate service issues. Other complaints can simply indicate dissatisfaction with an otherwise-valid claim settlement. Review of complaints received in a claim office can show whether problems exist with a particular claims representative, supervisor, or manager.

MEASURES USED TO ENSURE REGULATORY COMPLIANCE

Insurers institute compliance measures, which are various guidelines that insurers ask personnel to use or other actions that they take to ensure that legal and regulatory requirements are met and to promote good-faith claims handling practices.

Compliance measures include these:

- Claims guidelines, policies, and procedures
- Controls, such as reports, access security, authority levels, and tracking
- Supervisor and manager reviews
- Claims audits

A combination of compliance measures helps insurers enforce good-faith claims handling; encourages claims personnel to provide complete and accurate information to management, producers, reinsurers, lawyers, insureds, claimants, and others; and makes the insurer's operation run efficiently and with sound expense management.

Claims Guidelines, Policies, and Procedures

Some insurers have claims guidelines, which are policies and procedures that serve as a compliance measure. **Claims guidelines** specify how certain claims handling tasks should be performed by setting policies and procedures for claims handling. For example, claims guidelines might specify when an independent adjuster should be assigned to a claim. Such a guideline helps ensure that the insurer pays an independent adjuster only when necessary and helps claims managers control claims department expenses so that they can help meet corporate goals. A sample page from a hypothetical insurer's claims guidelines can be instructive. See the exhibit "Claims Guidelines Sample Page."

Steps for performing some tasks can be clearly specified in claims guidelines so that claims personnel ensure that information is accurate and that claims are handled properly and in good faith. Claims departments can use guidelines in training new claims personnel because they provide instruction for performing tasks properly. They are also useful as a reference for performing infrequent tasks or when one employee must perform another employee's duties because of vacation, illness, or another absence.

Claims guidelines

A set of guidelines and instructions that specify how certain claims handling tasks should be performed by setting policies and procedures for claim handling.

Claims Guidelines Sample Page

WORTHY INSURANCE COMPANY CLAIMS GUIDELINES

Subject:	Activity Log
Category:	File Documentation
Purpose:	The activity log is a chronological record of file development that describes the activities and analysis on the claim file.
Procedure:	The activity log form should be completed as events occur and include the day, month, year, time, and person making notes. The activity log should be a brief notation of file activities and analysis. Detailed explanations may appear in other documents and file reports.
Responsibility:	Anyone who conducts activity on the file must comply with this procedure.

[DA03173]

Claims guidelines can be in electronic or paper form. Some electronic guidelines give specific online directions for handling the file to ensure that all pertinent claim issues are addressed.

Claims guidelines, policies, and procedures can also be useful when an insurer must defend a bad-faith lawsuit. Evidence that good-faith claims handling procedures were prescribed and followed demonstrates that the insurer takes measures to help guarantee good-faith claims handling. When claims personnel consistently follow company policies and procedures, insureds and claimants are less likely to find fault with the claims handling.

Diary, or suspense

A system to remind claims personnel to perform a particular task on a claim.

Supervisors and managers often use diaries as reminders to review claim files or perform another activity. Claims representatives usually have many claims to handle at the same time; therefore, a reminder system is essential to helping them handle all of them properly. A **diary, or suspense**, is a system to remind claims personnel to perform a particular task on a claim. A diary might be as simple as a note on the calendar to call an insured about her claim and a note in the file of that date. An automated diary system might send a computer message at set intervals to remind the claims representative to review the file or reserves; to make a payment; to contact the insured, the claimant, or witnesses; or to request additional information from service providers. See the exhibit "Sample Automated Diary."

A claims information system might set an automatic diary entry when a claim is first reported. For example, an automatic diary of seven days might be set for each new claim. Claims representatives might modify that date, depending on the claim and their investigation plans.

Sample Automated Diary

Claim # 12345678

Pol # 78-02-3359   **Ins** Brown, Jackie   **DOL** 12/12/X0   **TOL** Collision

Diary 12/14/X1   **Claims rep** Stone   **Date set** 12/12/X1

Notes: Insured is to call today. Follow up if no response. Need vehicle location for inspection.

[DA03174]

An **activity log** is a record of all the activities and analyses that occur regarding a particular claim. See the exhibit "Sample Activity Log."

Activity log
A record of all the activities and analyses that occur while handling a claim.

Sample Activity Log

Activity Log

Claim # 12345678

Date	Activity	Diary
12/12/X1	Rec'd claim from home office. Called insured— no answer. Left msg on answering machine.	12/14/X1
12/14/X1	No response from Mrs. Darlington. Called again. Spoke with 16-yr.-old daughter. She will have her mother (the insured) call me tomorrow.	12/15/X1
12/15/X1	Spoke with insured. Took recorded statement. Mrs. Darlington backed out of her driveway and hit the neighbor's mailbox across the street, which belongs to Mr. Bounds, of 1220 NW 84th Street, Anytown, PA 19344. His evening phone number is 111-123-4567. The mailbox was mounted on a concrete post that suffered no damage, and Mr. Bounds told Mrs. Darlington that he would not file an insurance claim for damages. Mrs. Darlington's car is at Sam's Auto Repair. Arranged for inspection. Explained claims process to Mrs. Darlington. Phoned Mr. Bounds to verify that his mailbox was not damaged and that he will not file a claim.	12/20/X1
12/20/X1	Estimates rec'd and differences analyzed to ensure fair comparison. Called Mrs. Darlington and reviewed repair estimate with her. Agreed on settlement amount. Processed payment today. Closed file.	

[DA03175]

Because claims representatives handle a large volume of claims, the activity log is a crucial record of activity that has occurred on each claim. Claims representatives who rely on their memories to recall all the activity on a claim are likely to forget important information. A claim file should speak for itself so that anyone reading the activity log and other documents knows exactly what has occurred. Claims representatives should carefully document every activity on a claim. If insureds or claimants develop misunderstandings during the claims process, the claims representative can refer to entries in the activity log to remind himself or herself of previous conversations or other communications.

Many insurers use a team approach to claims handling and offer extended hours to provide better service to insureds and claimants. As a result, one claims representative might take an insured's statement during the day shift, and another claims representative might answer a question from the same insured during the evening shift. Without an accurate, complete activity log, the two claims representatives might give contradictory or confusing information to the insured. Especially when more than one claims representative might work on a claim, the activity log is crucial.

Activity logs are also useful in claims audits. Producers are sometimes interested in the details of how a claim was handled, and claims personnel can review activity logs to provide those details.

Controls

Claims departments can use various electronic controls as compliance measures, such as claims reports, access security, authority levels, and claims information tracking systems.

Most insurers' claims information systems can be used to generate periodic claims reports. Claims representatives, supervisors, and managers review those reports to ensure that claims have been entered correctly. Reports might include information such as this:

- Claims with reserves above a specified amount
- Claims assigned to independent adjusters
- Claims in litigation
- Claims closed by agents
- Claims with reserve changes larger than a specified amount
- Claims closed without payment by a claims representative

Reports can help insurer personnel monitor claims practices by indicating possible errors. For example, managers might review a daily report listing all claims with reserves above $100,000. If claims personnel mistakenly entered a $10,000 reserve as a $100,000 reserve, the daily report would alert managers to the error. The error could then be corrected before it affected reports produced for parties outside the insurer and agents' commission calculations.

Reports of claims assigned to independent adjusters can help an insurer meet corporate goals for expense management. If the reports indicate that many claims are assigned to independent adjusters, the insurer can examine the reasons for those assignments and determine whether a staff claims representative should be assigned to a different territory to reduce independent adjusting expenses. Similarly, claims in litigation can be reviewed to ensure that legal expenses are managed properly.

Access security refers to an individual's ability to review, enter, and change information in a claims information system. These systems limit access to claims information using three methods.

The first method of access security requires a person attempting to access claims information to enter a password maintained by the information systems department. The system will deny access to any person who does not have the password, thereby preventing unauthorized persons from reviewing or modifying claims information.

The second method of access security restricts access to certain data in the claims information system to managers only. For example, information provided by a lawyer might be considered highly confidential. Therefore, support staff would not be allowed to access that portion of the electronic claim file.

The third method of access security prevents unauthorized individuals from changing crucial information in the claims information system, such as reserve amounts or claims codes, and can prevent them from requesting payments. For example, a newly hired support person might be prohibited from requesting claim payments until that person has completed appropriate training.

These three methods of access security dictate which claims personnel can review or modify claim information. Authority levels restrict claims personnel from making changes to claims information that exceed their authority and are described next.

Authority levels refer to the reserve amounts and payment amounts that claims personnel are allowed to set and make. Claim information systems might be designed to allow different authority levels for different types of employees. For example, experienced personnel might be allowed to set reserves and request payments for larger amounts than inexperienced personnel. Supervisors might have an authority level that is higher than that for experienced claims personnel.

Authority levels help control claims in several ways. First, if a claim requires high reserves or payments, authority levels ensure that experienced, qualified personnel handle those reserves or payments. Second, if inexperienced claims personnel enter a reserve amount or payment inaccurately and the inaccurate amount exceeds their authority level, the claims system prevents the error.

While authority levels prevent claims personnel from exceeding their authority to review and modify claims information, claims information tracking

Access security
A security setting that controls an individual computer user's ability to review, enter, and change information in a claims information system.

Authority level
A designated dollar amount assigned to claims personnel to limit the reserve amounts they can set and the payment amounts they can make.

systems capture details of changes that were made to prevent fraud and help identify claims personnel training needs.

Claims information tracking systems can be designed to automatically capture information such as the date a reserve was changed, the name of the individual who made the change, the date a payment was requested, and the name of the individual who made the request. Such information is stored in the claims information system and cannot be altered. Tracking systems discourage fraud and are useful for identifying training needs. For example, if claims personnel often make unintentional errors, tracking systems can identify which employees might need additional training.

Supervisor and Manager Reviews

In addition to the various claims guidelines and controls, supervisor and manager reviews are another type of compliance measure that insurers can use. Supervisors and managers use diary systems as reminders to review claims. During a review, they might check the claims codes, reserves, and payments entered for the claim. They might review the claims representative's reports to the file; the activity log; and other file documentation, such as police reports, physician reports, and damage estimates. During the review, supervisors and managers might detect errors that can be corrected.

The review also allows supervisors and managers to coach claims representatives on how to handle claims, on additional investigation that might be needed, and on negotiation or settlement approaches. Supervisor and manager reviews are essential to helping claims personnel learn how to improve job performance.

Claims Audits

Claims audit

A review of claim files to examine the technical details of claim settlements; ensure that claims procedures are followed; and verify that appropriate, thorough documentation is included.

Internal claims audit

A review of claim files conducted by an insurer's staff to examine the technical details of claim settlements; ensure that claims procedures are followed; and verify that appropriate, thorough documentation is included.

Most insurers use claims audits as a type of compliance measure. **Claims audits** are a review of claim files, both paper and electronic, to ensure that claims are being handled properly. Claims audits can be conducted by an insurer's internal personnel or by others.

An **internal claims audit** is a review of claim files conducted by an insurer's staff to examine the technical details of claim settlements; ensure that claims procedures are followed; and verify that appropriate, thorough documentation is included. Generally, internal claims audits are conducted by claims personnel, but they might also be conducted by personnel from other departments, such as accounting, underwriting, or human resources and training.

Internal claims audits can be conducted by managers, supervisors, technical support staff, or other claims representatives. The reason for the audit determines which claim files are audited. For example, to ensure that claims representatives comply with procedures and policies, a random sample of claim files might be appropriate as a routine, regularly scheduled audit. If a specific catastrophe generated many claims complaints, managers might audit claims only from that catastrophe. A supervisor might audit a specific claims representative's claims to prepare for a performance review. Technical support staff might audit a sample of files involving only subrogated or only litigated claims.

An actuary might review claim files to examine how reserves are set, how frequently they are changed, and how accurate the initial reserves were compared to the final settlement amount. If reserves are habitually lower than the amount of the final claim settlement, the actuary might increase total reserves beyond the amounts set by the claims department. Such a change would help ensure that total reserves for all claims are adequate to maintain the insurer's financial condition.

The underwriting department might audit claim files to see the kinds of claims that are being reported; how much is being paid for those claims; and what, if any, coverage or underwriting standards should be changed to address those claims. For example, if an underwriter notices many claims for damage from sewer backup, the underwriter might decide that underwriting standards should be made more strict for properties likely to experience sewer backup.

Human resources and training might audit claim files to identify training needs for the claims department. For example, a trainer might discover that a claims code for a particular kind of loss is often entered incorrectly. Based on that finding, the trainer might develop a short class to teach support staff about that type of loss and how to code it correctly.

Internal claims audits might also be conducted to ensure that employee fraud is not occurring. In addition, if employees know that claims will be audited, it might deter them from committing fraud.

External claims audits are claim file reviews conducted by someone other than an insurer's own employees. External claims audits are conducted to review overall claims handling practices; to review reserves and other technical details of claim settlements; to investigate consumer complaints; to ensure that claims procedures were followed; and to verify that appropriate, thorough documentation was included.

External claims audit
A review of claim files conducted by organizations other than the insurer that involves reviewing overall claims handling practices; reviewing reserves and other technical details of claim settlements; investigating consumer complaints; ensuring that claims procedures were followed; and verifying that appropriate, thorough documentation was included.

State insurance regulators might conduct a claims audit to review an insurer's claims handling practices. The purpose of the review is to determine whether an insurer is violating any unfair claim settlement practices acts or laws and whether the insurer routinely engages in any illegal claims handling practices.

Many state insurance regulators are interested in insurers' reserving practices because adequate reserves are crucial to insurers' financial condition. Regulators can evaluate reserves based on an insurer's annual financial statement. However, if regulators need additional information, they might conduct a claims audit to review reserves and reserving practices. Regulators might find that an insurer routinely sets claims reserves lower than necessary and then increases the reserves in steps. On the other hand, regulators might find that an insurer routinely sets claims reserves higher than necessary so that the insurer owes fewer taxes. (Insurers do not pay taxes on premiums they have not yet earned.) Regulators would take action to correct either of these situations.

Insurance advisory organizations such as Insurance Services Office, Inc. (ISO) and the American Association of Insurance Services (AAIS) are also interested in insurers' reserves but rarely conduct a claim audit to study reserves or reserving practices. Instead, such organizations rely on the information provided in insurers' Annual Statements.

ACTIVITIES IN THE CLAIM HANDLING PROCESS

To provide consistent and effective claim handling, claim representatives follow a systematic process that helps ensure that claims are handled in a manner that conforms to legal and ethical standards.

Claim representatives are responsible for thoroughly investigating claims to determine how coverage applies. However, investigation is only one activity in the claim handling process. To ensure that every claim is handled in good faith from beginning to end, claim representatives must follow a systematic claim handling process.

The claim handling process consists of a series of typical activities. These activities are not always sequential; some can be performed concurrently, and others may need to be repeated as new facts are discovered. Although some claims may require unique treatment, the same basic activities are performed with every claim.

These activities provide a framework for handling all types of property, liability, and workers compensation claims:

- Acknowledging and assigning the claim
- Identifying the policy and setting reserves
- Contacting the insured or the insured's representative
- Investigating and documenting the claim
- Determining the cause of loss, liability, and the loss amount

The claim handling process begins when the insured reports the loss to the producer or to the insurer's claim center.

Acknowledging and Assigning the Claim

Once a loss notice has been received and the information has been entered into the insurer's claim information system, the insurer acknowledges the claim and assigns it to one or more claim representatives. The purpose of the acknowledgment is to advise the insured that the claim has been received and to provide the claim number and contact information of the assigned claim representative.

Insurers use different methods of assigning claims to claim representatives. Some insurers assign claims based on territory, type of claim, extent of damage, workload, or other criteria. In the case of more complex claims that involve multiple policy coverages, two or more claim representatives may be assigned to a claim, depending on the structure of the insurer's claim operations and the training and expertise of its representatives. For example, if an insured is responsible for causing a serious automobile accident, the claim may involve both damage to property and injuries. The insurer may assign the property damage portion of the claim to one claim representative and the liability portion to another. Regardless of the method used, claims must be acknowledged in a timely manner to comply with insurance regulations.

After receiving the claim assignment, the claim representative contacts the insured, and possibly the claimant (if it is a **third-party claim**), to acknowledge the claim assignment and explain the claim process. For insurers that do not make contact immediately after receiving the loss notice, this contact serves as the claim acknowledgment. For some types of losses, the claim representative may give the insured instructions to prevent further loss, such as to cover roof damage with a tarp. If the claim involves property damage, the claim representative may arrange a time with the insured to inspect the damage or the damage scene. As an alternative, the claim representative may advise the insured or claimant that an appraiser or an independent adjuster will be in contact to inspect the property damage. If the claim involves bodily injury, the claim representative should get information about the nature and extent of the injury.

Identifying the Policy and Setting Reserves

After receiving a claim assignment, a claim representative will identify the policy in force on the date of the loss to assess available coverage and determine whether the loss occurred within the policy period, whether coverage exists under the policy for the type of loss reported, and whether the insured followed the policy's terms and conditions. A basic identification of the policy must take place on all claims, including record-only claims, before the investigation begins.

The claim representative must thoroughly read the policy to determine what types of coverage apply to the loss. If it is apparent that coverage may not be available for the loss, the claim representative must notify the insured of this concern through a **nonwaiver agreement** or a **reservation of rights letter**. Both of these documents reserve the insurer's rights under the policy.

Often in conjunction with identifying the policy, the claim representative will establish claim or case reserves, also called **loss reserves**. The insurer's claim information system often determines the types of reserves that are established. Some systems require separate reserves for each claimant in a claim. Other systems require separate expense reserves for the costs of handling the claim. For example, in a claim for an auto accident, an individual reserve may be set

Third-party claim

A demand against an insured by a person or organization other than the insured or the insurer, seeking to recover damages that may be payable by the insured's liability insurance.

Nonwaiver agreement

A signed agreement indicating that during the course of investigation, neither the insurer nor the insured waives rights under the policy.

Reservation of rights letter

An insurer's letter that specifies coverage issues and informs the insured that the insurer is handling a claim with the understanding that the insurer may later deny coverage should the facts warrant it.

Loss reserve

An estimate of the amount of money the insurer expects to pay in the future for losses that have already occurred and been reported, but are not yet settled.

up for damage to the insured's vehicle, damage to the other party's vehicle, medical expenses for the insured, and bodily injury for the claimant.

Insurers can use different methods of setting reserves, including these six common methods: **individual case method, roundtable method, average value method, formula method, expert system method,** and **loss ratio method.** The individual case method and the roundtable method rely on the claim representative's judgment; the other methods rely on statistical analysis.

Setting accurate and adequate reserves is important to an insurer's continued solvency and capacity (ability to write new business). Inaccurate reserving often results when reserves are established based on limited or incomplete information, or when reserves are not reevaluated and adjusted as necessary when new facts come to light. See the exhibit "Stairstepping the Reserve."

Average value method

A case reserving method that establishes a predetermined dollar amount of reserve for each claim as it is reported.

Roundtable method

A method of setting reserves by using the consensus of two or more claims personnel who have independently evaluated the claims file.

Individual case method

A method of setting reserves based on the claim's circumstances and the claims representative's experience in handling similar claims.

Expert system method

A method of setting reserves with a software application that estimates losses and loss adjustment expenses.

Formula method

A method of setting claim reserves by using a mathematical formula.

Loss ratio method

A loss reserving method that establishes aggregate reserves for all claims for a type of insurance.

Stairstepping the Reserve

Reserve inaccuracy can sometimes be the result of the claim representative's poor planning, lack of expertise in estimating claim severity, or unwillingness to reevaluate facts. In these cases, the claim representative may set a modest initial reserve, but then raise the reserve by a few thousand dollars to issue payments. Later, the reserve is increased again when more bills arrive. This process is called stairstepping the reserve. On a claim that concludes in thirty, sixty, or ninety days, stairstepping has little effect. But if the claim remains open for several years, as many liability and workers compensation claims do, the incremental increase in reserves during those years is not properly reflected in the insurer's ratemaking process. Stairstepping can be avoided if proper claim handling practices and reserving methods are used.

[DA10549]

Although an occasional reserve may be inadequate or inaccurate with little or no effect on the insurer, consistently inaccurate or inadequate reserves on thousands of claims can distort the ratemaking process. This may eventually affect an insurer's ability to write business competitively and may ultimately affect solvency.

Contacting the Insured or the Insured's Representative

Soon after the loss has been assigned and initial reserves have been established, the claim representative contacts the insured or the insured's representative. This initial contact with the insured serves several purposes. It can reassure the insured that the claim will be investigated. It also provides the claim representative with an opportunity to explain the claim process and to begin the claim investigation.

Generally, the claim representative reviews the initial loss report and policy and then contacts the insured and schedules a time to speak with the insured or a party representing the insured about the facts of the loss. If the loss involves a third-party claimant, then the claim representative also contacts the claimant and schedules a meeting with the claimant or a party representing the claimant to discuss the facts of the loss.

At the initial contact, claim representatives frequently find that many insureds do not fully understand the details of their insurance coverages. The claim representative must be prepared to explain the policy terms and their meanings in relation to the loss. The claim representative must explain possible policy violations, exclusions, or limitations that can affect coverage. Withholding such information can be considered a breach of the claim representative's or insurer's duties. The claim representative must also be careful not to give the insured or claimant the impression that a claim will be paid if potential grounds exist to deny the claim.

Once contact is made, the claim representative normally takes these actions:

- Tell the insured what is required to protect damaged property and to document the claim. Be specific about what the insured must do and provide deadlines.

- Describe the inspection, appraisal, and investigation the claim representative will be conducting.

- Tell the insured what additional investigation is needed to resolve potential coverage issues and provide clear instructions if more information is needed.

- Explain potential coverage questions, policy limitations, or exclusions and obtain a nonwaiver agreement when necessary.

- If medical and wage-loss information is part of the claim, obtain the necessary authorizations.

- Explain the amount of time it will take to process and conclude the claim.

- Supply the insured with a blank **proof of loss** form for property damage and any necessary written instructions so that the insured can document the claim.

Proof of loss

A statement of facts about a loss for which the insured is making a claim.

Claim representatives must be aware of the legal implications of their words and actions when communicating with insureds. Claim representatives are required by law to act in **good faith**; they must be careful not to mislead the insured or the claimant about potential coverage for the claim or the amount of any claim payment.

Investigating and Documenting the Claim

Investigation and documentation occur throughout the life of the claim. The investigation of a claim can take many different forms, and all aspects of it must be documented to create a complete claim file.

Claim representatives begin investigating a claim as soon as it is assigned. The insurer's claim handling guidelines help claim representatives determine the

Good faith

The manner of handling claims that requires an insurer to give consideration to the insured's interests that is at least equal to the consideration it gives its own interests.

type and extent of investigation needed for a satisfactory claim settlement. These are among several types of investigations that are common to many types of claims:

- Claimant investigation—A claimant investigation, usually conducted by taking the claimant's statement, can help determine the value of the injury or damage, how it was caused, and who is responsible.

- Insured/witness investigation—Statements (either written or recorded) from the insured and witnesses can provide valuable information about the circumstances surrounding the loss.

- Accident scene investigation—An investigation of the accident scene may offer crucial clues about the loss and may help determine whether accounts of the loss are plausible or questionable.

- Property damage investigation—An investigation of damaged property is useful to confirm the cause of loss and the extent of damage, or, for business income claims, to determine lost profits or loss of business use resulting from covered property damage.

- Medical investigation—Investigations of bodily injury claims help determine the costs of medical treatment, the expected duration of medical treatment and disability, the need for rehabilitation, and the suitability of medical care for the type of injuries the claimant suffered.

- Prior claim investigation—A prior claim investigation is conducted on most claims using industry databases to avoid paying for property damage or bodily injury that has previously been paid through prior claims by the same insurer or by other insurers.

Along with the investigation, all aspects of a claim, including the results of all investigations, must be documented to create a complete claim file. Three crucial components of claim documentation are diary systems, activity logs, and file reports.

Diary systems, also called suspense systems or pending systems, are automated systems that aid the claim representative in handling multiple claims simultaneously. For example, the claim representative may request information from the insured and then establish a diary date for follow-up. Diary systems also ensure that mandated deadlines are met. For example, a state law may require that the insured receive a status letter on the claim every thirty days. The automated system would set the diary dates to meet this requirement.

Activity logs, also called file status notes, document all investigations, claim evaluations, and coverage decisions and include chronological accounts of the claim representative's activities. Regulators and attorneys may request access to activity logs, so information included in the logs must be accurate, complete, and unbiased.

File reports can take several different forms. Some file reports are prepared by claim representatives for others within the insurance organization. These internal reports may serve as status reports and may also alert others in the organization that follow-up is needed. For example, fraud investigators may review file reports to identify losses or loss trends that indicate potential fraud. In addition, insurers prepare external reports for producers; advisory organizations; and others outside the organization, such as reinsurers, who have an interest in certain claims or aggregated claim information.

Determining Cause of Loss, Liability, and Loss Amount

Claim representatives use the information gained during their investigation to determine the cause of loss, liability, and loss amount.

The facts of the loss determine the cause of the loss. For example, in a fire loss, the claim representative may find that a faulty toaster caused the fire. If there are several causes of loss, the claim representative should identify all of them and determine their relative importance in causing the loss, as well as the responsible party or event.

After the cause of loss has been determined, the claim representative must determine the liability for the loss based on the facts. For example, in an auto accident, the claim representative applies statutory and case law on negligence to determine liability of the parties involved. If the insured is liable, the claim representative must then determine whether coverage exists for that liability under the policy by reviewing all component parts of the policy and applying them to the facts of the case.

During the course of an investigation, the claim representative may discover that the insured was not liable and that a third party caused the accident. When an insurer pays a claim to an insured for a loss caused by a negligent third party, the insurer can recover that payment amount from the negligent third party through the right of **subrogation**.

Concurrent to the determination of the cause of and liability for the loss, the claim representative should determine both the type and amount of the loss and then decide whether they are covered under the policy. For a property damage claim, the amount of loss payable is usually limited to physical damage to, destruction of, or loss of use of tangible property, and the amount is usually based on the cost to repair or replace it with property of like kind and quality. For a bodily injury claim, the loss amount is usually based on the extent of the injury, the residual and lasting effects of the injury, and the amount of pain and suffering the individual has endured.

Once the amount of the loss has been determined, the claim representative must verify that the actual or anticipated damages are within the policy limits. The claim payment may also be subject to sublimits, deductibles, or **coinsurance** provisions in the policy.

Subrogation

The process by which an insurer can, after it has paid a loss under the policy, recover the amount paid from any party (other than the insured) who caused the loss or is otherwise legally liable for the loss.

Coinsurance

An insurance-to-value provision in many property insurance policies providing that if the property is underinsured, the amount that an insurer will pay for a covered loss is reduced.

Concluding the Claim

When the investigation has been completed and all documentation has been received, the claim representative must decide whether to pay the claim or deny it.

If the claim is to be paid, the claim representative often must negotiate the amount with the insured or the claimant. Negotiation involves discussing disputed matters and mutually agreeing on a settlement. In some cases, **alternative dispute resolution (ADR)** methods may be used to resolve a disagreement and, ultimately, the claim. After an agreement on the settlement amount is reached, the claim representative secures the necessary final documents so that payment can be made.

Alternative dispute resolution (ADR)

Procedures to help settle disputes without litigation, including arbitration, mediation, and negotiation.

When claim investigations reveal that a policy does not provide coverage for a loss, or when an insured fails to meet a policy condition, the claim may conclude with a denial rather than a payment. Insurers often have strict guidelines that must be followed when denying claims, and some insurers require a claim manager's approval to deny a claim. Once authority is given to deny a claim, the claim representative must prepare a formal denial letter in a timely manner. Denial letters must comply with state legal requirements. For example, most states require the letter to cite all known reasons for the denial.

Even with the variety of ADR methods available, many claims are concluded through litigation. Litigation can occur at almost any point during the life of a claim; however, it occurs most often when the parties to the claim are unable to reach an agreement by negotiation or ADR, or when a claim is denied. ADR reduces, but does not eliminate, the chance that a claimant will sue and take a case to trial. Accordingly, insurers must be prepared to litigate some claims.

When a claim is resolved, the claim representative may complete a closing or final report, which can include the claim representative's recommendations on subrogation, advice to underwriters, and other information required by the insurer or reinsurer.

FRAMEWORK FOR COVERAGE ANALYSIS

Coverage analysis is the process of examining a policy by reviewing all its component parts and applying them to the facts of a claim.

A claim representative begins the process of coverage analysis by carefully reading the policy form and all endorsements. With experience, claim representatives learn to recognize the types of losses covered under the policy forms. They are aware of the types of losses that insureds and claimants often believe are covered, but are not. This policy knowledge aids coverage analysis. But experience does not remove the necessity for the claim representative to read the applicable policy forms carefully and to analyze coverage systematically.

A systematic framework for coverage analysis can guide the claim representative to the parts of the policy that may provide or exclude coverage. It also ensures that all of the component parts are reviewed and reduces the incidence of erroneous coverage determinations. These questions outline a systematic framework for coverage analysis and the information it will yield:

- Is the person involved covered?
- Did the loss occur during the policy period?
- Is the cause of loss covered?
- Is the damaged property covered?
- Is the type of loss covered?
- Are the amounts of loss or damages covered?
- Is the location of the loss covered?
- Do any exclusions apply?
- Does other insurance apply?

The claim representative can follow this framework by answering the questions in the order they appear here. However, in some cases, the policy may prompt the claim representative to answer the questions in a different order. In any case, the answers help the claim representative make a coverage determination.

Is the Person Involved Covered?

Some policies cover only insureds named or listed in the policy. Most policies define "insured" broadly, so the claim representative must determine whether the persons who suffered the loss are covered. For example, the homeowners (HO) policy covers the financial loss that the insured suffers as the result of a fire. For coverage to apply, the policy must cover the person who has suffered the financial loss. For example, the Personal Auto Policy (PAP) Part A—Liability Coverage defines "insured" as:[1]

> B. "Insured" as used in this Part means:
> 1. You or any "family member" for the ownership, maintenance or use of any auto or "trailer".
> 2. Any person using "your covered auto".
> 3. For "your covered auto", any person or organization but only with respect to legal responsibility for acts or omissions of a person for whom coverage is afforded under this Part.
> 4. For any auto or "trailer", other than "your covered auto", any other person or organization but only with respect to legal responsibility for acts or omissions of you or any "family member" for whom coverage is afforded under this Part. This provision (B.4.) applies only if the person or organization does not own or hire the auto or "trailer".

According to the PAP definition, a friend who borrows your car and drives it is an insured. A friend who uses your car and pays you for that use is not an insured because of the last sentence in Item 4.

In contrast, the HO-3 defines "insured" in part as:[2]

> 3. "Insured" means:
>   a. You and residents of your household who are:
>   (1) Your relatives; or
>   (2) Other persons under the age of 21 and in the care of any person named above;...

According to the HO-3 definition, a sixteen-year-old international exchange student who lives in the household is an insured. An independent twenty-four-year-old friend who visits over the weekend is not an insured. "Insured" may be defined differently in other sections of the policy. For example, the definition of "insured" is expanded for Part B—Medical Payments Coverage of the PAP to include:[3]

> 1. You or any "family member":
>   a. While "occupying"; or
>   b. As a pedestrian when struck by;
>   a motor vehicle designed for use mainly on public roads or a trailer of any type.
> 2. Any other person while "occupying" "your covered auto".

Most property insurance policies limit recovery to the amount of a person's insurable interest in the damaged or destroyed property. However, insurable interest alone does not guarantee coverage. For example, an individual may have an insurable interest in a building but not be considered an insured under the policy because the person's name is not listed in the declarations or on an endorsement. Claim representatives determine whether the person making the claim is entitled to coverage under the policy and whether that person qualifies as an "insured."

For example, Kathy owns a house jointly with her parents, who live in another state. All three have an insurable interest in the house, but Kathy is the only named insured on the policy. If a tornado damages the house, Kathy would be paid for the loss because she has an insurable interest in the house and is a named insured. Kathy's parents are not residents of the house or named insureds, so even though they have an insurable interest, they are not insureds under the policy. See the exhibit "Adjusting Tip."

Did the Loss Occur During the Policy Period?

Many policies are written to cover only losses that occur during the policy period. The HO-3 states:[4]

Adjusting Tip

Claim representatives must determine whether others have an insurable interest in the property on which a claim is based. In Kathy's case, the claim representative, on discovering that Kathy's parents have an insurable interest in the house, should check with a supervisor or manager to determine how to handle the claim payment. Lienholders or mortgagees often have an insurable interest in property, and the claim representative must determine when they should be included as payees on any claim payments.

[DA03105]

P. **Policy Period**. The policy applies only to loss which occurs during the policy period.

The policy period typically begins and ends at one minute after midnight (for example, from 12:01 a.m. on January 25, 2006, to 12:01 a.m. of January 25, 2007). The Loss of Use section contains an exception to the policy period provision. For example, if a fire leaves a home unfit to live in, the insured can claim expenses for living elsewhere, even if the policy expires the next day. However, the fire must have begun during the policy period.

The date and time of loss occurrence is used to determine whether a loss occurred during the policy period. However, court decisions have offered different interpretations of date of occurrence. For example, a court may determine that the date of occurrence for an occupational disease is the first date of exposure to the harmful condition that caused the disease, the last date of exposure to the harmful condition that caused the disease, or the date the disease was diagnosed.

Is the Cause of Loss Covered?

Covered causes of loss, or perils, vary by type of policy and may include fire, theft, hail, windstorm, collision, or a legal obligation to pay damages.

Specified causes of loss coverage, also called named-perils coverage, covers a loss only if it is a direct result of a specifically listed or named cause of loss in the policy. For example, in the HO-3 policy, personal property is covered for specified perils.

Causes of loss are not often defined in the policy because the definitions are subject to court interpretation and therefore vary by state. For example, fire may seem easy to define, but does fire include smoke or excessive heat with no actual flame? Does it include damage the firefighters cause while extinguishing the fire? See the exhibit "Adjusting Tip."

Special form coverage, also called all-risks or open-perils coverage, covers every cause of direct physical loss that is not excluded. The HO-3 provides special form coverage on the dwelling and other structures. Section I—Perils

Specified causes of loss coverage

Coverage for direct and accidental loss caused by fire, lightning, explosion, theft, windstorm, hail, earthquake, flood, mischief, vandalism, or loss resulting from the sinking, burning, collision, or derailment of a conveyance transporting the covered auto.

Special form coverage

Property insurance coverage covering all causes of loss not specifically excluded.

Adjusting Tip

When the policy does not define a cause of loss or another term, claim representatives can use other resources to determine the meaning. For example, statutory provisions and court decisions have defined many terms that are not defined in policies. Standard dictionaries are also resources for defining terms.

[DA03107]

Insured Against in the HO-3 states, in part, "We insure against *risk of direct loss to property* described in Coverages A and B" [emphasis added].[5] Following that statement is a list of causes of loss that the policy does not cover, such as smog, rust, birds, and rodents. Any cause of loss that is not listed among the excluded causes of loss is covered. See the exhibit "An HO-3 Claim Example."

An HO-3 Claim Example

An insured accidentally spills a caustic chemical in the kitchen. The chemical splashes on the linoleum floor, table, chairs, and area rug. Because spills are not excluded under special form coverage on the dwelling, the damage to the linoleum floor is covered. Because spills are not a named peril under specified perils coverage on the contents, the damage to the table, chairs, and area rug is not covered.

[DA03108]

In answering the question "Is the cause of loss covered?", claim representatives should thoroughly investigate all the facts concerning the loss and apply them to the language in all the provisions of the policy.

Is the Damaged Property Covered?

In following the framework for coverage analysis, the claim representative must determine whether the damaged property is covered. Insurance policies may not cover all of the insured's property. Certain property must be specified in order for coverage to apply. For example, the PAP defines "your covered auto" as:[6]

1. Any vehicle shown in the Declarations.

2. A "newly acquired auto".

3. Any "trailer" you own.

4. Any auto or "trailer" you do not own while used as a temporary substitute for any other vehicle described in this definition which is out of normal use because of its:

   a. Breakdown;

   b. Repair;

   c. Servicing;

   d. Loss; or

   e. Destruction

If a claim investigation reveals that an auto involved in an accident does not appear in the declarations or fall within the definition of "your covered auto," a coverage question may exist. However, the question may be easily resolved if the insured can prove that the car was recently purchased but has not yet been added to the policy or is a temporary substitute vehicle.

In another example of property that must be specified for coverage to apply, the HO-3 describes the property covered under Coverage A—Dwelling as:[7]

   a. The dwelling on the "residence premises" shown in the Declarations, including structures attached to the dwelling; and

   b. Materials and supplies located on or next to the "residence premises" used to construct, alter or repair the dwelling or other structures on the "residence premises".

For example, if Jeff reported the theft of four bundles of shingles and two rolls of tar paper that were stored in his garage, and the claim representative's investigation revealed that Jeff planned to use those materials to repair his roof, then the stolen property would be covered based on the policy provision just mentioned. If the claim representative's investigation revealed that Jeff is a roofing contractor and planned to use those materials on a job, the loss would not be covered. Therefore, it is important to determine whether the damaged property is covered under the policy.

Is the Type of Loss Covered?

Losses can be classified as **direct losses** or **indirect losses**. A crumpled car fender is a direct loss. Indirect losses reduce future income, increase future expenses, or both. For example, if fire destroys an insured's home, the cost of rebuilding the home is a direct loss. The rental cost for temporary living quarters for the insured while the home is being rebuilt is an indirect loss. The loss of earnings and the extra expenses incurred over a period of time after a fire damages a business are also indirect losses.

Direct loss

A reduction in the value of property that results directly and often immediately from damage to that property.

Indirect loss

A loss that arises as a result of damage to property, other than the direct loss to the property.

Many property policies cover direct losses only. Other policies cover some types of indirect losses. Homeowners policies cover increases in living expenses after a covered loss renders the home untenable.

Are the Amounts of Loss or Damages Covered?

Claim representatives should always check the policy to determine whether the amounts of loss are covered. For property damage claims, the amount of loss payable is usually limited to physical damage to, destruction of, or loss of use of tangible property. The amount is usually based on the cost to repair or replace the damaged property with that of like kind and quality. Claims for indirect loss, such as loss of business income, can be payable if indirect loss coverage is included or has been added to the policy.

For liability claims, damages for which the insured may be liable are of two types:

Compensatory damages, which include **special damages** (which pay for specific, out-of-pocket expenses, such as medical expenses, wage loss, funeral expenses, or repair bills) and **general damages** (which pay for losses, such as pain and suffering, and do not involve specific measurable expenses), reimburse or compensate claimants for their bodily injury or property damage.

Punitive damages punish a wrongdoer for a reckless, malicious, or deceitful act and deter similar conduct. See the exhibit "Damages."

Special damages

A form of compensatory damages that awards a sum of money for specific, identifiable expenses associated with the injured person's loss, such as medical expenses or lost wages.

Compensatory damages

A payment awarded by a court to reimburse a victim for actual harm.

General damages

A monetary award to compensate a victim for losses, such as pain and suffering, that does not involve specific, measurable expenses.

Punitive damages (exemplary damages)

A payment awarded by a court to punish a defendant for a reckless, malicious, or deceitful act to deter similar conduct; the award need not bear any relation to a party's actual damages.

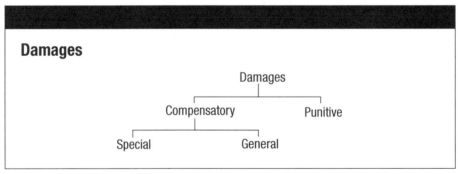

Damages

[DA03111]

Some policies do not define or list the types of damages payable under the policy. For example, the insuring agreement for the PAP liability coverage section begins, "We will pay damages for 'bodily injury' or 'property damage' for which any 'insured' becomes legally responsible because of an auto accident."[8]

Generally, the term "damages" refers only to compensatory damages, such as expenses for medical bills, lost wages, and pain and suffering. In some states, the insurer is not permitted to pay for punitive damages because such payment by an insurer would not punish the insured. For example, if a manufacturer of a defective product has insurance for punitive damages, imposition of punitive damages would not have the same deterrent effect as forcing the manufacturer to pay the damages directly from its assets. Therefore, some policies expressly exclude coverage for punitive damages.

In a liability insurance policy, the insurer agrees to pay judgments and settlements up to the policy limit. In addition, some liability policies contain deductibles. They may also include coverage for certain expenses, such as defense costs and bail bonds, outside the limit of liability. Others may have a self-insured retention (SIR) in which the insured organization adjusts and pays its own losses up to the SIR level. Once that SIR is exceeded, the insurer makes payment. The claim representative must verify all the policy limits applicable to a loss before making a settlement to ensure that any payment made falls within the available limits of coverage.

In addition to ensuring that the type of loss and types of damage are covered, claim representatives must verify that the amount of damages is within the policy limits. A first party property policy will have limits of liability and may also have sublimits for certain types of property or types of losses. For example, the HO-3 contains a limit on the dwelling and contents as well as special limits for loss of money and theft of jewelry and silverware. First-party losses are also subject to deductibles, provisions that specify how the loss is to be valued (either actual cash value or replacement cost), and coinsurance clauses designed to ensure that the appropriate amount of insurance is maintained on the property.

Is the Location of the Loss Covered?

The location where the loss occurred must be within the policy's territorial limits and, for property policies, be shown on the policy as a covered location. To illustrate, the PAP defines policy territory as:[9]

1. The United States of America, its territories or possessions;

2. Puerto Rico; or

3. Canada.

This policy also applies to loss to, or accidents involving, "your covered auto" while being transported between their ports.

Accidents occurring in Mexico would not be covered because they are outside the territory covered by the policy. Property policies cover buildings only at the locations listed in the declarations, but personal property can be covered at other locations.

Do Any Exclusions Apply?

Some losses may be excluded in the policy. For example, the HO-3 excludes losses caused by deterioration, such as a wooden garage door that rots. The

PAP excludes damage caused by wear and tear, such as the wear on a tire. Exclusions to coverage can involve these elements:

- Persons
- Causes of loss
- Types of property
- Types of damage
- Other circumstances

When claim circumstances fall within a specific exclusion, coverage does not apply. An exclusion applies even if other coverage requirements are met. For example, suppose that an insured uses his car as a taxi and is involved in an accident, severely damaging the driver's side door. The insured subsequently submits a claim. That claim appears to be covered according to these criteria:

- Is the person involved covered? The driver is the named insured.
- Did the loss occur during the policy period? In this case, it did.
- Is the cause of loss covered? The policy covers physical damage to the insured's car.
- Is the damaged property covered? The vehicle is listed in the policy's declarations.
- Is the type of loss covered? The policy covers collisions.
- Are the amounts of loss or damages covered? The amount of the loss is within the policy limits but more than the deductible.
- Is the location of the loss covered? The loss occurred within the policy's territorial limits.

Then the claim representative would ask another question: "Do any exclusions apply?" On reviewing the exclusions, the claim representative would find that the PAP excludes loss that occurs while the car is used as a public or livery conveyance, and the claim representative would rightfully deny the claim.

Sometimes exclusions contain exceptions, meaning they clarify what is excluded. For example, the PAP excludes liability coverage for damage to property used by the insured. However, an exception in the exclusion states that the exclusion does not apply to property damage to a residence used by the insured. Claim representatives who carefully read the policy can avoid incorrectly denying coverage based on an exclusion when an exception applies. See the exhibit "Adjusting Tip."

Adjusting Tip

A claim representative must make sure that the exclusion upon which the denial is based has not been declared invalid by a court having jurisdiction over the claim or by a state statute.

[DA05560]

Does Other Insurance Apply?

Some policies are intended to apply only if no other insurance applies or only above the limits provided by other insurance. For example, the PAP states that coverage provided under that policy is excess over other collectible insurance for vehicles the insured does not own. In other cases, a policy may pay a portion of the loss based on the limit of insurance available from other policies. Having answered all the questions in the framework for coverage analysis, the claim representative can apply the policy to the facts of the claim and make a coverage determination.

APPLYING THE CLAIM HANDLING PROCESS AND THE FRAMEWORK FOR COVERAGE ANALYSIS

To ensure good-faith handling of property and liability claims, insurers' claim departments adopt specific procedures and guidelines.

Claim representatives can use the claim handling process and apply the framework for coverage analysis as a guide for every claim they handle. Specific information about handling property, liability, and bodily injury claims will help dictate the procedures for each claim handling activity. Ultimately, the language of the policy and the facts of the claim provide the details to enable the claim representative to settle the loss in a timely and professional manner.

Case Facts

Susan and Thomas Reed live at 104 Fremont Street in Malvern, Texas. They have two children: Ann, age 16, who lives at home, and John, age 19, who lives at home when not attending Columbus College in New Mexico. Susan's mother, Marie, also lives with them. Susan is a schoolteacher. Thomas is the owner of a small company called Universal Widgets.

Susan and Thomas own their home and three cars. The ABC Loan Company holds a mortgage on their home. They also have a car loan, from Union Trust Company, on their 2010 Lexus. They do not have lienholders for their other two cars (a 2007 Toyota Camry and a 2006 Honda Civic).

Susan and Thomas have an HO-3 (2000) policy covering their home. They have a Personal Auto Policy (PAP) covering all three cars.

On April 12, 20XX, Susan and Thomas received a phone call from John's roommate informing them that John had been in an auto accident while driving the Honda Civic. John suffered minor injuries after failing to obey a stop sign and then hitting another car. The driver of the other car, Karen Jones, was hospitalized.

Case Analysis Tools

To handle a claim such as the one provided in this case study, a claim representative would need to have an understanding of the coverages provided in the HO-3 policy form and in the PAP form. However, to resolve the case study, only a thorough understanding of the activities in the claim handling process and the framework for coverage analysis is required.

Activities in the Claim Handling Process

A thorough understanding of these activities in the claim handling process will lead to the conclusion described in the Correct Answer section and other possible conclusions to this case study:

- Acknowledging and assigning the claim
- Identifying the policy and setting reserves
- Contacting the insured or the insured's representative
- Investigating the claim
- Documenting the claim
- Determining the cause of loss, liability, and the loss amount
- Concluding the claim

Acknowledging and Assigning the Claim

After talking with John, Thomas called his insurance agent and reported the claim. The agent then reported the claim to the insurer. Claim Representative Jim Smith was assigned to handle all aspects of the claim.

After he received the claim assignment, Jim acknowledged receipt of the claim to the agent. Then he entered the claim information into the insurer's claim-processing system.

Identifying the Policy and Setting Reserves

Jim identified the Reeds' auto policy and performed an initial review. He established that the 2006 Honda Civic had liability coverage, collision coverage with a $1,000 deductible, and Personal Injury Protection coverage. Based on the limited information on the first notice of loss, Jim set up these parts of the claim with preliminary reserves:

- Bodily injury liability claim from Karen Jones—reserve $5,000
- Property damage claim from Karen Jones—reserve $2,500
- Collision coverage for the 2006 Honda—reserve $2,500
- PIP coverage for John's injuries—reserve $1,000

Contacting the Insured or the Insured's Representative

Jim contacted Susan and Thomas Reed. They gave him a brief description of the accident and asked Jim to contact John for all of the details about what happened. While talking with Susan and Thomas, Jim confirmed that they are the registered owners of the car, that the car is registered in Texas, and that John was using the car with their permission.

Jim called John and took a recorded statement that provided these facts:

- John is a full-time college student in New Mexico. He lives in a dormitory on campus. He has had the Honda at school since the beginning of the semester and parks it on a campus parking lot.
- The accident occurred at 11:30 AM on a Saturday morning. John was driving to a sandwich shop. He did not see a stop sign or the car on his right because of sun glare, so he entered the intersection without slowing down or stopping.
- John's car struck the car driven by Karen Jones on the driver's side door. John was wearing his seatbelt at the time of the accident. His air bag deployed on impact. He was taken to the emergency room, treated for minor cuts, and released.
- Karen Jones was also taken to the emergency room. John believed she had a concussion and a deep laceration on her forehead. John received a ticket for careless driving.
- The Honda was taken to Sam's Auto Body Shop in Columbus, New Mexico.

Investigating the Claim

After concluding his conversation with John, Jim requested a police report and reviewed the PAP to answer some questions he had regarding coverage for this claim. Jim had already confirmed that the Honda is listed on the Reeds' policy and that it has collision coverage. (Is the damaged property covered? Is the cause of loss covered?) He also confirmed that the accident date occurred within the policy period. (Did the loss occur during the policy period?)

Jim determined who is covered by the PAP. According to the liability coverage part, "insured" is defined in this manner:

1. You or any "family member" for the ownership, maintenance or use of any auto or "trailer".

According to the definition of insured, John is covered by the policy. (Is the person involved covered?) The insuring agreement states that the insurer will pay damages for bodily injury or property damage for which any insured becomes legally responsible because of an auto accident. The insuring agreement also states that the policy will pay defense costs in addition to the limit of liability. (Is the type of loss covered?)

Jim then checked the Part A exclusions. None of the exclusions appear to apply. (Do any exclusions apply?)

Next, Jim examined the policy period and territory provision of the PAP. The loss occurred during the policy period and within the policy territory of the U.S. (Is the location where the loss occurred covered?)

Based on the information obtained from Thomas Reed and John Reed, no other auto policies are applicable to this accident because all of the Reeds' cars are insured under this policy. (Does other insurance apply?)

The PAP provides out-of-state coverage, so the policy complies with New Mexico's financial responsibility laws. New Mexico does not have no-fault laws, so the liability portion of the Reeds' coverage will apply to Karen's bodily injury and property claims. (Do any other policies apply to the loss?) Based on the limited medical information available at this time concerning Karen, Jim believes that the liability limit on the Reeds' policy is sufficient to cover the bodily injury and property damage that Karen sustained. (Are the amounts of loss or damages covered?) However, Jim will have to review this portion of the claim frequently as more information about Karen and her injuries becomes available

Jim confirmed that Karen was released from the hospital after she received treatment for her injuries and was kept for 24 hours of observation because of blood loss. He called her the next day to take her claim statement, which confirmed John's account of the accident. Karen's statement also revealed these details:

- Karen is 38 years old and single, and lives at 2227 North Casa Avenue, Apt. 215, Pueblo, New Mexico.

- Karen received sixty stitches for the wound in her forehead. While in the hospital, she received blood to replace blood she lost because of the laceration to her forehead. The emergency staff confirmed through an X-ray that she had suffered a minor concussion, and the physician prescribed a pain reliever for her headaches.

- Karen was placed under observation for one week to monitor any problems that might ensue because of the concussion.

- Karen's 2008 Buick Lucerne was taken to Roy's Auto Damage, where an estimate for $3,800 was prepared to cover repairs to the driver's-side door and front fender. Karen agreed to mail the estimate to Jim.

- Based on the estimate, Jim adjusted the property damage reserve for Karen's auto to $3,800.

Documenting the Claim

Jim recorded all of the information he learned through the investigation in his file status notes for this claim. He included the police report with a diagram of the scene (that matched John's and Karen's accident descriptions), Karen's auto estimate, and the recorded statements of the two claimants with the claim file documents.

The claim diary system created an automatic entry for follow-up two weeks after the date of Jim's initial entry. Jim changed the diary date to two weeks from the date he completed this phase of the investigation. Documentation of changes in the claim information, reserves, and settlements will be ongoing. Jim will also have to continue his investigation to determine who is liable for the accident.

Determining Cause of Loss, Liability, and Loss Amount

As part of his analysis of liability coverage, Jim answered some of the questions that needed to be asked when analyzing coverage for the damage to the Reeds' Honda:

- Did the loss occur during the policy period?
- Is the loss location covered by the policy?
- Do any other auto policies apply to this loss?

Based on the police report, the ticket issued to John, and John's own admission of fault, Jim determined that John was liable for the damages in the accident through tort liability. Because John is an insured under Susan and Thomas's policy, the policy will cover the damages up to the policy limits.

This investigation resolved the questions to which answers are required to ensure coverage under auto liability. (Did the claim arise out of the use of certain autos by certain individuals? Was the claim for bodily injury or property damage?) The investigation also addressed the PAP exclusion for intentional acts, as John did not intend the result of his actions or intend to commit the action that caused the injurious outcomes. After reviewing Part D—Coverage for Damage to Your Auto of the PAP, Jim confirmed that there is collision coverage on the Reeds' Honda. Based on the facts currently known, Jim reviewed the exclusions to Part D coverage and determined that none of the exclusions apply.

Property Damage Claims

Jim assigned an appraiser to assess the amount of damage to the Reeds' Honda and to Karen's Buick and to prepare estimates to repair the damages. Based on the description of the accident that John gave in his statement, Jim decided that the $2,500 reserve for the Honda is adequate. He will review the reserves after he receives the appraiser's estimates.

Jim changed the diary date to two weeks after the date he requested the estimate from the appraiser, so that he can follow up if he does not receive the reports. He also updated the file status notes with the cause of loss, liability, and coverage information.

Two days later, Jim received the appraiser's estimate for $3,700 in damages to the Reeds' Honda and an estimate for the damage to Karen's Buick that was $5 less than the estimate Karen submitted. He also received photos of the damage to both autos. Jim adjusted the reserve for this expected damage amount on the Reeds' auto to $2,700 (after application of the $1,000 deductible). The difference in the estimates for Karen's Buick was negligible, so he made no change to that reserve. Jim updated his file status notes and added the estimates and photos to the claim file.

John's Medical Claim

Jim reviewed the Personal Injury Protection (PIP) endorsement attached to the Reeds' auto policy. This endorsement provides unlimited medical expenses coverage to covered persons. Jim confirmed that the definition of insured applies to a family member. The insuring agreement states that PIP benefits will be paid to an insured who sustains bodily injury caused by an accident and resulting from the use of an auto. The medical expenses must be reasonable and necessary.

John had indicated that he suffered a laceration above his eye, which was treated at the emergency room. He also received treatment from a chiropractor for his sore neck and back. John will give his medical bills to Jim for review and reimbursement.

Jim also reviewed the exclusions in the endorsement and determined that none of them apply. Jim decided to raise the reserve on John's PIP claim to $2,500 to cover the emergency room bill and three months of chiropractic treatment.

Four months after the accident, Jim verified that John's treatment for his injuries had ended. John submitted medical bills and medical mileage expenses totaling $2,400. Jim examined the bills and mileage figures and determined that they were reasonable and necessary for John's injuries.

Karen's Medical Claim

Six weeks after the accident, Jim reviewed the medical receipts and medical mileage records he received from Karen for treatment of her injury. He determined that they were reasonable and necessary for the injuries she sustained. He reviewed an early photo of Karen's injured forehead and a recent photo showing that scarring was minimal.

Jim submitted a query in an injury database to which his employer subscribes. It showed that Karen had never sustained any injuries that were submitted to a workers compensation or liability insurer. This indicated that her injuries from this accident were new injuries.

Jim totaled the medical receipts and medical mileage claim at $4,200. Because she was hospitalized over a weekend and was able to report to work the following Monday, Karen incurred no loss of income. Jim added 10 percent to the total to compensate Karen for her "pain and suffering." Jim then confirmed that the total of $4,620 plus $3,800 for Karen's Buick, or $8,420, was within the Reeds' PAP liability policy limit.

Concluding the Claim

Before issuing any payments, Jim checked the federal and state databases to ensure that neither Karen nor any of the Reeds had any outstanding legal obligations that would require payment before they could receive any payment for their claims.

After Karen's auto was repaired, Jim issued a check payable to Roy's Auto Damage and to Karen Jones for $3,800. He then closed Karen's property damage reserve. After the Reeds' Honda was repaired, Jim issued a check payable to Sam's Auto Body and Thomas and Susan Reed for $2,700 and closed the Reeds' property damage reserve.

Jim arranged a settlement review with Karen, in which he offered her the calculated total of $4,620 for her medical expenses. Jim explained how he arrived at that amount and that he believed it was a reasonable settlement. He also showed Karen the total amount of the bodily injury and property damage claims paid by the Reeds' insurer for Karen's damages. (At this time, Jim noted that the scar on Karen's forehead was barely visible). Karen accepted Jim's settlement offer. He issued her a check for her medical expenses and obtained a full release from liability for the claim, which Karen signed. Later, Jim closed Karen's bodily injury claim reserve.

Jim contacted the Reeds and offered to pay $2,400 for John's PIP claim. Because John was at fault for the accident, no "pain and suffering" compensation was warranted. Jim noted that they had already paid $2,700 ($3,700 less the $1,000 deductible) for repairs to the Honda. The Reeds accepted Jim's settlement offer. He mailed them a check for $2,400, along with full releases for their property damage claim and for John's PIP claim. The Reeds signed the forms and returned them to Jim's office the following day. Jim closed John's PIP reserve.

Jim included the signed releases in the claim file and completed his file status notes to indicate the outcome of Karen's settlement meeting and the Reeds' settlements. Then he marked the claim file as closed on the insurer's claim information system. See the exhibit "Correct Answer*."

> ### Correct Answer*
>
> Claim Payments for Reed/Jones Accident, DOL: 04/12/20XX
>
> - Bodily injury liability claim payment for Karen Jones—Final payment, $4,620
> - Property damage claim for Karen Jones's 2008 Buick—Final payment, $3,800
> - Collision coverage for the Reeds' 2006 Honda—Final payment, $2,700
> - PIP coverage for John Reed's injuries—Final payment, $2,400
>
> *This solution might not be the only viable solution. Other solutions could be exercised if justified by the analysis. In addition, specific circumstances and organizational needs or goals may enter into the evaluation, making an alternative action a better option.

[DA06275]

SUMMARY

Two primary goals of the claim function are complying with the contractual promise and supporting the insurer's financial goals. The insurer fulfills its contractual promise to the insured through the claim handling process. Claim departments provide claim information that is used by marketing, underwriting, and actuarial departments to perform their functions. Additionally, the claim department must interact effectively with outside contacts, such as the public, lawyers, and state regulators.

Insurers and other insurance organizations have claim departments, which may be structured in various ways. Claims personnel who handle claims may be staff claims representatives, independent adjusters, employees of TPAs, or producers. In addition, public adjusters handle claims by representing the insured's interests to the insurer. Claims department performance can be measured by mathematical means and also qualitatively through the use of best practices, claim audits, and customer service comments.

Insurers use a combination of compliance measures to meet legal and regulatory requirements and promote good-faith claims handling practices. These measures include (1) claims guidelines, policies, and procedures; (2) controls, such as reports, access security, authority levels, and tracking; (3) supervisor and manager reviews; and (4) claims audits.

These activities in the claim handling process are performed on every claim to some degree to create consistency and to help ensure that claims are handled in a manner that conforms to legal and ethical standards:

- Acknowledging and assigning the claim
- Identifying the policy and setting reserves
- Contacting the insured or the insured's representative
- Investigating and documenting the claim
- Determining the cause of loss, liability, and the loss amount
- Concluding the claim

Claim representatives use a framework for coverage analysis that involves every policy component, ensuring that all parts of the policy will be considered when making a coverage determination. Using the framework, the claim representative answers these questions:

- Is the person involved covered?
- Did the loss occur during the policy period?
- Is the cause of loss covered?
- Is the damaged property covered?
- Is the type of loss covered?
- Are the amounts of loss or damages covered?
- Is the location where the loss occurred covered?
- Do any exclusions apply?
- Does other insurance apply?

Claim representatives can use the framework for coverage analysis and the claim handling process as guides for every claim they handle. The language of the policy and the facts of the claim will provide the details.

ASSIGNMENT NOTES

1. Includes copyrighted material of Insurance Services Offices, Inc., with its permission. Copyright, ISO Properties, Inc., 1997.
2. Includes copyrighted material of Insurance Services Offices, Inc., with its permission. Copyright, ISO Properties, Inc., 1999.
3. Includes copyrighted material of Insurance Services Offices, Inc., with its permission. Copyright, ISO Properties, Inc., 1997.
4. Includes copyrighted material of Insurance Services Offices, Inc., with its permission. Copyright, ISO Properties, Inc., 1999.
5. Includes copyrighted material of Insurance Services Offices, Inc., with its permission. Copyright, ISO Properties, Inc., 1999.
6. Includes copyrighted material of Insurance Services Offices, Inc., with its permission. Copyright, ISO Properties, Inc., 1997.
7. Includes copyrighted material of Insurance Services Offices, Inc., with its permission. Copyright, ISO Properties, Inc., 1999.
8. Includes copyrighted material of Insurance Services Offices, Inc., with its permission. Copyright, ISO Properties, Inc., 1997.
9. Includes copyrighted material of Insurance Services Offices, Inc., with its permission. Copyright, ISO Properties, Inc., 1997.

Actuarial Operations

Educational Objectives

After learning the content of this assignment, you should be able to:

▷ Describe the actuarial function in insurer operations and the actuarial services required by insurers.

▷ Describe the insurer goals of ratemaking and the ideal characteristics of rates.

▷ Describe the components of an insurance rate and common ratemaking terms.

▷ Explain how the following factors can affect ratemaking:

- Estimation of losses
- Delays in data collection and use
- Change in the cost of claims
- Insurer's projected expenses
- Target level of profit and contingencies

▷ Describe the following ratemaking methods:

- Pure premium
- Loss ratio
- Judgment

▷ Describe each of the following steps in the ratemaking process:

- Collect data
- Adjust data
- Calculate the indicated overall rate change
- Determine territorial and class relativities
- Prepare and submit rate filings to regulatory authorities as required

7

▸ Explain how the following ratemaking factors vary by type of insurance:

- Experience period
- Trending
- Large loss limitations
- Credibility
- Increased limits factors

▸ Describe the purpose and types of loss reserves, the importance of accurate estimation of loss reserves, and techniques used by actuaries in their analysis.

Actuarial Operations

7

THE ACTUARIAL FUNCTION

Actuaries are professionals who evaluate the financial consequences of future events. As such, they play a critical role in the fields of insurance and risk management.

The actuarial function is responsible for ensuring that the insurer operates effectively and conducts its operations on a financially sound basis. The two most prominent actuarial functions for an insurer involve ratemaking and estimation of unpaid liabilities and adequacy of loss reserves. Actuaries are also instrumental in developing an insurer's predictive models, and they perform other important functions for insurers, including analyzing reinsurance structure and participating in corporate planning and budgeting.

What Is an Actuary?

There are many definitions of what an actuary is. The American Academy of Actuary succinctly states, "Actuaries put a price tag on risk."[1] A more encompassing definition states, "An actuary is a business professional who deals with the financial impact of risk." The latter definition includes several terms that describe actuaries and their work.

First, actuaries are professionals; they have a formal educational process, a set of standards for performance, and a code of conduct. Focusing on the financial effects of risk, actuaries are found throughout the business world, often employed by either insurance companies or firms supplying services to insurers. Actuaries often rely heavily on mathematical models and statistical techniques, but their examination process also covers insurance operations, accounting, insurance law, and financial analysis.

In the United States, actuaries have several specialties, including life insurance, health insurance, pension, and property/casualty insurance. This discussion focuses on property/casualty actuaries specific to insurer operations.

Actuarial Functions

One of the major functions of actuaries is to direct insurer ratemaking operations. Actuaries also develop factors that are applied to loss costs in order to reflect individual insurer experience and expenses. The ratemaking process involves estimation of trends that will affect claim costs during the future effective period of the rates. Thus, the actuary must consider economic and regulatory factors that will affect the potential cost of coverage.

Another major function of an actuary involves the estimation of an insurer's unpaid liabilities and adequacy of its loss reserves. Insurers are required by both accounting standards and law to set aside funds for the future payments on claims for which they are liable. Actuaries use various methods to estimate the amount of these liabilities. In the U.S., insurers are required to submit, with their statutory annual statement, a statement of opinion by a qualified actuary as to whether the carried reserves make a reasonable provision for this liability. The actuary providing this statement must have been approved by the insurer's board of directors and is named individually in the statement.

Data mining

The process of extracting hidden patterns from data that is used in a wide range of applications for research and fraud detection.

Actuaries are also instrumental in developing insurer's predictive models using **data mining** tools. Predictive modeling is increasingly being applied in areas such as ratemaking, underwriting, claims analytics, customer segmentation, and target marketing, which can lead to increased profits for an insurer.

Because of their quantitative background and familiarity in dealing with uncertain events, actuaries often perform other tasks, primarily related to assessment of insurer risks, including these:

- Analyzing reinsurance needs to determine the level and concentration of risk the insurer can retain versus the cost of reinsurance
- Estimating future cash flows so that assets will be available when claims are to be paid
- Assessing corporate risk by testing the adequacy of surplus under potential adverse conditions (catastrophe, sudden change in asset values, soft pricing, and inflation, for example)
- Providing financial and statistical information to regulators and applicable statistical agents (with accounting and finance areas)
- Participating in corporate planning and budgeting

Actuarial Services

Many large insurers employ a number of actuaries. Although small insurers may have a few actuaries on staff, most tend to rely on actuarial consultants. Some actuaries are concentrated in specialized departments, such as reserving. Insurers may also use actuaries within regional offices or in other functional areas, such as underwriting.

Insurers that employ staff actuaries may also retain actuarial consultants. Outside actuaries can supplement staff knowledge with specialized expertise, provide independent opinion when needed, and ease workload peaks. Regulatory authorities and reinsurers sometimes require insurers to provide a consulting actuary's opinion verifying the accuracy and reasonableness of the staff actuaries' work.

Insurers with limited data for ratemaking rely on rates or loss costs prepared by actuaries at advisory organizations, such as Insurance Services Office, Inc. (ISO), the American Association of Insurance Services (AAIS), or the National Council on Compensation Insurance (NCCI). The actuaries at these organizations collect premium and loss data from many insurers to use in calculating expected loss costs for various types of insurance. Advisory organizations also maintain contact with regulatory authorities to facilitate approval of rate filings. Advisory organizations also provide some services that are not actuarial, such as drafting insurance policies.

INSURER RATEMAKING GOALS

Insurance ratemaking is challenging, because when rates are developed, the amounts of fortuitous future losses and their associated expenses are unknown. In light of this uncertainty, insurers try to develop rates that meet their goals.

With the ratemaking process, insurers strive to be profitable while also meeting all insurance policy obligations. An ideal insurance rate has a number of different characteristics, including some that are contradictory.

Ratemaking Goals

From the insurer's perspective, the primary goal of **ratemaking** is to develop a rate structure that enables the insurer to compete effectively while earning a reasonable profit on its operations. To accomplish this, the rates must result in premiums that adequately cover all losses and expenses and that leave a reasonable amount for profits and contingencies.

Ratemaking
The process insurers use to calculate insurance rates, which are a premium component.

This ratemaking goal complements the underwriting goal, which is to develop and maintain a profitable book of business. To be profitable, the insurer must have adequate rates. However, to maintain its book of business, the insurer's rates must be competitive. These goals can easily conflict with each other. The rate chosen by an insurer is often a compromise between maximizing profit and maintaining (or expanding) market share.

To be approved, rates must comply with applicable regulations. Rate regulation is generally based on having rates that are adequate, not excessive, and not unfairly discriminatory.

Ideal Characteristics of Rates

Ideally, rates should have five characteristics:

- Be stable
- Be responsive
- Provide for contingencies

- Promote risk control
- Reflect differences in risk exposure

Rates do not always have all of these characteristics. Also, some characteristics conflict with others, and compromises are often necessary. For example, rate stability could conflict with the characteristic of responsiveness, which suggests that rates should change promptly in response to external factors that affect losses.

Stable

Stable rates are highly desirable because changing rates is expensive. It takes a fair amount of time and expense to calculate rate indications, get needed approval, and implement them. Generally, rates are changed no more than annually. Rates should also be stable in the sense of not changing drastically from one rate change to the next. Sudden large rate changes cause dissatisfaction among customers and sometimes lead to regulatory or legislative actions.

Responsive

Rates should include the best possible estimates of losses and expenses that will arise from the coverage. Because external conditions change over time, the most recent claim experience ought to predict future experience better than older experience. For this reason, most insurers and advisory organizations review their rates at least annually.

Provide for Contingencies

Future events cannot be predicted accurately, and the insurer has a responsibility to pay all valid claims even if costs are higher than estimated. Rates should provide for contingencies, such as unexpected variations in losses and expenses. This provision will also provide greater security that the insurer will be able to meet its obligations to potential claimants.

Promote Risk Control

Ratemaking systems help to promote risk control by providing lower rates for policyholders who exercise sound risk control. For example, policyholders who install burglar alarm systems receive a reduction in their crime insurance rates. Lower fire insurance rates are charged to policyholders who install automatic sprinkler systems at their premises. However, policyholders who engage in activities that tend to result in more losses, such as persons who use their cars for business, generally pay higher rates.

Reflect Differences in Risk Exposure

A rate is a charge for the exposure to risk. If insureds have attributes that make them more or less susceptible to a risk, using a flat rate means that some will be overcharged and others will be undercharged. For example, the fire insurance rate should not be the same for a wood-frame building as for a steel and concrete building; an ideal rate reflects these differences. Moreover, if the rate could not reflect differences in exposure, the insurer would end up with only higher-risk insureds, a process called anti-selection. Using the preceding example again, owners of wood-frame buildings would gladly pay an "average" rate for fire insurance, while owners of steel buildings would find another insurer who would credit them for the lower risk. The first insurer would end up with only wood-frame insureds, and the average rate would be insufficient for that group. Because insurers have the ability to collect and analyze detailed data on each insured, they can incorporate exposure differences into the rates more accurately.

RATE COMPONENTS AND RATEMAKING TERMS

A rate is the basis for the premium charged by an insurer. To understand why a certain premium or rate is charged, the components that make up a rate must be understood. Knowledge of the components and terminology used in ratemaking will serve as a foundation to understanding the ratemaking process.

This section reviews the components of an insurance rate and discusses common ratemaking terms.

Rate Components

An insurance **rate** consists of three components:

- An amount needed to pay future claims and loss adjustment expenses (prospective loss costs)

- An amount needed to pay future expenses, such as acquisition expenses, overhead, and premium taxes (expense provision)

- An amount for profit and contingencies (profit and contingencies factor)

The first component of an insurance rate is related to the prospective loss costs developed by advisory organizations or by insurers with large pools of loss data. The second and third components are related to an expense multiplier. Once the insurance rate is calculated, it is multiplied by the appropriate number of exposure units to produce a **premium**.

Ratemaking Terms

These are common terms used in the ratemaking process:

Exposure base (sometimes just exposure) is a variable that approximates the loss potential of a type of insurance. For property coverage, the exposure base is the value being insured; for product liability, the exposure is sales.

Rate
The price per exposure unit for insurance coverage.

Premium
The price of the insurance coverage provided for a specified period.

Earned exposure unit is the exposure unit for which the insurer has provided a full period of coverage. The periods are typically measured in years.

Pure premium is the amount included in the rate per exposure unit required to pay losses. This component is also sometimes called the loss cost.

Expense provision is the amount added to the pure premium required to pay expenses. Such expenses include acquisition expenses; general expenses; premium taxes; and licenses and fees paid to government, regulatory, and advisory organizations. This component is sometimes referred to as **underwriting expenses**.

Loss adjustment expenses (LAE) are the expenses associated with adjusting claims. These expenses are often split into either **allocated** or **unallocated LAE**. Some allocated loss adjustment expenses, such as legal fees to defend a claim, may be included in the pure premium instead of in the expense provision. An example of loss adjustment expenses included in the expense provision is the cost of an insurer's in-house claims adjusters.

Insurers add a loading for profit and contingencies. This loading protects the insurer against the possibility that actual losses and expenses will exceed the projected losses and expenses included in the insurance rate. If excessive losses or expenses are not incurred, the funds generated by the loading produce additional profit for the insurer.

Investment Income

A property-casualty insurer performs two distinct operations: insurance operations and investment operations. The insurance operations write policies, collect premiums, and pay losses. The result of the insurance operations is called underwriting profit. The investment operations use the funds generated by the insurance operations to buy or sell bonds, stocks, and other investments to earn an investment profit. The return from these investments is called investment income.

Historically, property-casualty insurers did not consider their investment returns directly when calculating insurance rates. They may, however, have considered investment returns informally when determining allowances for profits and contingencies. Today, insurers commonly consider investment results explicitly in their rate calculations. Some states even require that investment income be considered explicitly. Sophisticated models are available that can be used to include investment returns in the insurance rate.

The investment return earned by an insurer depends largely on the types of insurance written, the loss reserves, and associated unearned premium reserves. Property losses are usually paid relatively quickly, while liability losses often are not paid until years after losses occur. Consequently, an insurer's loss reserves for liability insurance are usually much greater than its loss reserves for an equivalent amount of property insurance. Because the assets that support the loss reserves are invested to produce income for the insurer,

---

Pure premium

The average amount of money an insurer must charge per exposure unit in order to be able to cover the total anticipated losses for that line of business.

Expense provision

The amount that is included in an insurance rate to cover the insurer's expenses and that might include loss adjustment expenses but that excludes investment expenses.

Underwriting expenses

Costs incurred by an insurer for operations, taxes, fees, and the acquisition of new policies.

Loss adjustment expense (LAE)

The expense that an insurer incurs to investigate, defend, and settle claims according to the terms specified in the insurance policy.

Allocated loss adjustment expense (ALAE)

The expense an insurer incurs to investigate, defend, and settle claims that are associated with a specific claim.

Unallocated loss adjustment expense (ULAE)

Loss adjustment expense that cannot be readily associated with a specific claim.

investment returns have a much larger effect on liability insurance rates than property insurance rates.

FACTORS THAT AFFECT RATEMAKING

Various factors have considerable effect on the rate that is set for a particular insurance coverage.

Estimating future events and costs in the real world is subject to uncertainty. These areas of uncertainty affect ratemaking:

- Estimation of losses
- Delays in data collection and use
- Change in the cost of claims
- Insurer's projected expenses
- Target level of profit and contingencies

Estimation of Losses

The key to developing insurance rates that are adequate to pay future claims is estimating the amount of losses for those claims. Past loss experience is generally used as a starting point to estimate future losses. Ratemaking is based on estimating losses from past coverage periods and then adjusting those losses for future conditions. For example, adjustments could be made to past loss experience for anticipated future inflation or for changes in benefits mandated by legislation.

However, past loss experience may not be completely known because not all covered losses are paid immediately. At any point in time, many claims have been incurred but not yet paid. The difference between the estimated amount that will ultimately be paid for claims and the actual loss amount paid to date is the loss reserves. Insurers face the challenge of estimating **ultimate losses** for past experience as accurately as possible because of the difficulty of estimating future payments.

Ultimate loss
The final paid amount for all losses in an accident year.

Insurance rates are based partly on incurred losses. Incurred losses include both paid losses and outstanding loss reserves. Loss reserves are estimates of future payments for covered claims that have already occurred, whether the claims are reported or not. Insurers are legally required to set aside funds for these future payments; these are shown as liabilities on their balance sheets. Because loss reserves are estimates of future events, they are somewhat imprecise. Nonetheless, rates are based partly on such estimates. Therefore, if loss reserve estimates are too low, rates will probably be too low. If loss reserves are too high, rates will probably be too high.

To illustrate, assume that rates for auto liability insurance are calculated based on losses that occurred in the most recent three-year period. The insurer's past experience indicates that 25 percent of losses are paid in the year the accident occurs, 50 percent are paid in the second year, and 25 percent are paid in the third year. The exhibit shows the losses for each year in the three-year period, with Year 1 being the earliest year and Year 3, the most recent year. See the exhibit "Hypothetical Auto Liability Loss Experience at Year 3 End."

Hypothetical Auto Liability Loss Experience at Year 3 End

Year	(1) Paid Losses	(2) Loss Reserves	(3) Incurred Losses
1	$10,000,000	$0	$10,000,000
2	7,500,000	2,500,000	10,000,000
3	2,500,000	7,500,000	10,000,000
Total	$20,000,000	$10,000,000	$30,000,000

[DA03362]

The exhibit shows this information:

- The paid losses in Column (1) are the amounts paid from January 1 of Year 1 up to and including December 31 of Year 3. The insurer has already paid this money to claimants.
- The loss reserves shown in Column (2) are the insurer's best estimates, as of December 31 of Year 3, of the amounts it will pay in the future for losses that occurred during each one-year period. Because all losses that occurred in Year 1 have been paid, no loss reserve exists for Year 1.
- Column (3), which is incurred losses for a given period, is the sum of Columns (1) and (2).

If the insurer in this exhibit insured 100,000 cars each year during this three-year period, it provided 300,000 car-years of protection. A car-year represents the loss exposure of one car insured for one year. If the 300,000 car-years are divided into the $30 million of incurred losses, the insurer needs a pure premium—the amount needed to pay losses—of $100 per car per year ($30,000,000 ÷ 300,000 = $100) to pay its losses during this past three-year period. This example includes not only paid losses but also loss reserves.

If the pure premium indicated by this experience period were used to develop rates for a future year, any inadequacy in past loss reserves would also make future rates inadequate, assuming conditions remain the same. Using the preceding example, assume that the loss reserves were underestimated by 15 percent; that is, the company had only $8,500,000 in loss reserves at the end of Year 3 instead of $10,000,000. The total incurred losses for the years would then be $28,500,000, and the calculated pure premium would be only $95 per car per year ($28,500,000 ÷ 300,000). Rates based on underestimated losses could lead to underwriting losses and possibly even insolvency.

In theory, an insurer could avoid this problem by waiting for all claims to be paid before using loss experience to calculate rates. When all claims incurred during a given period have been paid, there is no need for loss reserves. In practice, however, waiting would create problems. If the rate filing were delayed for several years to permit all claims to be settled, then factors such as inflation, changes in traffic conditions, and so forth would have a greater chance of changing the loss exposure. The effects of these factors might be greater than the effects of errors in estimating loss reserves.

Delays in Data Collection and Use

Responsiveness is a desirable ratemaking characteristic. Because conditions are constantly changing, any delay between when data are collected and when they are used tends to reduce rate accuracy. A delay inevitably occurs between when losses are incurred and when they are reflected in rates charged to customers. The delay can span several years. During this period, economic or other factors can increase or decrease the rates the insurer should charge if the premium is to reflect the expected losses.

The delay in reflecting loss experience in rates stems from several sources, including these:

- Delays by insureds in reporting losses to insurers
- Time required to analyze data and prepare a rate filing
- Delays in obtaining state approval of filed rates
- Time required to implement new rates
- Time period during which rates are in effect, usually a full year

When a rate is in effect for a full year, the last policy issued under that rate could be issued 365 days (one year) after the effective date of the rate filing, and the policy's coverage under that rate continues until policy expiration, yet another year later. See the exhibit "Policy Year Time Frame."

Policy Year Time Frame

1/1/X1	12/31/X1	12/31/X2
Beginning of Policy Year First Policies Issued	Last Policies Issued for This Policy Year	Policies Issued 12/31/X1 Expire

[DA03368]

The "Chronology of a Rate Filing" exhibit shows a reasonably typical schedule for developing, approving, and implementing new rates for auto insurance. The exhibit assumes that the insurer is basing its new rates on its loss experience for a prior three-year period, called the **experience period**. Data from the experience period are collected and analyzed in the ratemaking process. See the exhibit "Chronology of a Rate Filing."

Experience period

The period for which all pertinent statistics are collected and analyzed in the ratemaking process.

Chronology of a Rate Filing

1/1,	Year 1	Start of experience period, first loss incurred
12/31,	Year 1	
12/31,	Year 2	
12/31,	Year 3	End of experience period
3/31,	Year 4	Start of data collection and analysis
7/1,	Year 4	Rates filed with regulators
9/1,	Year 4	Approval of rates received
1/1,	Year 5	New rates initially used
12/31,	Year 5	Rates no longer used
12/31,	Year 6	Last loss incurred under this rate filing

[DA03369]

The experience period in the exhibit begins on January 1 of Year 1. Data are collected for the three-year period beginning on that date and ending on December 31 of Year 3. The analysis phase of the ratemaking process begins three months after the end of the experience period. Some insurers wait longer to start the ratemaking process in order to permit loss data to mature because many claims incurred during the experience period would not yet have been reported to the insurer within three months.

The exhibit assumes that the new rates will become effective on January 1 of Year 5, one year after the end of the experience period. They will remain in effect until December 31 of Year 5, two years after the end of the experience period. However, the policies issued on December 31 of Year 5 will remain in force until December 31 of Year 6. Consequently, the last claim under these rates will be incurred three years after the end of the experience period, and six years after the beginning of the experience period, when the first losses on which the rate calculation was based occurred.

Some insurers shorten this process slightly by filing new rates every six months or issuing six-month policies. Others follow a longer cycle.

Change in Cost of Claims

Both loss severity and loss frequency affect an insurer's loss experience during any given period. Economic inflation or deflation during the inevitable delay also affects the average cost of a loss (severity). Finally, legislative or regulatory changes such as modification in rules governing claim settlement can affect the number of losses (frequency). Rates calculated without regard to these factors could prove to be grossly inadequate or grossly excessive.

These factors are difficult to quantify, but they clearly affect losses. Some factors that affect the size and frequency of losses cannot be identified or measured directly, but their aggregate effect on losses can be determined with reasonable accuracy by trending. The effects of historical changes can be used to adjust the experience used in the ratemaking analysis. In addition, the rates must include a provision for changes that may arise during the period rates will be in effect. For example, in the "Chronology of a Rate Filing" exhibit, the end of the experience period used is December 31, Year 3. However, the claims under the new rates will not start occurring until January 1, Year 5, and may occur as late as December 31, Year 6. Therefore, the filing made on July 1, Year 4, must make allowance for as much of two-and-a-half years of additional (estimated) trend.

Insurer's Projected Expenses

Insurance rates are also based on the insurer's projected expenses. Like losses, expenses can change over time, and any projected changes must be considered in the ratemaking process. Rather than past expenses, it is sometimes more relevant to use judgment or budgeted expenses, especially when conditions change dramatically. For example, if a new agent commission plan was introduced, past commission expense would not necessarily be a good estimate of the costs for new policies.

Ratemakers are also challenged to allocate general administrative expenses properly among different types of insurance. Changes in the allocation of these expenses may need to be reflected in the rates.

Target Level of Profit and Contingencies

The insurer must decide what provision for profit and contingencies should be included in the rate. Consideration is given to the overall desired rate of return, including likely returns from **investment income** versus underwriting profit, respectively. An insurer's target profit may also depend on other factors. For example, an insurer may initially accept a lower profit (and thus charge lower rates) for a new insurance product in order to build a customer base.

Investment income

Interest, dividends, and net capital gains received by an insurer from the insurer's financial assets, minus its investment expenses.

RATEMAKING METHODS

While there can be a myriad of data, adjustments, and other inputs to the ratemaking process, there are actually just a few methods for adjusting an existing rate or developing a new rate.

Insurers commonly use three ratemaking methods:

- Pure premium method
- Loss ratio method
- Judgment method

The three methods are compared in the exhibit. See the exhibit "Ratemaking Methods."

Ratemaking Methods

Method	Data Required	Uses
Pure premium method	• Incurred losses • Earned exposure units • Expense provision • Profit and contingencies factor	To develop rates from past experience (cannot be used without past experience)
Loss ratio method	Actual loss ratio, calculated from: • Incurred losses • Earned premiums Expected loss ratio, calculated as: 100%—Provision for expenses, profit, and contingencies	To modify existing rates (cannot be used without existing rates; cannot be used to determine rates for a new type of insurance)
Judgment method	Rates based on experience and judgment	To develop rates when data are limited (requires skilled judgment)

[DA03381]

Pure Premium Ratemaking Method

The first ratemaking method is the **pure premium method**. This method uses loss per exposure based on past experience as the basis for the rate. While this method relies on past experience, it is independent of any current rates.

The pure premium method has four steps. The first step is to calculate the pure premium. The pure premium (the amount needed to pay losses and, depending on the line of business, allocated loss adjustment expenses) is calculated by dividing the dollar amount of incurred losses by the number of earned exposure units.

$$\text{Incurred losses} = \$4 \text{ million}$$

$$\text{Earned car-years} = 100{,}000$$

$$\text{Pure premium} = \frac{\text{Incurred losses}}{\text{Earned car-years}}$$

$$\text{Pure premium} = \frac{\$4{,}000{,}000}{100{,}000} = \$40$$

The second step in the pure premium method is to estimate expenses per exposure unit based on the insurer's past expenses (except investment expenses and possibly loss adjustment expenses). Whatever loss adjustment expenses are included in the pure premium are excluded from the expenses. Investment expenses are not directly reflected in rate calculations. If expenses are $1.7 million, then expenses per exposure unit are as shown:

$$\frac{\$1{,}700{,}000}{100{,}000} = \$17$$

The third step is to determine the profit and contingencies factor. In this example, a factor of 5 percent is used. A provision for net investment income is generally included within the profit provision.

$$\text{Rate per exposure unit} = \frac{\text{Pure premium} + \text{Expenses per exposure unit}}{1 - \text{Profit and contingencies factor}}$$

$$= \frac{\$40 + \$17}{1 - 0.05}$$

The final step is to add the pure premium and the expense provision and divide by one minus the profit and contingencies factor. For example, if the pure premium is $40, the expenses per exposure unit are $17, and the profit and contingencies factor is 5 percent, the formula would be this:

$$\text{Rate per exposure unit} = \frac{\text{Pure premium} + \text{Expenses per exposure unit}}{1 - \text{Profit and contingencies factor}}$$

$$= \frac{\$40 + \$17}{1 - 0.05}$$

$$= \frac{\$57}{0.95}$$

$$= \$60$$

The rate per exposure unit of $60 is equal to the pure premium of $40 (the amount required to pay losses) plus an additional $17 (the amount required to pay expenses) and $3 (for profit and contingencies).

Some insurers separate their expenses into two components: fixed expenses and variable expenses. Fixed expenses are stated as a dollar amount per exposure unit. Variable expenses are stated as a percentage of the rate. For example, the insurer in the preceding example might decide that its cost for issuing a policy and collecting the premium is $2.50 per car-year, regardless of premium size, rating class, or rating territory. Its other underwriting expenses, such as commissions and premium tax, vary by premium size. The variable expenses equal 12 percent of the final premium. The rate per exposure unit in this case would be this:

$$\text{Rate per exposure unit} = \frac{\text{Pure premium} + \text{Fixed expenses per exposure unit}}{1 - \text{Variable expense percentage} - \text{Profit and contingencies factor}}$$

$$= \frac{\$40 + \$2.50}{1 - 0.12 - 0.05}$$

$$= \frac{\$42.50}{0.83}$$

$$= \$51 \text{ (rounded)}$$

The new rate per exposure unit of $51 is equal to the sum of pure premium of $40 (the amount required to pay losses or loss costs), fixed expenses of $2.50, variable expenses of $6 (rounded), and $2.50 (rounded) for profit and contingencies.

Loss Ratio Ratemaking Method

Loss ratio method

A method for determining insurance rates based on a comparison of actual and expected loss ratios.

The second ratemaking method is the **loss ratio method**. In its simplest form, the loss ratio method uses two loss ratios—the actual loss ratio and the expected loss ratio of the insurer during the selected experience period:

1. $\text{Actual loss ratio} = \dfrac{\text{Incurred losses}}{\text{Earned premiums}}$

2. $\text{Expected loss ratio} = 100\% - \text{Expense provision}$

In this method, profit and contingencies are included in the expense provision because the method modifies a current insurance rate. The expected loss ratio plus the provision for expenses, profit, and contingencies always add up to 100 percent.

This is the loss ratio ratemaking equation in its simplest form:

$$\text{Rate change} = \frac{\text{Actual loss ratio} - \text{Expected loss ratio}}{\text{Expected loss ratio}}$$

If the rate change percentage is negative, it indicates a rate reduction. If positive, it indicates a rate increase. For example, if the actual loss ratio equals 54 percent and the expected loss ratio equals 60 percent, then the rate change is a decrease of 10 percent.

$$\frac{\text{Actual loss ratio} - \text{Expected loss ratio}}{\text{Expected loss ratio}} = \frac{(0.54 - 0.60)}{0.60}$$

$$= \frac{-0.06}{0.60}$$

$$\text{Rate change} = -0.10 = -10\%$$

In this case, the insurer's actual loss ratio was better than expected. Based only on this information, it appears that the insurer could lower its rates and still make the desired profit on business subject to these rates. Lower rates would probably also attract additional business, which would produce greater profits.

The loss ratio ratemaking method cannot be used to calculate rates for a new type of insurance, because neither an actual loss ratio for the calculation nor an old rate to adjust is available. For a new type of insurance, either the pure premium method or the judgment method must be used.

Judgment Ratemaking Method

The third and oldest ratemaking method is the **judgment ratemaking method**. Though its use is no longer as widespread as it once was, this method is still used for some types of insurance, such as ocean marine insurance, some inland marine classes, aviation insurance and situations when limited data are available, as with terrorism coverage. Although the judgment ratemaking method might use limited or no loss experience data, an experienced underwriter or actuary generally has a sense of what rates have produced desired results in the past.

Judgment ratemaking method

A method for determining insurance rates that relies heavily on the experience and knowledge of an actuary or an underwriter who makes little or no use of loss experience data.

RATEMAKING PROCESS OVERVIEW

Ratemaking can involve a number of complex technical issues. An understanding of the process involved reveals the importance and contribution of each step in the ratemaking process.

When creating or revising insurance rates, an insurer's staff, or an advisory organization on behalf of the insurer, follows a series of steps:

1. Collect data
2. Adjust data
3. Calculate overall indicated rate change
4. Determine territorial and class relativities
5. Prepare rate filings and submit to regulatory authorities as required

An insurer follows a similar process when reviewing loss costs, rather than rates. The provisions for expense and for profit and contingencies are excluded from the process, but all other adjustments and parts of the process are unchanged.

For companies that rely on loss cost filings made by advisory organizations, the ratemaking process involves calculating and filing an appropriate **loss cost multiplier**.

Loss cost multiplier

A factor that provides for differences in expected loss, individual company expenses, underwriting profit and contingencies; when multiplied with a loss cost, it produces a rate.

Collect Data

To obtain and maintain usable data, each insurer must code data when transactions occur. Some coding is prescribed by advisory organizations, but many insurers collect more data than advisory organizations require. Information about specific policies is collected most conveniently when policies, endorsements, and invoices are issued. Claim data are collected when claims are reported, reserves are established or changed, checks or drafts are issued, or claims are closed.

Before collecting ratemaking data, the insurer must determine the kinds of data needed. The data fall into three general categories:

*   Losses, both paid and incurred (including any loss adjustment expenses to be included in the pure premium)
*   Earned premium and/or exposure information
*   Expenses, including a profit and contingencies factor

If rates are to vary by rating class and/or territory, data must be identified for each class and territory. For example, if an insurer is considering establishing a new class of business, it would first identify experience for this class separately so there would be data to calculate a separate class rate.

Ideally, the incurred losses, earned premiums, and earned exposure units should be based on the same group of policies. Because this is not always practical, approximation techniques are used. For example, sometimes it is most practical to compare premiums during one twelve-month period with losses for a slightly different twelve-month period, even if these two periods do not involve exactly the same policies.

Different aggregations of data may be used, depending on the line of business. For example, loss payments for a single claim could be made over several successive calendar years. Consequently, the **calendar-year method** is unsuitable for collecting ratemaking data for liability and workers compensation insurance, because the delay in loss payment can be long and the loss reserves can be large relative to earned premiums. For those types of insurance, either the **policy-year method** or **accident-year method** should be used.

For fire, inland marine, and auto physical damage insurance, losses are paid relatively quickly, and loss reserves tend to be small relative to earned premiums. Consequently, the calendar-year method may be satisfactory for ratemaking data collection, although it is still not as accurate as the other two methods.

Adjust Data

After data have been collected, they must be adjusted. Adjustment is necessary because the raw exposure, premium, and loss data reflect conditions from present and past periods, whereas the rates being developed will be used in the future.

Actuaries use several ways of adjusting premium and loss data:

- Adjust premium to current rate level
- Adjust historic experience for future development
- Apply trending to losses and premium

Adjust Premiums to Current Rate Level

If rates charged in the experience period were written at different rate levels, premiums will need to be adjusted to the current level.

The ideal way to adjust premiums to current rate level is to calculate the premium for each policy in the experience period at current rate level. For example, the 20X1 personal auto premiums at 20X4's rate level would be calculated by pricing each auto insured in 20X1 at 20X4 rates. However, re-rating every exposure requires storing, retrieving and using every rating factor for each policy of each exposure, possibly making this method economically unfeasible. An alternative is to adjust historic premiums in total to current levels.

As an illustration of this approach, assume that a book of business has $100 of losses each year. In Year 1, a premium of $200 is charged, but the insurer decreases rates by 20 percent in each of the next two years. Therefore, an insured that paid $1,000 premium in the first year would pay only $640 after the two rate decreases. If the insurer had a 50 percent loss ratio the first year, 63 percent the second year, and 78 percent the third year, it would be inappropriate to project the coming year's loss ratio as the average of those loss ratios. The 50 percent loss ratio in Year 1 was based on premiums that would

Calendar-year method
A method of collecting ratemaking data that estimates both earned premiums and incurred losses by formulas from accounting records.

Policy-year method
A method of collecting ratemaking data that analyzes all policies issued in a given twelve-month period and that links all losses, premiums, and exposure units to the policy to which they are related.

Accident-year method
A method of organizing ratemaking statistics that uses incurred losses for an accident year, which consist of all losses related to claims arising from accidents that occur during the year, and that estimates earned premiums by formulas from accounting records.

not be charged as of Year 3, so it should not be used directly for ratemaking. The premium that had been charged must be adjusted to what would be charged in Year 3, the most recent year. See the exhibit "Effect of On-Level Premium Adjustment."

Effect of On-Level Premium Adjustment

Year	(1) Developed Losses	(2) Collected Premium	(3) = (1)/(2) Collected Loss Ratio	(4) Rate Level Index	(5) On-Level Factor	(6) = (2)×(5) On-Level Premium	(7) = (1)/(6) On-Level Loss Ratio
1	$100	$200	50%	1.00	0.64	$128	78%
2	$100	$160	63%	0.80	0.80	$128	78%
3	$100	$128	78%	0.64	1.00	$128	78%

[DA06289]

On-level factor

A factor that is used to adjust historical premiums to the current rate level.

Column 4 in the table shows the rate level relative to Year 1. This rate level index reflects the assumption that rates decreased 20 percent from the prior year in both Year 2 and Year 3. The **on-level factor** in Column 5 adjusts rate levels for each year to the most recent period's rate levels. It equals the rate level index for the most recent period (Year 3) divided by the rate level index for each year. At the most recent year's rate level, each year's losses would have produced a 78 percent loss ratio.

Premiums may also have to be adjusted for different levels of coverage purchased. For example, an automobile liability insurer finds that it is now selling much more of its $100,000 per accident limits than the $25,000 limit it had in the past. The premiums (and perhaps losses) need to be adjusted for this change in coverage provided.

Adjust Historic Experience for Future Development

When policy-year or accident-year experience is used to predict future results, one must remember that the experience might not be complete. There may still be open claims that require future payment or the possibility of a late-reported claim for which the insurer is liable. The insurer must estimate the values of these future payments and add it to the payments to date in order to estimate the ultimate losses of each period.

For example, at the end of a year, payments for medical malpractice claims that occurred during that year may be only 10 percent of the ultimate payment. Because of the complexity and long discovery period of such claims, even the incurred losses tend to increase over time. Conversely, for automobile physical damage, an insurer's net loss payments might decrease over time as it collects salvage and subrogation recoveries on claims it has paid.

The future development of the losses can be estimated by several actuarial methods. The most common method used is applying **loss development factors** to the current experience. With any method, the goal is to estimate the final, total cost to pay all the claims within each year. These projections are then used as the basis for estimating the losses that will be incurred in the proposed policy period.

Apply Trending to Losses and Premium

Another way losses are adjusted for ratemaking is through trending. Trending is the review of historic environmental changes and projecting such changes into the future. Examples of such changes would be inflation of claim costs, the increasing safety of newer cars, or changes in legal liability.

Trend adjustments can come from various sources. In some instances, external indexes such as the Consumer Price Index or one of its components may be used in trending. The most frequently used source of trends is historical experience. This experience can be reviewed by an insurer using its own data or by a statistical agent, such as Insurance Services Office, Inc. (ISO) or the National Council on Compensation Insurance (NCCI), using the combined experience of numerous companies. The trend adjustment commonly uses historical experience to project past trends into the future. Loss trending is usually reviewed in separate severity and frequency components.

These trends can be projected into the future using an exponential trending method. **Exponential trending** assumes that data being projected will increase or decrease by a fixed percentage each year as compared with the previous year. For example, claim frequency will increase 1.3 percent each year, or claim severity will increase 8.2 percent each year. Exponential trends have a compounding effect over time. For example, price inflation would be expected to follow an exponential trend. See the exhibit "Claim Severity Trend Calculation."

Losses may need to be adjusted to current conditions if other significant external changes have affected loss payouts in recent years. For example, workers compensation insurance benefits are established by statute. If legislation or a court decision changes these benefits, past losses must be adjusted to current benefit levels.

Premiums may also need to be trended to reflect changing conditions. For example, the amount of homeowners insurance purchased tends to change with the value of the home. If home prices have risen, more premiums might be collected on the same house just because of its increase in value. Trending factors would be applied to adjust for past and future changes in premium due to these external factors.

Loss development factor
An actuarial means for adjusting losses to reflect future growth in claims due to both increases in the incurred amount for reported losses and incurred but not reported (IBNR) losses.

Exponential trending
A method of loss trending that assumes a fixed percentage increase or decrease for each time period.

Claim Severity Trend Calculation

	(1)	(2)	(3)	(4)	(5)
			Developed	= (3)/(2)	
		Developed	Number of	Average Claim	Change From
	Accident Year	Losses	Claims	Severity	Prior Year
	20X1	$11,000,000	9,167	$1,200	
	20X2	$10,287,750	7,913	$1,300	8.3%
	20X3	$11,112,000	7,880	$1,410	8.5%
	20X4	$10,659,000	6,995	$1,524	8.1%
	20X5	$11,275,000	6,860	$1,644	7.9%
				Average	8.2%

The losses and claims are the estimated final values for each accident year, projected using development factors or other methods.

[DA06290]

Calculate Overall Indicated Rate Change

The purpose of adjustments, development, and trending is to bring prior experience to a level comparable to the future rate's policy period. Based on the adjusted experience, an overall rate indication is calculated. In some cases, a new rate is calculated directly. However, in most cases, the indication shows a change from the current rate level, for example, an overall 2.7 percent increase.

Several different methods, such as the loss ratio method and the pure premium method, can be used to produce an indication. These methods depend on the amount and type of experience available.

Determine Territorial and Class Relativities

If rates vary by territory and/or class, they are reviewed after the calculation of the overall rate change. Further analysis is performed to determine territorial and/or class relativities. These relativities reflect the extent to which various subsets of insureds in a state deserve rates that are higher or lower than the statewide average rate. For example, in a territory with many congested highways, auto insurance rates might be 8.6 percent higher than the statewide average rate, while in a rural territory rates might be 20.2 percent lower. Similarly, a frame-constructed building has a different exposure to fire loss than a fire-resistive steel and concrete building, so different rates are warranted.

Territorial relativities can be determined by comparing the estimated loss ratio (or pure premium) for each geographic territory to the statewide average loss ratio (or pure premium). This comparison produces factors that are applied to the statewide average rate to reflect experience in each geographic territory. If a given territory has limited experience, its territorial loss ratios are likely to vary widely. Differences from the overall average rate must be supported by credible experience. If a class has only a few exposures, even very good (or very poor) experience will produce only minimal difference from the average rate; because of the limited exposures, the difference could be a result of mere chance.

Class relativities are used to develop rates for each rating class. Class relativities are determined similarly to territorial relativities. Once class relativities have been determined, the insurer can prepare a rate table showing rates for each territory and each rating class.

Prepare and Submit Rate Filings

After data have been collected and adjusted, and after any territorial and class relativities have been determined, rate filings must be prepared. A rate filing is a document submitted to state regulatory authorities. The form for and the amount of information required in a filing vary by state.

Generally, the filing must include at least these seven items:

- Schedule of the proposed new rates
- Statement about the percentage change, either an increase or a decrease, in the statewide average rate
- Explanation of differences between the overall statewide change in rate and the percentage change of the rates for individual territories and/or rating classes (if any)
- Data to support the proposed rate changes, including territorial and class relativities
- Expense provision data
- Target profit provision included in the rates, if applicable, and any supporting calculations
- Explanatory material to enable state insurance regulators to understand and evaluate the filing

Depending on state law, formal approval of the filing by regulators might not be required. In some states, approval must be obtained before the rates are used. In other states, formal approval is not required by law, but many insurers prefer to obtain approval before use to avoid the possibility of having to withdraw the rates if regulators decide that rates do not meet statutory requirements.

Actuaries are best qualified to answer any technical questions that the regulators might raise. However, some insurers prefer to delegate most of the contact with regulators to the legal department or filing specialists and to involve actuaries only as needed.

If an advisory organization files rates or loss costs on behalf of an insurer, it handles any follow-up or negotiations. Generally, companies that use an advisory organization are assumed to adopt the filings made by that organization automatically. When loss costs are filed by an advisory organization, the insurer is responsible for filing its expense provisions, which would yield its final rates.

RATEMAKING FACTOR VARIANCES FOR DIFFERENT TYPES OF INSURANCE

Ratemaking can vary widely by type of insurance. These variations can result from the characteristics of loss exposures, regulatory requirements, and other factors.

Major differences between ratemaking for different lines of business can be found in experience period, trending, large loss limitations, credibility, and increased limits factors.

Experience Period

Using an experience period of one to three years is common for auto insurance and other types of liability insurance. For fire insurance, a five-year experience period is used almost universally because it is required by law in many states. The experience for each of the five years is usually not given equal weight. The experience for the most recent years is given greater weight to promote rate responsiveness.

The experience period used for other property causes of loss, such as wind, is even longer—frequently twenty years or more. The purpose of such a long experience period is to avoid the large swings in rates that would otherwise result when a major hurricane, a series of major tornadoes, or another natural catastrophe strikes an area.

Three factors can be considered in determining the appropriate experience period: (1) legal requirements, if any; (2) the variability of losses over time; and (3) the credibility of the resulting ratemaking data. The second and third factors are related to some degree.

Trending

Trending practices also vary by type of insurance. Trending may be based on experience or external indices. Moreover, trending may be needed for premiums as well as losses.

For property insurance, loss claim frequency is low and generally stable, so trending may be restricted to claim severity. However, the average claim is not used to measure claim severity because the average property insurance claim may be distorted by infrequent large claims. Consequently, an external composite index, composed partly of a construction cost index and partly of the consumer price index, is used for trending.

For liability insurance, separate trending of claim severity and claim frequency is common because of the different factors that affect them. Economic inflation or deflation over the course of payments can affect the average cost of a claim (severity). Legislative, regulatory or other external changes, such as modification in rules governing claim settlement, can affect the number of losses (frequency).

In some lines, such as fire insurance, trending both losses and premiums is necessary. Losses are trended partly to reflect any effects of inflation on claim costs. For example, inflation can elevate property values, and people tend to increase the amount of property insurance purchased to reflect the increased values. This increases insurer premium revenue. Increases in amounts insured tend to lag somewhat behind inflation during certain periods. Consequently, insurers trend both losses and premiums and offset the growth in premiums against the growth in losses. Premiums are also trended in other types of insurance for which the exposure units are affected by inflation. Examples include workers compensation (which uses payroll as its exposure base) and some general liability insurance (which uses sales).

A special trending problem exists in workers compensation insurance. Because the benefits for such insurance are established by statute, legislation or a court decision can change the benefits unexpectedly. A law amendment factor is used to adjust rates and losses to reflect statutory benefit changes. Actuaries can estimate with reasonable accuracy the effects of a statutory benefit change on the losses that insurers will incur under their policies. Unlike other trending, rate changes in statutory benefits might apply to outstanding policies as well as new and renewal policies.

For equipment breakdown insurance, inspection and risk control services are a significant portion of the rate, often exceeding the pure premium component. In this case, trending is applied to the risk control expenses because they constitute such a large portion of the rate.

Large Loss Limitations

Unusual rate fluctuations could result from occasional large losses, whether from large individual losses or from an accumulation of smaller losses from a single event, such as a hurricane. In liability insurance, these fluctuations are controlled by using only basic limit losses in calculating incurred losses. **Basic limit** losses are losses capped at some predetermined amount, such as $100,000.

A similar practice is followed in workers compensation insurance ratemaking. Individual claims are limited to a specified amount for ratemaking purposes.

Basic limit

The minimum amount of coverage for which a policy can be written; usually found in liability lines.

Another limitation applies to multiple claims arising from a single event. Both limitations vary over time and by state.

Loss limitations also apply in ratemaking for property insurance. For example, when a large single loss occurs in fire insurance, only part of it is included in ratemaking calculations in the state in which it occurred. The balance is spread over the rates of all the states. The amount included in the state depends on the total fire insurance premium volume in that state, so it varies substantially by state.

Most losses from catastrophic events, such as hurricanes, are excluded from ratemaking data and replaced by a flat catastrophe charge in the rates. The amount of the catastrophe charge is determined by catastrophe data collected over a long time period to smooth the fluctuations that would otherwise result. A **catastrophe model**, which incorporates past experience with scientific theory, is often used to calculate an appropriate charge for these potential losses.

Catastrophe model

A type of computer program that estimates losses from future potential catastrophic events.

Commercial insurers may also be required to quote a separate charge applicable to the terrorism loss exposure. Because past loss experience with terrorism losses in the United States has been extremely limited, terrorism ratemaking presents a special challenge.

Credibility

Credibility is a measure of the predictive ability of data. In ratemaking, the credibility of past loss data is important in projecting future losses. Fully credible ratemaking data have sufficient volume to provide an accurate estimate of the expected losses for the line, state, territory, and/or class being reviewed. The volatility of the loss data determines how much volume is needed to be fully credible—the higher the volatility, the more data are required to provide a reasonable projection of future losses. For example, a smaller amount of automobile liability experience is needed for full credibility than for fire insurance, because the larger number of claims per exposure and smaller average claim size leads to more stable results.

Credibility

The level of confidence an actuary has in projected losses; increases as the number of exposure units increases.

Credibility assumptions vary by type of insurance. In auto insurance, advisory organizations and some larger insurers consider the statewide loss data to be fully credible. That assumption might be inappropriate for some small insurers who base their rates solely on their own loss data. For territories and classes with loss data that the advisory organization determines are not fully credible, rates are calculated as a weighted average of the indicated rate for the territory or class and the statewide average rate for all classes and territories combined. The **credibility factor** is used as the weight in the weighted average. It indicates the amount of weight to give to the actual loss experience for the territory or class as compared with an alternative source—in this case, the statewide average loss experience. A credibility factor is a number between 0 (no credibility) and 1 (full confidence).

Credibility factor

The factor applied in ratemaking to adjust for the predictive value of loss data and used to minimize the variations in the rates that result from purely chance variations in losses.

For property insurance, because of the low average claim frequency, advisory organizations might determine that even the statewide loss data are not fully credible. In that case, a three-part weighted average could be used, combining the state loss data for the rating class, regional (multistate) loss data of the rating class, and state loss data for a major group encompassing several rating classes. Again, credibility factors are used as weights.

The pure premiums for workers compensation insurance developed by the National Council on Compensation Insurance (NCCI) are composed of pure premium charges for medical and indemnity costs. Separate credibility standards exist for each of these categories.

Increased Limits Factors

Liability insurance coverage is provided at various limits of coverage. Actuaries use a number of ratemaking techniques for pricing coverage amounts in excess of the basic limit. Although it would be possible to develop separate rates for each limit of liability coverage offered, that approach would require credible ratemaking experience at each limit, as well as significant, often duplicative, efforts.

The most common approach to establishing rates for coverage greater than the basic limit is to develop **increased limits factors**. A base rate is first developed using losses capped at the basic limit. Increased limits factors can then be applied to the basic limit rate. For example, the additional charge to increase the general liability limit to $2 million for any one occurrence might be expressed as 70 percent of the basic coverage limit rate, producing an increased limits factor of 1.70.

Increased limit factor
A factor applied to the rates for basic limits to arrive at an appropriate rate for higher limits.

Charges to increase liability limits can, and frequently do, exceed 100 percent of the charge for basic coverage limits. Several reasons exist for the large increased limits factors for several lines of business, such as general liability and auto liability. First, the additional coverage purchased by the customer can be much higher than the basic limit. For example, in personal auto liability, the basic limit might be $50,000 per accident, but the customer purchases $1 million in coverage to protect his or her assets. Although loss severity does not increase uniformly with increased coverage limits, the exposure to loss is substantially greater at higher limits. Second, higher limits can also require a portion of the coverage to be reinsured, with the additional expense of reinsurance included in the rate. Finally, because large losses occur less frequently than small losses and take longer to settle, the variability of losses in higher coverage layers is greater than for the basic limit losses, and the credibility is lower. This greater variability requires a greater **risk charge** at higher levels of coverage.

Risk charge
An amount over and above the expected loss component of the premium to compensate the insurer for taking the risk that losses may be higher than expected.

LOSS RESERVES AND ANALYSIS

A matter of critical concern to an insurer is the holding of the appropriate amount of loss reserves.

Loss reserves for future claim payments are generally the largest liability on the insurer's balance sheet and a significant part of an insurer's financial condition. They represent the security that an insured's claim will be paid. Accurate estimation of these future liabilities provides the insurer with an understanding of the actual costs of business and ensures its ability to pay the claims in the future. Actuaries use various techniques to estimate the liability for these future payments.

Purpose of Loss Reserves

Insurers are required by law and good accounting practice to establish reserves for losses that reasonably can be assumed to have been incurred. These reserves are not just for reported claims but also for claims that have occurred but that have not yet been reported to the insurer. The reserves set aside part of current income (premiums) for the losses to be paid in the future.

Loss reserves are also needed to provide a complete picture of an insurer's financial status. Unlike manufacturers, insurers do not completely know their costs of doing business in advance of the sale of the product. Future payments on current claims may stretch out over years. An insurer must estimate these future payments in order to calculate its profit or loss.

The liability carried on an insurer's books for future payments on incurred claims is commonly called loss reserve. However, the liability is not just for payments of claimants' losses; the insurer is also responsible for future loss adjustment expenses (LAE). Such expenses include both allocated loss adjustment expenses (ALAE) and unallocated loss adjustment expenses (ULAE).

The responsibility for selecting the amount of loss reserves held by an insurer rests with the company's senior management. Actuaries and other professionals provide estimates of the liability (estimated unpaid claims) to management to assist them in this decision.

Types of Loss Reserves

The principal types of loss reserves established by insurers are case reserves and bulk reserves.

Case reserves are amounts that represent the estimated loss value of each individual claim. An insurer's claim department usually sets these reserves, but the actuarial department might assist with some complex claims. Case reserves are set according to the specific characteristics of each claim. When a claim is first reported, the claim representative's estimate might be based on very little information. Over time, as the specific characteristics of the claim become known, the case reserve becomes more accurate.

The claim department is responsible for setting case reserves on each of the individual claims. However, the insurer cannot identify specific claims with inadequate or excessive case reserves or predict which claims will reopen. Therefore, insurers make general provision for additional reserves, called bulk reserves (in contrast to case reserves). For some types of insurance, the bulk reserves can be a substantial part of an insurer's total liabilities.

The bulk (or aggregate) reserves can have three components:

- **Incurred but not reported (IBNR) reserves**
- Reserves for losses that have been reported but for which the established case reserves are inadequate (sometimes called IBNER (incurred but not enough recorded) reserves)
- Reserves for claims that have been settled and then reopened

Reserves specifically for unreported claims are sometimes called "pure IBNR." An example of a pure IBNR claim is a general liability claim for injuries suffered in a slip and fall inside an insured's premises, unknown to the insurer until a lawsuit is brought months after the accident. In practice, the term "IBNR reserves" is often used to mean all of the bulk reserves.

Importance of Accurate Loss Reserves

The purpose of loss reserve analysis is to determine whether the carried loss and loss adjustment expense reserves can be expected to adequately cover the losses that have been incurred but not yet been paid. Such analysis might be undertaken by a number of parties for various reasons:

- Management, as part of its analysis of costs of doing business
- The insurer's auditors, to determine whether the insurer's financial statements accurately indicate its financial condition and performance
- Rating agencies (such as A. M. Best or Standard & Poor's), on behalf of potential investors or creditors
- Regulators (on behalf of policyholders), to assure that claims will be paid

The National Association of Insurance Commissioners (NAIC) Annual Statement instructions require insurers to have their loss reserves certified by an **actuary** or another qualified professional. Those who provide such certification may be exposed to potential professional liability claims. Consequently, they ordinarily provide such opinions only after carefully analyzing the reserves.

The effect of inaccurate loss reserves can be substantial. Loss reserves (including LAE reserves) often exceed the total surplus for an insurer and are usually a considerable multiple of the earnings in a year. A significant change in

Incurred but not reported (IBNR) reserves
A reserve established for losses that reasonably can be assumed to have been incurred but not yet reported.

Actuary
A person who uses mathematical methods to analyze insurance data for various purposes, such as to develop insurance rates or set claim reserves.

reserves for prior years not only affects the current year's profitability but can even risk the insurer's solvency.

An overestimation of loss reserves (higher than ultimately paid) can lower an insurer's financial strength ratings, reduce statutory limits on premiums that can be written, or lead to dissolution of an insurer. If loss reserves are underestimated, the insurer can become insolvent when it becomes apparent that the future payments will exceed the reserve level.

Analysis of Loss Reserves

Because of the size and potential effect of loss reserves, close attention is given to the estimation of these unpaid liabilities. The analysis is usually done by an actuary, using a variety of methods and techniques. In most cases, estimates are made of the ultimate losses to be paid on the exposures to date; the loss reserve is then estimated by subtracting payments to date. Sometimes separate projections of the reserve are required for known claims and for IBNR claims, and those results are added together.

ALAE reserves may be estimated with or separately from the loss reserve estimate. ULAE reserves are usually analyzed separately from those of loss and ALAE.

Among the most common methods used to estimate ultimate losses are these:

- Expected loss ratio method
- Loss development method
- Bornhuetter-Ferguson method

The expected loss ratio method uses a prior estimate of ultimate losses rather than current experience. It is often used when current experience is limited or of little predictive value, and in fact, the method ignores the experience to date.

The loss development method assumes that future changes in the loss will occur in a similar manner as in the past. This method assumes that the experience to date is an indicator of what future payments will be.

The Bornhuetter-Ferguson method uses parts of the other two methods. It accepts the experience to date (unlike the expected loss ratio method), but assumes that future results are independent of the current experience. The ultimate projection from this method is the sum of actual results to date plus expected future results. See the exhibit "An Illustration of Reserving Methods."

The selection of the appropriate method to be used depends on the data available, timing, and other characteristics of the experience reviewed. For example, it would usually be inappropriate to apply the loss development method to the experience of only the first week of a policy period.

An Illustration of Reserving Methods

An illustration may help clarify how the three common methods of estimating ultimate losses work. Assume Josh wishes to estimate the number of home runs Ethan will hit this season. Before the season starts, Josh looks at Ethan's record and finds that he has hit 40 home runs a year, spread about evenly through the season. Suppose that, after a quarter of the season has gone, Ethan has hit 15 home runs. How many home runs would Ethan be expected to hit for the whole season?

The expected loss method would stay with the initial estimate of 40 home runs. The 15 hit so far could be just a random fluctuation, which might be offset by a slump later in the season. The initial estimate remains.

The loss development method would note that Ethan usually hits 10 home runs in the first quarter and ends the season with 40 home runs, or four times the quarterly experience. Using this method would produce an estimate of 15 (home runs to date) × 4 = 60 home runs for the year. The estimate is based entirely on past patterns applied to current experience.

The Bornhuetter-Ferguson method combines these two approaches. For the three quarters of the year remaining, Ethan had been expected to hit 40 × ¾ = 30 home runs. Adding them to the 15 hit so far produces an estimate of 45 home runs for the year.

[DA06341]

Because the reserve analysis is an estimate of future events, there is inherent uncertainty in any reserve estimate. An actuarially sound reserve estimate should be based on reasonable assumptions using appropriate and generally accepted methodology. Even so, actuaries cannot and do not guarantee that actual future payments will be at or near the estimate.

Loss Development—A Closer Look

Because of the widespread use of the loss development method and underlying loss development triangles, it is useful to take a closer look at this method. Although most commonly used to project losses (both paid and reported) to ultimate values, this technique is also used to project allocated loss adjustment expenses, claim counts, and even premiums.

The loss development method involves four steps:

1. Compile the experience into a loss development triangle
2. Calculate the age-to-age development factors
3. Select the development factors to be used
4. Apply factors to experience to make projections

The loss development triangle is a table showing values for a specific group of claims at different points in time. The table is arranged so that it is easy to see values and changes of different groups at similar ages of development. The claims are usually grouped by accident year or policy year.

A simple example shows how the loss development triangle is created. Assume that accident year 20X1 has three claims, with payments made as shown. See the exhibit "Payments Made on Accident Year 20X1 Claims."

Payments Made on Accident Year 20X1 Claims

Claim	Payment Made	Payment Amount
A	3/14/X1	$425
A	7/21/X2	$200
A	2/12/X3	$192
B	1/04/X2	$75
B	9/04/X2	$25
C	11/29/X2	$75

Paid as of 12/31/X1 = $425

Paid as of 12/31/X2 = Paid @ 12/31/X1 + Paid during 20X2

= 425 + (200 + 75 + 25 + 75)

= $800

Paid as of 12/31/X3 = Paid @ 12/31/X2 + Paid during 20X3

= 800 + 192

= $992

[DA06342]

The payments at the end of each year can be summarized. See the exhibit "Cumulative Paid Loss as of Calendar Year-End."

Cumulative Paid Loss as of Calendar Year-End

Accident Year	Year-End 20X1	Year-End 20X2	Year-End 20X3	Year-End 20X4
20X1	$425	$800	$992	$992

[DA06343]

By the end of 20X4, payments have also been made for later accident years, so a more complete table of payments can be assembled. See the exhibit "Cumulative Paid Loss as of Calendar Year-End, Multiple Years."

It is easier to compare the different years' experience at the same "age"; for example, comparing accident year 20X1 at the end of 20X1 to accident year

Cumulative Paid Loss as of Calendar Year-End, Multiple Years

Accident Year	Year-End 20X1	Year-End 20X2	Year-End 20X3	Year-End 20X4
20X1	$425	$800	$992	$992
20X2		450	750	870
20X3			500	850
20X4				600

[DA06344]

20X2 at the end of 20X2. Standard practice starts the age of a period from its start, so at 12/31/X1, the accident year 20X1 (which began January 1) is twelve months old.

Rearranging the experience so that the columns now are the age of the experience produces a loss development triangle. See the exhibit "Cumulative Paid Loss as of Year-End by Age."

Cumulative Paid Loss as of Year-End by Age

Accident Year	After 12 Mos.	After 24 Mos.	After 36 Mos.	After 48 Mos.
20X1	$425	$800	$992	$992
20X2	450	750	870	
20X3	500	850		
20X4	600			

[DA06345]

This loss development triangle can be built up year after year. For analysis purposes, there should be enough data so that the amounts in the columns on the right do not change from the prior value; that is, there is no further development.

The second step, to calculate the age-to-age factors, is based on the information presented in the loss development triangle. The triangle provides an overview of how each accident year's losses develop over time. Comparison between years is easier by looking at the change from one evaluation period to the next. For example, at 24 months the losses paid for accident year 20X1 were 800, compared with 425 at 12 months. The ratio of the two values is 800/425 = 1.88; therefore, losses increased by 88 percent from twelve months to twenty-four months. This ratio is called an age-to-age factor. Similar factors can be calculated for each accident year's development, producing a loss development triangle of age-to-age factors. See the exhibit "Hypothetical Development of Loss Payments."

Hypothetical Development of Loss Payments

	Months of Development			
Accident Year	12	24	36	48
20X1	$425	$800	$992	$992
20X2	450	750	870	
20X3	500	850		
20X4	600	992	992	

	Age-to-Age Development Factors		
Accident Year	12 to 24	24 to 36	36 to final
20X1	1.88	1.24	1.00
20X2	1.67	1.16	
20X3	1.70		
Average	1.75	1.20	1.00

[DA06346]

If the age-to-age factors down the column are relatively consistent, a pattern of development may be revealed that can be used to estimate how future development will occur.

The third step is selection of the loss development factors to be used. Assume that the average factors shown are a reasonable estimate of development. In an actual analysis, the factors selected might vary from the means. For example, if the accident-year multipliers indicated an increasing trend, the analyst might use selected values higher than the mean. The expected development from each age to the final value can be derived by multiplying the factors together. See the exhibit "Expected Development Factors to Ultimate."

The results are cumulative loss development factors that project from an age of development to a projected final value, or age-to-ultimate factors.

In the simplified example presented, the experience shows that there is no further development. In some cases, development may appear to continue beyond the last age for which there is experience. For example, liability claims may take many years to settle. An indication of further development is that factors for the most mature periods are still significantly different from 1.00. In such cases, a "tail" factor to account for this further development would have to be estimated using other information.

Expected Development Factors to Ultimate

Expected development from 36 months to 48 months (final) =1.00

Expected development from 24 months to final
= Expected development from 24 to 36 months × Expected development from 36 months to final
= 1.20 × 1.00 = 1.20

Expected development from 12 months to final
= Expected development from 12 to 24 months × Expected development from 24 months to final
= 1.75 x 1.20 = 2.10

[DA06347]

Finally, the ultimate development factors selected can be used to project immature loss data to full maturity. The respective factors multiply the losses to produce a projected ultimate loss. See the exhibit "Projected Ultimate Losses Using Development Factors."

Projected Ultimate Losses Using Development Factors

Accident Year	Paid Loss at 12/31/X4	Development Age at 12/31/X4	Factor to Ultimate	Projected Ultimate Losses
20X1	$992	48 mos.	1.00	$ 992
20X2	$870	36 mos.	1.00	$ 870
20X3	$850	24 mos.	1.20	$1,020
20X4	$600	12 mos.	2.10	$1,260

[DA06348]

An estimated loss reserve can be calculated by subtracting the current paid losses from the projected ultimate losses.

The loss development method does have limitations. Because it assumes that future experience will develop the same way it has in the past, any changes in business practices or external conditions could affect the usefulness of this method. Examples of such changes are changes in mix of business, policy limits purchased, and how case reserves are set. Also, large one-time events such as catastrophes would disrupt the historical pattern of development. There may be adjustments that can be made to the data, such as excluding catastrophe losses, which can correct for these different conditions. Other types of trends may be addressed by careful selection of the development factors. The power and usefulness of the development method more than offset these limitations in most circumstances.

SUMMARY

Actuaries are trained professionals who estimate the cost of risk for insurers. Major responsibilities for an insurer include ratemaking and estimation of unpaid liabilities and adequacy of loss reserves. Actuaries are also instrumental in developing predictive models, and perform other important functions for insurers. These functions can be performed within an insurer, an advisory organization, or a consulting firm.

Ratemaking is an important component of the overall insurance mechanism. From the insurer's perspective, rates should enable the insurer to be competitive and earn a reasonable profit. Insurers are also concerned about stability, responsiveness, and reflection of differences in risk exposure, as well as the potential to promote risk control. Rates should provide for unanticipated contingencies, such as actual losses being greater than projected. Ratemaking goals often conflict with each other, requiring compromise.

An insurance rate consists of three components: (1) an amount needed to pay losses and loss adjustment expenses (prospective loss costs); (2) an amount needed to pay expenses, such as acquisition expenses, overhead, and premium taxes (expense provision); and (3) an amount for profit and contingencies (profit and contingencies factor).

Common terms used in the ratemaking process are exposure, earned exposure unit, pure premium, expense provision, loss adjustment expenses, profit and contingencies, and investment income.

Ratemaking is based on estimating losses from past coverage periods and then adjusting those losses for future conditions. However, past loss experience may not be completely known because not all covered losses are paid immediately. Because conditions are constantly changing, any delay between when data are collected and when they are used tends to reduce rate accuracy.

Other factors that affect ratemaking include changes in the cost of claims, the insurer's projected expenses, and the target level of profit and contingencies.

There are three ratemaking methods: the pure premium method, the loss ratio method, and the judgment method. The pure premium method involves calculating a pure premium, the amount needed to pay losses, and then adding an expense provision and applying a profit and contingencies factor. The loss ratio method determines a new rate by modifying an old rate, using a comparison of actual and expected loss ratios. The judgment method is used when little or no loss experience data are available for ratemaking, and it relies heavily on the knowledge and experience of an actuary or underwriter.

The complexities of real-world ratemaking arise from variations in policyholders and loss exposures as well as from time-related changes in the insurance environment. The ratemaking process includes these steps:

1. Collect data
2. Adjust data
3. Calculate overall indicated rate change
4. Determine territorial and class relativities
5. Prepare rate filings and submit them to regulatory authorities as required

Ratemaking factors can vary significantly by type of insurance. These variations can result from the characteristics of loss exposures, regulatory requirements, and other factors. Some of the factors that can vary among types of insurance include these:

- Experience period
- Trending
- Large loss limitations
- Credibility
- Increased limits factors

An insurer's loss reserves provide for estimating future claim payments. Estimating the liabilities as accurately as possible is important for understanding the actual costs of business and ensuring the insurer's ability to pay the future claims. Actuaries use various techniques to estimate the liability for these future payments, including the expected loss ratio method, the loss development method, and the Bornhuetter-Ferguson method.

ASSIGNMENT NOTE

1. American Academy of Actuaries, www.actuary.org/becoming.asp (accessed August 9, 2010).

8

Reinsurance Principles and Concepts

Educational Objectives

After learning the content of this assignment, you should be able to:

▷ Describe reinsurance and its principal functions.

▷ Describe the three sources of reinsurance.

▷ Describe treaty reinsurance and facultative reinsurance.

▷ Summarize the types of pro rata reinsurance and excess of loss reinsurance and their uses.

▷ Describe finite risk reinsurance and other methods that rely on capital markets as alternatives to traditional and nontraditional reinsurance.

▷ Describe the factors that should be considered in the design of a reinsurance program.

▷ Given a case, identify the reinsurance needs of an insurer and recommend an appropriate reinsurance program to address those needs.

Reinsurance Principles and Concepts

8

REINSURANCE AND ITS FUNCTIONS

A single insurer that sells a $100 million commercial property policy and a $100 million commercial umbrella liability policy to the owners of a high-rise office building may appear to be jeopardizing its financial stability. Insurers who provide billions of dollars of property insurance in wind-prone Florida and earthquake-prone California may seem similarly imperiled. However, such transactions are possible when the insurers use reinsurance as a tool to expand their capacity.

No insurer intentionally places itself in a situation in which a catastrophic event could destroy its net worth. Additionally, insurance regulators attempt to prevent insurers from being left in such a position. Reinsurance is one way insurers protect themselves from the financial consequences of insuring others. This section introduces basic reinsurance terms and concepts, including the principal functions of reinsurance.

Basic Terms and Concepts

Reinsurance, commonly referred to as "insurance for insurers," is the transfer from one insurer (the **primary insurer**) to another (the **reinsurer**) of some or all of the financial consequences of certain loss exposures covered by the primary insurer's policies. The loss exposures transferred, or ceded, by the primary insurer could be associated with a single subject of insurance (such as a building), a single policy, or a group of policies.

An insurer that transfers liability for loss exposures by ceding them to a reinsurer can be referred to as the reinsured, the ceding company, the cedent, the direct insurer, or the primary insurer. Although all these terms are acceptable, "primary insurer" will be used to denote the party that cedes loss exposures to a reinsurer.

Reinsurance is transacted through a **reinsurance agreement**, which specifies the terms under which the reinsurance is provided. For example, it may state that the reinsurer must pay a percentage of all the primary insurer's losses for loss exposures subject to the agreement, or must reimburse the primary insurer for losses that exceed a specified amount. Additionally, the reinsurance agreement identifies the policy, group of policies, or other categories of insurance that are included in the reinsurance agreement.

Reinsurance
The transfer of insurance risk from one insurer to another through a contractual agreement under which one insurer (the reinsurer) agrees, in return for a reinsurance premium, to indemnify another insurer (the primary insurer) for some or all of the financial consequences of certain loss exposures covered by the primary's insurance policies.

Primary insurer
In reinsurance, the insurer that transfers or cedes all or part of the insurance risk it has assumed to another insurer in a contractual arrangement.

Reinsurer
The insurer that assumes some or all of the potential costs of insured loss exposures of the primary insurer in a reinsurance contractual agreement.

Reinsurance agreement
Contract between the primary insurer and reinsurer that stipulates the form of reinsurance and the type of accounts to be reinsured.

Insurance risk

Uncertainty about the adequacy of insurance premiums to pay losses.

Retention

The amount retained by the primary insurer in the reinsurance transaction.

The reinsurer typically does not assume all of the primary insurer's **insurance risk**. The reinsurance agreement usually requires the primary insurer to retain part of its original liability. This **retention** can be expressed as a percentage of the original amount of insurance or as a dollar amount of loss. The reinsurance agreement does not alter the terms of the underlying (original) insurance policies or the primary insurer's obligations to honor them. See the exhibit "Risk."

Risk

Although "risk" is often defined as uncertainty about the occurrence of a loss, risk has several other meanings that are useful in understanding reinsurance practices. In reinsurance, the term risk often refers to the subject of insurance, such as a building, a policy, a group of policies, or a class of business. Reinsurance practitioners use the term risk in this way and include it in common reinsurance clauses.

[DA05756]

Reinsurance premium

The consideration paid by the primary insurer to the reinsurer for assuming some or all of the primary insurer's insurance risk.

Ceding commission

An amount paid by the reinsurer to the primary insurer to cover part or all of the primary insurer's policy acquisition expenses.

Retrocession

A reinsurance agreement whereby one reinsurer (the retrocedent) transfers all or part of the reinsurance risk it has assumed or will assume to another reinsurer (the retrocessionaire).

Retrocedent

The reinsurer that transfers or cedes all or part of the insurance risk it has assumed to another reinsurer.

Retrocessionaire

The reinsurer that assumes all or part of the reinsurance risk accepted by another reinsurer.

The primary insurer pays a **reinsurance premium** for the protection provided, just as any insured pays a premium for insurance coverage, but, because the primary insurer incurs the expenses of issuing the underlying policy, the reinsurer might pay a **ceding commission** to the primary insurer. These expenses consist primarily of commissions paid to producers, premium taxes, and underwriting expenses (such as policy processing and servicing costs, and risk control reports).

Reinsurers may transfer part of the liability they have accepted in reinsurance agreements to other reinsurers. Such an agreement is called a **retrocession**. Under a retrocession, one reinsurer, the **retrocedent**, transfers all or part of the reinsurance risk that it has assumed or will assume to another reinsurer, the **retrocessionaire**. Retrocession is very similar to reinsurance except for the parties involved in the agreement. The discussions of reinsurance in the context of a primary insurer-reinsurer relationship also apply to retrocessions.[1]

Reinsurance Functions

Reinsurance helps an insurer achieve several practical business goals, such as insuring large exposures, protecting policyholders' surplus from adverse loss experience, and financing the insurer's growth. The reinsurance that an insurer obtains depends mainly on the constraints or problems the insurer must address to reach its goals. Although several of its uses overlap, reinsurance is a valuable tool that can perform six principal functions for primary insurers:

- Increase large-line capacity
- Provide catastrophe protection
- Stabilize loss experience

- Provide surplus relief
- Facilitate withdrawal from a market segment
- Provide underwriting guidance

Depending on its goals, a primary insurer may use several different reinsurance agreements for these principal functions.

Increase Large-Line Capacity

The first function of reinsurance is to increase **large-line capacity**, which allows a primary insurer to assume more significant risks than its financial condition and regulations would otherwise permit. For example, an application for $100 million of property insurance on a single commercial warehouse could exceed the maximum amount of insurance that an underwriter is willing to accept on a single account. This maximum amount, or **line**, is subject to these influences:

- The maximum amount of insurance or limit of liability allowed by insurance regulations. Insurance regulations prohibit an insurer from retaining (after reinsurance, usually stated as net of reinsurance) more than 10 percent of its policyholders' surplus (net worth) on any one loss exposure.
- The size of a potential loss or losses that can safely be retained without impairing the insurer's earnings or policyholders' surplus.
- The specific characteristics of a particular loss exposure. For example, the line may vary depending on property attributes such as construction, occupancy, loss prevention features, and loss reduction features.
- The amount, types, and cost of available reinsurance.

Reinsurers provide primary insurers with large-line capacity by accepting liability for loss exposures that the primary insurer is unwilling or unable to retain. This function of reinsurance allows insurers with limited large-line capacity to participate more fully in the insurance marketplace. For example, a primary insurer may want to compete for homeowners policies in markets in which the value of the homes exceeds the amount the primary insurer can safely retain. Reinsurance allows the primary insurer to increase its market share while limiting the financial consequences of potential losses.

Provide Catastrophe Protection

Without reinsurance, catastrophes could greatly reduce insurer earnings or even threaten insurer solvency when a large number of its insured loss exposures are concentrated in an area that experiences a catastrophe. Potential catastrophic perils include fire, windstorm (hurricane, tornado, and other wind damage), and earthquakes. Additionally, significant property and liability losses can be caused by man-made catastrophes, such as industrial explosions, airplane crashes, or product recalls.

Large-line capacity

An insurer's ability to provide larger amounts of insurance for property loss exposures, or higher limits of liability for liability loss exposures, than it is otherwise willing to provide.

Line

The maximum amount of insurance or limit of liability that an insurer will accept on a single loss exposure.

The second function of reinsurance is to protect against the financial consequences of a single catastrophic event that causes multiple losses in a concentrated area. For example, an insurer might purchase reinsurance that provides up to $50 million of coverage per hurricane when the total amount of loss from a single hurricane exceeds the amount the insurer can safely retain.

Stabilize Loss Experience

An insurer, like most other businesses, must have a steady flow of profits to attract capital investment and support growth. However, demographic, economic, social, and natural forces cause an insurer's loss experience to fluctuate widely, which creates variability in its financial results. Volatile loss experience can affect the stock value of a publicly traded insurer; [2] alter an insurer's financial rating by independent rating agencies; cause abrupt changes in the approaches taken in managing the underwriting, claim, and marketing departments; or undermine the confidence of the sales force (especially independent brokers and agents who can place their customers with other insurers). In extreme cases, volatile loss experience can lead to insolvency.

Reinsurance can smooth the resulting peaks and valleys in an insurer's loss experience curve. In addition to aiding financial planning and supporting growth, this function of reinsurance encourages capital investment because investors are more likely to invest in companies whose financial results are stable.

Reinsurance can be arranged to stabilize the loss experience of a line of insurance (for example, commercial auto), a class of business (for example, truckers), or a primary insurer's entire book of business. In addition, a primary insurer can stabilize loss experience by obtaining reinsurance to accomplish any, or all, of these purposes:

- Limit its liability for a single loss exposure
- Limit its liability for several loss exposures affected by a common event
- Limit its liability for loss exposures that aggregate claims over time

The exhibit illustrates how reinsurance can stabilize a primary insurer's loss experience. See the exhibit "Stabilization of Annual Loss Experience for a Primary Insurer With a $20 Million Retention."

Provide Surplus Relief

Insurers that are growing rapidly may have difficulty maintaining a desirable capacity ratio, because of how they must account for their expenses to acquire new policies. State insurance regulation mandates that, for accounting purposes, such expenses be recognized at the time a new policy is sold. However, premiums are recognized as revenue as they are earned over the policy's life. When an insurer immediately recognizes expenses while only gradually

Stabilization of Annual Loss Experience for a Primary Insurer With a $20 Million Retention

(1)	(2)	(3)	(4)
	Actual	Amount	Stabilized
Time Period	Losses	Reinsured	Loss Level
(Year)	($000)	($000)	($000)
1	15,000	—	15,000
2	35,000	15,000	20,000
3	13,000	—	13,000
4	25,000	5,000	20,000
5	40,000	20,000	20,000
6	37,000	17,000	20,000
7	16,500	—	16,500
8	9,250	—	9,250
9	18,000	—	18,000
10	10,750	—	10,750
Total	$219,500	$57,000	$162,500

The total actual losses are $219.5 million, or an average of $21.95 million each time period. If a reinsurance agreement were in place to cap losses to $20 million, the primary insurer's loss experience would be limited to the amounts shown in the stabilized loss level column. The broken line that fluctuates dramatically in the graph below represents actual losses, the dotted line represents stabilized losses, and the horizontal line represents average losses.

Graph of Hypothetical Loss Data

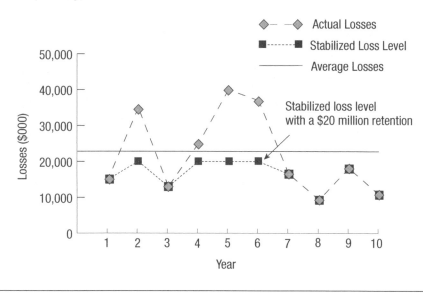

[DA03016]

recognizing revenue, its policyholders' surplus will decrease as its capacity ratio increases.

Surplus relief

A replenishment of policyholders' surplus provided by the ceding commission paid to the primary insurer by the reinsurer.

Many insurers use reinsurance to provide **surplus relief**, which satisfies insurance regulatory constraints on excess growth. State insurance regulators monitor several financial ratios as part of their solvency surveillance efforts, but the relationship of written premiums to policyholders' surplus is generally a key financial ratio and one considered to be out of bounds if it exceeds 3 to 1 or 300 percent. Policyholders' surplus (also called "surplus to policyholders" or simply "surplus") is an insurer's net worth as reported on the financial statement prescribed by state insurance regulators. It represents the financial resource the primary insurer can draw on to pay unexpected losses.

Some reinsurance agreements facilitate premium growth by allowing the primary insurer to deduct a ceding commission on loss exposures ceded to the reinsurer. The ceding commission is an amount paid by the reinsurer to the primary insurer to cover part or all of a primary insurer's policy acquisition expenses. The ceding commission immediately offsets the primary insurer's policy acquisition expenses for the reinsured policies and often includes a profit provision, or an additional commission, if the reinsurance ceded is profitable.

Because the ceding commission replenishes the primary insurer's policyholders' surplus, the surplus relief facilitates the primary insurer's premium growth and the increase in policyholders' surplus lowers its capacity ratio.

Facilitate Withdrawal From a Market Segment

Reinsurance can also facilitate withdrawal from a market segment, which may be a particular class of business, geographic area, or type of insurance. A primary insurer may want to withdraw from a market segment that is unprofitable, undesirable, or incompatible with its strategic plan. When withdrawing from a market segment, the primary insurer has these options:

- Stop writing new insurance policies and continue in-force insurance until all policies expire (often referred to as "run-off")
- Cancel all policies (if insurance regulations permit) and refund the unearned premiums to insureds
- Withdraw from the market segment by purchasing portfolio reinsurance

To withdraw from a market segment, an insurer can stop writing new business or, to the extent permitted by applicable cancellation laws, cancel all policies in effect and return the unearned premiums to its insureds. However, these approaches can be unwieldy and expensive and could create ill will among insureds, producers, and state insurance regulators. They also create uncertainty about the insurer's outstanding claims, which must be settled, and about new claims, which might continue to be filed even after the insurer ceases operations.

Another approach available to the primary insurer is to transfer the liability for all outstanding policies to a reinsurer by purchasing **portfolio reinsurance**. Portfolio reinsurance can facilitate withdrawal from a market segment and prevent the formation of ill will due to policy cancellation. It is an exception to the general rule that reinsurers do not accept all of the liability for specified loss exposures of an insurer.

In portfolio reinsurance, the reinsurer accepts all of the liability for certain loss exposures covered under the primary insurer's policies, but the primary insurer must continue to fulfill its obligations to its insureds. For example, the primary insurer may decide to use portfolio reinsurance to withdraw from the errors and omissions insurance market. In this situation, the reinsurer typically agrees to indemnify the primary insurer for all losses incurred as of, and following, the date of the portfolio reinsurance agreement. However, the primary insurer continues to pay claims to (or on behalf of) its insureds who are covered by the underlying insurance.

Portfolio reinsurance can be expensive, particularly if the portfolio has been unprofitable and is expected to incur additional losses for the reinsurer. In many states, portfolio reinsurance must be approved by the state insurance department.

Sometimes a primary insurer wants to completely eliminate the liabilities it has assumed under the insurance policies it has issued. This can be accomplished through a **novation**. A novation is not considered portfolio reinsurance because the substitute insurer assumes the direct obligations to insureds covered by the underlying insurance. Usually, the approval of state insurance regulators or the insured is required to effect a novation.

Provide Underwriting Guidance

Reinsurance may also provide underwriting guidance. Reinsurers work with a wide variety of insurers in the domestic and global markets under many different circumstances. Consequently, reinsurers accumulate a great deal of underwriting expertise. A reinsurer's understanding of insurance operations and the insurance industry can assist other insurers, particularly inexperienced primary insurers entering new markets and offering new products. For example, one medium-size insurer reinsured 95 percent of its umbrella liability coverage over a period of years and relied heavily on the reinsurer for technical assistance in underwriting and pricing its policies. Without such technical assistance, certain primary insurers would find it difficult to generate underwriting profits from coverages with which they have limited expertise.

Reinsurers that provide underwriting assistance to primary insurers must respect the confidentiality of their clients' proprietary information. Reinsurers often learn about the primary insurer's marketing and underwriting strategies but should not reveal insurer-specific information to other parties.

Portfolio reinsurance

Reinsurance that transfers to the reinsurer liability for an entire type of insurance, territory, or book of business after the primary insurer has issued the policies.

Novation

An agreement under which one insurer or reinsurer is substituted for another.

REINSURANCE SOURCES

The reinsurance market is international in scope, with many participants. In the United States, licensed insurers can market reinsurance unless prohibited by statute or charter. Few such prohibitions exist, and many primary insurers sell some reinsurance. If an insurer is too small to provide reinsurance on its own, it can participate in various reinsurance pools and syndicates.

Reinsurance can be purchased from three sources:

- Professional reinsurers
- Reinsurance departments of primary insurers
- Reinsurance pools, syndicates, and associations

Additionally, the reinsurance business has several professional and trade associations that serve member companies and provide information to interested parties.

Professional Reinsurers

Professional reinsurer

An insurer whose primary business purpose is serving other insurers' reinsurance needs.

Direct writing reinsurer

A professional reinsurer whose employees deal directly with primary insurers.

Reinsurance intermediary

An intermediary that works with primary insurers to develop reinsurance programs and that negotiates contracts of reinsurance between the primary insurer and reinsurer, receiving commission for placement and other services rendered.

The first source of reinsurance is **professional reinsurers**, which interact with other insurers either directly or through intermediaries as primary insurers do.

A reinsurer whose employees deal directly with primary insurers is called a **direct writing reinsurer**. However, most direct writing reinsurers in the U.S. also solicit reinsurance business through reinsurance intermediaries.

Reinsurance intermediaries generally represent a primary insurer and work with that insurer to develop a reinsurance program that is then placed with a reinsurer or reinsurers. The reinsurance intermediary receives a brokerage commission—almost always from the reinsurer or reinsurers—for performing other necessary services in addition to placing the reinsurance, such as disbursing reinsurance premiums among participating reinsurers and collecting loss amounts owed to the insurer.

Although the variety of professional reinsurers leads to differences in how those reinsurers are used and what they can offer, some broad generalizations may be made about professional reinsurers:

- Primary insurers dealing with direct writing reinsurers often use fewer reinsurers in their reinsurance program.
- Reinsurance intermediaries often use more than one reinsurer to develop a reinsurance program for a primary insurer.
- Reinsurance intermediaries can often help secure high coverage limits and catastrophe coverage.
- Reinsurance intermediaries usually have access to various reinsurance solutions from both domestic and international markets.
- Reinsurance intermediaries can usually obtain reinsurance under favorable terms and at a competitive price because they can determine

prevailing market conditions and work repeatedly in this market with many primary insurers.

Professional reinsurers evaluate the primary insurer before entering into a reinsurance agreement because the treaty reinsurer underwrites the primary insurer as well as the loss exposures being ceded. In evaluating the primary insurer, the reinsurer gathers information about the primary insurer's financial strength by analyzing the primary insurer's financial statements or by using information developed by a financial rating service. Other information about the primary insurer may be obtained from state insurance department bulletins and the trade press.

Reinsurers also consider the primary insurer's experience, reputation, and management. The reinsurer relies on the quality of the management team, and a relationship of trust must underlie any reinsurance agreement. Whether it involves a one-time facultative agreement or an ongoing treaty agreement, the relationship between the primary insurer and the reinsurer is considered to be one of "utmost good faith." This is because each party is obligated to and relies on the other for full disclosure of material facts about the subject of the agreement. It would be considered a breach of this duty of utmost good faith if the primary insurer withheld material facts relevant to the reinsurer's underwriting decision, intentionally underestimated prior losses, or failed to disclose hazardous conditions affecting loss exposures.

Just as the reinsurer should evaluate the primary insurer, the primary insurer should evaluate the reinsurer's claim-paying ability, reputation, and management competence before entering into the reinsurance agreement.

Reinsurance Departments of Primary Insurers

Some primary insurers also provide treaty and facultative reinsurance, and the reinsurance departments of these companies serve as the second source of reinsurance.

A primary insurer may offer reinsurance to affiliated insurers, regardless of whether it offers reinsurance to unaffiliated insurers. To ensure that information from other insurers remains confidential, a primary insurer's reinsurance operations are usually separate from its primary insurance operations.

Many primary insurers are groups of commonly owned insurance companies. Intragroup reinsurance agreements are used to balance the financial results of all insurers in the group. The use of intragroup reinsurance agreements does not preclude using professional reinsurers.

Reinsurance Pools, Syndicates, and Associations

The third source of reinsurance is **reinsurance pools, syndicates, and associations**. These entities provide member companies the opportunity to participate in a line of insurance with a limited amount of capital—and a

Reinsurance pools, syndicates, and associations

Groups of insurers that share the loss exposures of the group, usually through reinsurance.

proportionate share of the administrative costs—without having to employ the specialists needed for such a venture. Whether a pool is a reinsurance device is determined by the organizational structure, the type of contract issued, and the internal accounting procedures. The terms "pool," "syndicate," and "association" are often used interchangeably, although there are some fine differences.

Reinsurance pool

A reinsurance association that consists of several unrelated insurers or reinsurers that have joined to insure risks the individual members are unwilling to individually insure.

In a **reinsurance pool**, a policy for the full amount of insurance is issued by a member company and reinsured by the remainder of the pool members according to predetermined percentages. Some pools are formed by insurers whose reinsurance needs are not adequately met in the regular marketplace, while others are formed to provide specialized insurance requiring underwriting and claim expertise that the individual insurers do not have. Reinsurance intermediaries also form reinsurance pools to provide reinsurance to their clients. A reinsurance pool may accept loss exposures from nonmember companies or offer reinsurance only to its member companies. Some reinsurance pools restrict their operations to narrowly defined classes of business, while others reinsure most types of insurance.

Syndicate

A group of insurers or reinsurers involved in joint underwriting to insure major risks that are beyond the capacity of a single insurer or reinsurer; each syndicate member accepts predetermined shares of premiums, losses, expenses, and profits.

In a **syndicate**, each member shares the risk with other members by accepting a percentage of the risk. These members collectively constitute a single, separate entity under the syndicate name. For example, syndicates are a key component of Lloyd's (formerly Lloyd's of London), an association that provides the physical and procedural facilities for its members to write insurance. Each individual investor of Lloyd's, called a "Name," belongs to one or more syndicates. The syndicate's underwriter, or group of underwriters, conducts the insurance operations and analyzes applications for insurance coverage. Depending on the nature and amount of insurance requested, a particular syndicate might accept only a portion of the total amount of insurance. The application is then taken to other syndicates for their evaluations.

Association

An organization of member companies that reinsure by fixed percentage the total amount of insurance appearing on policies issued by the organization.

An **association** consists of member companies that use both reinsurance and risk-sharing techniques. In many cases, the member companies issue their own policies; however, a reinsurance certificate is attached to each policy, under which each member company assumes a fixed percentage of the total amount of insurance. One member company is usually responsible for inspection and investigation, while a committee comprising underwriting executives from the member companies establishes the association's underwriting policy. Organizations of this type allow members to share risks that require special coverages or special underwriting techniques, and can increase the primary insurer's capacity to insure extra-hazardous risks.

Reinsurance Professional and Trade Associations

Unlike many primary insurers, reinsurers do not use service organizations such as Insurance Services Office, Inc. (ISO) and the American Association of Insurance Services (AAIS) to develop loss costs and draft contract wording. However, the reinsurance field has several associations that serve member companies and provide information to interested parties.

Intermediaries and Reinsurance Underwriters Association (IRU)

The Intermediaries and Reinsurance Underwriters Association (IRU) was founded in 1967 and is composed of intermediaries and reinsurers that broker or assume non-life treaty reinsurance. IRU publishes the *Journal of Reinsurance*, which discusses concepts and research affecting the reinsurance market. IRU conducts claim seminars, sponsors an internship program for college students, and holds conferences for members.[3]

Brokers & Reinsurance Markets Association (BRMA)

The Brokers & Reinsurance Markets Association (BRMA) represents intermediaries and reinsurers that are predominately engaged in U.S. treaty reinsurance business obtained through reinsurance brokers. BRMA seeks to identify and address industry-wide operational issues through various member committees and is described as a forum for treaty reinsurance professionals.

Of particular importance are BRMA's efforts in the area of reinsurance contract wording. The organization has compiled the *Contract Wording Reference Book*, which has become a benchmark for treaty reinsurance contracts. It is available on BRMA's website.[4]

Reinsurance Association of America (RAA)

The Reinsurance Association of America (RAA), headquartered in Washington, D.C., is a not-for-profit trade association of professional reinsurers and intermediaries. All members are domestic U.S. companies or U.S. branches of international reinsurers.

The RAA engages in many activities, serving its members and providing information on reinsurance issues to interested parties outside the industry. In addition to member advocacy and lobbying at both the state and federal levels, the RAA analyzes aggregate data and conducts seminars countrywide.[5]

REINSURANCE TRANSACTIONS

No single reinsurance agreement performs all the reinsurance functions. Instead, reinsurers have developed various types of reinsurance, each of which is effective in helping insurers meet one or more goals. A primary insurer often combines several reinsurance agreements to meet its particular needs. Each reinsurance agreement is tailored to the specific needs of the primary insurer and the reinsurer.

There are two types of reinsurance transactions: treaty and facultative.

Treaty reinsurance uses one agreement for an entire class or portfolio of loss exposures and is also referred to as obligatory reinsurance. The reinsurance agreement is typically called the treaty.

Facultative reinsurance uses a separate reinsurance agreement for each loss exposure it wants to reinsure and is also referred to as nonobligatory reinsurance.

Treaty Reinsurance

In treaty reinsurance, the reinsurer agrees in advance to reinsure all the loss exposures that fall within the treaty. Although some treaties allow the reinsurer limited discretion in reinsuring individual loss exposures, most treaties require that all loss exposures within the treaty's terms must be reinsured.

Primary insurers usually use treaty reinsurance as the foundation of their reinsurance programs. Treaty reinsurance provides primary insurers with the certainty needed to formulate underwriting policy and develop underwriting guidelines. Primary insurers work with reinsurance intermediaries (or with reinsurers directly) to develop comprehensive reinsurance programs that address the primary insurers' varied needs. The reinsurance programs that satisfy those needs often include several reinsurance agreements and the participation of several reinsurers.

Treaty reinsurance agreements are tailored to fit the primary insurer's individual requirements. The price and terms of each reinsurance treaty are individually negotiated.

Treaty reinsurance agreements are usually designed to address a primary insurer's need to reinsure many loss exposures over a period of time. Although the reinsurance agreement's term may be for only one year, the relationship between the primary insurer and the reinsurer often spans many years. A primary insurer's management usually finds that a long-term relationship with a reinsurer enables the primary insurer to be able to consistently fulfill its producers' requests to place insurance with them.

Most, but not all, treaty reinsurance agreements require the primary insurer to cede all eligible loss exposures to the reinsurer. Primary insurers usually make treaty reinsurance agreements so their underwriters do not have to exercise discretion in using reinsurance. If treaty reinsurance agreements permitted primary insurers to choose which loss exposures they ceded to the reinsurer, the reinsurer would be exposed to **adverse selection**.

Adverse selection

The decision to reinsure those loss exposures that have an increased probability of loss because the retention of those loss exposures is undesirable.

Because treaty reinsurers are obligated to accept ceded loss exposures once the reinsurance agreement is in place, reinsurers usually want to know about the integrity and experience of the primary insurer's management and the degree to which the primary insurer's published underwriting guidelines represent its actual underwriting practices.

Facultative Reinsurance

In facultative reinsurance, the primary insurer negotiates a separate reinsurance agreement for each loss exposure that it wants to reinsure. The primary insurer is not obligated to purchase reinsurance, and the reinsurer is not obligated to reinsure loss exposures submitted to it. A facultative reinsurance agreement is written for a specified time period and cannot be canceled by either party unless contractual obligations, such as payment of premiums, are not met.

The reinsurer issues a **facultative certificate of reinsurance** (or facultative certificate) that is attached to the primary insurer's copy of the policy being reinsured.

Facultative reinsurance serves four functions:

Facultative certificate of reinsurance
An agreement that defines the terms of the facultative reinsurance coverage on a specific loss exposure.

- Facultative reinsurance can provide large-line capacity for loss exposures that exceed the limits of treaty reinsurance agreements.

- Facultative reinsurance can reduce the primary insurer's exposure in a given geographic area. For example, a marine underwriter may be considering underwriting numerous shiploads of cargo that are stored in the same warehouse and that belong to different insureds. The underwriter could use facultative reinsurance for some of those loss exposures, thereby reducing the primary insurer's overall exposure to loss.

- Facultative reinsurance can insure a loss exposure with atypical hazard characteristics and thereby maintain the favorable loss experience of the primary insurer's treaty reinsurance and any associated profit-sharing arrangements. Maintaining favorable treaty loss experience is important because the reinsurer has underwritten and priced the treaty with certain expectations. A loss exposure that is inconsistent with the primary insurer's typical portfolio of insurance policies may cause excessive losses and lead to the treaty's termination or a price increase. The treaty reinsurer is usually willing for the primary insurer to remove high-hazard loss exposures from the treaty by using facultative reinsurance. These facultative placements of atypical loss exposures also benefit the treaty reinsurer. For example, an insured under a commercial property policy may request coverage for an expensive fine arts collection that the primary insurer and its treaty reinsurer would not ordinarily want to cover. Facultative reinsurance of the fine arts collection would eliminate the underwriting concern by removing this loss exposure from the treaty. Often, the treaty reinsurer's own facultative reinsurance department provides this reinsurance. The facultative reinsurer knows that adverse selection occurs in facultative reinsurance. Consequently, the loss exposures submitted for reinsurance are likely to have an increased probability of loss. Therefore, facultative reinsurance is usually priced to reflect the likelihood of adverse selection.

- Facultative reinsurance can insure particular classes of loss exposures that are excluded under treaty reinsurance.

Primary insurers purchase facultative reinsurance mainly to reinsure loss exposures that they do not typically insure or on exposures with high levels of underwriting risk. Consequently, primary insurers use facultative reinsurance for fewer of their loss exposures than they use treaty reinsurance. Primary insurers that find they are increasingly using facultative reinsurance may want to review the adequacy of their treaty reinsurance.

The expense of placing facultative reinsurance can be high for both the primary insurer and the reinsurer. In negotiating facultative reinsurance, the primary insurer must provide extensive information about each loss exposure. Consequently, administrative costs are relatively high because the primary insurer must devote a significant amount of time to complete each cession and to notify the reinsurer of any endorsement, loss notice, or policy cancellation. Likewise, the reinsurer must underwrite and price each facultative submission. See the exhibit "Hybrids of Treaty and Facultative Reinsurance."

Hybrids of Treaty and Facultative Reinsurance

Reinsurers sometimes use hybrid agreements that have elements of both treaty and facultative reinsurance. The hybrid agreements usually describe how individual facultative reinsurance placements will be handled. For example, the agreement may specify the basic underwriting parameters of the loss exposures that will be ceded to the reinsurer as well as premium and loss allocation formulas. Although hybrid agreements may be used infrequently, they demonstrate the flexibility of the reinsurance market to satisfy the mutual needs of primary insurers and reinsurers. The two hybrid agreements briefly described next illustrate common reinsurance agreement variations.

- In a *facultative treaty*, the primary insurer and the reinsurer agree on how subsequent individual facultative submissions will be handled. A facultative treaty could be used when a class of business has insufficient loss exposures to justify treaty reinsurance but has a sufficient number of loss exposures to determine the details of future individual placements.

- In a *facultative obligatory treaty*, although the primary insurer has the option of ceding loss exposures, the reinsurer is obligated to accept all loss exposures submitted to it. Facultative obligatory treaties are also called *semi-obligatory treaties*.

[DA05757]

TYPES OF PRO RATA AND EXCESS OF LOSS REINSURANCE

Each reinsurance agreement negotiated between a primary insurer and reinsurer is unique because its terms reflect the primary insurer's needs and the willingness of reinsurers in the marketplace to meet those needs. Several types of reinsurance have been developed to serve the functions of reinsurance and to help insurers meet their goals.

Two types of reinsurance transactions are treaty reinsurance and facultative reinsurance. These types can be further categorized based on the manner in which the primary insurer and the reinsurer divide the obligations under the reinsurance agreements. The principal approaches that reinsurers use to allocate losses are broadly defined as pro rata reinsurance and excess of loss reinsurance. These types of reinsurance reflect how the primary insurer and reinsurer will share premiums, amounts of insurance, and losses. See the exhibit "Types of Reinsurance."

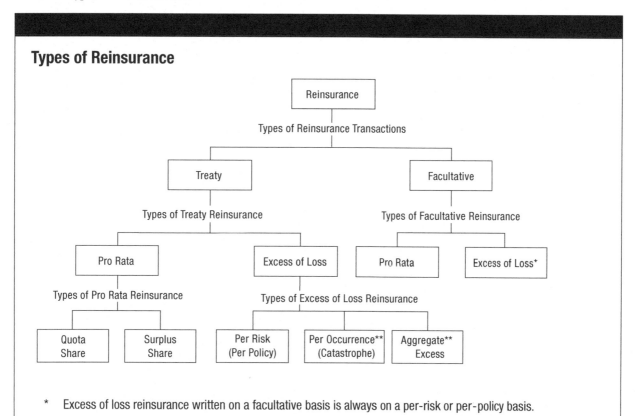

[DA05080]

In practice, a primary insurer's reinsurance program usually combines several of the various types of reinsurance agreements to meet the specific needs of a primary insurer. Unlike primary insurance contracts, reinsurance agreements are not standardized.

Pro Rata Reinsurance

Pro rata reinsurance

A type of reinsurance in which the primary insurer and reinsurer proportionately share the amounts of insurance, policy premiums, and losses (including loss adjustment expenses).

Under **pro rata reinsurance**, or proportional reinsurance, the amount of insurance, premium, and losses (including loss adjustment expenses) are divided between the primary insurer and the reinsurer in the same proportions as the loss exposure. For example, if the reinsurer covers 60 percent of the liability for each loss exposure that the primary insurer insures, then the reinsurer is entitled to 60 percent of the policy premiums and is responsible for 60 percent of each loss. The primary insurer also incurs loss adjustment expenses. Loss adjustment expenses that can be related to a specific loss are also usually shared proportionately.

Flat commission

A ceding commission that is a fixed percentage of the ceded premiums.

Profit-sharing commission

A ceding commission that is contingent on the reinsurer realizing a predetermined percentage of excess profit on ceded loss exposures.

Sliding scale commission

A ceding commission based on a formula that adjusts the commission according to the profitability of the reinsurance agreement.

The reinsurer usually pays the primary insurer a ceding commission for the loss exposures ceded to reimburse the primary insurer for the acquisition expenses involved in selling, underwriting, and issuing the underlying policies. A **flat commission** is commonly used in pro rata reinsurance treaties; however, **profit-sharing commission** or **sliding scale commission** arrangements are also commonly used and provide an incentive to the primary insurer for ceding profitable business. The amount of ceding commission paid to the primary insurer is usually negotiated and is taken from the reinsurance premium remitted to the reinsurer.

Pro rata reinsurance is generally chosen by newly incorporated insurers or insurers with limited capital because it is effective in providing surplus relief. Its effectiveness results from the practice of paying ceding commissions under pro rata treaties, a practice not common under excess of loss treaties.

Pro rata reinsurance can be identified as either quota share or surplus share. The principal difference is how each indicates the primary insurer's retention.

Quota Share Reinsurance

Quota share reinsurance

A type of pro rata reinsurance in which the primary insurer and the reinsurer share the amounts of insurance, policy premiums, and losses (including loss adjustment expenses) using a fixed percentage.

The distinguishing characteristic of **quota share reinsurance** is that the primary insurer and the reinsurer use a fixed percentage in sharing the amounts of insurance, policy premiums, and losses (including loss adjustment expenses). For example, an insurer may arrange a reinsurance treaty in which it retains 45 percent of policy premiums, coverage limits, and losses while reinsuring the remainder. This treaty would be called a "55 percent quota share treaty" because the reinsurer accepts 55 percent of the liability for each loss exposure subject to the treaty. Quota share reinsurance can be used with both property insurance and liability insurance but is more frequently used in property insurance. See the exhibit "Quota Share Reinsurance Example."

Quota Share Reinsurance Example

Brookgreen Insurance Company has a quota share treaty with Cypress Reinsurer. The treaty has a $250,000 limit, a retention of 25 percent, and a cession of 75 percent. The following three policies are issued by Brookgreen Insurance Company and are subject to the quota share treaty with Cypress Reinsurer.

- Policy A insures Building A for $25,000 for a premium of $400, with one loss of $8,000.
- Policy B insures Building B for $100,000 for a premium of $1,000, with one loss of $10,000.
- Policy C insures Building C for $150,000 for a premium of $1,500, with one loss of $60,000.

Division of Insurance, Premiums, and Losses Under Quota Share Treaty

	Brookgreen Insurance Retention (25%)	Cypress Reinsurance Cession (75%)	Total
Policy A			
Amounts of insurance	$6,250	$18,750	$25,000
Premiums	100	300	400
Losses	2,000	6,000	8,000
Policy B			
Amounts of insurance	$25,000	$75,000	$100,000
Premiums	250	750	1,000
Losses	2,500	7,500	10,000
Policy C			
Amounts of insurance	$37,500	$112,500	$150,000
Premiums	375	1,125	1,500
Losses	15,000	45,000	60,000

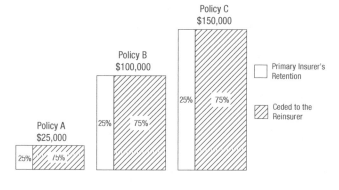

[DA05081]

Because the primary insurer cedes a fixed percentage under a quota share treaty, even policies with low amounts of insurance that the primary insurer could safely retain are reinsured. However, one type of quota share treaty, a **variable quota share treaty**, has the advantage of enabling a primary insurer to retain a larger proportion of the small loss exposures that are within its financial capability to absorb, while maintaining a safer and smaller retention on larger loss exposures.

Variable quota share treaty

A quota share reinsurance treaty in which the cession percentage retention varies based on specified predetermined criteria such as the amount of insurance needed.

Most reinsurance agreements specify a maximum dollar limit above which responsibility for additional coverage limits or losses reverts back to the primary insurer (or is taken by another reinsurer). With a quota share reinsurance agreement, that maximum dollar amount is stated in terms of the coverage limits of each policy subject to the treaty. For example, a primary insurer and a reinsurer may share amounts of insurance, policy premiums, and losses on a 45 percent and 55 percent basis, respectively, subject to a $1 million maximum coverage amount for each policy.

In addition to a maximum coverage amount limitation, some quota share reinsurance agreements include a per occurrence limit, stated as an aggregate dollar amount or as a **loss ratio** cap, which restricts the primary insurer's reinsurance recovery for losses originating from a single occurrence.

Surplus Share Reinsurance

A distinguishing characteristic of **surplus share reinsurance** is that when an underlying policy's total amount of insurance exceeds a stipulated dollar amount, or line, the reinsurer assumes the surplus share of the amount of insurance (the difference between the primary insurer's line and the total amount of insurance). Surplus share reinsurance is typically used only with property insurance.

Under surplus share reinsurance, the primary insurer and the reinsurer share the policy premiums and losses proportionately. The primary insurer's share is the proportion that the line bears to the total amount of insurance; the reinsurer's share is the proportion that the amount ceded bears to the total. For example, if the line is $50,000 and the amount ceded is $200,000, the primary insurer would receive 20 percent ($50,000 ÷ $250,000) of the policy premium and pay 20 percent of all losses, while the reinsurer would receive 80 percent ($200,000 ÷ $250,000) of the policy premium and pay 80 percent of all losses. A surplus share treaty does not cover policies with amounts of insurance that are less than the primary insurer's line (in this case, $50,000).

The **reinsurance limit** of a surplus share treaty is expressed in multiples of the primary insurer's line. A primary insurer with a nine-line surplus share treaty has the capacity under the treaty to insure loss exposures with amounts of insurance that exceed its retention by a multiple of nine. For example, if the line is $300,000 for a nine-line surplus share treaty, the primary insurer has a total underwriting capacity of $3 million, calculated as the $300,000 line, plus nine multiples of that $300,000 line. In addition to being expressed as a number of lines, the reinsurance limit of a surplus share treaty can be expressed as an amount of insurance the reinsurer is willing to provide, such as $2.7 million ($300,000 multiplied by nine lines).

Unlike the simplified example shown in the exhibit, many surplus share treaties allow the primary insurer to increase its line from a minimum amount to a maximum amount, depending on the potential loss severity of the exposed limit. For example, Brookgreen's surplus share treaty may allow the company

Loss ratio

A ratio that measures losses and loss adjustment expenses against earned premiums and that reflects the percentage of premiums being consumed by losses.

Surplus share reinsurance

A type of pro rata reinsurance in which the policies covered are those whose amount of insurance exceeds a stipulated dollar amount, or line.

Reinsurance limit

The maximum amount that the reinsurer will pay for a claim and that is commonly stated in the reinsurance agreement.

to increase its line on a quality loss exposure from $25,000 to $50,000. In this case, the nine-line surplus share treaty would give Brookgreen large line capacity to insure loss exposures with amounts of insurance as large as $500,000, which is calculated as the $50,000 line, plus nine multiplied by the $50,000 line. The primary insurer's ability to vary its line also allows it to retain some loss exposures it may otherwise be required to cede. See the exhibit "Surplus Share Reinsurance Example."

Excess of Loss Reinsurance

Under an **excess of loss reinsurance** agreement, also called nonproportional reinsurance, the reinsurer responds to a loss only when the loss exceeds the primary insurer's retention, often referred to as the **attachment point**. The primary insurer fully retains losses that are less than the attachment point and will sometimes also be required by the reinsurer to retain responsibility for a percentage of the losses that exceed the attachment point. The purpose of this requirement is to provide the primary insurer with a financial incentive to manage losses efficiently that exceed the attachment point.

An excess of loss reinsurer's obligation to indemnify the primary insurer for losses depends on the amount of the loss and the layer of coverage the reinsurer provides. The reinsurer providing the first layer of excess of loss reinsurance shown in the exhibit would indemnify the primary insurer for losses that exceed $250,000 (the attachment point) up to total incurred losses of $500,000. This reinsurer describes its position in the primary insurer's excess of loss reinsurance program as being "$250,000 in excess of (denoted as 'xs') $250,000." The reinsurer in the second layer of the excess of loss reinsurance program would indemnify the primary insurer for losses that exceed $500,000 up to total incurred losses of $1 million, or "$500,000 xs $500,000." Losses that exceed the capacity of the primary insurer's excess of loss reinsurance (in this case, $25 million) remain the primary insurer's responsibility unless otherwise reinsured. See the exhibit "How Excess of Loss Reinsurance Is Layered."

Excess of loss reinsurance premiums are negotiated based on the likelihood that losses will exceed the attachment point. The reinsurance premium for excess of loss reinsurance is usually stated as a percentage (often called a rate) of the policy premium charged by the primary insurer (often called the **subject premium**, or underlying premium). Therefore, unlike quota share and surplus share reinsurance, the excess of loss reinsurer receives a nonproportional share of the premium.

Generally, reinsurers do not pay ceding commissions under excess of loss reinsurance agreements. However, the reinsurer may reward the primary insurer for favorable loss experience by paying a profit commission or reducing the rate used in calculating the reinsurance premium.

The primary insurer's attachment point is usually set at a level where claims that are expected are retained. However, if the primary insurer's volume of losses is expected to be significant, an excess of loss reinsurance agreement

Excess of loss reinsurance (nonproportional reinsurance)

A type of reinsurance in which the primary insurer is indemnified for losses that exceed a specified dollar amount.

Attachment point

The dollar amount above which the reinsurer responds to losses.

Subject premium

The premium the primary insurer charges on its underlying policies and to which a rate is applied to determine the reinsurance premium.

Surplus Share Reinsurance Example

Brookgreen Insurance Company has a surplus share treaty with Cypress Reinsurer and retains a line of $25,000. The treaty contains nine lines and provides for a maximum cession of $225,000. Therefore, the retention and reinsurance provide Brookgreen with the ability to issue policies with amounts of insurance as high as $250,000. The following three policies are issued by Brookgreen Insurance Company and are subject to the surplus share treaty with Cypress Reinsurer.

- Policy A insures Building A for $25,000 for a premium of $400, with one loss of $8,000.
- Policy B insures Building B for $100,000 for a premium of $1,000, with one loss of $10,000.
- Policy C insures Building C for $150,000 for a premium of $1,500, with one loss of $60,000.

Division of Insurance, Premiums, and Losses Under Surplus Share Treaty

	Brookgreen Insurance Retention	Cypress Reinsurance Cession	Total
Policy A			
Amounts of insurance	$25,000 (100%)	$0 (0%)	$25,000
Premiums	400	0	400
Losses	8,000	0	8,000
Policy B			
Amounts of insurance	$25,000 (25%)	$75,000 (75%)	$100,000
Premiums	250	750	1,000
Losses	2,500	7,500	10,000
Policy C			
Amounts of insurance	$25,000 (16.67%)	$125,000 (83.33%)	$150,000
Premiums	250	1,250	1,500
Losses	10,000	50,000	60,000

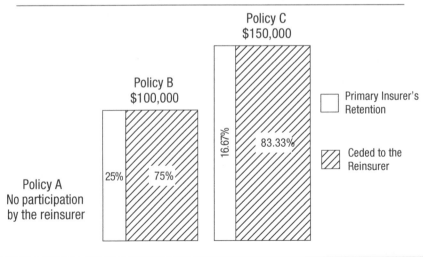

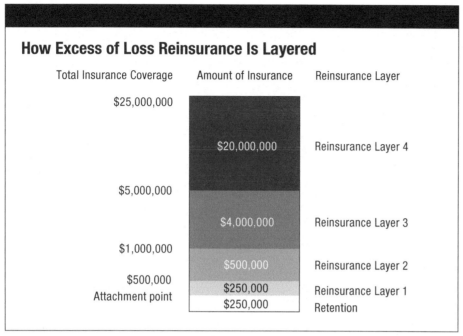

How Excess of Loss Reinsurance Is Layered

Total Insurance Coverage   Amount of Insurance   Reinsurance Layer

$25,000,000

$20,000,000   Reinsurance Layer 4

$5,000,000

$4,000,000   Reinsurance Layer 3

$1,000,000

$500,000   Reinsurance Layer 2

$500,000
Attachment point $250,000   Reinsurance Layer 1
$250,000   Retention

[DA05084]

may have a low attachment point. This type of reinsurance agreement is sometimes referred to as a **working cover**. A working cover enables the primary insurer to spread its losses over several years. Primary insurers selling a type of insurance with which they have little expertise may choose to purchase a working cover until they better understand the frequency and severity of losses that the portfolio for that type of insurance produces.

There are five types of excess of loss reinsurance, each of which usually has a specific use:

- **Per risk excess of loss reinsurance** is often referred to as property per risk excess of loss and is generally used with property insurance. The attachment point and reinsurance limit apply separately to each loss occurring to each risk (loss exposure), with the primary insurer usually determining what constitutes one risk. The attachment point and reinsurance limit are stated as a dollar amount of loss.

- **Catastrophe excess of loss** protects the primary insurer from an accumulation of retained losses that arise from a single catastrophic event, such as a tornado, hurricane, or earthquake. As with per risk excess of loss reinsurance, the attachment point and reinsurance limit are stated as a dollar amount of loss. The attachment point is subject to negotiation, but it is usually set high enough to be exceeded only if the aggregation of losses from a catastrophe would impair the policyholders' surplus of a primary insurer. Additionally, losses exceeding the attachment point are usually subject to a **co-participation provision**.

Working cover

An excess of loss reinsurance agreement with a low attachment point.

Per risk excess of loss reinsurance

A type of excess of loss reinsurance that covers property insurance and that applies separately to each loss occurring to each risk.

Catastrophe excess of loss reinsurance

A type of excess of loss reinsurance that protects the primary insurer from an accumulation of retained losses that arise from a single catastrophic event.

Co-participation provision

A provision in a reinsurance agreement that requires the primary insurer to retain a specified percentage of the losses that exceed its attachment point.

Per policy excess of loss reinsurance

A type of excess of loss reinsurance that applies the attachment point and the reinsurance limit separately to each insurance policy issued by the primary insurer regardless of the number of losses occurring under each policy.

Per occurrence excess of loss reinsurance

A type of excess of loss reinsurance that applies the attachment point and reinsurance limit to the total losses arising from a single event affecting one or more of the primary insurer's policies.

Aggregate excess of loss reinsurance

A type of excess of loss reinsurance that covers aggregated losses that exceed the attachment point, stated as a dollar amount of loss or as a loss ratio, and that occur over a specified period, usually one year.

Finite risk reinsurance

A nontraditional type of reinsurance in which the reinsurer's liability is limited and anticipated investment income is expressly acknowledged as an underwriting component.

- **Per policy excess of loss reinsurance** is used primarily with liability insurance; it applies the attachment point and the reinsurance limit separately to the losses occurring on each insurance policy and is triggered when a loss on a policy exceeds the attachment point.

- **Per occurrence excess of loss reinsurance** is also typically used for liability insurance; it applies the attachment point and the reinsurance limit to the total losses arising from a single event, regardless of the number of policies or risks involved. A per occurrence excess of loss treaty covering liability insurance usually has an attachment point that is less than the highest liability policy limit offered by the primary insurer.

- **Aggregate excess of loss reinsurance** can be used for property or liability insurance and covers aggregated losses that exceed the attachment point and occur over a stated period, usually one year. The attachment point can be stated as a dollar amount of loss or as a loss ratio. When the attachment point is stated as a loss ratio, the treaty is called "stop loss reinsurance." Most aggregate excess of loss treaties also contain a coparticipation provision of 5 percent to 10 percent to provide the primary insurer with an incentive to handle claims efficiently that exceed the attachment point.

ALTERNATIVES TO TRADITIONAL REINSURANCE

While the demand for traditional reinsurance continues to evolve as the industry adapts to new economic and regulatory pressures, alternatives to traditional reinsurance have emerged.

Some types of risk, particularly catastrophe risk, cannot always be suitably addressed through traditional reinsurance. Alternatives to traditional reinsurance include finite risk reinsurance and instruments that use the capital market as a source for risk financing, such as insurance-linked securities and various exchange-traded products.

Finite Risk Reinsurance

Finite risk reinsurance is a nontraditional type of reinsurance in which the reinsurer's liability is limited (or "finite") and anticipated investment income is expressly acknowledged as an underwriting component. Because this type of reinsurance transfers a limited amount of risk to the reinsurer with the objective of improving the primary insurer's financial result, it is often called financial reinsurance.

Finite risk reinsurance can be arranged to protect a primary insurer against a combination of a traditionally insurable loss exposure and a traditionally uninsurable loss exposure. For example, the traditionally insurable loss could be building loss caused by an explosion, while the traditionally uninsurable exposure could be the possibility of loss due to economic variables such as product demand and market competition. It also effectively handles extremely large and unusual loss exposures, such as catastrophic losses resulting from an oil rig explosion or an earthquake.

A finite risk reinsurance agreement typically has a multi-year term (for example, three to five years). This allows the risk and losses to be spread over several years, while being subject to an aggregate limit for the agreement's entire term. With finite risk reinsurance, the primary insurer can rely on long-term protection and a predictable reinsurance cost over the coverage period, while the reinsurer can rely on a continual flow of premiums. Because of these benefits, both the primary insurer and the reinsurer tend to be flexible in negotiating the price and terms.

Finite risk reinsurance premiums can be a substantial percentage of the reinsurance limit (for example, 70 percent). This relationship between premium and reinsurance limit reduces the reinsurer's potential underwriting loss to a level that is much lower than that typically associated with traditional types of reinsurance.

Generally, finite risk reinsurance is designed to cover high severity losses. The reinsurer commonly shares profits with the primary insurer when it has favorable loss experience or has generated income by investing the prepaid premium. This profit-sharing income can compensate the primary insurer for the higher-than-usual premium for finite risk reinsurance. The reinsurer will not assess any additional premium even if losses exceed the premium.

Capital Market Alternatives to Traditional and Nontraditional Reinsurance

Capital markets have emerged as tools that primary insurers can use to finance risk as an alternative to insurance. Instead of purchasing reinsurance to cover its potential liabilities, the primary insurer uses traded security instruments to finance insurance risk.

Some of the capital market instruments are rooted in the concepts of **securitization of risk** and **special purpose vehicles (SPVs)**, which allow primary insurers to exchange assets for cash. Others are based on **insurance derivatives** or **contingent capital arrangements**.

Although these products are expanding and evolving rapidly, these are among the methods most often used:

- Catastrophe bond—A type of **insurance-linked security** that is specifically designed to transfer insurable catastrophe risk to investors. A bond is issued with a condition that if the issuer suffers a catastrophe loss greater than specified amount, the obligation to pay interest and/or repay principal is deferred or forgiven. As long as catastrophe-related losses do not exceed the specified amount, investors earn a relatively high interest rate

Capital market

A financial market in which long-term securities are traded.

Securitization of risk

The use of securities or financial instruments (for example, stocks, bonds, commodities, financial futures) to finance an insurer's exposure to catastrophic loss.

Special purpose vehicle (SPV)

A facility established for the purpose of purchasing income-producing assets from an organization, holding title to them, and then using those assets to collateralize securities that will be sold to investors.

Insurance derivative

Financial contract whose value is based on the level of insurable losses that occur during a specific time period.

Contingent capital arrangement

An agreement, entered into before any losses occur, that enables an organization to raise cash by selling stock or issuing debt at prearranged terms after a loss occurs that exceeds a certain threshold.

Insurance-linked security

A financial instrument whose value is primarily driven by insurance and/or reinsurance loss events.

and receive a return of their principal. If catastrophe losses exceed the specified loss amount, the interest and/or principal forgone by bondholders is used to pay losses. Catastrophe bonds are typically issued by the SPVs of insurers, large reinsurers, or large corporations for any type of catastrophic insurable risk, such as hurricanes, earthquakes, and other adverse weather and environmental risks.

- Catastrophe risk exchange—A means through which a primary insurer can exchange a portion of its insurance risk for another insurer's. The exchange can be, for example, an Internet-based forum on which risks available for trade are advertised, negotiated, and completed. The insurance risk traded may differ by geographic area, type of property, or cause of loss insured against. A primary insurer with a geographic concentration of loss exposures can use a catastrophe risk exchange to reduce its losses from a single loss occurrence. A primary insurer can also diversify the kinds of property insured to make it less susceptible to heavy losses from a single cause of loss.

Surplus note

A type of unsecured debt instrument, issued only by insurers, that has characteristics of both conventional equity and debt securities and is classified as policyholders' surplus rather than as a liability on the insurer's statutory balance sheet.

- Contingent surplus note—A **surplus note** that has been designed so a primary insurer, at its option, can immediately obtain funds by issuing notes at a pre-agreed rate of interest. A benefit of surplus notes is that they increase a primary insurer's assets without increasing its liabilities.

- Industry loss warranty (ILW)—An insurance-linked security that covers the primary insurer in the event that the industry-wide loss from a particular catastrophic event, such as an earthquake or hurricane, exceeds a predetermined threshold. The distinguishing characteristic of this instrument is that its coverage is triggered by industry losses as a whole, rather than only on the primary insurer's losses.

- Catastrophe option—An agreement that gives the primary insurer the right to a cash payment from investors if a specified index of catastrophe losses reaches a specified level (the **strike price**). The catastrophe loss index, such as that provided by Insurance Services Office, Inc.'s (ISO's) Property Claim Services, keeps track of catastrophe losses by geographic region, by cause of loss, and by time of occurrence.

Strike price

The price at which the stock or commodity underlying a call option (such as a warrant) or a put option can be purchased (called) or sold (put) during a specified period.

- Line of credit—An arrangement in which a bank or another financial institution agrees to provide a loan to a primary insurer in the event the primary insurer suffers a loss. The credit is prearranged so that the terms, such as the interest rate and principal repayment schedule, are known in advance of a loss. In exchange for this credit commitment, the primary insurer taking out the line of credit pays a commitment fee. A line of credit does not represent any risk transfer; they simply provide access to capital.

- Sidecar—A limited-existence SPV, often formed as an independent company, that provides a primary insurer additional capacity to write property catastrophe business or other short-tail lines through a quota share agreement with private investors. Investors in the SPV assume a proportion of the risk and earn a corresponding portion of the profit on the primary insurer's book of business. The primary insurer charges a ceding commission and may receive a profit commission if the book of business is profitable.[6]

REINSURANCE PROGRAM DESIGN

A well-planned, well-executed reinsurance program plays a key role in meeting specific primary insurer goals. It can help stabilize loss experience while providing large-line capacity, catastrophe protection, and surplus relief. In a catastrophe, an effective reinsurance program can mean the difference between a primary insurer's survival or failure.

Many kinds of reinsurance exist, and, with rare exceptions, any primary insurer can find a combination of reinsurance agreements that meets its needs. Designing an optimal **reinsurance program** requires careful analysis of a primary insurer's needs, retentions, and reinsurance limits. Assistance in this could come from reinsurers, reinsurance intermediaries, and consultants.

Reinsurance program
The combination of reinsurance agreements that a primary insurer purchases to meet its reinsurance needs.

Factors Affecting Reinsurance Needs

Primary insurers consider several factors to determine their reinsurance needs, all of which interact to increase or decrease a primary insurer's need for reinsurance:

- Growth plans
- Types of insurance sold
- Geographic spread of loss exposures
- Insurer size
- Insurer structure
- Insurer financial strength
- Senior management's risk tolerance

Growth Plans

A primary insurer that expects rapid premium growth is likely to need more reinsurance than a primary insurer that expects premium volume to remain stable or to decrease. There are three reasons for the need for additional reinsurance:

- Rapid growth can cause a drain on a primary insurer's policyholders' surplus. Pro rata reinsurance provides a replenishment of the primary insurer's policyholders' surplus because of the ceding commission paid by the reinsurer to the primary insurer.
- The loss ratio for a primary insurer's new business is likely to be less stable than the loss ratio for its established business, which has undergone renewal underwriting. This instability may be severe if the primary insurer is growing by selling types of insurance that it has not previously

sold or by selling in markets in which it has no previous operating experience. For a rapidly growing primary insurer, new insurance sold may constitute a substantial part of total premium volume relative to renewals of existing policies. Consequently, the variability of the loss ratio on the new policies could cause instability in the primary insurer's overall loss ratio. Reinsurance, while not abrogating the total loss amount, limits the amount of this loss to the primary insurer's retention amount.

- Growth often entails expanding into markets with greater coverage requirements. To compete effectively in new markets, a primary insurer may have to offer coverage limits higher than it offered previously or insurance coverages it has not offered before. For example, a primary insurer may decide to enter the segment of the homeowners insurance market in which it must offer a personal umbrella with limits up to $2 million to match its competitors' products. Reinsurance enables primary insurers to provide larger amounts of coverage than they otherwise would be able to provide.

Pro rata reinsurance is the appropriate choice if a rapidly growing primary insurer needs only surplus relief. If the major concern is loss ratio stability or large line capacity, excess of loss reinsurance may be an appropriate choice.

While a primary insurer might reduce its long-term profits by entering into a reinsurance agreement because it has potentially ceded away profitable loss exposures, sacrificing these profits is a short-term strategy that enables the primary insurer to grow and possibly earn greater future profits.

Types of Insurance Sold

The types of insurance that a primary insurer sells are a major determinant of its reinsurance needs. The insurance products offered by primary insurers vary in loss stability, which affects the primary insurer's ability to project loss experience. A reinsurance program must be tailored to the loss characteristics of the insurance that the primary insurer sells.

Generally, primary insurers selling personal insurance need less reinsurance than those selling commercial insurance because personal insurance loss exposures need relatively lower coverage limits. Additionally, personal insurance loss exposures are more homogeneous and subject to fewer severe hazards than commercial insurance loss exposures. Because of the homogeneity among personal insurance loss exposures, the loss experience is usually more stable than that of commercial insurance loss exposures and therefore more predictable. Both personal and commercial insurance loss exposures are subject to catastrophic loss, but primary insurers usually address catastrophe reinsurance needs separately from reinsurance agreements designed only to smooth loss experience fluctuations.

Some types of insurance require a greater commitment of policyholders' surplus (capital) than do others. State insurance regulators use a risk-based capital system to establish an insurer's minimum capital requirements. This system has several components, but it gives the greatest weight to **under-writing risk**; some types of insurance require the insurer to maintain more policyholders' surplus than other types of insurance. For example, medical malpractice insurance is subject to severe losses that are difficult to forecast from past loss experience. A primary insurer selling medical malpractice insurance is therefore required to have sufficient policyholders' surplus to absorb unexpected fluctuations in losses. Using reinsurance that provides surplus relief can help primary insurers reduce demands on their policyholders' surplus.

Underwriting risk
A measure of the loss volatility of the types of insurance sold by an insurer.

The number of different types of insurance a primary insurer sells also affects its reinsurance needs. A primary insurer that sells several types of insurance is more diversified and therefore more likely to have a stable loss ratio than a primary insurer selling only a few types of insurance.

Geographic Spread of Loss Exposures

Another determinant of a primary insurer's reinsurance needs is the geo-graphic spread of its loss exposures. A wide geographic spread may stabilize the insurer's loss ratio and minimize reinsurance needs, especially in property insurance. While no part of the world is completely immune to natural catas-trophes, the nature of catastrophe loss exposures differs by geographic area and catastrophes seldom strike all geographic areas simultaneously. Consequently, if a property insurer's insured loss exposures are spread over a wide geographic area, poor loss experience in one area may be offset by good loss experience in another area during a given period.

Geographic diversification is an especially effective tool when property insur-ance is spread worldwide, but it can still be effective even if diversification is limited to the United States. For example, the West Coast is vulnerable to earthquakes, the South Atlantic and Gulf Coasts are vulnerable to hurricanes, and the middle of the country is vulnerable to tornadoes. However, these natural forces are not usually all at their worst in the same year.

Primary insurers selling property insurance in a single geographic area are especially vulnerable to fluctuations caused by catastrophe losses and need reinsurance to cover such losses. For example, devastating hurricanes that struck the South Atlantic and Gulf Coasts led to the insolvency of several insurers, including some that had been considered financially strong. These insurers had concentrations of loss exposures in the hurricane area and inad-equate reinsurance to cover their losses.

Geographic diversification can also stabilize loss ratios for reasons other than limiting losses from natural catastrophe loss exposures. Insurance regula-tion, laws governing tort liability, law enforcement practices, and other factors affecting property or liability insurance losses vary by geographic area. Adverse changes in these factors in one geographic area may be offset by favorable developments in another if the loss exposures are geographically diverse.

Insurer Size

Insurer size is also an important determinant of reinsurance needs. Typically, small primary insurers need proportionately more reinsurance to stabilize loss ratios than large primary insurers. According to the law of large numbers, actual losses tend to approach expected losses as the number of loss exposures increases. Therefore, the loss ratio of a large primary insurer is likely to be more stable than the loss ratio of a small one even if the mix of business sold is identical.

Insurer Structure

The legal form of a primary insurer may affect its reinsurance needs. For example, stock insurers have more access to capital markets than mutual and reciprocal insurers. They may consequently be willing to accept less stability in their loss ratios and depend on capital markets to replace the policyholders' surplus depleted by adverse loss fluctuations. This could be risky, however, because the providers of capital may not look favorably on an insurer that has just sustained heavy losses.

Insurer Financial Strength

An insurer that is financially strong needs less reinsurance than a financially weaker one for two reasons. First, it does not need surplus relief to increase its premium capacity. Second, it needs less reinsurance to stabilize its loss ratio. A stronger surplus position enables the primary insurer to absorb more adverse loss ratio variations. The resulting lower reinsurance costs are an added advantage for a financially strong primary insurer.

One aspect of evaluating an insurer's financial strength involves assessing the stability and liquidity of its invested assets. If a primary insurer's strategy is to rely on its policyholders' surplus to absorb abnormal losses, that policyholders' surplus must be invested in assets that are readily marketable and not subject to wide fluctuations in market price. Otherwise, the primary insurer's financial resources may be insufficient to pay losses in a timely manner.

Because common stock may be marketable only at a substantial loss in an unfavorable market, a primary insurer that holds large amounts of it in an investment portfolio needs to be more heavily reinsured than one that holds short-term bonds. However, a large portfolio of long-term bonds could also sustain substantial market losses due to interest rate risk. A primary insurer that invests a large portion of its funds in wholly-owned subsidiaries needs to have a substantial reinsurance program because the stock of subsidiaries is not generally marketable.

Senior Management's Risk Tolerance

The decision of how much reinsurance and what types to buy is made by the primary insurer's senior management. Although the decision may be supported by statistical data and financial models, it usually reflects the senior management's risk tolerance, which is their willingness to assume risk. Senior management must be comfortable with the insurance risk assumed, particularly when setting retentions or changing the reinsurance program.

Senior management must be confident that other stakeholders are comfortable with the adequacy of the primary insurer's reinsurance program. For example, the reinsurance program should reflect the risk tolerance of the board of directors, stockholders, or policyholders in a mutual company. Senior management must be sensitive to those stakeholders' views.

The practical effect of any proposed reinsurance program changes on supervisors and underwriters must also be considered. For example, if treaty reinsurance is used to increase large-line capacity, then individual underwriters must adjust to the higher amounts of insurance that the primary insurer can now safely offer. If the underwriters are not comfortable with the additional large-line capacity available under the reinsurance treaty, they may continue to purchase facultative reinsurance when they do not need to. Those actions could negate the cost savings of the treaty.

Factors Affecting Retention Selection

The primary insurer's selection of its retention is an essential and sometimes complex step in designing a reinsurance program. Although the retention is based on the primary insurer's financial needs and the types of insurance that the primary insurer sells, it is also negotiable by the primary insurer and the reinsurer. Cost is always a factor in selecting a retention, and the cost of a reinsurance treaty usually increases as the size of the retention decreases.

In addition to cost, four factors are considered when selecting a retention:

- Maximum amount the primary insurer can retain
- Maximum amount the primary insurer wants to retain
- Minimum retention sought by the reinsurer
- Co-participation provision

Maximum Amount the Primary Insurer Can Retain

The first factor to consider in selecting a retention is the maximum amount that the primary insurer can retain. This amount is a function of two aspects: regulatory requirements and the primary insurer's financial strength.

State insurance regulations effectively limit premium capacity to three dollars of net written premiums for each dollar of policyholders' surplus. Large-line capacity is limited by a statutory provision that an insurer cannot retain a net amount for a single loss exposure greater than 10 percent of its policyholders' surplus. These statutes and regulations determine the upper limits of the amount that an insurer can retain. Many conservative primary insurers retain significantly less than those limits, especially the statutory limit of 10 percent of policyholders' surplus.

Subject to the statutory and regulatory limits, a primary insurer's ability to retain loss exposures is also limited by its financial strength. An insurer should not retain loss exposures so large that the losses under a worst-case scenario can threaten its solvency. Determining the loss size that could threaten the primary insurer's solvency involves some judgment. The primary insurer must consider not only the losses within the retention of the possible reinsurance agreement, but also the retentions of closely related reinsurance agreements. For example, in setting the retention of a property per risk excess of loss treaty, potential retained losses under the related catastrophe excess of loss treaty must be considered and vice versa.

Maximum Amount the Primary Insurer Wants to Retain

The second factor to consider in selecting a retention is the maximum amount the primary insurer is willing to retain. Possible maximum retentions are rarely accepted. This may be partly because of the uncertainty of determining how much loss exposure can safely be assumed and partly because of the conservatism of some managers.

In the case of publicly held stock insurance companies, market pressures may keep retentions well below the maximum that the insurer could legally or financially bear. Investors favor insurers that report growing, or at least stable, earnings. A primary insurer that assumes large retentions under its reinsurance agreements risks alienating investors because its earnings are likely to vary widely from year to year.

Minimum Retention Sought by the Reinsurer

The third factor to consider in selecting a retention is that reinsurers sometimes demand a minimum retention as a condition of providing reinsurance. This demand is especially likely for excess of loss treaties, particularly catastrophe treaties. The purpose of the minimum retention requirement is to encourage the primary insurer to implement sound risk control, underwriting, and loss adjustment practices. Occasionally, for profitable pro rata treaties, the reinsurer may seek a lower retention in order to participate more fully in the profitable business.

Co-Participation Provision

The fourth factor in selecting a retention is the co-participation provision, which requires the primary insurer to participate in losses beyond the retention for risk control, underwriting, and loss adjustment reasons previously described.

Factors Affecting Reinsurance Limit Selection

Selecting treaty limits can be as complex as selecting retentions. There are five factors to consider in selecting treaty limits, which vary depending on the kind of treaty involved:

• Maximum policy limit
• Extracontractual obligations
• Loss adjustment expenses
• Clash cover
• Catastrophe exposure

Maximum Policy Limit

The first factor to consider in selecting reinsurance limits is the maximum policy limit sold by the primary insurer. The maximum policy limit sold by the primary insurer may seem like a natural maximum reinsurance limit for a treaty that applies separately to each policy because this practice would ensure coverage for any loss incurred. However, this may not be the most economical way to provide full reinsurance coverage. For example, if a primary insurer has many policies outstanding with limits of $500,000 or less and relatively few with limits between $500,000 and $1 million, setting the treaty limit at $500,000 and relying on facultative reinsurance to provide the remaining protection on the few larger loss exposures may be more economical than setting the reinsurance treaty limit at $1 million.

The limit for a stop loss treaty is stated as a loss ratio. Ideally, the limit should be set at the highest loss ratio that the primary insurer is likely to reach. Cost may force the primary insurer to settle for a lower limit, even if the reinsurer is willing to provide a higher limit.

Extracontractual Obligations

The primary insurer's potential exposure to extracontractual obligations is the second factor to consider in selecting reinsurance limits. If a reinsurance treaty is to provide protection against extracontractual damages and excess of policy limit losses, the reinsurance treaty limit should be substantially higher than the primary insurer's highest policy limit. Damages resulting from extracontractual obligations may be several multiples of the highest coverage limit offered.

Loss Adjustment Expenses

The third factor to consider in selecting reinsurance limits is the potential magnitude of loss adjustment expenses. Loss adjustment expenses can be a significant loss component in per risk and per occurrence excess of loss treaties, depending on the type of underlying policy. Because loss adjustment expenses are generally added to the amount of loss and not pro rated between the primary insurer and reinsurer, loss adjustment expenses should be considered when selecting retentions and reinsurance limits. A primary insurer selling medical malpractice insurance, which has significant loss adjustment expenses, may exhaust the coverage provided by a casualty per occurrence excess of loss treaty with the loss adjustment expenses alone and have no reinsurance available to provide loss indemnification. Consequently, the primary insurer must carefully consider reinsurance limits and add an additional layer of reinsurance to accommodate the loss adjustment expenses.

Clash Cover

The primary insurer's potential exposure to multiple policies responding to the same occurrence is the fourth factor to consider in selecting reinsurance limits. Clash cover applies when claims from two or more policies arise as a result of the same occurrence. Clash cover limits should be set by considering the highest limits offered by the primary insurer and the perceived likelihood that multiple policies may be involved in a single occurrence.

Catastrophe Exposure

The fifth factor to consider in selecting reinsurance limits is the primary insurer's potential exposure to catastrophe losses. Selecting the limit for a catastrophe treaty is a more complex task than selecting limits for per risk excess of loss treaties because catastrophe losses involve an accumulation of losses arising from a single occurrence. The primary insurer's liability for such losses has no stated limit. The effective limit is set by the number and face amount of policies subject to losses by a single catastrophic occurrence that the primary insurer has in force in a geographic area. In the case of a hurricane, the area affected may cover hundreds of square miles.

Statistics on hurricanes have been collected for many years and show the paths that hurricanes have followed and the wind forces that have been involved. If an insurer has data on the loss exposures that it has previously assumed in a storm area, it can estimate future losses from a hurricane of a given intensity following a specified path. Insurers can do similar analyses for flood and earthquake losses because severe losses from those causes are likely limited to known flood zones and geological faults. Extensive data on the occurrence and intensity of floods, hurricanes, tornadoes, earthquakes, and other natural catastrophes are available from various government agencies such as the National Oceanic and Atmospheric Administration (NOAA) and other industry organizations. Catastrophe models that estimate catastrophe losses are also often used to help set treaty limits.

REINSURANCE PROGRAM DESIGN CASE STUDIES

The various ways in which the different types of reinsurance can be used to address a primary insurer's business constraints are best illustrated through case studies.

These case studies illustrate how reinsurance programs are applied to specific situations and how combinations of various forms of reinsurance are useful in property and liability insurance. The programs outlined are realistic for the circumstances shown but are not necessarily the only appropriate reinsurance options for the hypothetical insurers.

Two caveats should be considered when reading these cases. First, reinsurance program design is a function of conditions in the reinsurance market and who is developing the program. Second, reinsurance program design is usually based on an in-depth analysis of several factors, such as the primary insurer's historical loss experience, financial condition, and types of insurance, as well as such subjective factors as senior management's aversion to risk.

The facts presented in these cases may be used to answer these questions:

- What factors lead Atley's reinsurance intermediary to recommend a reinsurance program that includes surplus relief and catastrophe protection?
- Why does Med-Mal's reinsurance intermediary recommend that Med-Mal purchase clash cover?

Atley Insurance Company

Two situations describe how Atley Insurance Company has used reinsurance to meet its objectives.

Situation 1

Atley Insurance Company has developed a program for insuring office condominiums that has proven to be very popular with its producers. One producer in particular has been aggressive in selling this program and is attempting to write accounts that need high property coverage limits. Atley is concerned about the rapid growth of this program and the negative consequences if Atley is unable to accept large accounts.

Atley and its reinsurers developed a reinsurance program that provides both large-line capacity and financing to aid future growth. The program consists of a four-line surplus share reinsurance treaty with Atley retaining $75,000. Two reinsurers participate in the program, each with two lines. Atley's underwriters must arrange facultative reinsurance for accounts with coverage limits that exceed $375,000 (the capacity of the four-line treaty). Atley's reinsurance program has a $1 million per occurrence limit. The exhibit illustrates how coverage limits, premiums, and losses will be shared on two of the accounts written under Atley's office program. The coverage limit of the first account is within the four-line treaty, and the second account exceeds the capacity of the four-line treaty. See the exhibit "Illustration of Situation 1."

Situation 2

Atley is concerned that its existing reinsurance program will not adequately handle its growing catastrophe exposure. Atley amends its reinsurance program by adding a catastrophe excess of loss reinsurance agreement that provides $5 million in excess of $750,000. (Atley's relationship with a facultative reinsurer is sound, and Atley believes it can arrange facultative limits up to $750,000 for almost any account eligible under the office program.) The exhibit includes a substantially larger account and shows how this amended reinsurance program would respond to a catastrophe that affects all three risks. See the exhibit "Illustration of Situation 2."

Medical Malpractice Insurance Company

Medical Malpractice Insurance Company (Med-Mal) sells medical professional liability insurance for physicians and surgeons in one state. Med-Mal insures physicians and surgeons statewide, but its policy portfolio is concentrated in the state's two largest cities. Its medical professional liability policy has a $1 million limit that applies on a per occurrence and on an aggregate basis.

Med-Mal is concerned about an increase in the number of successful lawsuits against physicians and surgeons in the state. One significant loss for another insurer operating in the same state involved several surgeons who were insured under separate policies with the insurer and were successfully sued for injuries arising from a common incident. Because of this loss and the unfavorable legal environment for medical malpractice insurance, Med-Mal wants to avoid potential catastrophic occurrences in which multiple insureds, with multiple limits of liability, would be involved in the same occurrence.

Med-Mal's reinsurance intermediary recommends per occurrence excess of loss reinsurance of $750,000 xs $250,000 to limit the effect of any one claim. Med-Mal's reinsurance intermediary also recommends that the reinsurance program address the possibility that more than one insured could be sued as the result of a single occurrence, and that extracontractual damages or excess policy limits judgments could be awarded. The reinsurance intermediary suggests clash cover with a $500,000 attachment point (applies to the retention after the per occurrence excess of loss treaty) to restrict the use of the clash cover to occurrences with more than one physician. It also suggests a $5 million limit to recognize the possibility of multiple insured doctors being involved in a common incident and/or the awarding of extracontractual damages or excess policy limits judgments. See the exhibit "Application of Med-Mal's Reinsurance Program."

Illustration of Situation 1

Account With Limits Within the Surplus Share Treaty

The Doctor's Office account has a policy limit of $200,000. Coverage, premiums, and losses would be retained by Atley and shared with its reinsurers as shown below.

Atley Reinsurance Program	Assumption of Liability	Percentage Assumption of Liability
Retention	$75,000	37.5
First Surplus Treaty (2 lines)	$125,000	62.5
Second Surplus Treaty (2 lines)		
Facultative Reinsurance ($750,000 Maximum)		
Total Assumption of Liability	$200,000	100.0

Account With Limits That Exceed the Surplus Share Treaty

The Chesterbrook Office Park account has property coverage needs of $650,000. Because the coverage needs of this account exceed the limits of Atley's surplus share treaty reinsurance program, Atley arranges facultative reinsurance that is also on a surplus share basis. Coverage, premiums, and losses would be retained by Atley and shared by its reinsurers as shown below.

Atley Reinsurance Program	Assumption of Liability	Percentage Assumption of Liability
Retention	$75,000	11.5
First Surplus Treaty (2 lines)	$150,000	23.0
Second Surplus Treaty (2 lines)	$150,000	23.0
Facultative Reinsurance	$275,000	42.0
Total Assumption of Liability	$650,000	100.0*

*This column actually totals 99.5. A primary insurer and its reinsurers would likely determine an exact percentage, but in this illustration we have not.

Assume that Doctor's Office and Chesterbrook Office Park both sustain substantial losses (50 percent) caused by a tornado. Atley's reinsurance program would respond as shown below.

Atley Reinsurance Program	Doctor's Office Account $100,000 Loss	Chesterbrook Office Park $325,000 Loss
Retention	$37,500	$37,375
First Surplus Treaty (2 lines)	$62,500	$74,750
Second Surplus Treaty (2 lines)		$74,750
Facultative Reinsurance		$136,500
Total	$100,000	$325,000*

*This column actually totals $323,375 because it uses the rounded percentages calculated previously.

[DA06161]

Illustration of Situation 2

In addition to the Doctor's Office account and the Chesterbrook Office Park account, Atley writes the Technology Office Complex account for $4 million.

Atley Reinsurance Program	Assumption of Liability	Percentage Assumption of Liability
Retention	$75,000	10.0
First Surplus Treaty (2 lines)	$150,000	20.0
Second Surplus Treaty (2 lines)	$150,000	20.0
Facultative Reinsurance ($750,000 Maximum)	$375,000	50.0
Total	$750,000	100.0
Catastrophe Excess ($5 million × $750,000)	$3,250,000	
Total Assumption of Liability	$4,000,000	

Had the tornado occurred and damaged 50 percent of Technology Office Complex as well, Atley's reinsurance program would have responded as shown below. The catastrophe excess of loss reinsurance applies net after other available reinsurance.

Atley Reinsurance Program	Doctor's Office Account $100,000 Loss	Chesterbrook Office Park $325,000 Loss	Technology Office Complex $2,000,000 Loss
Retention	$37,500	$37,375	$75,000
First Surplus Treaty (2 lines)	$62,500	$74,750	$150,000
Second Surplus Treaty (2 lines)		$74,750	$150,000
Facultative Reinsurance		$136,500	$375,000
Total	$100,000	$323,375	$750,000
Catastrophe Excess ($5 million × $750,000)			$1,250,000
Total	$100,000	$323,375	$2,000,000

Atley's reinsurance program includes a $1,000,000 per occurrence limit. The total losses under the reinsurance program, before the application of the catastrophe excess agreement, are $1,173,375, or $173,375 higher than the per occurrence limit. Atley's reinsurance program provides that the catastrophe reinsurer will include losses that exceed its per occurrence limit. The catastrophe reinsurer in this case will pay $1,423,375 ($1,250,000 plus $173,375).

[DA06162]

Application of Med-Mal's Reinsurance Program

Med-Mal must pay a medical malpractice claim involving three surgeons insured under separate policies. The injured parties are awarded damages that total $2 million. The losses from this single occurrence are paid as indicated:

Policy	Damages	Med-Mal's Retention	Per Occurrence Reinsurer	Clash Cover Reinsurer
1	$500,000	$250,000	$250,000	$0
2	500,000	-----	500,000	0
3	$1,000,000	$250,000	Limit exhausted	$750,000
Total	$2,000,000	$500,000	$750,000	$750,000

[DA06163]

SUMMARY

Reinsurance is the transfer of insurance risk from one insurer to another through a contractual agreement under which the reinsurer agrees, in return for a reinsurance premium, to indemnify the primary insurer for some or all the financial consequences of the loss exposures covered by the reinsurance contract. Reinsurance performs these principal functions for primary insurers: increase large-line capacity, provide catastrophe protection, stabilize loss experience, provide surplus relief, facilitate withdrawal from a market segment, and provide underwriting guidance.

Reinsurance is available from professional reinsurers; reinsurance departments of primary insurers; and reinsurance pools, syndicates, and associations. A direct writing reinsurer is a professional reinsurer that deals directly with primary insurers. Reinsurers also may deal with primary insurers through reinsurance intermediaries. Some primary insurers also serve as reinsurers, either only to affiliates or to both affiliated and unaffiliated insurers.

Reinsurance pools, syndicates, and associations are groups of insurers that share the loss exposures of the group. Several reinsurance professional and trade associations serve member companies and provide information to interested parties.

The two types of reinsurance transactions are treaty reinsurance and facultative reinsurance. Treaty reinsurance agreements provide coverage for an entire class or portfolio of loss exposures and involve an ongoing relationship between the primary insurer and the reinsurer. Treaty reinsurance agreements are usually obligatory; loss exposures must be ceded to and accepted by the reinsurer. Facultative reinsurance agreements insure individual loss exposures. Under a facultative agreement, the reinsurer is usually not obligated to accept the loss exposure submitted by the primary insurer.

Reinsurance agreements can be categorized as either pro rata (proportional) or excess of loss (nonproportional) reinsurance. Pro rata reinsurance involves the proportional sharing of amounts of insurance, policy premiums, and losses (including loss adjustment expenses) between the primary insurer and the reinsurer. Pro rata reinsurance can either be on a quota share basis or a surplus share basis. With excess of loss reinsurance, the reinsurer responds to a loss only when the loss exceeds the primary insurer's retention (often referred to as the attachment point). Types of excess of loss reinsurance include per risk excess of loss, catastrophe excess of loss, per policy excess of loss, per occurrence excess of loss, and aggregate excess of loss.

Finite risk reinsurance is a nontraditional type of reinsurance that can be arranged to protect a primary insurer against large and unusual loss exposures. Although premiums for finite risk reinsurance are typically higher than for other forms of reinsurance, the finite risk reinsurer usually shares profits with the primary insurer when it has favorable loss experience or has generated income by investing the prepaid premium. Organizations also can use capital markets to finance risk as an alternative to insurance and traditional reinsurance, particularly for catastrophe risk financing. Although the number of these products is increasing rapidly, the methods most often used are catastrophe bonds, catastrophe risk exchanges, contingent surplus notes, industry loss warranties, catastrophe options, lines of credit, and sidecars.

Reinsurance program design is a process through which primary insurers analyze their reinsurance needs to develop an optimal reinsurance program that meets their specific goals. In designing a reinsurance program, primary insurers or their reinsurers, reinsurance intermediaries, or consultants compare existing reinsurance agreements with ever-changing needs. To be effective, reinsurance programs must be flexible enough to meet known and anticipated needs. Designing a reinsurance program involves determining reinsurance needs, setting retentions, and setting limits.

Applying a reinsurance program to a specific situation requires understanding many characteristics of the primary insurer, such as its historical loss experience, financial condition, and the types of insurance it sells. Subjective factors such as senior management's aversion to risk must also be understood. A variety of reinsurance programs may be equally effective in a given scenario.

ASSIGNMENT NOTES

1. Many of the definitions of terms in this section were adapted from the Reinsurance Association of America's (RAA) *Glossary of Terms*. The RAA's website is www.reinsurance.org (accessed March 31, 2010).

2. Insurers that are publicly traded are usually referred to as "stock insurers" to differentiate them from "mutual insurers," which are owned by their policyholders.

3. Intermediaries and Reinsurance Underwriters Association, www.irua.com (accessed May 12, 2010).

4. Brokers & Reinsurance Markets Association, www.brma.org (accessed May 12, 2010).

5. Reinsurance Association of America, www.reinsurance.org (accessed May 12, 2010).

6. Definition adapted from Reinsurance Association of America, www.reinsurance.org (accessed June 15, 2010).

9

Business Needs and Information Technology Alignment

Educational Objectives

After learning the content of this assignment, you should be able to:

▷ Describe the importance of information technology to an insurer in terms of the following:

- Gaining competitive advantage

- Optimizing operations and resources

- Providing information to support strategy and decision making

- Facilitating governance, risk, and compliance initiatives

▷ Explain how data quality practices enable insurers to meet operational-, managerial-, and strategic-level information needs.

▷ Explain how insurers use these technology systems to optimize decision making, customer service, and daily transactions:

- Transaction processing systems

- Decision support systems

- Expert systems

- Customer-focused collection and safety systems

- Electronic and mobile commerce

▷ Describe the security risks in information systems, appropriate responses to the risks, and measures for controlling the integrity of information.

▷ Explain why an insurer's information technology strategy should align with its overall business strategy.

Business Needs and Information Technology Alignment

IMPORTANCE OF INFORMATION TECHNOLOGY TO AN INSURER

The role of information technology (IT) in business has evolved from a tool for storing, organizing, and retrieving data to a crucial resource to support and drive nearly all areas of a business. The chief information officer (CIO), who manages the IT function, has gained executive status and collaborates with other executives to determine the vision and mission of the organization.

To be successful, insurers must investigate ways to improve their operational efficiency and drive growth while meeting and exceeding customers' expectations. Insurers are more likely to meet these challenges if business and IT professionals understand each other's goals, capabilities, and limitations and collaborate to leverage IT capabilities. The importance of IT to an insurer is demonstrated in the ways it uses IT to pursue its business goals; gain a competitive advantage; increase operational efficiency; support strategy and decision making; and facilitate governance, risk, and compliance initiatives.

Gaining a Competitive Advantage

Information is essential to effectively underwrite an insurance policy or a book of business; consequently, insurers are major consumers of information. IT capabilities improve the speed with which information can be stored, processed, and retrieved. These capabilities enable insurers to collect and validate data using outside sources—such as motor vehicle registration and licensing records or an individual's claims history—to create a rich data resource that can become the basis for enhanced business decisions.

IT encompasses the tools that insurers use to successfully compete against other insurers. IT capabilities that deliver the right data to the insurer or customer at the right time, in the right place and form, provide an insurer with a competitive advantage.

In the modern insurance environment, insurer differentiation hinges on intelligence, customer relationships, and speed. Business and IT professionals should collaborate to exploit predictive analytics that can develop intelligence using **database** information such as customer behaviors and preferences, the markets the insurer serves or might consider, and the risks and opportunities that it might encounter. For example, analytics might show the percentage of insurance consumers below the age of fifty who request

Database

A collection of information stored in discrete units for ease of retrieval, manipulation, combination, or other computer processing.

insurance quotes using smartphone applications and the frequency with which they shop for insurance products. Analytics that incorporate medical information, claims history, and fraud incidence might suggest that an insurer withdraw from writing auto liability insurance in a particular region. As these examples demonstrate, IT intelligence gives insurers better insight for underwriting, product development, and pricing.

IT could support a decision to deploy new tools, such as smartphone applications offering policy self-service, auto maintenance reminders, and route planning for vacations. The intelligence could suggest solutions that improve collaboration and communication with insurers' stakeholders, such as a web portal for producers that aggregates customer information to suggest **endorsements**, new policy features, and other products, customized for each insured. IT intelligence can also assist the insurer with governance. For example, building code requirements could be embedded in a database to help claims representatives accurately estimate the cost to replace commercial buildings destroyed by covered causes of loss. As demonstrated, the blending of business and IT can combine **business intelligence (BI)** with web-enabled capabilities, social media, and innovation to craft marketing programs, explore distribution channels, and develop new products and services that entice customers and boost **retention** and loyalty by engaging producers and policyholders.

Business and IT personnel must work together to manage the quality of the insurer's data. Successful insurers identify data that have the greatest impact in their business strategy and focus on defining and validating that data. Accurate, current customer data create opportunities for insurers and producers. An insurer might discover purchasing trends or demographics from its data that suggest a profitable emerging or **niche market**. For example, analytics might reveal locations with aging populations that have strong financial resources and an interest in fitness. This information may suggest a commercial policy offering customizations to fitness and spa facilities that cater to customers who are over age fifty-five. Unique companion products could be offered, such as cosmetic procedure insurance and discounts on products that impede aging—which could become a profitable niche that other insurers overlooked.

Insurers increasingly use analytical engines with predictive modeling to help underwriters examine and price insurance products that meet the demands of knowledgeable consumers while providing profitability. Predictive modeling enables underwriters to experiment with pricing changes and predict outcomes as they affect key performance indicators. It integrates the costs of providing insurance policies with intelligence on consumer behavior. Predictive modeling can enable underwriters to integrate cost and demand to find the optimum premium that is likely to gain regulatory approval, to be low enough that customers will positively associate the cost of the policy with its benefits, and to be high enough to meet or exceed the organization's profit and growth objectives.

Endorsement

A document that amends an insurance policy.

Business intelligence (BI)

The skills, technologies, applications, and practices used to improve decision-making insights and reinforce information integrity.

Retention

The percentage of policies in force that are renewed at the policy anniversary.

Niche market

A small segment of a total market.

For example, an underwriter might cull an insurer's data to prove that parents of young drivers are likely to shop for low-cost auto insurance. To encourage customer retention and reduce the risk of claims from young drivers' errors, an underwriter might use a predictive model to determine a premium discount that encourages young drivers to take a safe-driver course every two years. The insurer might also negotiate a discount with a national course provider.

Business personnel—from underwriting, claims, and accounting—and their IT partners must examine the needs of insurance consumers who use web-enhanced tools and mobile applications to get instant insurance quotes from multiple insurers and price changes on their current policies, as well as to submit new applications, change requests, and cancellation requests. These capabilities can be enhanced through IT's collaboration with outside entities such as motor vehicle departments, credit rating agencies, and insurance subscriber services that share information from their own databases. This partnering reduces customer entries and provides accurate quotations through a channel that speeds delivery of insurance products.

Increasing Operational Efficiency

IT capabilities can increase the operational efficiency of nearly every functional area of an insurer's business. Accounting, finance, human resources, internal auditing, loss control, information services, and operations (inventory control, mail center, security, and so forth) are all functions that use IT tools to improve efficiency in their work processes and to store and access appropriate data.

When considering whether to develop or purchase new technology, business and IT personnel should collaborate to weigh the costs of efficiency enhancements against the savings and benefits that the new IT would produce to determine the return on investment (ROI). In addition to the cost of purchasing and installing the equipment, as well as any development costs, insurers should consider these costs when calculating ROI: the value of staff's time for training and any associated fees or materials costs; the value of time lost until staff become proficient using the new technology; the costs of maintaining the technology; the costs for any required services associated with the IT; and any costs associated with building or structural modifications and equipment needed to house and protect the new IT equipment. The savings/benefit calculations should consider any salary and benefit costs eliminated through staff reductions; the savings from eliminated expenses incurred for the use, support, and maintenance of the old technology; the realized value of employees' reduced time once the learning curve has been eliminated; the value of customers' satisfaction with the improved technology; and new business volume that results from the IT upgrade.

Insurers that align all of their objectives with their organization's vision, mission, and goals might decide to use a transformational approach for evaluating IT system and process upgrades rather than a cost/benefit approach, or they might combine the approaches. In a transformational approach, insurers focus on the future state of the organization based on its vision and strategic goals. If IT initiatives align with the organization's goals, then they are worthy of pursuit. For example, if a corporate goal is to improve operational efficiency by reducing costs and risk, and a technology improvement allows the insurer to use online, real-time monitoring of its operations to identify backlogs and workflow bottlenecks; to better track inventory and reduce waste; and to identify loss-control issues and propose solutions before losses or injuries occur, then that IT improvement is appropriate for the organization.

Claims representative

A person responsible for investigating, evaluating, and settling claims.

Recent improvements in mobile technology and declining costs have made adoption of portable IT enhancements imperative for operational efficiency. The benefit is evident for field **claims representatives** who access and verify policy information and transmit claims information while adjusting property losses at storm sites. IT features enable claims representatives to settle losses or make partial payments immediately so that displaced families can return to their homes as soon as possible. The customer service and satisfaction benefits of this technology are exponential compared with the costs of the technology. As the storm claim example illustrates, emerging technology can improve operational efficiency. Insurers' business and IT personnel should be alert to new technologies and explore their potential uses to increase efficiency and meet the organization's goals.

Increased operational efficiencies can also be derived from exploring enhanced IT models. Insurers might use cloud computing and storage to eliminate the costs of purchasing and owning expansive computer equipment and to enjoy the processing speeds of newer equipment. However, they must also consider the potential trade-offs. These include the insurer's loss of control over its data and the risk that the cloud vendor might not properly protect the data. Insurers should weigh these considerations carefully, and, if they proceed, IT staff should locate a reputable vendor that provides data security measures, such as encryption, to protect customers' data.

Insurers might benefit from external IT services. They might explore pay-per-use services for infrequent access to external data sources rather than pay expensive, recurring subscription fees. Software-as-a-service—leasing computer software—might save insurers the costs of purchasing commercial business software (such as word-processing and spreadsheet applications) and avoid the costs of software upgrades as they become available. These services allow insurers to use the latest software enhancements for cutting-edge speed and capabilities while minimizing operational costs.

Insurance Services Office, Inc. (ISO)

An advisory organization that provides analytical and decision-support products and services to the property-liability insurance industry.

Apply Your Knowledge

Andy is the new manager of the Claims Division of a regional insurance company. At a recent claims association conference, he learned about a user-friendly, image-enabled workflow system with built-in analytics and networking capability that integrates with **Insurance Services Office, Inc.'s (ISO's)** database services for improved fraud detection, theft recovery, and exposure analysis. Andy is not certain that the system is compatible with his company's current network operating system or database, but he is so impressed by it and the value he believes it would deliver to his employer that he thinks the organization should purchase it and let the IT Division work out any compatibility issues later. What flaw in Andy's thinking could undermine adoption of this new system?

Feedback: Andy's expectations are short-sighted. Before considering any new technology purchase, business professionals should collaborate with their IT professionals to determine user needs and current system capabilities. Together, they should explore system options, their costs and benefits, and the feasibility of adopting new technology. In Andy's scenario, even if the new system were compatible with his company's existing network, the insurer would still be likely to incur IT costs to integrate the new system with the existing system. If conversions were required to adapt data for the new system, reduced retrieval speeds would create operating inefficiencies. In either case, the time to complete the integration might outdate the proposed claims system, as technology continually evolves.

Supporting Strategy and Decision Making

Management decision-making requires analyzing complex business information from multiple sources that often change. Unfortunately, human decision makers have limitations. The volume of information to be analyzed increases the time needed for people to make informed decisions, whereas the pace of change makes timely business decisions essential. Further complicating these decisions are people's bounded views of reality, which are based on individuals' experiences, education, values, and biases. Although a manager with considerable education and experience could potentially make superior decisions, his or her personal biases and values may negatively influence those decisions, rendering them less effective.

IT decision-support capabilities can help people overcome these limitations. Decision-support systems analyze large databases of BI to supply managers with suggested fact-based outcomes for the business problem the manager inputs. Each database is logically organized for efficient processing, and the results can include graphics and other tools that support a decision. The number of outputs is limited to a few that are best supported by the data. The manager must still exercise good judgment to select the best solution, but the software improves the speed and quality of decisions and may help the manager recognize flaws in his or her thinking. Another benefit is that the manager can add to or change details of the problem and then rerun the application to produce better-defined or more specific solutions. In addition to the speed with which decision-support applications produce results, they incorporate business rules with knowledge that has developed over time, and they easily transfer the knowledge to new managers, resulting in more consistent, rational decision making by one individual or many.

Modern decision-support systems incorporate Internet use, allowing individuals to access tools through personal computers (PCs) or handheld devices, and enable groups of decision makers to use real-time collaboration for effective decisions.

Because decision-support systems include business rules and vast databases of BI, they have become essential tools for developing business strategy. Predictive analytics tools are often paired with decision-support functionality. When managers input data that they deem strategic to the organization, these systems can project the outcomes of various strategies. Managers can examine the suggested results in conjunction with the organization's vision, mission, and objectives to produce optimum strategies that will help set the insurer apart from its competition.

At various points during the year, managers can reassess their strategies by rerunning the analytical decision-support systems—using new and developing data that have periodically been added to the database—to ensure that the strategy remains effective to meet the insurer's goals or to tweak its strategies based on new BI. For example, an insurer's business strategy was to release a new interface for mobile devices that run on a particular provider's network. In recent weeks, however, news accounts revealed that the selected provider has filed for bankruptcy. A subsequent run of the decision-support system should acknowledge the pending bankruptcy and suggest alternatives. Managers can use the output to adapt or eliminate the affected strategy and redirect their efforts to agendas that will better meet their mission.

Facilitating Governance, Risk, and Compliance Initiatives

The most successful organizations align their people, processes, and tools to support the organization's vision, mission, and strategies. IT tools and processes are two of these components; however, insurers' technology is controlled by IT staff, who often lack business and insurance knowledge and who may not understand the needs of insurers' stakeholders or insurers' missions and goals. To ensure organizational success, IT staff should learn about basic business principles and the nuances of the insurance business—its stakeholders and their needs and demands. Conversely, an insurer's business staff should expand their knowledge of technology, its capabilities and limitations, and the importance of data quality to support effective strategy and decision making.

An insurer's governance, risk, and compliance programs create rules, processes, and controls that support the insurer's operating policies and strategic goals. They create transparency that offers the insurer's management and stakeholders a macro view of all of the organization's daily activities and helps them identify any potential credit, market, or operational risk exposures so that they can react quickly and appropriately.

Modern IT support and decision-making tools enable insurers to proactively analyze various scenarios and conduct tests for corporate exposures to risk. Results of these tests and analysis help insurers anticipate and identify risk and react to it promptly and effectively. IT controls help insurers better understand financial **market risks** and changes in laws and regulations; threats and vulnerabilities to IT systems; and threats caused by environmental issues, political unrest, and terrorism.

IT provides insurers with a means to integrate risk assessment into their financial processes. For example, insurers can identify risks to properties in geographic areas based on their zip codes, but new technology can also enable them to track locations based on longitude and latitude to determine property elevations. Accordingly, an insurer may target lower-risk properties in a given zip code. IT tools make this type of risk assessment possible and provide a way to identify new, profitable loss exposures.

Governance, risk, and financial reporting features that are embedded in an insurer's IT-enabled end-to-end processes and controls on an enterprise-wide basis are, in effect, integrated into that insurer's daily processing. This integration can reduce the insurer's administrative burden and provide ongoing **compliance** and risk monitoring. This holistic view of enterprise risk allows the insurer to respond promptly to changes in its environment and markets, enabling it to use strategic risk and return to sustain a competitive advantage.

The National Association of Insurance Commissioners (NAIC) monitors insurers' corporate governance practices through annual and quarterly reports that insurers develop and transmit. The NAIC guides insurers on corporate governance. It requires them to have adequate top-level controls, checks, established structures, and communications.

IT capabilities can assist with auditing by preventing unauthorized entries, such as **reserves** that are set by claims representatives that exceed their authority level. Control features might also select files for auditing based on preset criteria and provide the list of files to a manager or an internal auditor. Control functions can even audit the IT systems to provide real-time alerts to IT staff concerning system problems and errors; unauthorized attempts to access secured data or systems; and failures of other systems, such as malfunctions of the cooling and humidity controls that protect computer equipment.

Accurate data reporting is crucial for government oversight, the industry, and stakeholders. State insurance regulators require the use of statutory accounting principles (SAP) for insurers' financial statements that assist them with monitoring insurer **solvency**. SAP accounting uses a conservative approach to the valuation of assets and liabilities (the insurer's obligations) and the recording of income to ensure that the insurer has adequate capital to meet solvency requirements. Accurate solvency data protect policyholders and public interests, ensuring that insurers have the capital to meet their claim

Market risk

Uncertainty about an investment's future value because of potential changes in the market for that type of investment.

Compliance

The process of documenting an organization's adherence to external legal and regulatory requirements as well as to internal policies and standards.

Reserve

The amount the insurer estimates and sets aside to pay on an existing claim that has not been settled.

Solvency

The ability of an insurer to meet its financial obligations as they become due, even those resulting from insured losses that may be claimed several years in the future.

obligations and remain solvent, even when disaster strikes or the economy slumps. IT tools and capabilities simplify categorizing data according to SAP requirements and developing standardized SAP reports that are required by state insurance regulators. Standardized data formats and electronic report submissions improve regulators' ability to maintain oversight of all insurers.

Generally accepted accounting principles (GAAP)

A common set of accounting standards and procedures used in the preparation of financial statements to ensure consistency of presentation and reported results.

Accurate data are equally important for insurers' **generally accepted accounting principles (GAAP)** financial reporting. GAAP reporting provides investors, members, or other stakeholders with financial information in a uniform format, enabling them to analyze and compare an insurer's profitability and earnings with data from other insurers and types of business organizations. Credit rating agencies, such as Moody's, analyze insurers' GAAP financial reports to assign ratings that assist investors, creditors, and additional stakeholders in making sound financial decisions. IT tools and capabilities also categorize information for GAAP reporting. Credit rating agencies require standardized data formats for GAAP reporting. They run IT analytics to apply rules and algorithms consistently and, in so doing, to develop and assign a financial strength rating for each insurer. IT ensures the reliability of the ratings so that agency customers can use them to make sound business decisions.

THE IMPORTANCE OF DATA QUALITY IN MEETING INSURER INFORMATION NEEDS

Computer data are captured information that has been broken down into distinct, logical, defined units (or details) that can be combined, rearranged, selected, processed, and/or analyzed to provide intelligence—increased understanding, knowledge, or facts that may be applied to manipulate some aspect of the user's environment. This intelligence can be used to make decisions or as input for more complex computer processing.

Almost every crucial insurance decision is based on data. Examples include insurers' daily evaluations, such as pricing and reserving, as well as less-frequent questions about which markets to serve, when to buy reinsurance, how to control risk, and how best to ensure funding to protect policyholders. Because these decisions greatly affect an insurer's success, data quality is imperative to meeting operational, managerial, and strategic information needs.

Usage and Characteristics of Quality Data

Quality data are pieces of information that suit their intended purposes. In insurance, data serve many purposes, and in many cases, the same data serve multiple purposes. For example, a policyholder's zip code is stored as part of the address; however, insurers often use zip codes to evaluate known loss exposures in a given region for policy pricing or for decisions to expand or withdraw from writing insurance coverages.

Quality data should be appropriate, reasonable, and comprehensive for a given use. Certain dimensions of data determine whether the data are appropriate, such as the timeliness or historic value, the source from which the data were collected or derived, the independence or dependence on other appropriate data, and the suitability of the data to produce a reliable result or assessment. Reasonable data represent or are similar to other data (or knowledge) both within and outside of the organization; in other words, it is internally and externally homogenous. Reasonable data have been validated with outside sources or audited for consistency and accuracy (error-free quality). Comprehensive data contain the full range of data needed to produce a reliable result or analysis.

For example, data for evaluating auto rates by insured age must include age groupings that have been used consistently within the organization and in nationwide claims databases. The data must also include claims data that helps determine rates for various coverages, such as claims for which losses were paid; their settlement amounts; and data that may explain the results, such as the territory, types of claims (property damage or bodily injury) paid, and causes of loss. A quality control audit should be performed on the selected data to ensure accuracy, validity (quality as a permitted value in a data set), and consistency. For example, in a claim selected for a random audit, all policy details in the claim should accurately compare with those in the policy information file, the payment amount must be at least zero (a valid number), and the cause of loss should be one that is used consistently within the industry.

Quality data should be free of any material limitations. If limitations exist and reasonable alternatives are viable, alternatives should be used. For example, when selecting data for a study to determine the number of auto accidents that occurred while the driver was texting, claims that occurred before the year 2005 would be materially limited because of the infrequency of texting before that year. Viable alternative data to reflect current trends would be claims from the two most recent years.

When selecting a representative sample for data analysis, the user should consider the validity of the sampling method. In the texting example, claims that occurred more than two years prior would produce an invalid sample because the cost of texting services has steadily decreased and more people use text features; however, efforts to halt texting while driving could have reduced the incidence of such texting over the past eighteen months. A sample selected from the previous eighteen months or less may be valid.

Insurance Services Office, Inc. (ISO) has developed standards for the data it collects from insurers. ISO advocates for insurers to preserve and enhance their data quality by enforcing data standards and applying best practices, and it offers a number of tools to assist insurers in these endeavors. Similarly, the National Association of Insurance Commissioners (NAIC) encourages insurers to adopt standards and best practices for ensuring data quality.

As quality data have become a valuable asset for insurers, actuarial, business, and information technology professionals have collaborated to form business associations that develop and propagate data quality standards and best practices for insurers. Two such organizations are the Casualty Actuarial Society (CAS) and the Insurance Data Management Association (IDMA). These organizations have both defined data quality and established best practices for gathering, organizing, analyzing, and distributing information for insurers' decision support.

The IDMA Value Proposition explains that poor data quality can be costly and harmful for insurers. The best approach is to avoid the costs of mitigating and correcting bad data by proactively addressing quality at the moment data are created—by engineering the processes to create quality data. See the exhibit "The IDMA Value Proposition."

The IDMA Value Proposition

With every advance in technology, the value of data increases. Evolving and new technologies make sharing data fairly simple, but if bad information moves through a process, the costs grow exponentially at each step. Data must be managed to ensure quality and to ensure maximum benefit to the organization. If senior managers receive bad data, how can they properly manage? If marketing receives incorrect information, the dollar value of lost opportunities can only be guessed. In the realm of regulatory or statutory reporting, bad data may create a liability for your organization. All of the Actuarial, Claims, Compliance, Finance, and Information Technology functions need reliable data to work with. The data manager's function is to provide other managers with the information they need to fulfill their role.

Insurance Data Management Association, "Value Proposition," www.IDMA.org (accessed July 29, 2013). [DA10557]

The goal of data management is to manage data supplied to business processes and use it in the best way possible. The data manager acts as an intermediary between business and information technology (IT) personnel, striving to increase both groups' understanding of the capabilities and weaknesses of the data.

Data warehousing

The use of a database or a collection of databases developed for an organization or an enterprise for analysis and support of management decisions.

Modeling

In data analysis, a system of calculating known outcomes based on current data and then applying these calculations to new data to predict future outcomes.

Data governance goes beyond managing data to include rules, processes, and controls that are developed to protect and enhance an organization's data. Traditionally, insurers have used a two-level approach to managing data: an organizational-level group of senior managers and a group of data stewards appointed to provide governance at the line-of-business level. Many insurers have added a third, central level of data governance and appointed a data manager to lead that charge.

Data managers achieve data governance by creating and documenting data definitions and metadata (information describing the data); developing and documenting data standards; ensuring data quality and compliance with standards; and monitoring and assisting with data analysis, **data warehousing**, predictive **modeling**, business intelligence, and risk management. Data managers advocate for standardized data across the insurance industry, which supports statistical reporting and regulatory compliance.

A data manager develops comprehensive, enterprise-wide data management strategies and processes that improve reuse of data. Data management ensures accurate booking of premium, loss accounting, and financial transactions, as well as timely and accurate statistical reporting to comply with insurers' state solvency regulations. To effectively manage the quality of an insurer's data, a data manager must understand the insurer's information needs, which can be classified into three levels: operational, managerial, and strategic.

Operational-Level Information Needs

Insurers' operational-level needs derive from their basic activities: determining rates; underwriting and producing policies; collecting premiums; reserving and paying claims; defending insureds and claims decisions; supporting producers; developing customer and sales information; marketing products; managing human resources (hiring, payroll, and benefit administration, and so forth); accounting for income and expenses; performing financing and related functions; maintaining facilities and inventory; auditing internally; controlling losses; and developing, purchasing, and maintaining information systems. Insurers need vast amounts of operational data to contend with all of these ongoing activities. A more in-depth examination of some operational insurance functions depicts the extent and types of information required.

Customer Information

Both producers and insurers benefit from learning as much as possible about their customers and prospects. This information drives product development, sales, and customer service. Basic customer information includes details such as names, addresses, phone numbers, tax-ID/social security numbers, and employment or business information. Insurers need customers' current and past insurance information to underwrite and rate coverages, including detailed exposure information and details of customers' risk retention and risk management efforts. Quality data are crucial for understanding customers' preferences and meeting customers' needs.

Underwriting Information

Underwriters are charged with selecting profitable **exposures** and developing rates that cover losses and expenses and produce a profit. Therefore, underwriters need specific, detailed data on the coverage requested and claims history. Selection and rating data must be accurate, complete, and granular enough to provide flexibility for use with decision support and predictive modeling. Underwriters need data covering the insurer's underwriting rules and guidelines; unique rating formulas; reinsurance guidelines and criteria; ISO loss costs; and, for workers compensation cases, National Council on

Exposure

Any condition that presents a possibility of gain or loss, whether or not an actual loss occurs.

Compensation Insurance (NCCI) classification codes. Poor quality rating data result in improper pricing.

Underwriters also need data produced by outside organizations, such as credit ratings; loss experience data; motor vehicle and driver records; authorized medical records; wildfire, flood plain, and National Weather Service data; vehicle valuation data; stolen equipment or art registry data; and many others. These types of data are called structured data because they can be defined. Underwriters also need to store and access unstructured data, such as claims representatives' notes; digital images of correspondence and forms; photos; and audio and video files.

Claims Information

Claims representatives and claims departments need a tremendous amount of information to handle claims and for overall claims administration. When a claim is reported, claims representatives gather information from numerous sources. They get policy information from the insurer's database and the loss notice to verify that coverage existed at the time of the loss, identify the **policy limits**, and determine whether **aggregate limits** or reinsurance applies. Claims representatives should resolve entry or processing errors to ensure data quality.

When conducting an investigation, claims representatives collect more data. They develop the claim information using additional loss details, claimant information, investigation details, claim reserves, loss payments, and **salvage** and reinsurance recoveries. This information is recorded in the insurer's database along with documentation, diary entries, and electronically transmitted data from outside sources. Claims representatives' notes, digital images of photos and correspondence, audio or video recordings, and other items are stored in claims systems and may be referenced in the database. Outside data sources include fire and police departments; motor vehicle departments; medical providers; claims history and fraud databases; property damage estimators; valuation services and salvage buyers; stolen property registries; social media; independent adjusters; lawyers, verdict research systems, and the courts; and many others. The insurer's claim file must provide documentation to support its decisions and avoid or provide defense against **bad faith**.

In addition to requiring policy and claims information, claims managers need information from the insurer's defense and corporate legal counsel, the insurer's other IT systems, and state insurance departments. Ideally, all of an insurer's data are stored in a central database, but for many insurers, some functions have independent databases. Claims managers need information developed through queries, analytical engines, and predictive-modeling tools. These IT tools can help claims managers monitor claims expenses and the use of legal counsel, independent adjusters, and appraisal and valuation providers.

Aggregate limit

The maximum amount an insurer will pay for all covered losses during the covered policy period.

Policy limits

The maximum that can be paid on the claim, regardless of the actual value of the property damaged.

Salvage

The process by which an insurer takes possession of damaged property for which it has paid a total loss and recovers a portion of the loss payment by selling the damaged property.

Bad faith

An insurer's denial of coverage without cause, which can result in extracontractual damages, punitive damages, or both.

Apply Your Knowledge

Greg, an insurer's claims representative, reviewed a property damage claim submitted by a producer. When Greg contacted the insured, he was surprised to learn that she did not report a loss. Greg then called the producer, who realized she had entered the claim on the wrong policy. Greg learned that his colleague, Carrie, that morning took a loss report from the correct insured, who was frustrated that the insurer had no claim for her policy. Greg noted the error and closed the claim assigned to him. What went wrong, and what could prevent this error? What costs likely accrued from this error?

Feedback: This claim resulted from human error: the producer entered the claim on the wrong policy. Agency software provides validation to ensure that the policy number is correct; the producer should have verified this. Most agency software generates a daily report of claims entered that day, including the policy information, which should have alerted the producer to her error. Claims systems assign a claim number for new claims. The producer should have given the insured that number; this would have helped Carrie find the problem.

In this case, the insurer incurred financial costs from handling the errone-ous claim and will incur future costs when staff examine it. If the dissatisfied insureds complain to others—especially through social media, which allows messages to reach many people quickly—the nonfinancial costs could damage the reputations of the insurer and the industry, and the extra claim record could misrepresent claims counts that the insurer and producer use to make operational and strategic decisions.

Accounting and Financial Information

Whether billing and collections are handled electronically or through printed and mailed statements with collections through paper or electronic transac-tions, accounting staff need all information stored in the insurer's database, as well as access to stored premium and claims information. Accounting and financial staff also need information available from banks and other finan-cial institutions. Many banking and investment functions can be performed electronically, including automated clearing house (ACH) payments, bank statements and reconciliation, investment transactions, and monitoring.

Finance extracts most federal, state, and local tax reporting information from the insurer's database(s), but also needs information and systems for track-ing depreciation on business property; processing and filing state statistical and rating information; and completing and filing tax returns and reporting payments to employees and vendors, including tax rules and regulations. Financial staff need data from IT tools, such as analytic engines and predic-tive modeling, for investment planning and for meeting reporting and legal requirements.

Managerial-Level Information Needs

Managers need accurate information to control and monitor the performance of the enterprise. This information should indicate the insurer's progress toward meeting objectives and suggest changes to improve performance and achieve profitability.

Financial Reporting and Premium Determination

Accountants need complete, accurate, and detailed current and historical data for tracking the insurer's assets and liabilities to complete financial reporting, including any acquisitions, mergers, separations, or disposals. Consolidated financial statements covering all of a corporation's subsidiaries are especially challenging to develop. Financial reports are required by state insurance departments to evaluate insurers' solvency and are submitted to financial rating bureaus to assist investor decision making. Managers use financial reports to analyze the insurer's profitability. These evaluations illuminate any problems that might require managers' attention, as well as areas in which results are satisfactory.

Managers also use financial reports to prepare budgets based on expected premiums, losses, and expenses. This information supports the organization's planning process and ensures that department goals are aligned with the organization's strategic goals. Managers use budgets to periodically compare actual results to budgeted amounts and to determine how well the organization is meeting its financial goals.

Actuaries need premium and loss information for ratemaking to determine the insurer's standard premiums. Ideal premiums should appeal to customers; satisfy state insurance regulators; cover insurers' losses, expenses, and required reserves; and allow for producer contingencies, while providing profit for the insurer. Financial reports enable underwriters to monitor premium and loss data and to discover new loss exposures that may merit a premium change.

Product Development and Pricing, Producer Relations, and Reinsurance

Underwriters and actuaries often monitor sales trends and profit margins to identify markets in which the insurer can leverage its market advantage. Insurers can use predictive modeling to simulate market conditions and change policy terms and coverages to estimate future loss patterns and develop appropriate pricing structures for new products. Quality historical data must form the foundation of these new product prices to ensure their profitable market introduction. Insurers' data must be flexible to adapt to the ever-changing uses of marketing information.

Insurers analyze their policy and financial data to determine the volume and profitability of business provided by each producer. They also analyze premium and loss information to determine the type and level of reinsurance protection the insurer should seek for its book of business. Insurers analyze data on exposures by geographic concentration, industry, and coverage limits to suggest the appropriate mix of reinsurance protection. They use financial data to monitor their books of business for new patterns in risk assumption and to review their reinsurance programs regularly for continued adequacy and cost-effectiveness.

Strategic-Level Information Needs

Insurers examine their vision, mission, and goals and align their strategies to achieve them. An insurer needs collective data and output from analytics and predictive modeling to determine what products to produce, what processes to adapt, what customers to serve, and the optimum size and character of the organization.

Executive managers need extensive quality information resources and IT analytics to determine the insurer's strategic path. Specialists may assist them by monitoring outside sources, gathering information, and using analytics and predictive models to recommend future developments. Executive information systems combine the insurer's financial data with data from external databases containing news feeds, market research, population trends, trade activity, and economic activity for powerful decision-support systems that provide a competitive edge.

Strategic use of quality data and IT tools enable insurers to leverage intelligence to improve their customers' experiences and determine which IT capabilities to use. Insurers' IT capabilities should provide intelligence on the IT resources and capabilities adopted by their producers that help them locate prospects, cross sell, and upsell to their customers. An insurer's use of faulty data for customer-facing tools could alienate customers and become a liability.

TYPES OF BUSINESS INFORMATION SYSTEMS

A business information system (BIS) encompasses information and the many technology tools that insurers use to successfully compete against other insurers.

A BIS includes one or more databases, decision-support tools, and all of the system processes, applications, and information structures needed for an organization's information management and business analysis needs. Transaction processing systems, decision support systems, customer-focused collection and safety systems, and electronic and mobile commerce are subsets of a BIS that assist insurers in delivering information and products, making sound decisions, and providing customer service.

Transaction Processing Systems

A transaction processing system (TPS) is a collection of software, databases, procedures, and devices that perform high-volume routine and repetitive business transactions. A TPS can include database management, document management, and automated workflow systems. A TPS is useful for policy and claim processing, managing purchasing and inventory, accounting within an insurer's general ledger systems, and managing financial investments. Insurers can leverage a TPS for efficient collection, modification, and retrieval of all transaction data. An example explains how this occurs.

After receiving an insurance application, a producer enters the customer's name, address, and contact information; vehicle identification numbers (VINs); policy limits; **deductibles**; and so forth into the agency's TPS, which stores the data in the insurer's database so that consistent information will be used by all of the insurer's systems. The insurer's underwriting TPS retrieves the information from the database for underwriting review and policy issuance; there is no need to reenter information, and potential data entry errors are avoided. Any updates for the policy, including final premium information, are entered in the underwriting TPS and updated in the database. These data are then fed into the insurer's accounting TPS, which uses them to generate billing information and financial reports, handle electronic payments, and so on. Each functional TPS may be accessed from different locations, yet they all use the same database, allowing efficient, accurate transaction processing.

Database Management Systems

A database management system (DBMS) is a group of programs that organizes data in a database and provides a user interface for retrieving information. The DBMS controls the database structure, and security features control access.

Insurers use a DBMS to store and access information developed within a functional TPS (such as accounting, claims, or underwriting) or from other sources. A DBMS manages information from each functional TPS and stores it in a central repository database or in individual databases functioning together as a central repository. A DBMS collects data at the beginning of a policy life cycle for reuse in other systems, such as premium billing, finance, and claims. Sharing data avoids duplicate entries and errors or confusion created by conflicting information entered in multiple systems, such as addresses, policy limits, and VINs.

For example, an underwriter or producer enters an insured's name, address, coverage, and other basic policy information into its TPS to create a policy record that is stored in the DBMS. When the insured reports a claim, a customer service representative (CSR) keys the policy number into the claims TPS, and the policy and premium information that was previously entered into the TPS and stored in the DBMS is automatically fed into the claims TPS for reuse. No one in the claims department must retype the information to process claim payments because it was already captured in the underwriting TPS, passed to the DBMS, and made available for the claims TPS and other systems. This DBMS functionality ensures that crucial information is accurate

Deductible

A portion of a covered loss that is not paid by the insurer.

and consistent among each TPS. See the exhibit "Interaction Between Functional Transaction Processing Systems and a Central Database."

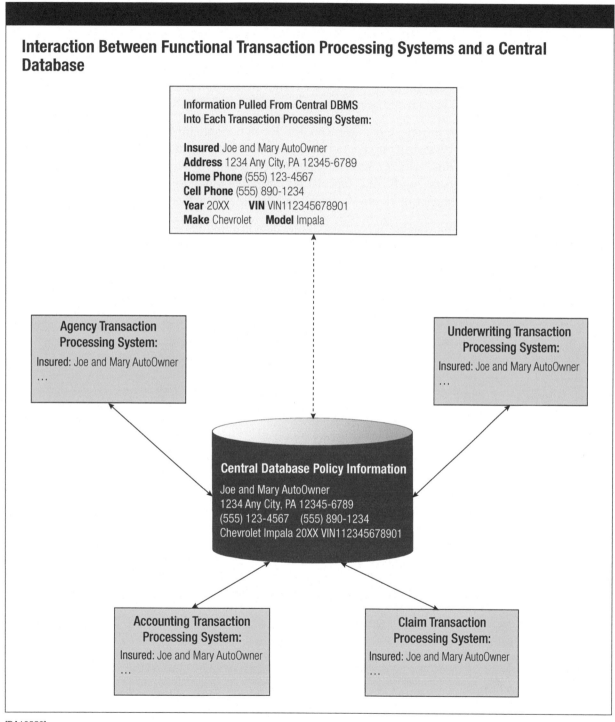

Interaction Between Functional Transaction Processing Systems and a Central Database

Information Pulled From Central DBMS Into Each Transaction Processing System:

Insured Joe and Mary AutoOwner
Address 1234 Any City, PA 12345-6789
Home Phone (555) 123-4567
Cell Phone (555) 890-1234
Year 20XX   **VIN** VIN112345678901
Make Chevrolet   **Model** Impala

Agency Transaction Processing System:
Insured: Joe and Mary AutoOwner
...

Underwriting Transaction Processing System:
Insured: Joe and Mary AutoOwner
...

Central Database Policy Information
Joe and Mary AutoOwner
1234 Any City, PA 12345-6789
(555) 123-4567   (555) 890-1234
Chevrolet Impala 20XX VIN112345678901

Accounting Transaction Processing System:
Insured: Joe and Mary AutoOwner
...

Claim Transaction Processing System:
Insured: Joe and Mary AutoOwner
...

[DA10558]

Technological advancements have led to massive databases that recognize, organize, store, and provide access through user-interface tools to various types of data and the methods or processes used within a DBMS. These data include files, digital images, audio and video recordings, and so on. Multipurpose databases, or data warehouses, can be used for structured and unstructured data. Structured data are made up of defined fields, whereas unstructured data can include open text fields and objects such as emails, audio and video files, web pages, customer intelligence retrieved through social media (such as "likes" and group affiliations), and data transmitted from vehicles and smartphones.

An insurance manager can develop actionable information by selecting and sorting structured data by territory code, policy limits, loss amount, or policy term. However, searching unstructured data for such key terms as "fraud," "arson," and "SIU" **(special investigative unit)**, for example, could enable the manager to identify suspicious claims that may be related.

Special investigation unit (SIU)

A division set up to investigate suspicious claims, premium fraud, or application fraud.

Data warehouse features enable data mining, the analysis of large quantities of data to find patterns, trends, and correlations. Data mining offers users new perspectives on information, leading to better decisions, new products, new customer groups, and recognition of emerging exposures, all of which can create a marketing advantage. Data mining has been used in insurance to identify fraud activity, predict customer buying patterns, and increase operating productivity. For example, data mining can generate a report of a city's suspicious rear-end collision claims, including those involving injured pedestrians, in which the injured are treated by the same physicians and specialists and the treatments extended beyond six months. Another example of a data mining report is one of claims in which all damaged autos were repaired by one of three auto repair facilities for less than $2,000. Such patterns could suggest that fraud rings are involved.

Large database systems are termed "big data" because of the vastness of the systems and the variety of data they capture, manage, and mine. Big data stored in scalable base systems improve the ease of access and enable insurers to leverage volume, velocity, and variety to create value. Velocity relates to the speed with which data can be transmitted, and variety refers to various types of structured and unstructured data.

Telematics

The use of technological devices in vehicles with wireless communication and GPS tracking that transmit data to businesses or government agencies; some return information for the driver.

The variety, volume, and velocity of data involved in **telematics** exemplify the dimensions of big data. A telematics device installed in an auto or a mobile device senses driving behaviors, such as hard braking, fast turns, quick acceleration, speed, miles driven, location, and the time of day driven (variety and volume), in real time (high velocity), then transmits these data wirelessly to an insurer, enabling the insurer to offer usage-based rating for auto insurance.

A drawback of big data is that managing the versions and locations of the various files can be time consuming. One solution is a sophisticated enterprise-wide index that can tag (label) data and store their location and metadata (information about the data and their attributes); a user-friendly interface then helps locate particular data. Another drawback is the need to secure sensitive data. A variety of tools can usually protect data from hackers and thieves.

Document Management Systems

A document management system (DMS) stores, organizes, and retrieves image files that were created electronically or on paper and converted into digital images using scanners or image conversion software. Staff then records index-ing information, which becomes part of the file, for identification, location, and retrieval. Insurers use a DMS to manage the volume of correspondence, applications, forms, legal notices, photos, and other documents and to provide easy retrieval, access, and simultaneous use. For example, an underwriter can review claims information on a large loss to determine whether to nonrenew the policy while a claims manager audits the claims file.

A DMS saves the insurer the time and expense previously incurred filing and retrieving paper files for delivery to one individual at a time, and it eliminates the time and expense of making duplicate copies of the files for offsite stor-age—a risk management measure. Instead, electronic files with digital images can be electronically transmitted to an offsite storage location. Another benefit is that the electronic documents or files can be sent electronically to producers, field claims representatives, outside adjusting firms, lawyers, appraisal firms, the courts, and others to eliminate the time and cost of send-ing them through other means and to reduce the chances of losing customers' confidential information. At some insurers, producers, field claims represen-tatives, and other authorized individuals can log into the system and access electronic files directly.

Automated Workflow Systems

Automated workflow systems (workflows) are used with a DMS to distribute documents according to processing rules, which differ for various transac-tions. Workflows enable insurers to maximize the benefits of electronic images and files. Workflows deliver the transaction and links to all of its associated files into a work queue—a virtual inbox—for the next performer, who can select the transaction, open all needed files, complete his or her work on it, and then send it to the next performer. As new information arrives, it can be added to the file immediately by scanning an image and/or keying in new information, and every performer will have access to the current version of the file immediately, with no need to locate the file, wait for another person to complete his or her tasks, or update multiple copies of the file.

For example, a policy application with photos is indexed and then sent to an underwriting assistant, who orders various reports. When the reports are collected, the transaction, along with links to the reports, is routed to the underwriter for evaluation. If the underwriter approves the application, the transaction is sent to an automated policy printing or transmission queue for delivery to the producer. If the underwriter declines the application, the transaction is sent to an automated queue to produce a denial letter, which is mailed or electronically sent to the producer or applicant. Work flows smoothly and quickly through the workflow process; delays associated with physically transporting a paper document, delivery to the wrong party, and misplacement of the file are reduced or eliminated. Also, the files are stored electronically; the space, materials, and equipment needed to store paper files are unnecessary; and the cost of labor to organize, file, or locate them is eliminated.

Workflows also create a log showing details such as the transaction status, the current step in the process, the user(s) to whom the transaction was sent, the dates and times it reached each step and was sent to the next, and comments about the transaction. Workflows have features that enable managers to monitor the transactions' progress and redistribute work as needed. Some workflows alert users or managers if the transaction remains in a queue longer than a specified amount of time or if a queue has an excessive number of transactions.

Scanning and workflows speed the processing of applications and claims by immediately delivering files to the appropriate personnel at each step in the process and by automating the retrieval of necessary data and other electronic documents. For example, some systems retrieve specific data based on a caller's phone number. The workflow delivers the information to the CSR. In other systems, user interface and search engines provide the information. These systems enable insurers to respond to producers, customers, claimants, and other callers promptly and efficiently.

Decision Support Systems

In addition to data mining, a BIS also uses analytical tools that help managers or other staff examine and manipulate vast, detailed data from numerous perspectives to support strategic decisions. A decision support system (DSS) is an organized collection of hardware, software, databases, and procedures that support decision making. It typically uses information collected in a TPS. A DSS is used to solve problems at all levels of an organization.

The typical DSS is applied to specific problems, which may be simple or complex. The database system used in a DSS contains relevant information, rules, and modeling and analytical tools. A DSS provides a user interface that allows users to enter details about the problem and obtain suggested solutions. Insurers can also use a DSS to more accurately predict return on investment (ROI) from various strategic changes the insurer might make, as well as the time it will take to realize that ROI, by entering details on the new markets they are considering. Further, a DSS can help identify declining markets that the insurer should abandon.

A DSS can perform analyses based on changes to one or more situational details (what if), repeated changes to a single detail (sensitivity), and changes to several details aimed at achieving a target result (goal-seeking). It can also experiment to find the best combination of details subject to certain constraints (optimization). For example, an insurer might ask, "What if we reduce the insured's deductible by $50 for one year of accident-free driving? [what if]"; "How would the insured react if we increased premium by 10 percent each year? [sensitivity]"; "At what premium and deductible amount will insureds be willing to purchase a vanishing (decreasing) deductible feature? [goal seeking]"; or "How much can we increase the premium and deductible before a ten-year policyholder will price policies with another insurer? [optimization]"

These examples help explain an insurer's use of a DSS. A DSS can predict the ROI from offering alternatives for auto identification cards, such as transmitting insurance details to an electronic device installed in an auto so that, in the event of an accident, the information can be accessed by police and transmitted to a handheld device or another insurer. A DSS can identify consumers' needs for a certain type of insurance coverage or policy features. A DSS also can predict the number of insureds willing to purchase such coverages or features and determine the ROI for providing them.

Expert Systems

An expert system (ES) stores knowledge and makes inferences. It is designed to emulate human decision making using **artificial intelligence (AI)**. An ES knowledge base contains case-based or hierarchical facts about a specific subject and rules that use and explain expert reasoning. An ES analyzes complex information and either recommends solutions or actually makes decisions.

Artificial Intelligence (AI)
Computer processing or output that simulates human reasoning or knowledge.

The benefits of using an ES to supplement or support human decision making include speed and consistency, its preservation and use of the knowledge of multiple experts, and the fact that it does not suffer human limitations (distraction, stress, or fatigue). Some notable limitations are that an ES cannot learn from its errors, it is costly, and it can only solve problems related to specific subjects in a limited domain. Insurers can use an ES to underwrite complex accounts, handle complex claims, offer medical diagnoses, and detect fraud.

Customer-Focused Collection and Safety Systems

Insurers are increasingly using information developed by systems that interface directly with their customers. These systems are geared toward data collection or safety. They enable insurers to collaborate with their customers to provide individualized pricing or discounts.

Telematics is one example. Telematics, used in what is called pay-as-you-drive or pay-how-you-drive insurance, enables insurers to rate drivers based on their driving habits rather than assumptions based on segmentation (such as age, gender, marital status, and auto model). Some regulators are prohibiting insurers from using personal characteristics as the bases of price because doing so penalizes law-abiding drivers in those segments. Telematics provides a solution with individualized pricing. Because safe drivers are attracted to telematics' benefits, insurers can gain a competitive advantage by attracting the most profitable insurance customers.

Cutting-edge safety and security features are increasingly being installed in motor carriers, personal autos, homes, and commercial buildings. These technologies may use cameras, sensors, global positioning systems, and other devices to transmit data to insurers and/or security vendors and local protection authorities. Information transmitted and/or collected by these devices can be used by insurers' claims departments to investigate losses, determine causes of loss, and serve as evidence that can potentially bring to justice those who have committed fraud and secure recoveries that offset insurers' losses. Insurers can offer attractive policy pricing to more-profitable prospects that have these safety devices and are less likely to suffer a loss.

Electronic and Mobile Commerce

Electronic commerce (e-commerce) enables insurers to conduct business using the Internet and other networks. Nearly all aspects of insurance sales and customer service can be conducted electronically, including marketing, sales, delivery of quotes, application submission, collection of underwriting and claims information, billing and premium collection, policy delivery and maintenance, claims submission, and even claim payment. Mobile commerce (m-commerce), which is e-commerce conducted through mobile devices, places all of these functionalities at the fingertips of consumers.

E-commerce and m-commerce enable customer-facing benefits, such as click-through advertising that attracts business through well-crafted websites or applications that educate consumers on the benefits and drawbacks of insurance, local insurance requirements, and insurance trends. Customers can use these applications to rate and comment on their experiences, potentially persuading applicants to consider that insurer's products. Intuitive, user-friendly, online applications with prefilled information (obtained through an insurer's subscriber services) that are easy to complete and that help prospects choose appropriate options demonstrate that the insurer is customer driven and capable of delivering an optimum experience.

E-commerce and m-commerce provide premium and renewal reminders for insureds, offering online or automated payment options using automated clearing houses and credit or debit cards. They allow the insured to update contact information and price policy changes, improving the ease of doing business with the insurer. These systems offer claimants immediate claim reporting by scanning codes on insurance identification cards using their cell phones or by entering claim information into mobile applications or websites. These applications allow users to easily attach photos of damaged property, driver's licenses, and others' insurance cards, making it easy to file claims.

Insurer websites and applications provide customers twenty-four-hour access to their information.

E-commerce and m-commerce features that collect and mine customer browsing information can offer insureds customized tips to reduce premiums, explain discount programs and additional exposures, suggest other insurance products, or recommend affinity groups (such as antique car or motorcycle discussion boards). These features might encourage tech-savvy insureds to purchase additional products and services. This differentiation may help retain business.

On the insurer-facing side, e-commerce and m-commerce provide seamless transmission of claim information into the insurer's DSS, which eliminates or minimizes claims entry, quickly delivers relevant details and documents to a claims representative, and enables an insurer to respond to a claim promptly, thus improving customer experience and reducing cost. These features improve the accuracy of insurers' data, ease claims reporting, and increase customer satisfaction.

Aggregators offer competitive quotes to consumers. Aggregators collect and deliver contact information to subscribing insurers, who can follow up with a customized quote based on the insurer's discounts and price offerings. Some aggregators provide a link to an insurer's applications for a detailed quote or to alert the insurer to call the prospect to provide more information.

SECURITY AND CONTROL IN INFORMATION SYSTEMS

There have been news reports of cyberattacks on credit card companies, banks, and educational facilities that resulted in assets being stolen or personal information being revealed. All organizations, including insurers, are vulnerable to such attacks, but can control these risks to minimize resulting damage.

Data security can be threatened by internal sources, external sources, and **collusion** between both. Security risks for insurers can come from the destruction of data or programs, espionage, invasion of privacy, social networks, employee fraud, human error, **cloud computing**, and mobile devices. An organization's security team can minimize data security risks and subsequent losses by remaining vigilant about ongoing security concerns and emerging and changing risks. Employees should be made aware of these concerns, trained in best practices, and held accountable for their own data safety as directed by the security team.

Aggregator

A business that offers similar products or services from several organizations on its customers' comparison website and then collects a referral fee from those organizations when a customer uses the site tools or links.

Collusion

An agreement by two or more people to defraud another.

Cloud computing

Information, technology, and storage services contractually provided from remote locations, through the Internet or another network, without a direct server connection.

Sources of Security and Control Risks

Weaknesses in data security allow risks from three sources: internal, external, and collusive. For an organization, internal sources of risk are employees at all levels who might exploit weaknesses in data security. When an organization implements appropriate segregation of duties, no one person has both custody of an asset and access to the records concerning that asset. This separation restricts the ability of operations-level employees, such as accounting clerks and sales clerks, to steal an asset and then conceal the theft by altering computer records. Managers and supervisors have greater access to and can more easily falsify records, but they have fewer opportunities to steal assets.

External sources of risk include business contacts and potential criminals who have opportunities to steal the organization's assets. Two major sources of risk are customers and vendors that process transactions with an organization and have indirect access to assets and records. Former employees also constitute a risk to computerized data, as they may have intimate knowledge of data systems and their control weaknesses and may hold a grudge against their previous employer. Unknown criminals include hackers, who may be more motivated by the challenge than the theft; a company's competitors attempting to gain an advantage; or members of organized crime, who may want to exploit weaknesses in data security to defraud an organization of its assets.

Collusive sources of risk exist when two or more individuals conspire to defraud an organization and to conceal the theft by altering records. Internal collusion occurs when two or more employees of an organization cooperate to bypass its controls, steal an asset, and conceal the theft. External collusion exists when an employee acts with a nonemployee to defraud the organization.

In organizations with sound control policies, practices, and procedures, managers and collusive sources are the primary sources of risk. Without good internal control, risks exist from all sources.

Security Risks and Responses

From internal, external, and collusive sources, specific organizational risks may arise.

Destruction of Data or Programs

Although all of an organization's internal information is important, certain data and files are vital to its operation and may be difficult to reconstruct accurately if destroyed.

Data can be destroyed by computer viruses entering an organization's system from outside. This intentional data or program destruction may arise from disgruntled employees or former employees, who can gain unauthorized access to various systems and destroy or modify files as a form of revenge, or from hackers, proving they can bypass the security features of the system. For general network security, it is important to invest in and run quality antivirus and spyware software on a regular basis.

The destruction of data or programs may be accidental. This risk is minimized by hiring capable, trained, and responsible employees; by continually retraining and updating their skills; by providing manuals and resources for safeguarding data; and by maintaining high standards and adhering to them. Following prescribed backup policies ensures that data can be retrieved in the event of a fire, flood, or other physical damage to the computer hardware. See the exhibit "Best Practices for Backup."

Best Practices for Backup

To ensure data integrity and restoration, an organization can adopt best practices for backup, including these:

- Determine what data on which computers will be backed up
- Select the appropriate program(s) for backing up the data
- Determine an offsite location for backup archives
- Set up a regular backup schedule
- Periodically monitor the backups for occurrence and accuracy
- Periodically pursue data restoration in a test environment

To ensure data integrity during the backup process, an organization can adopt best practices for employees, including these:

- Save data often and always at the end of the workday
- Report any scheduled backups that are missed
- Do not alter or change the scheduled backup times
- Store data in designated locations (such as certain drives or certain folders) to maximize backup efforts
- If overnight backup is scheduled, leave computers in the correct mode

If data backup will be on the cloud, organizations should ensure that the above best practices align with those of the cloud provider.

[DA10517]

Espionage

Managers are concerned about the actions and plans of competing companies. They can acquire useful information about competitors, such as financial, production, or employee records, by gaining access to computerized data. Information can be stolen by using a simple Universal Serial Bus (USB) flash drive, also called a thumb drive, or by using a keystroke logger, often marketed to parents and employers, to monitor a company's emails, passwords, viewed website addresses, and newly inputted data. See the exhibit "USB Flash Drives and Security Failures."

USB Flash Drives and Security Failures

The United States Department of Homeland Security conducted a security check by leaving Universal Serial Bus (USB) flash drives in the parking lots of federal buildings and private contractors. The majority of those that were found were plugged into company computers, particularly the flash drives that had official logos on them. While this was only a test, it did confirm that hackers can leave tempting USB flash drives in the paths of individuals and wreak potentially devastating results. A flash drive can introduce an executable program to collect information or spread a virus. In addition, it can be programmed to accomplish its activities weeks later, convincing the user in the short term that it is safe and can continue to be used. A damaging flash drive may appear on screen to be blank, luring the user into a false sense of security.

[DA10518]

Companies operating on an international level may be victims of espionage from competitors in a foreign country, where spying may be legal and promoted.

Wireless connections should be secured by encrypting all information between wireless devices and a router. Because the router may be set up with a default setting that is commonly available to anyone on the Internet, it is important to secure a wireless access key and to change or view the router settings often.

Although espionage is primarily an external threat, a competitor may gain access to sensitive data by collusion with an employee.

Invasion of Privacy

Computerized data files contain much personal information about individuals. Disclosure of this information is an invasion of privacy, with implications of possible criminal or civil liability at the local, state, and federal levels. Employees want their information, such as age, address, wages, and pension records, kept private. Customers expect confidentiality concerning current balances, credit ratings, and payment histories.

Threats to privacy come from hackers and employees. General network security procedures can stop some hackers from obtaining private data that should remain confidential. Routine employee training regarding company standards and the applicable laws addressing privacy issues can be good reminders to keep personal file information secure.

Insurers, because of their gathering of personal information of applicants, insureds, and claimants, should be particularly aware of invasion of privacy and the legal and regulatory requirements affecting the industry. One statute regarding consumer privacy is the **Health Insurance Portability and Accountability Act (HIPAA).** For insurers, only requesting, receiving, and storing the personal information necessary for a claim or an insurance application limits loss exposures by reducing the amount of acquired and stored personal information.

Social Networks

The explosion of social networking sites is a concern to employers. These sites encourage communication and connections, which create an atmosphere of sharing and trust.

An organization's internal secrets may be obtained indirectly by analyzing employees' public postings on social networking sites. Employees visiting these sites during business hours or detailing company plans or projects can leave their employers vulnerable to information leaks, no matter how unintentionally. Posted company information can become public information within minutes over the Internet.

Organizations may find an explicit social media policy helpful in educating their employees of the potential threats, providing them with detailed standards and guidelines, and proactively minimizing their exposures before any damage occurs.

Employee Fraud

Fraud is the risk that most often affects the accuracy of accounting records by misstating assets and expenses in financial statements. Major fraud endangers the ability of an organization to continue its operations. Although many controls protect against fraud by lower-level employees, managers may be in a position to override these controls. Additionally, when employees collude internally or externally, controls may fail to prevent or detect fraud. Accountants and auditors may be helpful in detecting the concealment of fraud.

Human Error

Human error is the cause of many incidents of information loss, including unintentional errors from users, programmers, and service providers. Human error, not technical failure, is generally considered the most frequent cause of security lapses. This risk can be minimized by hiring technicians with the appropriate amount and type of experience and by emphasizing security training and certifications for information technology (IT) employees.

Human error or carelessness can be a factor in security breaches involving passwords. If someone casually reveals a personal password and that same password is used for all his or her business applications, a company's security could be jeopardized. Other examples of human error or carelessness are never changing (or only slightly changing) passwords, selecting easy-to-guess

Health Insurance Portability and Accountability Act (HIPAA)
Federal legislation establishing standards for health insurance information exchanges and health coverage protection when jobs are lost or changed.

passwords, or using laptops displaying sensitive information in public places without a privacy screen.

Employees who are uneducated about phishing expeditions may put their business data at risk. In a phishing scheme, a person targets a company by obtaining employees' email addresses, perhaps from a list of work friends publicly posted by an employee. A carefully crafted email is sent to each employee to persuade the recipients to either open a harmful link or provide company information or passwords. Spear phishing, which specifically targets certain individuals at one company, and whale phishing, which specifically targets managers or senior officials of a company, prey on the trust and gullibility of employees. Training that explains these activities and equips employees to be vigilant in identifying them is a good defense against phishing attacks.

Cloud Computing

Cloud computing, or the cloud, enables a company to access and run many programs and applications without buying or maintaining them for each employee and without needing to install the best and fastest computer hardware.

The cloud allows employees to sign in from any location and stores data on remote computers. The cloud also provides data backup with digital storage devices and keeps a copy of all company information to ensure retrieval in case of a breakdown. This backup and redundancy saves time and storage space for a company and provides assurance that full access to all information will be available at any time. The risk is allowing others to have this access—there is uncertainty in placing a company's ideas and secrets in someone else's control.

Distributed computing

An arrangement consisting of multiple computers that are interconnected and work together on a common project.

Other risks to consider are a cloud provider's security standards and procedures, which can vary by provider. A company must be vigilant in understanding and scrutinizing the contract entered into with a provider and its regulatory, compliance, jurisdictional, and privacy implications. Cloud computing is a type of **distributed computing** and shares many of the same types of risks. To date, little conclusive research exists on the cost of losses from cloud computing. Insurance for covering these losses, offered as part of a service agreement, is an option to consider when choosing a provider.

If a company's files are stored on the cloud, that company is dependent on the servicing company or network to provide its data. If the service is disrupted, for example, by damage to a fiber-optic cable, the network will be down. Although backup data would be available, and thus no actual information lost, a company would at best be inconvenienced, with possibly devastating results depending on when the disruption occurred and for how long.

Important actions for a company entering into a cloud servicing contract are to determine the value of the data on the cloud and then to match the protection measures to the data value. These determinations could influence decisions made regarding encryption levels or the complexity of passwords.

Mobile Devices

Many companies are providing company-issued mobile devices such as smartphones or tablets, some with mobile payment technology (digital wallets), to employees. Other companies are allowing employees to access business emails and files from their personal devices (known as bring your own device, or BYOD), thereby mingling personal emails and applications with business emails and applications.

Risks to an organization include the loss of data or, if the device is lost or stolen, a security breach. When payments can be made from the device, there is an added financial risk. The same concerns as those for human error and invasion of privacy exist but now for a device that leaves the office building and is used by the employee after leaving that building. It is important for companies to ensure that employees conform to established business practices regarding the use of these devices.

Some organizations are using encryption programs for business-related information, requiring strict password standards, and remotely wiping the mobile devices of business data when they are reported lost or stolen. Employers may ask their employees to keep business emails separate from personal emails. Companies can also train employees how to change the settings on their devices for greater security and protection against viruses. Employees should take the same corporate-level precautions when using their mobile devices that they take when using their in-office computers.

Security and Control Measures

Companies of all sizes are vulnerable to security breaches from inside and outside their organizations. Internal controls include the methods, policies, and procedures used by an organization to ensure the safeguarding of assets, the accuracy and reliability of financial records, the promotion of administrative efficiency, and compliance with management and regulatory standards. External controls include a well-maintained network with firewalls and **access control lists (ACLs)**.

A company should have in place a security team that understands senior management's goals for the company and integrates a security plan to help meet those goals. In this way, the security team is supported by senior management and can enlist the help of the entire organization. A security team that familiarizes itself with all aspects of an organization's departments can more easily identify and respond to emerging risks.

An education and training program is especially important for organizations such as insurers, which value their stakeholders' trust by safeguarding personal information. Employees must understand the reasons that safety measures are created, the structure and hierarchy of the security system, and the need for periodic audits to measure and improve compliance. An insurer can reinforce this approach by impressing upon employees that they are partners with senior

Access control list (ACL)
A set of permissions linking a user with a specific information system object and specifying the level of access to that object, such as read, write, execute, or delete.

management and the security team in accomplishing the goal of attracting new customers, retaining existing insureds, and continuing an insurer's reputation for privacy and confidentiality.

A technology usage statement is an important policy that identifies levels, responsibilities, and roles for all internal employees and external partners, such as vendors or contract workers. All practices deemed essential, such as access to the Internet, password requirements, and use of mobile devices, should be presented in writing, explained in detail with corrective actions for noncompliance, and signed off by the employees. This agreement should be revisited, revised, reinforced, and resigned as needed.

It is important for an organization to have a process in place for identifying, approving, implementing, and monitoring security changes with identified task owners and chains of command. A process for addressing security breaches or violations includes steps for detection of the breach, correction of the problem, restoration of the system, and analysis and revision of the process for any future incidents.

To the extent possible, a company should be forward-thinking and aware of emerging technology, new risks, and possible solutions. Issues such as whether to allow BYODs and access to social media sites during work hours should be addressed long before they have become problematic and threaten company security.

ALIGNING INSURER AND IT STRATEGY

Practically every insurer, whether large or small, must address the challenges of aligning information technology (IT) strategies with business strategies. Despite the difficulty of the task, aligning current and new technologies with business objectives can result in more efficient and expanded operations in all departments.

Key subjects concerning the alignment of business and IT strategy include these:

- Importance of IT and business strategy alignment
- Benefits and challenges
- Plan for alignment
- Metrics of successful alignment

Importance of IT and Business Strategy Alignment

How IT is aligned with core insurer operations and the integral relationships between IT and senior leadership are essential to the success of an insurer. Insurers are continually evolving operationally in response to market and regulatory influences as well as new trends in technology. Technology can create a competitive advantage as an insurer's dependencies on information and data increase.

As insurers become more transaction-focused, the value of IT investments increases. IT is no longer a stand-alone cost center. For an insurer to grow to its full potential, IT initiatives must be aligned closely with an insurer's key strategic goals and objectives. See the exhibit "Example of an IT Initiative That Is Not Aligned With an Insurer's Business Goals."

Example of an IT Initiative That Is Not Aligned With an Insurer's Business Goals

An insurer's chief information officer (CIO) visited the vendor booths at an underwriting conference, where he found a workers compensation policy processing system he believed could replace the outdated system the insurer was currently using. The new, off-the-shelf application would be easy for the IT staff to master and was designed to interface easily with several external databases and state workers compensation rating bureaus. The CIO conferred briefly with the vice president of workers compensation underwriting, and she concurred.

Only after purchasing this software package and migrating policy processing off the old system did they realize that the new system did not capture and store key data elements necessary for both internal reports and external regulatory reports.

What went wrong? Although the CIO did consult with the underwriting vice president, the new system still did not align with business needs. In this instance, they failed to consult with personnel in the business units who use the system: underwriters, data quality managers, business analysts, and compliance staff.

[DA10559]

Benefits and Challenges

Alignment of IT goals with business goals creates both benefits and challenges. Part of the responsibilities of each of an insurer's department managers is to identify what benefits can be expected from an IT initiative and what challenges may prevent its successful implementation.

Benefits

These are among the numerous potential benefits to all of an insurer's departments of increasing alignment between IT and business objectives:

- Sustainable improvements in service level realized for internal and external customers
- Cost reduced
- Compliance with a state's insurance department regulations attained
- Private or privileged information protected
- Best practices standardized

- Productivity increased
- Communications enhanced
- Production workflows expedited
- Competitive advantage obtained via faster implementation of new technology

These benefits can result from an IT initiative's helping an insurer reach a business goal, such as operational excellence, that promotes efficient operations. An example of a sustainable improvement in service level for internal and external customers is the use of cost-of-repair estimating software that can generate more consistently accurate estimates. An example of cost reduction is a program that allows employees to report their monthly expenses more quickly than the previous method, which should result in more available time for employees to perform productive tasks.

Properly aligned and successfully implemented IT projects can create a chain reaction of benefits. Elevated performance can lead to improved customer satisfaction, which, in turn, may lead to fewer complaints to the insurer and state department of insurance, a lower loss ratio and lower loss adjustment expenses, and higher revenue and market share. By selecting IT investments based on their probability of helping the insurer succeed, the insurer improves its performance and also sees the IT Department's overall success enhanced. The success of the IT Department is predominantly determined by its ability to ensure that the insurer's business needs drive the technology.

Challenges

Every insurer has its own set of unique challenges, which can hinder the complete alignment of IT and business strategies. Challenges that can affect IT and the business functions it serves include these:

- Controlling expenses—This is often the primary concern. The benefit delivered by the investment in the IT project must exceed its expense. To determine whether the investment will earn an acceptable return, assess the insurer's ability to implement the IT project successfully.
- Changing IT or business metrics—Frequently, in IT, when a trend that management may want to act on is detected, a change occurs that causes current metrics to become obsolete. Be ready to make adjustments mid-cycle. For example, changes in traffic regulations—such as increasing the legal speed limit on a state highway—will change the predicted frequency and severity of insured bodily injuries and property damage.
- Clearly understanding customers' needs—This is essential for both internal and external customers. Understanding their needs will help IT guide customers through the learning curve and encourage acceptance of IT initiatives. When IT is aligned to serve the business, the business can best align with customer needs.

- Management financial support—Substantial infrastructure changes can be a significant investment for an insurer. Senior management may not always see the enterprise-wide picture and may have varying opinions about how to spend budget dollars. Showing a positive correlation between successfully implementing IT initiatives and achieving business goals can help obtain IT funding.

- Lack of prioritization—IT project to-do lists do not get shorter. Projects must be prioritized to ensure that adequate resources will be available for successful implementation. Projects without a high enough priority and sufficient resources may cause the insurer to incur unnecessary costs and consumption of time. Time, capital, and outcomes should be considered when prioritizing projects.

- Lack of trust—Because an insurer's IT professionals may not believe their jobs are secure, they may pursue training to obtain skills that would be desirable to another employer rather than the IT skills the current employer needs. Assurances of job security can help prevent this inefficiency.

- Overly complex IT infrastructure—A **legacy system** that is retrofitted onto the business structure can become difficult to modify and can have trouble supporting overlying business functions. In such a case, comparative analysis should be performed to determine the costs and benefits of retaining the old infrastructure as opposed to updating to a new one.

  Legacy system

  Typically an outdated computer system that continues to meet users' needs and is still in use even though newer technology is available that can meet those needs more efficiently.

- IT as a separate unit—IT personnel too often see themselves as a separate unit apart from the rest of the organization, rather than as people who can help a customer perform a business function. It should be emphasized to IT personnel that, for an IT initiative to be considered a success, it must have a business driver; there is a business need for an IT solution rather than an interesting state-of-the-art technology seeking an application.

- Lack of understanding of insurer and its needs—Some IT personnel need to better understand the insurance business and the insurer's operations to be able to more effectively align business needs with an IT solution. The corporate culture needs to be one in which IT personnel are considered part of the business. Training, education, and job rotation and shadowing can help resolve this concern. In addition, a competent business analyst who can speak the language of business and the language of technology could be hired to help bridge the communication gap.

- Lack of understanding of IT and its capabilities—Businesspeople need to understand the technology and what it is, and is not, capable of. The same solutions that have been suggested for improving understanding of an insurer can be applied here.

Plan for Alignment

To substantially increase the chances of success, IT management must be involved in the insurer's strategic planning. Insurers that make a significant investment in the planning process in the beginning will likely save time and money as the alignment continues. These savings are probable for a variety of reasons, which include the insurer's being able to more quickly and accurately anticipate challenges to the implementation of an alignment plan. This advance knowledge regarding which challenges will be problematic allows management to allocate resources more economically and to have them available when needed. Initially, the planning process should focus on determining the insurer's business needs.

Once the insurer's strategic goals have been established, a plan should be drafted in which the business objectives are mapped with measurable IT services. Preferably, business and IT management do this jointly. By charting a path that aligns business and IT objectives, they can be prioritized and placed in the order of execution that optimizes allocation of IT resources and the business value of each IT initiative. The charted path should be a map that also shows the key touch points and interdependencies between business processes and technological opportunities.

Key resources, both internal and external, should be identified. These resources should be aligned so that the entire staff can function efficiently. The vision and strategy created through the planning process should be shared with the entire staff, as well, so they can see the direction in which the insurer intends to go.

Finally, the functionality of each project should be determined, and how it supported or improved a business process in the organization should be measured. IT should not be doing projects just for the sake of doing projects. Baseline measurements must be taken so that significant changes can be detected and reported to management.

Metrics of Successful Alignment

Some insurers measure the value of a project by selecting an internal baseline with a goal of improving it by a certain percentage. Other insurers may supplement that measurement by using industry benchmarks to compare their performance with competitors'. However, when performing this analysis, management should not lose sight of the key issue of whether an IT project is enabling the associated business goal to be met and business benefits to be realized. An IT initiative may be implemented successfully, but if it does not support or improve a process that results in a business benefit or attainment of a goal, it has failed. Tracking and measuring value from a project's design throughout its implementation should help avoid such a situation and support the realization of benefits.

An important way to track and measure the success of an IT project is to evaluate the efficiency and effectiveness of the business process it is intended to improve and to show tangible results. Although it is recommended that metrics be developed that are tailored to a specific insurer's objectives, some standard metrics can work well for any organization:

- Percentage of uptime—Consider how downtime affects the functionality and value of the system. What costs are incurred, including missed opportunities, because of the downtime of the system?

- Functionality—What is the purpose of the project, and which business process is it supporting or improving? Determine whether the project is meeting that purpose.

- Problem resolution—Are the concerns of internal and external (if applicable) customers being addressed efficiently? Is there one central office or point of contact to which customers can go for the project? How long does it usually take for a customer's problem to be resolved?

SUMMARY

IT capabilities that deliver the right data to the insurer or customer at the right time, in the right place and form, provide an insurer with a competitive advantage. IT capabilities can increase the operational efficiency of nearly every functional area of an insurer's business and support that insurer's strategy and decision making. Insurers that take a holistic, strategic approach to corporate governance, risk, and compliance and incorporate that approach into their IT processes meet regulatory requirements and are more likely to achieve a competitive advantage.

Quality data are essential for an insurer's information needs. Many organizations have established a data manager role to ensure that quality standards are met and best practices are followed. To effectively manage the quality of an insurer's data, a data manager must understand the insurer's information needs, which can be classified into three levels: operational, managerial, and strategic.

A BIS offers insurers a competitive advantage through transaction processing systems, decision support systems, expert systems, customer-focused collection and safety systems, and electronic and mobile commerce systems. These systems can improve the efficiency of processing and data collection, and they create value for customers.

An organization's data security can be threatened internally from employees, externally from business contacts and potential criminals, and collusively when two or more individuals conspire to harm a company. Risks to a company can come from the destruction of data or programs, espionage, invasion of privacy, social networks, employee fraud, human error, cloud computing, and mobile devices. An organization's security team plans and executes its control measures in response to these specific risks and in accordance with the organization's needs and goals.

Key subjects concerning the alignment of business and IT strategy include these:

- Importance of IT and business strategy alignment
- Benefits and challenges
- Plan for alignment
- Metrics of successful alignment

Direct Your Learning ▶▶

Insurer Strategic Management

Educational Objectives

After learning the content of this assignment, you should be able to:

▷ Describe the stages in the strategic management process.

▷ Explain how the Five Forces and SWOT methods can be used to analyze the environment in which an insurer operates.

▷ Explain how strategies are developed at the corporate, business, functional, and operational levels.

▷ Describe the strategic reasons, considerations, and approaches for insurers to expand their operations globally.

▷ Given information about an insurer's business strategies, conduct a SWOT analysis of its strategy.

▶▶

Insurer Strategic Management

STRATEGIC MANAGEMENT PROCESS

The strategic management process is critical to any organization's success. However, effective strategic management is especially important for insurers because they must distinguish themselves in a highly regulated business where products may not widely vary.

Organizations can be successful in the long term if they have effective strategies that efficiently deploy resources. Therefore, the heart of any successful business strategy is the alignment between the internal resources of the organization and external factors. This alignment allows an organization to create a sustainable competitive advantage.

The **strategic management process** involves three interdependent stages:

- Strategy formulation—creating a plan
- Strategy implementation—putting the plan into action
- Strategy evaluation—monitoring the results to determine whether the plan works as envisioned

Strategic management process
The process an organization uses to formulate and implement its business strategies.

Strategy Formulation

Strategy formulation depends on an organization's mission or value statements. Throughout the strategic management process, these statements should serve as a focal point for the organization's management and board of directors.

Mission and Vision Statements

A **mission statement** is a broad expression of an entity's purpose or goals, while reflecting the entity's character and spirit. The mission statement specifies the products or services the organization provides, its stakeholders, and what is important to the organization. Mission statements frequently refer to customers, shareholders, employees, and other corporate stakeholders. For insurers, mission statements frequently mention financial strength, customer service, and integrity.

Mission statements may also include, or be accompanied by, vision or value statements that provide additional information about company values or principles important to the organization. Values such as integrity, honesty,

Mission statement
A broad expression of an entity's goals.

customer focus, flexibility, and compassion are often included in these statements. See the exhibit "Example of Insurer Mission/Vision Statements."

Example of Insurer Mission/Vision Statements

STATE FARM INSURANCE

Our Mission, Our Vision, and Our Shared Values

State Farm's mission is to help people manage the risks of everyday life, recover from the unexpected, and realize their dreams.

We are people who make it our business to be like a good neighbor; who built a premier company by selling and keeping promises through our marketing partnership; who bring diverse talents and experiences to our work of serving the State Farm customer.

Our success is built on a foundation of shared values—quality service and relationships, mutual trust, integrity and financial strength.

Our vision for the future is to be the customer's first and best choice in the products and services we provide. We will continue to be the leader in the insurance industry and we will become a leader in the financial services arena. Our customers' needs will determine our path. Our values will guide us.

Source: http://www.statefarm.com/about/mission.asp (accessed June 22, 2010).

AMICA INSURANCE

Mission Statement

Amica's mission is to enhance the financial security of our customers by offering personal insurance protection and other related services at the lowest reasonable cost, consistent with sound financial management.

In accomplishing this mission, we are dedicated to the following principles:

Exceeding customer expectations by providing the highest quality service in the industry.

Offering superior products and services that respond to the needs of our customers.

Maintaining financial strength through sound business practices and the aggressive pursuit of efficient operations.

Promoting well-being, dedication, and professionalism in our employees by providing them with equal opportunity for personal growth and recognition in a pleasant, healthy, and safe work environment.

Adhering to the highest ethical, moral, and legal standards in our business and civic activities.

Source: http://www.amica.com/about_us/amica_advantage/missionStatement.html (accessed June 22, 2010).

[DA06246]

Strategy Formulation Steps

Considering the organization's mission and vision statements, board members and senior-level executives develop strategies through a three-step process. Although business theorists differ over the labeling and numbering of the steps (and some divide individual steps into more than one), strategy formulation has these basic components:

- Analysis of external and internal environments
- Development of long-term strategies and organizational goals
- Determination of strategy at different organizational levels

The first step of strategy formulation involves an internal analysis of the organization and an analysis of external factors including competitors, current and prospective customers' needs, the current and anticipated economy, and government regulations. Typically, a **SWOT analysis** may enable executives to determine how receptive the market would be to its products and services and its competitive position within the market. Opportunities can be categorized as those that "can" or those that "should" be pursued. With this approach, the framework for a strategic plan begins to emerge.

SWOT analysis
A method of evaluating the internal and external environments by assessing an organization's internal strengths and weaknesses and its external opportunities and threats.

The second step in the process involves development of long-term strategies and organizational goals to support the mission statement within the framework developed during the analysis step. An organization's goals should reflect an understanding of its identity, customers, and purpose. Companies establish these goals to set the priorities or direction for the organization, to establish a measurement of success, and to align its people and actions.

Normally, the chief executive officer (CEO) and executive officers will develop these strategies and goals, often with input from the board and operational-level managers. Depending on the organization, executives and others in management will then develop short-term financial objectives that are aligned with long-term strategies and goals.

The third step in strategy formulation is to determine strategies at different levels of the organization. This involves agreement on more specific action and delegation of responsibilities to achieve long-term strategies and goals. These strategies are based on an organization's core competencies, the competitive nature of the business, the potential customer base, and other factors. This step in the strategic management process involves formulating the "who," "what," and "when" responsibilities.

Strategy Implementation

The second stage of the strategic management process is strategy implementation, also called strategy execution. Strategy implementation is the process of making strategies work. In relation to the strategy formulation stage, this stage is more difficult to complete and requires more time.

Functional structure

An organizational structure in which departments are defined by the operation they perform.

Multidivisional structure

An organizational structure in which divisions are organized into separate profit centers.

Cost leadership

A business-level strategy through which a company seeks cost efficiencies in all operational areas.

The first consideration and a crucial component of strategy implementation is designing the structure of the organization. The most appropriate organizational structure for a company will be determined by its strategic goals. In a single-business company, a **functional structure** might be most suitable, with departments defined by the operation they perform. Examples of such departments would be claims, underwriting, and marketing and sales, among others. A diversified company is more likely to use a **multidivisional structure** to organize its operations and to segregate each division into separate profit centers.

Other possible structures organize company operations by region or by type of product or customer. A large insurer, for example, might have separate underwriting departments for commercial, marine, and personal lines insurance. This way, the expertise and resources required for specific customers is concentrated within the related department. Such an approach supports a differentiation strategy, in which the company seeks to provide unique products for specific market segments.

Structure can also determine the reporting relationships or the company's level of vertical differentiation, which is the extent to which an organization is stratified from its lowest to highest levels. Some companies are tall organizations, with many levels between functional-level positions and executive-level positions. Conversely, a flat organization has fewer levels from the top of the organization to the bottom. When following a **cost leadership** strategy, a flat organization helps to eliminate costs related to maintaining multiple reporting relationships within the company.

Companies should also decide what degree of centralization is needed to operate efficiently and to meet organizational goals. The degree of centralization determines whether authority is maintained at top levels of the organization or is delegated throughout headquarters, into regions, or even to the local level. For example, some insurers retain underwriting authority at the headquarters level, while others extend authority to local offices or to managing general agents. Their claim departments make similar decisions about whether claim-settling authority resides with home office claim staff or is extended to regional claim managers or local company adjusters.

Ultimately, the entire organization is responsible for successful strategy implementation. However, the plans for implementation begin with a filtering-down process, where organizational goals are communicated by top management. Often, managers at each successive level must "sell" organizational goals to their employees.[1] See the exhibit "Strategy Implementation Steps."

Strategy implementation and evaluation are intertwined—a company cannot achieve its goals if its strategies are not implemented effectively. Because of this, there must be a way to measure this effectiveness. Strategies also need to be continually evaluated and modified based on market, economic, and competitive conditions.

Strategy Implementation Steps

Mid-level managers are typically responsible for strategy implementation and may follow these five steps:

- Create a documented roadmap of the specific processes, tasks, and responsibilities necessary to disseminate the corporate strategies throughout the organization.

- Communicate information regarding the strategies clearly, frequently, and completely throughout the organization.

- Assign specific responsibilities, tasks, authority, and accountability throughout the organization.

- Allocate adequate resources for successful implementation. Resources include finances, staff, training, time, equipment, data, and technology.

- Manage variances between the goals and the mid-year results; make necessary adjustments to achieve the goals.

[DA06247]

Strategy Evaluation

Strategy evaluation, also called strategic control, provides a method for measuring a strategy's success. Control mechanisms allow management at each level to gauge the progress of the integration of established strategies into the organization's activities and toward achieving the goals that have been set. The control process has four steps:

1. Establish standards
2. Create and apply measurements
3. Compare actual results to standards
4. Evaluate and implement corrective actions if goals are not met

Following these steps provides a structured approach to strategy implementation. See the exhibit "Example of Steps in the Control Process Applied to an Underwriting Department."

> ## Example of Steps in the Control Process Applied to an Underwriting Department
>
> 1. Establish standards—A combined ratio of under 100 was established as the standard. Combined ratios are usually readily available, which makes the ratio an appropriate and easily-applied standard.
>
> 2. Create and apply measurements—Measurement would consist of compiling all premium, expense, and loss data required to develop a combined-ratio figure for this individual office, as well as determining a format for reporting the data.
>
> 3. Compare actual results to standards—An inherent part of this process is for managers to communicate the importance of meeting this standard to all employees and to motivate them to do so. These premium, expense, and loss reports would then be used in comparing actual results to the established standard of a combined ratio under 100. If the standard has not been met, managers will need to determine the reason and then implement changes.
>
> 4. Evaluate and implement corrective actions if goals are not met—Depending on the results of this comparison, corrective actions might involve training initiatives for employees, strengthening communications with producers, examining marketing activities, or taking other corrective actions. If the goal has been met, management should reward and recognize all employees involved to provide motivation to achieve future strategic goals.

[DA06248]

These are categories of organizational controls that may be used to monitor goals:

- Financial controls—In the insurance industry, loss ratios, expense ratios, and combined ratios are financial controls typically used to evaluate overall corporate performance. They also measure the performance of business units, regional offices, and individual books of business. Other financial controls include stock price, return on investment formulas, cost/benefits analysis, or budget measurements.

- Operational or process controls—These include processes to monitor work flow, production processes, and customer service. In an insurance claims department, such controls could include the average cost of settlement, average case load per adjuster, or file turnover rates for individual adjusters.

- Human or behavior controls—This category includes rules, policies, and procedures that provide operating guidelines for employees within an organization, including measurement of individual performance.

As a result of evaluation, strategic plans may be reformed, and/or the manner in which they are implemented may need to be adjusted. The evaluation may indicate that results are off target in ways that cannot be addressed through moderate adjustments. Or it may reveal that the plan's concepts were not completely connected in the implementation stage, which requires an adjustment to the implementation approach.

Unexpected outside economic forces also may make achievement of a strategic plan impractical or impossible. For example, significant events such as the September 11, 2001, terrorist attacks; Hurricane Katrina and related litigation; and the recession that started at the end of the first decade of the 2000s required many insurers to revise strategic management plans.

THE FIVE FORCES AND SWOT METHODS OF ANALYZING THE ENVIRONMENT

An insurer's success depends on its ability to analyze changing environmental factors and influences and to formulate sound business strategies based on its analysis.

Insurers rely on the strategic management process to achieve long-term goals. Strategy formulation is a crucial component of the strategic management process and involves the interrelated steps of analysis of external and internal environments, development of long-term strategies and organizational goals, and determination of strategy at different organizational levels.

In the first step of the process, managers consider factors in both the general environment and the task environment. The general environment affects all businesses, regardless of the specific industry in which they operate, and includes demographic, sociocultural, legal, technological, economic, and global factors. The task environment, which includes an organization's customers, competitors, and suppliers, describes the environmental factors specific to the industry in which the organization operates. The task environment for an insurance company might include customers, competitors, suppliers, reinsurance providers, and regulators.

Many methods can be used to analyze the environment in which an organization operates. Two commonly used methods are the Five Forces Model and SWOT analysis.

The Five Forces Model

The widely used **Five Forces Model**, developed by Harvard Business School professor Michael E. Porter, deals with the external task, or competitive, environment and is often used to analyze customers, competitors, and suppliers. Porter describes five forces that drive competition:[2]

- Threat of new entrants
- Threat of substitute products or services
- Bargaining power of buyers

Five Forces Model
A method of evaluating the external environment in which a company operates. Involves assessing five forces that drive competition: threat of new entrants, threat of substitute products or services, bargaining power of buyers, bargaining power of suppliers, and rivalry among existing firms.

- Bargaining power of suppliers
- Rivalry among existing firms

By analyzing these forces and their effect on the organization, managers can better understand their company's position in the industry. This increased understanding allows management to construct strategies that build a competitive advantage.

Threat of New Entrants

The threat of new entrants in a market is one force that drives competition, although the strength of this force depends on how difficult it is for outsiders to enter the market. Barriers to entry include economies of scale, which contribute to lower overall costs by decreasing the unit cost of products as volume increases. Many insurers writing homeowners or personal auto policies have achieved economies of scale through technology. The standardized nature of personal insurance policies allows some insurers to use automated processes to issue large numbers of policies with relatively low overhead costs. These insurers have lower expenses than insurers relying on more labor-intensive processes, allowing them to charge lower premiums and thus raise barriers to entry for this market segment.

Insurers can also raise barriers to entry by offering unique products or services through the establishment of leadership in certain distribution methods (for example, having a long-term relationship with producers or creating an online direct application system known for its ease of use) or by having established advertising or group marketing programs. The ability for one insurer to access distribution channels in a marketing system can create barriers to entry for others and pose a competitive disadvantage for potential new entrants. For insurance products, the insurance distribution system and channel can be important components of the overall marketing plan.

State statute and regulatory policy can act as a barrier to entry if they deter potential entrants from considering the highly regulated insurance industry. Regulatory requirements within a given jurisdiction can also discourage insurers from entering certain states. For example, the state of Massachusetts once discouraged new entrants to the personal auto insurance market with state-made rates and restrictions on distribution.

Other potential barriers to entry include the presence of switching costs, cost disadvantages independent of scale, and the need to invest large amounts of capital for production facilities for research and development.[3] All of these conditions increase costs for potential entrants, raising the barriers for them.

Threat of Substitute Products or Services

A second force that drives competition is the threat of substitute products or services. This threat arises when products that are capable of performing the same function as those from another industry become widely available. This threat makes it difficult for any one seller to substantially increase prices and tends to hold down profits for all participants in the original industry.

The threat of substitute products or services to the insurance industry has been limited thus far, but remains an important force for insurers to consider. One example of such a threat is alternative risk transfer mechanisms including self-insured retention, formation of captive insurance companies, catastrophe bonds, and finite risk transfer. On a more limited scale, an example of such a threat is the state-run Florida Citizens Property Insurance Corporation (Citizens). Citizens, originally intended as a market of last resort, could pose a threat to private insurers to the extent that it seeks to compete with the private market.

Bargaining Power of Buyers

The third force that drives competition is the bargaining power of buyers. When buyers have significant power, they can increase competition within an industry and demand lower prices. According to Porter, "consumers tend to be more price sensitive if they are purchasing products that are undifferentiated, expensive relative to their incomes, or of a sort where quality is not particularly important to them."[4] This force affects the insurance industry, principally in the personal insurance market, in which customers have exerted great pressure on insurers to lower prices and increase availability. The bargaining power of buyers is the reason that many government-sponsored or -mandated residual market plans were created. Auto assigned risk plans and property insurance plans (particularly those serving coastal markets) were created where the market would not support the prices needed for insurers to voluntarily offer coverage. Further, the bargaining power of buyers led to the explosive growth in a number of coastal property insurance plans and wind pools as property owners would not, or could not, pay rates sought by the private market.

The bargaining power of customers is also affected by the cyclical nature of the insurance business. In a soft market, many insurers vie for business and provide undifferentiated products. Insurance consumers have greater bargaining power and can negotiate for broader coverages at lower premiums. In a hard market, limited capacity results in rising prices and makes it difficult for customers to bargain for broader coverage.

When formulating strategy, companies should consider customer buying power. In some cases, insurers might decide not to enter markets where they feel pressure from buyer groups would inhibit their ability to be profitable.

Bargaining Power of Suppliers

A fourth force driving competition is the bargaining power of suppliers. In some industries, suppliers can exert power over companies by increasing prices, restricting supply, or varying product quality. For example, in the energy industry, oil-producing countries can exert tremendous power over the supply and price of petroleum products.

In the insurance industry, reinsurers are a supplier to primary insurers. Without access to reinsurance, many insurers would lack sufficient capacity to write certain types and amounts of insurance. Reinsurers are in a position to control the price and amount of capacity they provide depending on the market conditions. For example, after consecutive years of devastating hurricanes in the United States (Charley, Francis, Ivan, and Jeanne in 2004; Katrina, Rita, and Wilma in 2005), reinsurers were faced with enormous losses and uncertainty as to whether losses might even be worse if post-Hurricane Katrina litigation resulted in an unanticipated expansion of coverage. At the same time, many insurers found that they had been underestimating worst-case loss scenarios. Such uncertainty in the marketplace generally results in tighter capacity, rising rates, and more restrictive terms. In this case, demand for reinsurance increased at the same time that reinsurers limited capacity, resulting in reduced capacity and higher rates for primary insurance.

Another example of the bargaining power of suppliers is the power exerted by auto manufacturers to mandate use of original equipment manufacturer (OEM) parts for auto physical damage repairs. Where suppliers have successfully limited the acceptance or use of less expensive non-OEM (aftermarket) parts, physical damage loss costs may increase for insurers.

Rivalry Among Existing Firms

Rivalry among existing companies is the fifth force that drives competition. Rivalry is reflected in pricing wars, aggressive advertising campaigns, and increased emphasis on customer service. Competitors are constantly striving to be at the top of their industry and to outperform other companies. This type of rivalry exists among personal lines auto insurers.

A high level of competition can be expected in industries having many companies, little product differentiation, or high exit costs. All of these characteristics are present in the insurance industry, making the market strongly competitive. While some insurers can use economies of scale to gain a competitive edge, the individual market share of insurers at the top of the market is still relatively small compared to that of other industries. No single insurer has enough market share to dominate the overall property-casualty market. For example, the leading property-casualty insurer's market share is only approximately 10 percent.

SWOT Analysis

SWOT analysis, or situational analysis, is another method used to analyze the competitive environment. SWOT (Strengths, Weaknesses, Opportunities, and Threats) analysis allows organizations to consider both the general environment and the task environment. This method was devised by Albert S.

Humphrey, a business scholar and management consultant who specialized in business planning and change.

Strengths and Weaknesses

Identifying internal strengths and weaknesses involves consideration of financial, physical, human, and organizational assets.[5] Managers use SWOT analysis to determine the current state of their companies. These are some of the assets that management considers:

- Managerial expertise
- Available product lines
- Skill levels and competencies of staff
- Current strategies
- Customer loyalty
- Growth levels
- Organizational structure
- Distribution channels

It would be a strength if an organization has an executive training program that is considered an industry standard. If a company is having financial difficulty or is experiencing unfocused growth, it would be a weakness. In an insurance operation, an insurer that had been cutting prices to gain market share might identify loss of premium volume as a substantial weakness when an unanticipated rise in losses is projected as part of the SWOT analysis. Unfavorable loss results cause financial constraints.

For example, in 2002, several major property-casualty insurers conducted studies to determine the accuracy of reserves for asbestos-related claims. As a result of these studies, many of these insurers were required to increase their reserves significantly. These increases highlighted a key internal weakness for the insurers and had a negative effect on their earnings and stock prices.

Opportunities and Threats

Managers determine potential opportunities or threats by analyzing the external environment, including both general and task environment factors. One way to achieve this is through **trend analysis**, which identifies patterns related to specific factors in the past and then projects those patterns into the future to determine potential threats or opportunities. Insurers might determine opportunities and threats through trend analysis. Opportunities might be presented by new markets, possible acquisition targets, or a reduction in competition, while threats might include new competitors, an increase in competition levels, economic downturns, or changes in customer preferences.

Trend analysis
An analysis that identifies patterns in past data and then projects these patterns into the future.

For example, projection of various demographic trends might reveal new marketing opportunities or a shrinking market for an existing core product. See the exhibit "SWOT Analysis Table."

SWOT Analysis Table

	Strengths	Weaknesses
Internal	List assets, competencies, or attributes that enhance competitiveness	List lacking assets, competencies, or attributes that diminish competitiveness
	Prioritize based on the quality of the strength and the relative importance of the strength	Prioritize based on the seriousness of the weakness and the relative importance of the weakness
	Opportunities	**Threats**
External	List conditions that could be exploited to create a competitive advantage	List conditions that diminish competitive advantage
	Prioritize based on the potential of exploiting the opportunities	Prioritize based on the seriousness and probability of occurrence
	Note strengths that can be paired with opportunities as areas of competitive advantage	Note weaknesses that can be paired with threats as risks to be avoided

[DA03626]

The approach used by organizations varies based on each company's needs. A company should not only identify strengths, weaknesses, opportunities, and threats, but should also thoroughly analyze how they affect its strategic plan.

Once the SWOT analysis has been completed, managers can develop strategies that position the company to gain a competitive advantage by leveraging organizational strengths and offsetting or reducing weaknesses. The company should also find ways to capitalize on identified opportunities and to neutralize existing threats.

DETERMINING STRATEGY AT DIFFERENT ORGANIZATIONAL LEVELS

Strategic plans encompass a variety of organizational activities. Because organizations vary widely, every organization requires its own approach. Strategies can be categorized based on the levels at which they are carried out within an organization, how they relate to the development stage of the organization, and how they align with the organization's overall business approach.

Different kinds of strategies are carried out at various levels within an organization. Strategies at all levels should be aligned to support the organization's overall mission and vision. On any given day, insurance professionals may participate in implementing multiple strategies simultaneously. See the exhibit "Types of Organizational Strategies."

[DA06291]

These are the most prevalent types of organizational strategies:

- Corporate-level strategy represents the highest strategy level for a diversified organization. It determines the types and potential profitability of businesses or activities the organization will undertake.
- Business-level strategy may be implemented by a single operation or, in the case of a diversified corporation, a strategic business unit (SBU). Managers develop strategies at this level to support the corporate-level strategy, to be competitive, and to respond to changes in the external environment.
- Functional-level strategy is carried out by individual departments performing specific organizational functions, such as marketing or underwriting.
- Operational-level strategy relates to a department's narrowly defined day-to-day business activities. Operational strategies include workflows and production processes.

Corporate-Level Strategy

At the corporate level, the chief executive officer (CEO) and the executive team determine the businesses in which the company will be involved, allocate organizational resources properly, and coordinate strategies at all company levels to maximize profits. Corporate-level strategies are relatively long term, established for a five-year period and beyond.

Competitive advantage is reinforced when each department or unit in an organization creates value for the customer. In insurance operations, the marketing, underwriting, claim, customer service, and other departments must align to build value and to support corporate-level strategy in a continuous chain. This alignment can also provide additional advantages in the form of reduced operating expenses or increased differentiation of products and services through the interaction of various departments, such as marketing and underwriting.

Three generic corporate-level strategies are available for companies in a growth mode:

- Single business
- Vertical integration
- Diversification

There are different corporate-level strategies for companies in a decline mode, such as the bankruptcy, divestiture, turnaround, and harvest strategies.

Concentration on a Single Business

Based on a business environmental assessment, a company might determine that the best corporate-level strategy for it to pursue is concentration on a single business. By concentrating its efforts and resources on one industry, product, or market, a company can build distinctive competencies and gain a competitive advantage. Many property-casualty insurers pursue a single-business strategy, even though they write many types of insurance.

Concentrating on a single business, however, has some potential disadvantages. Most are related to missing opportunities to build a competitive advantage through either vertical integration or diversification into related areas.

Vertical Integration

Vertical integration strategy

A corporate-level strategy through which a company either produces its own inputs or disposes of its own outputs.

A **vertical integration strategy** can be either backward or forward. If an organization produces inputs for processing (such as an insurer printing policy forms in-house instead of purchasing them from a printing supplier), it is backward integration. When an organization sells its product directly to the customer rather than through a wholesaler, it is called forward integration. Direct writer insurers are an example of forward integration being put to use.

Companies choose vertical integration to decrease expenses or increase efficiency. However, vertical integration could have an opposite effect due to a lack of expertise or the cost of resources in different stages of the production process.

Diversification

Diversification for the property-casualty insurance industry can be advantageous. Because the industry is affected by the weather cycles, diversifying into lines of insurance or financial products that are unaffected by the weather can help smooth the demand for both financial and human resources. Because the insurance underwriting cycle does not coincide with the general business cycle, some insurers may benefit from diversification into non-insurance businesses to offset lower insurer profits during troughs in the insurance profit cycle. In pursuit of diversification, companies can pursue either related or unrelated diversification strategies.

Related diversification allows companies to gain economies of scope by sharing resources, such as the same distribution system or research and development facilities. For example, a property-casualty insurer may also provide life or health insurance and thus utilize its existing technology and agency system to grow its business while spreading risk. Another benefit of related diversification is the ability to leverage fixed expenses with additional revenues from diversified operations, resulting in a lower unit cost for each product or service offered. For example, insurers may enter into third-party administration of claims as some of their customers choose alternative risk financing approaches instead of traditional insurance. This allows the insurers to obtain additional revenue from their existing technology platforms, claim expertise, and other internal resources.

Related diversification strategy
A corporate-level strategy through which a company expands its operations into areas that are similar to its existing operations.

Unrelated diversification strategy (also referred to as conglomerate diversification strategy) involves acquiring companies that have no relationship to the existing business operations and is riskier than related diversification. The negative aspects of unrelated diversification include additional costs of coordinating the divergent businesses, a loss of synergy among business units, and diminishing returns from any economies of scale or scope. Companies that have succeeded with an unrelated diversification strategy excel at making the right types of acquisitions. These companies have also developed strong structure and control mechanisms to offset some of the difficulties stemming from managing an extensive and varied group of profit centers.

Unrelated diversification strategy
A corporate-level strategy through which a company expands its operations into areas that have no relation to its existing operations.

Decline Mode Strategies

All of the strategies discussed to this point involve companies operating in growing markets. However, some companies might not be growing, might be encountering substantial marketplace obstacles, or might have numerous internal weaknesses and external threats. The problems that these companies encounter could include decreasing profits, loss of market share, or changing economic conditions. When a company is operating in a market in which demand for its products or services is decreasing, it is in a decline mode and its strategic options are different than those of companies in a growth mode.

Corporate-level strategies for such companies are defensive. In the worst-case scenario, the company might determine that the only option is bankruptcy or liquidation. In bankruptcy, companies seek court protection from creditors to reorganize and improve their financial standing. If a company cannot recover from bankruptcy, it is liquidated and any remaining proceeds are used to satisfy outstanding obligations.

There are other corporate-level strategies that can be used in a decline mode. In the **harvest strategy**, for example, an insurer might sell real estate, such as office buildings, while it phases out an unprofitable line of insurance. In a **turnaround strategy**, an insurer might reorganize and reduce the number of offices and redundant administrative staff. In a **divestiture strategy**, an insurer will sell businesses or divisions to increase profits through the sale of assets or to reduce losses from unprofitable business. AIG provides an example of the divestiture strategy, having divested its stake in London City airport in 2008 and sold AIG Life of Canada and Hartford Steam Boiler in 2009.

Business-Level Strategy

Business-level strategies are developed at the business or division level by managers who are responsible for supporting the stated corporate-level strategy. These managers must find ways for their business units to be competitive and to respond to changes in the external environment. Business-level management also budgets for needed resources and coordinates the functional-level strategy within the division. The time frame for business-level strategies, sometimes referred to as tactical strategies, is three to five years in most organizations. There are three business-level strategies:

- Cost leadership
- Differentiation
- Focus

Cost Leadership

Cost leadership enables a company to charge a lower price for its products or services. It involves eliminating costs in every aspect of the operation, from product development and design to distribution and delivery. However, cost leadership involves more than just charging the lowest price in the industry. Even when prices for similar products are comparable, the cost leader can earn higher overall profits than its competitors because of its lower costs. Cost leaders can also better withstand prolonged price wars.

One requirement of a cost leadership strategy is that most products or services must be fairly standardized. Introducing varied types of products increases expenses and erodes any cost leadership advantages, so cost leaders do not tend to be first movers within an industry.

For insurers, price cutting might be limited by regulatory constraints. Insurers must closely examine the three components of an insurance rate (allowances for loss payments, expenses, and profit) to determine where costs can

Harvest strategy
A corporate-level strategy through which a company seeks to gain short-term profits while phasing out a product line or exiting a market.

Turnaround strategy
A corporate-level strategy through which a company rebuilds organizational resources to return to profitable levels.

Divestiture strategy
A corporate-level strategy through which a company sells off a portion of an operation, usually a division or profit center that is not performing to expectations.

be reduced. When evaluating how to decrease costs, insurers can consider reducing acquisition expenses by lowering producers' commissions, using a direct writer system for some or all of their marketing, or exploring alternative distribution channels.

Loss expenses can be reduced by streamlining claim adjusting processes, managing litigation expenses, or implementing cost containment practices, such as negotiation of repair or medical reimbursement rates with vendors. Underwriting expenses can be reduced by using expert computer systems or standardizing underwriting guidelines. Technology can automate processes, improve interaction among departments, and speed policy processing times. All of these efforts combine to execute the cost leadership strategy.

Differentiation

A successful **differentiation strategy** requires products and services that customers perceive as distinctive and that are difficult for rivals to imitate. Companies using this strategy must accurately determine the needs and preferences of their customers, or revenue and market share will be lost. Market share will also be lost if competitors can match or improve upon the product's unique features.

Insurers employing this strategy may choose to differentiate products or services to gain market share and to establish a competitive advantage. Insurers that offer special programs for commercial or homeowners insurance are examples. When an insurer writes only homeowners or personal auto insurance and targets multiple markets (such as teachers, retired persons, and military personnel), it is following a differentiation strategy. If an insurer offers a wide range of specialized coverages, but offers them only to municipalities, it is following a focus strategy.

Focus

A focus strategy involves concentrating on a group of customers, a geographic area, or a narrow line of products or services while using a low-cost approach or a differentiation strategy. The two types of this strategy are **focused cost leadership strategy** and **focused differentiation strategy**.

Many insurers follow one of the focus strategies. Niche marketing programs, which offer tailored coverages to specific groups of customers, are examples of focused differentiation. Alternatively, an example of a focused cost leadership approach is when an insurer that sells to a specific group of customers, such as retail hardware stores, and offers discounted commercial packages or automobile policies using standard forms. The use of standard forms is an important factor because any significant level of specialization increases costs and erodes profits.

Differentiation strategy

A business-level strategy through which a company develops products or services that are distinct and for which customers will pay a higher price than that of the competition.

Focused cost leadership strategy

A business-level strategy through which a company focuses on one group of customers and offers a low-price product or service.

Focused differentiation strategy

A business-level strategy through which a company focuses on one group of customers and offers unique or customized products that permit it to charge a higher price than that of the competition.

Functional-Level Strategy

Functional-level strategies are the plans for managing a particular functional area, such as finance, marketing, underwriting, actuarial, risk control, premium audit, and claims. These strategies establish how functional departments support the organization's business-level and corporate-level strategies. The time frame for these strategies is short term, usually one year.

Companies build value and competitive advantage through efficiency, quality, customer responsiveness, and innovation. Some combination of these factors must be incorporated into its activities at the functional level for a company to pursue either a cost leadership or differentiation strategy at the business level. For example, without efficiency and innovation, cost leadership cannot be attained. Similarly, quality and customer responsiveness must be included in the development, production, and marketing functions for a company to execute a differentiation strategy effectively.

In insurance operations, functional-level strategies specify how the underwriting, claim, actuarial, and other departments advance business-level strategies. For an insurer to be successful at garnering market share using a cost leadership strategy, it must become a highly efficient organization. For example, human resources, in cooperation with the underwriting, claim, customer service, and marketing departments, should find ways to improve productivity. The information technology department should provide innovative solutions to lower overall production costs and improve the speed of organizational communications, both internally and externally. Likewise, an insurer that is pursuing a differentiation strategy will consider innovation and quality at all functional levels to be critical to providing a distinctive product that meets the customer's needs.

Operational-Level Strategy

Operational-level strategies involve daily business processes and workflows, and are implemented at the department level to support the strategies of the functional, business, and corporate levels. For example, a claim office with a high volume of claims and a functional-level strategy to improve efficiency might decide to obtain more information through the claim reporting process in order to assign the claim properly and eliminate redundant communication with insureds. A premium auditing department, striving to achieve a functional-level budget strategy, might use pre-audit screening as an operational-level strategy to make the most effective use of resources to achieve its budget goals.

INSURERS' GLOBAL EXPANSION

Global competition is now a factor in virtually every industry. Advances in communication and transportation, international trade agreements to lower trade barriers, and growth in emerging markets have led many businesses to expand into global markets. Global investment and expansion in the insurance industry, both by insurers based in the United States entering foreign markets and by foreign insurers entering U.S. markets, have increased significantly in recent years and are likely to continue to do so.

Insurers are increasingly expanding operations to foreign markets. These four topics provide a basic understanding of why and how insurers engage in global expansion:

- Trends in global expansion
- Strategic reasons for global expansion
- Global market considerations
- Approaches to global expansion

Trends in Global Expansion

Global commerce has been growing since the end of World War II. During the past two decades, this growth accelerated as a result of numerous trade agreements throughout the world, advances in transportation and communication, the influence of the Internet, and financial innovation. The insurance market, like the markets in other industries, has become a global market where U.S. insurers compete in many other countries and where insurers domiciled in other countries compete in the U.S.

The U.S. experiences a trade deficit in global insurance trade that has increased steadily since 1995. In 1995, the deficit was approximately $1 billion, less than 1 percent of the U.S. global insurance trade. In 2006, the deficit was about $24.3 billion, almost 10 percent.[6] In 2006, foreign-owned insurers wrote 13.6 percent of the nonlife U.S. insurance premiums, and U.S. insurers ceded 53.1 percent of reinsurance premiums to foreign-domiciled entities.

Meanwhile, the U.S. also continued to increase exports of insurance with a 19 percent increase in 2006 (reinsurance comprised 60 percent of this total). However, in the same year, imports of insurance into the U.S. increased by 18 percent (reinsurance comprised 90 percent of the total).[7]

These statistics express the increased global competition within the international insurance industry. While there is greater competition for U.S. insurers from foreign insurers within the U.S. market, growth of the U.S. market has been slowing. From a low rate of growth of 2.1 percent for all insurance premiums (life and nonlife), to a decline of 7.8 percent in 2009, the U.S. market offers low growth potential along with increased competition.

As indicated in the chart in the exhibit, almost all of the premium growth in property and casualty insurance is occurring in emerging markets. For example, the Chinese nonlife market grew by 18.6 percent in 2009. There is, therefore, a growth opportunity for U.S. insurers in global markets, especially in emerging markets. See the exhibit "Global Insurance Markets—2009."

Global Insurance Markets—2009

	Nonlife Premiums USD billion	Change versus 2008
Industrialized Countries	1486	-0.6%
United States	647	-1.8%
Germany	127	1.0%
Japan	107	-2.0%
United Kingdom	92	-3.1%
France	89	0.9%
Italy	54	-2.5%
Hong Kong	3	6.1%
Emerging Markets	249	2.9%
Latin America and Caribbean	67	4.3%
Central and Eastern Europe	67	-7.5%
South and East Asia	75	13.9%
Middle East and Central Asia	22	4.7%
Africa	17	0.4%
World	1735	-0.1%

swissre.com/media/media_information/pr_sigma2_2010.html [DA06391]

Strategic Reasons for Global Expansion

Key strategic reasons why insurers pursue global expansion are revenue growth, financial stability, and building global competitiveness.

Revenue Growth and Financial Stability

Revenue growth is the primary reason that insurers look to global expansion. Some insurance markets, including the U.S., are considered mature markets, meaning that there are few new potential customers. In a mature market, competition for market share results in shrinking profit margins and companies will look for new opportunities for revenue growth. However, worldwide nonlife premium growth increased from $671 billion to more than $1.7 trillion between 1991 and 2009. Therefore, global markets, especially those in emerging economies (developing countries where the economy is growing rapidly) offer such growth opportunities.

Global expansion, particularly into emerging economy markets, also allows insurers to diversify operations and risks. Expanding into foreign markets has the benefit of allowing insurers to achieve these objectives:

- Greater stability during economic downturns—Spreading risks worldwide helps to counter the effects of economic downturn in a particular country. Furthermore, even in a worldwide recession, the potential for growth in emerging markets can offset loss of income from declines in premiums and investment returns. For example, in 2009, nonlife premiums dropped in the developed countries of the U.S., United Kingdom, and Japan, but increased in emerging markets.

- Diversification of risk—Spreading risk over a larger and more diverse base minimizes the impact of heavy losses in any one segment of the operation. This has long been the business model of international reinsurers who spread the risk of extreme natural catastrophes through globalization.

Global Competitiveness

Global expansion can increase an insurer's competitiveness in several ways. Through the growth from global expansion, an insurer may achieve economies of scale and efficiencies that allow it to compete more effectively in its domestic market as well as in the global market.

A global expansion strategy also provides an insurer with the technology and strategic resources to quickly expand into additional foreign markets or offer additional products when there is an opportunity. If an insurer waits to begin expansion until a market is developing, that insurer may lag behind other organizations that were more nimble in their ability to enter that market.

Insurers may also choose to expand in order to remain competitive in a specific specialty market. For example, an insurer specializing in mining risks or oil exploration may be better able to compete if it markets such coverage globally.

Global Market Considerations

Many companies pursue international growth strategies to build long-term financial strength. However, the decision to operate globally involves many variables. Management needs to determine the global markets to target, what products could be sold in other countries, what distribution channels should be used, and how regulations and government restrictions might affect global operations. Making these determinations is essential for an insurer to decide whether operating globally would improve its competitive advantage.

There are three key areas for an insurer to evaluate in making a strategic decision about expansion into a global market:

- Market analysis
- Economic considerations
- Political risks

Market Analysis

When a company is considering global expansion, it must analyze the insurance market in the country it plans to enter. Financial requirements, including capital and surplus, need to be evaluated. The company must also assess whether the potential return is worth the amount of capital that will need to be committed. Other factors include the ease of entry and the difficulty of withdrawal from the market. The competition from other insurers will also be included in this analysis. The insurer will consider whether it has any competitive advantage that it can use to provide leverage in the country where it plans to expand, such as a product offering that fits well in the market.

Distribution channels, the availability of producers, and underwriting practices are additional factors to analyze as well as whether these practices are compatible with the insurer's marketing and underwriting philosophy.

Other factors include cultural and language differences, and whether the insurer has the staff or can hire and manage the appropriate staff to overcome any linguistic or cultural barriers.

Economic Considerations

Insurers evaluating global expansion must also consider the host country's economic environment. Important considerations include the level of economic stability, monetary policies, the prevailing attitude toward foreign investors, and the potential for exchange-rate volatility. Other economic factors such as the country's gross domestic product or national income are also important, as is specific information including regulation, taxation, and premium tax requirements. Insurers will want to evaluate whether the country's economy is growing and whether there are any significant risks to economic growth on the horizon. For example, some countries that were growing rapidly may experience high levels of private and public debt that will restrain future growth potential.

Insurers need to have information regarding average personal income, disposable income, and the prevailing wages for various occupations in any country that is a potential market. This information is important, along with other demographic factors, to determine how many of the country's residents are potential consumers. Insurers also need to understand the wages they would need to pay employees in that country. Additionally, insurers considering expansion need to understand the laws and regulations that may affect them as potential employers.

Political Risks

Political risks are uncertainties faced by companies doing business in foreign countries that arise from the actions of host-country governments. These risks are greater in developing or emerging countries than in established countries with stable governments. Serious concerns include kidnap and ransom, terrorism, civil unrest, acts of war, revolution, and changes in government. Foreign nationals and their businesses can be at great risk in unsettled parts of the world. When considering global expansion, insurers often work with consultants who provide country reports or political risk scores to determine what political risks are present and how dangerous those risks are for foreign businesses.

Of greatest financial concern is the potential for the confiscation of business assets by a foreign government or other interference with the rights of ownership of corporate assets, such as confiscation of inventory. Expropriation occurs when a foreign government takes property without compensating its owners. This occurred in Cuba during the 1960s, when many U.S. firms had business properties and inventory expropriated as part of Cuba's regime change. This can also occur when a cash-strapped government seeks to seize businesses that generate high returns.

Foreign governments might also nationalize a business and compensate the owners, usually at a lower rate than the market value of the assets. For example, in 1956 the government of India enacted legislation to nationalize insurance, resulting in the takeover of all insurers including several foreign companies.

Companies are also concerned when countries treat local businesses more favorably than foreign businesses regarding taxes, government contracts, or access to required financing. Insurers will also evaluate the nature and extent of regulation. Several countries prohibit nonadmitted insurance or have laws requiring insurance to be written by local insurers for designated classes of business. For example, China requires insurers to be licensed by the China Insurance Regulatory Commission (CIRC) before they can write insurance in China.

Approaches to Global Expansion

Insurers who, after careful consideration, decide to expand into a global market may decide to form an alliance or joint venture with an existing insurer in that country, to merge with another insurer, to begin a new operation, or to acquire an existing foreign company.

- **Strategic alliance**—Strategic alliances have the advantages of bringing together separate areas of expertise and of gaining a host-country

Strategic alliance

An arrangement in which two companies work together to achieve a common goal.

participant, who can access local markets and who is familiar with local laws, regulations, and customers. Such an alliance can provide a low-risk approach to quickly entering a new market. Strategic alliances include international licensing agreements (contractual agreement allowing one party to use another party's distribution system or trademark), and co-marketing/co-development agreements.

Joint venture

A business association formed by an express or implied agreement of two or more persons (including corporations) to accomplish a particular project, such as the construction of a building.

- **Joint venture**—A joint venture is a specific type of strategic alliance that involves shared ownership, shared responsibilities, and often joint management of the foreign venture. A joint-venture agreement brings together two companies to form a new organization that is legally separate and distinct from the parent companies, with its own management and directors. The most common form of joint venture occurs when a domestic company joins with a company from the country in which the operation is located. Joint ventures with governments or state-owned industries are referred to as public-private ventures and are common in India, China, Russia, and the former Soviet republics. Joint ventures allow companies to enter markets (both geographic and product markets) that would otherwise be beyond the reach of an individual company. For example, insurers wishing to expand into India commonly enter into joint venture agreements because India's law caps foreign direct investment for insurance.

Merger

A type of acquisition in which two or more business entities are combined into one.

- **Merger**—The advantage to merger is the ability to combine resources and reduce overhead expenses, allowing the new company to be more successful than the sum of the parties to the merger. International mergers carry a high degree of risk and are complicated by compliance with the regulations and antitrust laws of more than one country.

Subsidiary

A company owned or controlled by another company.

- Wholly owned **subsidiary**—Acquisition of, or formation of, a wholly owned subsidiary allows for direct ownership and control of assets in a foreign country. This presents the highest degree of business, political, and economic risk. Operating a subsidiary in a foreign country requires more capital than other methods of entering a foreign market, such as a joint venture, but also gives the domestic company greater control over operations. Acquiring an existing company generally results in faster entry into a market. However, establishment of a new company gives an insurer the greatest level of control over foreign affiliates because the parent company makes decisions about management, distribution channels, product mix, and other organization issues.

STRATEGIC MANAGEMENT CASE STUDY

A SWOT (strengths, weaknesses, opportunities, and threats) analysis can improve an insurer's planning process and the resulting outcome, particularly if those participating in the process represent a variety of perspectives and ask and find answers to difficult questions. It also may be used to evaluate whether an insurer's business strategies will contribute to its success.

A SWOT analysis can be used to examine an insurer's internal and external environment, and is frequently used in the strategic management planning process. The analysis is a step in action planning—not an end in itself. Results of SWOT analyses can change over time; therefore, the first step in the process of evaluation of business strategies should be to complete a current analysis. The current analysis can then be used to examine the insurer's business strategies, placing emphasis on any issues that have prompted the current evaluation. Strategies can then be evaluated to determine whether they are appropriate in guiding the insurer to meet its goals and objectives.

Case Facts

To evaluate an insurer's strategies, the reviewer or team of reviewers needs information about the insurer's strategic goals, as well as its internal and external environment. In addition, an understanding of the purpose of the evaluation will help narrow the review's focus.

Given background information on an insurer, the overall question to be answered is, "Will this insurer's current business strategies allow it to achieve its goals, or is a change required?"

Greenly Insurance Company—Internal and External Environment

Greenly Insurance Company (Greenly) is a sixty-year-old regional mutual insurance company authorized and operating in eight states. The company is headquartered in Pennsylvania, but maintains at least one satellite claims office in each state in which it writes.

Greenly writes only personal lines risks, with automobile insurance being the core of its business. Auto customers may be offered coverage in Greenly's "preferred" automobile insurance company, or in its "nonstandard" (high risk) company. The company offers generous discounts for drivers between the ages of thirty-five and sixty, based on the favorable loss ratios of this group. Greenly does not offer a rating discount based on longevity, although long-term households also show consistently favorable loss ratios.

The company's operations are consistent with core values it established sixty years ago: to protect policyholder assets, to gain customer loyalty, be a good corporate citizen, and to comply with all legal requirements. Throughout its existence, the company has enjoyed a consistently superior financial rating. A conservative investment strategy, favorable underwriting results, and conservative policy growth have allowed Greenly to maintain ample policyholder surplus even in years of high catastrophe losses and lackluster returns on investments. Greenly does not compete based on price, but rather on financial strength and core values.

Greenly uses independent agents to sell its products, and a monthly policyholder magazine accounts for the majority of its advertising. Greenly's customer-focused philosophy stresses personalized service to gain customer trust and loyalty. Therefore, Greenly's website does not provide quotes, direct purchase options, claim reporting, or premium payment options.

Over the past decade, the automobile insurance market has changed dramatically. Policyholders demand customer service, yet also want lower premiums. The line between "preferred" and "nonstandard" companies has blurred as the use of credit-based insurance scoring and other tools effective in predicting risk of loss have resulted in more refined pricing and increased use of rating tiers. More sophisticated coverage and rating options mean that insurers are able to rate and compete for segments of business that they may not have in the past.

Some automobile insurers invest millions of dollars annually in high-profile advertising. Celebrity spokespersons, mascots, special effects, and humor have led to name recognition for certain companies and remind consumers that they can easily switch companies. More than one-half of "Generation Y" insurance consumers (those born between 1977 and 1992) seek information from insurers' websites when shopping for automobile insurance, and those shoppers are almost twice as likely to seek an automobile insurance quote directly from a website as are Baby Boomers (those born between 1946 and 1964). At the same time, however, "Generation Y" shoppers are less likely than Baby Boomers to shop for new coverage based on price.[8]

Greenly Insurance Company—Goals

An organization's goals provide the overall context for what the organization seeks to achieve. Greenly's goals have remained fairly constant for many years, and it establishes metrics based on these goals annually:

- Maintain financial strength to protect insureds
- Build long-term customer loyalty and maintain high customer satisfaction by meeting customer needs
- Contribute to charitable community efforts through time and financial support
- Comply with legal requirements

Greenly Insurance Company—Business Strategies

Based on its goals of financial strength, customer loyalty and satisfaction, and charitable giving, Greenly has developed business strategies to direct its actions. See the exhibit "Greenly Insurance Company—Business Strategies."

Issues That Prompted the Evaluation

Greenly has failed to meet its automobile insurance written premium and policy growth goals for the past two years. Greenly's new business has declined steadily over the past few years, and **retention ratios** of existing business have decreased at an even greater pace. After accounting for the impact of the

Retention ratio

The percentage of insurance policies renewed.

Greenly Insurance Company—Business Strategies

1. Financial Strength: We will protect our policyholders' security by maintaining financial strength. To accomplish this, we will:

   - Increase policyholders surplus and maintain our superior financial rating

   - Achieve a combined ratio of 98% or less (automobile and homeowners)

   - Increase written premium by 5%

   - Gain a net increase of automobile policies in force by 2%

2. Customer Focus: We will commit to providing the outstanding customer service that our customers deserve and demand, and will strive to build long-term relationships with our policyholders. To accomplish this, we will:

   - Offer quality products, while meeting or exceeding established product delivery goals

   - Increase average household longevity by providing consistently superior service

   - Achieve 98% customer satisfaction as expressed on post-claim settlement and annual policyholder renewal surveys

3. Technology and Data Management: We will provide the best service possible to our agents and policyholders by adopting current and efficient technologies intended to enhance our business. To accomplish this, we will:

   - Safeguard all customer data

   - Expand use of data-driven products in the claims settlement process

4. Corporate Leadership: We will show leadership in the communities in which we operate through organizational effort and through the dedication of our employees. To accomplish this, we will:

   - Dedicate our time and financial support to community activities

   - Encourage employee participation in community charitable efforts

   - Achieve a 50% positive response on recognition of our community efforts as measured by annual policyholder renewal surveys

[DA06385]

economic downturn, it has become clear that the negative trends likely stem from its current business practices.

A survey of Greenly's agents has revealed that Greenly insureds who were insured under their parent's policies seem increasingly less likely to stay with Greenly when they establish their own households. Further, many cited customer dissatisfaction with claims service as a primary reason for obtaining coverage elsewhere, despite the fact that post-claim surveys continue to show acceptable results. See the exhibit "SWOT Analysis Table."

SWOT Analysis Table

	Strengths	Weaknesses
Internal	List assets, competencies, or attributes that enhance competitiveness	List lacking assets, competencies, or attributes that diminish competitiveness
Internal	Prioritize based on the quality of the strength and the relative importance of the strength	Prioritize based on the seriousness of the weakness and the relative importance of the weakness
	Opportunities	**Threats**
External	List conditions that could be exploited to create a competitive advantage	List conditions that diminish competitive advantage
External	Prioritize based on the potential of exploiting the opportunities	Prioritize based on the seriousness and probability of occurrence
	Note strengths that can be paired with opportunities as areas of competitive advantage	Note weaknesses that can be paired with threats as risks to be avoided

[DA03626]

Case Analysis Tools and Information

To evaluate business strategies for Greenly Insurance Company, the reviewer or review team will need these:

- A current SWOT analysis
- The company's business strategies
- An explanation of the reason for the evaluation
- The company's goals and objectives that relate to the reason for the evaluation

Case Analysis Steps

Evaluating an organization's strategies involves a series of decision-making steps. Following these steps minimizes the effort required by focusing on the issues, strategies, and desired outcome:

1. Conduct a current SWOT analysis of the organization's internal and external environments

2. Determine the business strategies relevant to the business issue that generated the need for evaluation

3. Evaluate the relevant business strategies using the SWOT analysis

Conduct a Current SWOT Analysis

The SWOT analysis is a methodical assessment of an organization and its business environment that usually is completed by those involved in planning and decision-making for the organization. While determination of strengths and weaknesses may be based on subjective criteria, the overall process allows for an objective view of the environments in which the organization operates. See the exhibit "SWOT Analysis Process."

SWOT Analysis Process

One method of conducting a SWOT analysis is through a group activity that involves an organization's managers and is organized by a facilitator.

Brainstorming

- If the group is large, the facilitator may divide the managers into smaller groups to encourage participation.
- Through brainstorming, factors are listed under each of the SWOT headings.
- This activity will produce many factors randomly organized under each SWOT heading.

Refining

- To make the list easier to examine, similar items are clustered together.
- Items of high importance are noted under each of the SWOT headings.

Prioritizing

- Strengths are ordered by quality and relative importance.
- Weaknesses are ordered by the degree to which they affect performance and by their relative importance.
- Opportunities are ordered by degree and probability of success.
- Threats are ordered by degree and probability of occurrence.
- Strengths that require little or no operational changes and can be paired with opportunities are designated for potential action to maximize competitive advantages that entail low risk.
- Weaknesses that can be paired with threats are designated in the prioritized list for potential action to minimize consequences that entail high risk.

[DA03650]

The SWOT analysis of Greenly reveals that the company faces a high-risk threat because it has not kept pace with the needs of existing customers or the buying preferences of prospective customers. Customer satisfaction surveys may be unreliable because they are outdated and fail to ask the right questions, or fail to reach a broad enough audience. Further, the company's normal avenue of direct communication with policyholders, the monthly magazine, may have little impact on customer relations or loyalty.

A review of the survey questions asked and their target audience may reveal whether such surveys need to be revised. For example, Greenly could be relying only on input from current satisfied customers rather than from former customers who may have left due to dissatisfaction, which would skew responses toward positive results. To prevent this, Greenly could utilize focus groups of current customers, former customers, and producers to determine how it is perceived and any areas needing improvement. See the exhibit "SWOT Case Table—Greenly Insurance."

Determine Business Strategies to Be Evaluated

The organization's business strategies are its long-term approach to attaining its goals and objectives. Because an organization's strategies can be extensive, it is helpful to narrow the focus of the examination by understanding the business issue that has prompted the evaluation. The strategies relevant to the issue can then be targeted for evaluation.

Which business strategies have contributed to the failure of Greenly to meet its customer satisfaction and loyalty goals and policy growth target?

Assuming that customers are leaving because they are either dissatisfied with the company's products, services, or prices, the company may need to reevaluate its customer-focused strategy:

> 2. Customer Focus: We will commit to providing the outstanding customer service that our customers deserve and demand, and will strive to build long-term relationships with our policyholders. To accomplish this, we will:
>
> · Offer quality products, while meeting or exceeding established product delivery goals
>
> · Increase average household longevity by providing consistently superior service
>
> · Achieve 98% customer satisfaction as expressed on post-claim settlement and annual policyholder renewal surveys

This goal seeks to meet the needs of customers but fails to address identification of changes in the marketplace. The company's business strategies also lack commitment to respond to the changing needs or buying habits of insurance consumers.

Evaluate Relevant Business Strategies

After an organization's internal and external environments and its business strategies have been examined, the next step is to determine whether a change in course is required to achieve its goals.

Will the current business strategies for Greenly continue to be the most effective approach toward attaining its goals, or should its business strategies be changed?

SWOT Case Table—Greenly Insurance

	Strengths	Weaknesses
Internal	Strengths are apparent in the organization's financial stability: • Superior financial rating and policyholders' surplus • Branding based on customer satisfaction allows the company to focus on financial stability • Commitment to charitable efforts and community involvement • Established method of monthly communication with policyholders • Representation by independent agents fosters goal of customer loyalty (for example, trust and service) • Experienced employees	Weaknesses have emerged in the types of services that the organization has not developed and the needs it is not meeting: • Customer surveys are inadequate in measuring customer feedback • Technology in use has not kept pace with consumer demands/lack of development of website options for quotes and applications • Claim handling complaints increasing (distant locations may have resulted in inadequate oversight, training, or focus on company values) • Inadequate advertising/lack of branding • Reliance on products with few unique options/lack of new products (for example, "green" insurance options)
	Opportunities	**Threats**
External	Opportunities provide potential actions that the organization can take to meet the needs of its current and potential policyholders. • Generation Y insurance consumers less sensitive to price—ability to target younger prospective policyholders based on factors other than price • Ability to enhance branding through focus on charitable and community involvement efforts • Ability to pilot discounts or incentives based on customer longevity • Claims staff can be retrained and customer evaluation materials can be revised to improve reliability of results • Ability to expand into additional states • Ability to pilot direct writing option, and Internet-based partnership options with independent agents	Threats have surfaced as some are better positioned to meet the needs of the company's customers. • Current business is vulnerable to price leaders' advertising efforts, particularly of national writers • Agency force may lean toward better-recognized brands or companies that advertise lower prices • Increasing percentage of consumers looking for direct purchase options and interactive website capability • Dissatisfaction with claims processes may damage the company reputation, particularly if dissatisfied customers tell others or if complaints are filed with state departments of insurance • Competitors offer more pricing options, reducing likelihood of declinations and nonrenewals and enhancing customer stability

[DA06389]

Greenly's current customer-focused strategy will not lead to successful achievement of the company's growth goals. Greenly has committed to customer satisfaction but has not devised an effective method of determining customer needs and opinions. Although the company is committed to soliciting feedback through renewal and post-claim surveys, those surveys may not be worded appropriately to invite the type of feedback needed for the company to truly evaluate its operations. For example, if the surveys only request feedback on current issues, the company will not have the benefit of hearing how customers believe the company has changed, improved, or even declined over time—or the benefit of hearing suggestions for the future. Perhaps even more important, Greenly has no established method of seeking input from former customers to determine why they left.

If the company revises its customer surveys and establishes additional methods of reaching out to current and former customer and agents, it may determine that additional changes are needed as well. For example, the company may wish to revise its business strategies to include opportunities identified to attract and retain policyholders and to help meet the company's goals. Such changes may include these: See the exhibit "SWOT Case Correct Answer."

- Redesign its website to add online quote capability or other interactive options
- Expand into a new state as a direct writer
- Implement a pilot program to test new products or coverage options
- Redesign the company magazine to emphasize new developments and to better target second-generation policyholders
- Refocus community involvement efforts on issues more likely to appeal to second generation policyholders and effectively promote those efforts
- Retrain claims staff to improve customer satisfaction

SWOT Case Correct Answer

The Greenly Insurance Company has failed to meet its automobile insurance written premium and policy growth goals for the past two years because customer satisfaction goals are not being met and lapse ratios are increasing. A SWOT analysis indicates that Greenly has not adequately identified or kept pace with the changing needs of customers.

Using that information to evaluate its business strategies, Greenly must revise its customer-focused strategy to meet its goals. As a well-capitalized company, Greenly is in a good position to implement changes, including updating technology and implementing pilot marketing programs designed to attract and retain business.

[DA06390]

SUMMARY

The strategic management process is employed by organizations to align external factors and internal resources to create a sustainable competitive advantage. Mission and value statements define a company's purpose and overarching goals, and provide the framework for the strategic management process. The strategic management process includes strategy formulation, strategy implementation, and strategy evaluation. Implementation and evaluation phases are closely linked, and may reveal the need for adjustment to the strategic management plan.

The Five Forces Model can be used to thoroughly assess an organization's external environment by identifying factors related to customers, competitors, and suppliers. The "Five Forces" that drive competition are the threat of new entrants, the threat of substitute products or services, bargaining power of buyers, bargaining power of suppliers, and rivalry among existing firms. Evaluating these forces also helps management to better understand the organization's position within its industry.

A SWOT analysis can then be used to determine internal strengths and weaknesses related to the company's financial, physical, human, and organizational assets. An examination of the external environment is then conducted to determine opportunities and threats.

Strategy is planned and implemented at the organization's corporate, business, functional, and operational levels. Corporate-level strategies in a growing company include concentration on a single business, vertical integration, and either related or unrelated diversification. When a company is encountering a decreasing market, corporate management is faced with a different set of strategies from those available to a growing company. For organizations in a decline mode, bankruptcy or liquidation may be undertaken as a last resort. Other options are the harvest, turnaround, or divestiture strategies.

Business-level strategies are employed by divisional managers within the organization. These strategies include cost leadership, differentiation, and focus. At the functional level, strategies focus on integrating efficiency, quality, customer responsiveness, and innovation in each functional process or operation. Functional areas of insurers include marketing, underwriting, claim, risk control, premium audit, actuarial, and finance. Operational-level strategies are implemented at the department level to support the strategies of the functional, business, and corporate levels; these strategies focus on daily business operations.

The strategic reasons for global expansion include revenue growth and financial stability along with global competitiveness. However, there are significant risks associated with expanding into global markets, and insurers need to perform a market analysis and evaluate economic considerations along with political risks before deciding to expand into a global market. Insurers can enter a foreign market by forming a strategic alliance, joint venture, or merger with an insurer operating in that country. Alternatively, insurers can form a new company or acquire an existing one to establish a subsidiary in a new global market.

A SWOT analysis is a structured examination of an organization's internal and external environment as a prelude to action planning. When used to evaluate an organization's business strategies, the SWOT analysis focuses on the event that prompted the evaluation. The results of the business strategies relevant to the cause of the event are examined to determine whether those strategies will continue to be effective in achieving the organization's goals.

ASSIGNMENT NOTES

1. Robert Kreitner, *Management Principles and Practices*, 3rd ed. (Atlanta: LOMA, 1997), p. 203.

2. Michael E. Porter, *Competitive Strategy: Techniques for Analyzing Industries and Competitors* (New York: The Free Press, 1980), p. 4.

3. Porter, *Competitive Strategy*, pp. 9–12.

4. Porter, *Competitive Strategy*, p. 26.

5. Kathryn M. Bartol and David C. Martin, *Management*, 3rd ed. (New York: McGraw-Hill Cos., Inc., 1998), p. 228.

6. U.S. Department of Commerce, *Survey of Current Business*, October 2007, pp. 114-115 and 132.

7. U.S. Department of Commerce, *Survey of Current Business*, pp. 114–115 and 132.

8. "Study: Overall Purchase Beats Price in Auto Insurance Satisfaction," *Insurance Journal*, May 2010, www.insurancejournal.com/news/national/2010/05/26/110212.htm (accessed July 15, 2010).

Index

Page numbers in boldface refer to pages where the word or phrase is defined.